Foreign direct investment and governments

The recently concluded Uruguay round of GATT underscores the changing structure of the world economy and the growing significance of multinational enterprises to economic growth. This book examines the dynamic relationship between foreign direct investment, governments and economic development, and demonstrates the nature of their interaction through a set of eleven country studies at various stages of development.

The volume describes the catalytic role governments and multinationals may play in determining the evolution, restructuring and upgrading of the competitive and comparative advantages of countries. The fact that multinationals' activities and government policy are highly interdependent is highlighted in the country studies. The countries examined include the UK, USA, Sweden, Japan, New Zealand, Mexico, Spain, Taiwan, India, Indonesia and China.

The increasing globalization of production and the crucial role of technology in enhancing the competitive advantages of both firms and countries at all stages of economic development is firmly demonstrated with a detailed, in-depth evaluation of the chosen countries.

John H. Dunning is State of New Jersey Professor of International Business at Rutgers University, USA, and Professor Emeritus in International Business at the University of Reading, UK. **Rajneesh Narula** is Research Fellow at the Maastricht Economic Research Institute on Innovation and Technology (MERIT) in the Netherlands. He is the author of *Multinational Investment and Economic Structure*, also published by Routledge.

Routledge Studies in International Business and the World Economy

1 States and firms
Multinational enterprises in institutional competition
Razeen Sally

2 Multinational restructuring, internationalization and small economies
The Swedish case
Thomas Andersson, Torbjörn Fredriksson and Roger Svensson

3 Foreign direct investment and governments
Catalysts for economic restructuring
John H. Dunning and Rajneesh Narula

4 Multinational investment and economic structure
Globalisation and competitiveness
Rajneesh Narula

Foreign direct investment and governments

Catalysts for economic restructuring

Edited by John H. Dunning and Rajneesh Narula

London and New York

332.673
F7147

First published 1996
by Routledge
11 New Fetter Lane, London EC4P 4EE

Simultaneously published in the USA and Canada
by Routledge
29 West 35th Street, New York, NY 10001

Reprinted 1996

First published in paperback 1998

© 1996 John H. Dunning and Rajneesh Narula for the
collection; individual chapters the contributors

Typeset in Times by
J&L Composition Ltd, Filey, North Yorkshire
Printed and bound in Great Britain by
Clays Ltd, St Ives PLC

British Library Cataloguing in Publication Data
A catalogue record for this book is available from the British
Library

Library of Congress Cataloguing in Publication Data
Foreign direct investment and governments: catalysts for
   economic restructuring/edited by John Dunning and
   Rajneesh Narula.
        p.   cm.—(Routledge studies in international business
   and the world economy)
      Includes bibliographical references and index.
      1. Investments, Foreign—Case studies.   2. Economic
   policy—Case studies.   3. Economic development—Case
   studies.   I. Dunning, John H.   II. Narula, Rajneesh, 1963–
   III. Series.
   HG4538.F61917   1997
   332.67'3—dc21   97–21653

ISBN 0–415–11820–4 (hbk)
ISBN 0–415–17355–8 (pbk)
ISSN 1359–7930

Contents

List of figures   vii
List of tables   ix
List of contributors   xii
Acknowledgements   xiv

1 **The investment development path revisited:
   some emerging issues**
   John H. Dunning and Rajneesh Narula   1

2 **The United Kingdom: a** *par excellence* **two-way direct
   investor**
   Jeremy Clegg   42

3 **The United States: some musings on its investment
   development path**
   Edward M. Graham   78

4 **Sweden: a latecomer to industrialization**
   Ivo Zander and Udo Zander   101

5 **Japan: the macro-IDP, meso-IDPs and the technology
   development path (TDP)**
   Terutomo Ozawa   142

6 **New Zealand: the development of a resource-rich
   economy**
   Michèle Akoorie   174

7 **Spain: a boom from economic integration**
   José Manuel Campa and Mauro F. Guillén   207

 8 **Mexico: foreign investment as a source of international competitiveness**
    Alvaro Calderón, Michael Mortimore and Wilson Peres   240

 9 **Taiwan: foreign direct investment and the transformation of the economy**
    Roger van Hoesel   280

10 **Indonesia: the critical role of government**
    Donald J. Lecraw   316

11 **India: industrialization, liberalization and inward and outward foreign direct investment**
    Nagesh Kumar   348

12 **China: rapid changes in the investment development path**
    Hai-Yan Zhang and Danny Van Den Bulcke   380

13 **The investment development path: some conclusions**
    Sanjaya Lall   423

    Index   442

Figures

1.1 The pattern of the investment development path   2
1.2 NOI and GDP for 1992   30
1.3 Outward FDI and GDP   34
1.4 Inward FDI and GDP   35
3.1 Net US FDI position   79
3.2 Net, gross inward and outward FDI position   82
3.3 US manufacturing FDI position   84
3.4 FDI flows to the United States by component   86
3.5 FDI flows from the United States by component   89
3.6 1989 stock and 1990–1993 flow by region   90
3.7 1989 stock and 1990–1993 flow; US direct investment
    abroad by industry   92
3.8 US net direct investment position as fraction of US
    direct investment abroad   98
4.1 Sweden's investment development path   104
Appendix 4.3 The share of foreign technological activity
    in major Swedish MNEs   135
5.1 Flying-geese paradigm and the meso-IDP   145
5.2 Structural upgrading and meso-IDPs   150
5.3 Japan's balance of technology trade as a technology
    development path (TDP)   154
5.4 Japan's technology trade with other major countries   155
5.5 Japan's balance of technology trade by manufacturing
    industry   156
5.6 Japan's structural upgrading and outward FDI   165
7.1 Foreign direct investment and manufacturing direct
    investment in Spain   213
7.2 Outward FDI by mode and by goal   215
7.3 Inward FDI by mode   216

7.4 Receipts and payments for patents, royalties and fees   228
8.1 Foreign investment and GDP growth   247
8.2 Mexico: automotive industry exports   257
8.3 Mexico: passenger car sales   257
8.4 Mexico: total exports of in-bond industry   267
9.1 Inward direct investment flows   282
9.2 Outward direct investment flows   294
9.3 Inward and outward investment flows in the electronics
     and electronic appliances industry   306
9.4 Accumulated inward and outward FDI in the
     electronics and electronic appliances industry   307
11.1 Stock of inward FDI in India   350
11.2 Stock of Indian outward FDI   350
12.1 Evolution of the Chinese investment development path   383
12.2 Regional pattern of the investment development path
     in China   411

Tables

1.1 Linear regression equations for NOI 31
1.2 FDI activity and GDP 31
1.3 Log–linear regression equations for inward and
  outward FDI against GDP 34
2.1 The aggregate FDI position of the United Kingdom and
  investment development path coefficient 46
2.2 Technological and mineral royalty transactions' trade
  performance for the UK 49
2.3 The UK's aggregate IDP position with the major
  regions of the world 55
2.4 The UK's aggregate IDP position with selected
  European countries 59
2.5 The UK's aggregate IDP position with selected
  developed countries outside Europe 62
2.6 The UK's aggregate annual IDP position and IDP
  position by industry group 68
2.7 Components of annual NOI flows in the UK's IDP
  position 70
3.1 Earnings before interest and tax of US affiliates of
  foreign firms 87
3.2 Net FDI flows from and to United States 99
4.1 Swedish outward and inward foreign direct investment 102
Appendix 4.1 Major Swedish firms established around
  the turn of the century 133
Appendix 4.2 Early mechanical engineering workshops in
  Sweden 134
Appendix 4.4 Flows of outward and inward foreign direct
  investment in Sweden 136
5.1 Structural changes in industry, exports and FDI 166

Appendix 5.1 Japan's outward and inward FDI and GDP   169
Appendix 5.2 Japan's technology trade   171
  6.1 Inward and outward FDI, New Zealand   175
  6.2 Foreign direct investment, New Zealand   192
  6.3 Net FDI inflows to New Zealand   193
  6.4 Sectoral patterns of inward investment, New Zealand   194
  6.5 New Zealand, direct investment by country and
       destination   198
  7.1 Annual flows of inward and outward FDI   208
  7.2 Stocks of foreign direct investment and number of
       large firms for selected countries   209
  7.3 Total outward FDI by purpose and country of
       destination   220
  7.4 Outward manufacturing FDI by form of investment and
       industry   222
  7.5 Inward manufacturing FDI by form of investment and
       country of origin   224
  7.6 Inward manufacturing FDI by form of investment and
       industry   225
  7.7 Internalization advantages of Spanish firms   230
  8.1 Foreign direct investment flows   241
  8.2 Cumulative foreign investment   248
  8.3 Share of foreign investment in Mexico's gross fixed
       investment   250
  8.4 Indicators of Mexico's international competitiveness   252
  8.5 Share of foreign firms in Mexico's foreign trade   254
  8.6 Mexico: passenger car sales, by principal market   260
  8.7 Mexico: passenger car sales, in export and domestic
       markets   261
  8.8 Main economic indicators of the *maquiladora* industry   266
  8.9 Total value of US imports under HTS provision
       9802.00.80   268
  9.1 Approved inward investment flows   284
  9.2 Approved inward investment flows per industry   288
  9.3 Destination of approved outward investment flows   295
  9.4 Approved outward investment flows per industry   296
  9.5 Trade and investment between China and Taiwan   301
 11.1 Sectoral distribution of the stock of FDI in India   352
 11.2 Investments made by Indian enterprises in overseas
       subsidiaries and joint ventures by year of approval   360

11.3 Investments made by Indian enterprises in overseas subsidiaries and joint ventures by industry and year of approval   364

11.4 Indian outward FDI by region and sector   368

11.5 Summary of foreign collaboration approvals   374

11.6 FDI approvals by foreign equity ownership   375

12.1 Inward and outward foreign direct investment of China   382

12.2 Some indications of the impact of inward foreign direct investment on the Chinese economy   384

12.3 Forms of inward FDI in China   390

12.4 Location pattern of inward FDI in China   393

12.5 Sectoral distribution of inward FDI in China   394

12.6 Foreign direct investment in China by countries of origin   398

12.7 Geographic pattern of Chinese outward non-trade FDI   403

12.8 China's foreign investment position by country   412

13.1 Foreign direct investment: inflows and outflows   428

Contributors

Michèle Akoorie is Senior Lecturer in International Management at the University of Waikato, New Zealand.

Danny Van Den Bulcke is Professor of International Management and Development at the University of Antwerp (RUCA) and Ghent, and Director of the Centre of International Management and Development – Antwerp (CIMDA).

Alvaro Calderón has worked for eight years in the ECLAC/UNCTAD Joint Unit on Transnational Corporations. He is now Sub-Director of the Institute for European–Latin American Relations in Madrid, Spain.

José Manuel Campa is Assistant Professor of Economics and International Business in the Stern School of Business at New York University.

Jeremy Clegg is Jean Monnet Lecturer in European Integration and International Business in the Centre for International Business Research, School of Management, at the University of Bath, UK.

John H. Dunning is State of New Jersey Professor of International Business at Rutgers University, USA, and Professor Emeritus in International Business at the University of Reading, UK.

Mauro F. Guillén is the Edward Pennell Brooks Career Development Assistant Professor of International Management and Sociology in the Sloan School of Management at the Massachusetts Institute of Technology.

Edward M. Graham is Senior Research Fellow at the Institute for International Economics, Washington, DC.

Roger van Hoesel is Research Associate at the Tinbergen Institute of the Erasmus University Rotterdam, The Netherlands.

Nagesh Kumar is currently on the faculty of the United Nations University – Institute for New Technologies (UNU/INTECH) in Maastricht, The Netherlands.

Sanjaya Lall is a University Lecturer in Development Economics at Oxford University.

Donald J. Lecraw is Professor of Business Administration at the University of Western Ontario.

Michael Mortimore is Transnational Corporations Officer at the ECLAC/UNCTAD Joint Unit on Transnational Corporations, Division of Production, Productivity and Management, ECLAC, in Santiago, Chile.

Rajneesh Narula is Assistant Professor at the University of Limburg, Maastricht, and Research Fellow at MERIT.

Terutomo Ozawa is Professor of Economics at Colorado State University.

Wilson Peres is the Chief Technical Adviser of the ECLAC/UNDP Regional Project on Innovation and Competitiveness in the Latin American Business Sector.

Ivo Zander is Assistant Professor at the Institute of International Business, IIB, at the Stockholm School of Economics.

Udo Zander is Assistant Professor at the Institute of International Business (IIB), at the Stockholm School of Economics.

Hai-Yan Zhang is a Ph.D. student and research assistant at the University of Antwerp (RUCA).

Acknowledgements

The first drafts of the chapters were presented at a workshop held at the Tinbergen Institute, Rotterdam, 11–13 December 1994. This provided the perfect environment for considerable discussion and the interchange of ideas. We are most grateful to all the participants in helping us develop a more focused set of chapters.

Much of the mammoth task of organising this workshop was shouldered by Roger van Hoesel, and all the participants were most appreciative of his role as a gracious, tireless and generous host. We would also like to thank the Tinbergen Institute for hosting the workshop, and Nagesh Kumar for his assistance in organising it. We would like to express our appreciation to the Royal Netherlands Academy of Arts and Sciences, Erasmus University, the Vereniging Trostfonds Erasmus Universiteit Rotterdam and the United Nations University Institute for New Technologies (UNU/INTECH), Maastricht, for their financial support towards the workshop.

Special thanks are also due to Karin Kamp who assisted in compiling, editing and proofreading the various versions of all the chapters. Her (largely unpaid) assistance has been crucial in the timely completion of this volume. We also wish to thank Phyllis Miller of Rutgers University and Eva Nelissen at the University of Limburg for their secretarial and administrative support.

John H. Dunning
Reading and Rutgers Universities

Rajneesh Narula
University of Limburg, Maastricht

Chapter 1

The investment development path revisited
Some emerging issues

John H. Dunning and Rajneesh Narula

PART 1: THE THEORY

The nature of the investment development path

The notion that the outward and inward direct investment position of a country is systematically related to its economic development, relative to the rest of the world, was first put forward by John Dunning in 1979, at a conference on 'Multinational Enterprises from Developing Countries' which took place at the East–West Center at Honolulu.[1]

Since then the concept of the investment development path (IDP)[2] has been revised and extended in several papers and books (Dunning 1981, 1986, 1988a, 1993; Narula 1993, 1995; Dunning and Narula 1994). The following paragraphs summarize the state of thinking – prior to this volume – on the nature and characteristics of the IDP.

The IDP suggests that countries tend to go through five main stages of development and that these stages can be usefully classified according to the propensity of those countries to be outward and/or inward direct investors. In turn, this propensity will rest on the extent and pattern of the competitive or ownership specific (O) advantages of the indigenous firms of the countries concerned, relative to those of firms of other countries; the competitiveness of the location-bound resources and capabilities of that country, relative to those of other countries (the L specific advantages of that country); and the extent to which indigenous and foreign firms choose to utilize their O specific advantages jointly with the location-bound endowments of home or foreign countries through internalizing the cross-border market for these advantages,[3] rather than by some other organizational route (i.e. their perceived I advantages).

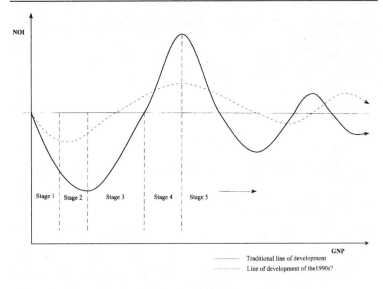

Figure 1.1   The pattern of the investment development path
Note: Not drawn to scale – for illustrative purposes only

A diagrammatic representation of the IDP, which relates the net outward investment (NOI) position of countries (i.e. the gross outward direct investment stock less the gross inward direct investment stock) – as a continuous line – is presented in Figure 1.1. We shall briefly summarize the main features of these stages, but pay particular attention to Stage 5, which we did not consider in our earlier writings.

Stage 1

During the first stage of the IDP path, the L specific advantages of a country are presumed to be insufficient to attract inward direct investment, with the exception of those arising from its possession of *natural* assets. Its deficiency in location-bound *created* assets[4] may reflect limited domestic markets – demand levels are minimal because of the low per capita income – inappropriate economic systems or government policies; inadequate infrastructure such as transportation and communication facilities; and, perhaps most important of all, a poorly educated, trained or motivated labour force. At this stage of the IDP, there is likely to be very little outward direct investment. *Ceteris paribus*, foreign firms will prefer to export to and import from this market, or conclude cooperative non-equity arrangements with indigenous firms. This is because the O specific advantages of domestic firms are few and far between, as there is little or no indigenous technology accumulation and hence few created assets. Those that exist will be in labour-intensive manufacturing and the primary product sector (such as mining and agriculture), and may be government influenced through infant industry protection such as import controls.

Government intervention during Stage 1 will normally take two forms. First it may be the main means of providing basic infrastructure, and the upgrading of human capital via education and training. Governments will attempt to reduce some of the endemic market failure holding back development. Second, they engage in a variety of economic and social policies, which, for good or bad, will affect the structure of markets. Import protection, domestic content policies and export subsidies are examples of such intervention at this stage of development. At this stage, however, there is likely to be only limited government involvement in the upgrading of the country's created assets, e.g. innovatory capacity and human resources.

Stage 2

In Stage 2, inward direct investment starts to rise, while outward investment remains low or negligible. Domestic markets may have grown either in size or in purchasing power, making some local production by foreign firms a viable proposition. Initially this is likely to take the form of import substituting manufacturing investment – based upon their possession of intangible assets, e.g. technology, trademarks, managerial skills, etc. Frequently such inbound foreign direct investment (FDI) is stimulated by host governments imposing tariff and non-tariff barriers. In the case of export-oriented industries (at this stage of development, such inward direct investment will still be in natural resources and primary commodities with some forward vertical integration into labour-intensive low technology and light manufactures) the extent to which the host country is able to offer the necessary infrastructure (transportation, communications facilities and supplies of skilled and unskilled labour) will be a decisive factor. In short, a country must possess some desirable L characteristics to attract inward direct investment, although the extent to which foreign firms are able to exploit these will depend on its development strategy and the extent to which it prefers to develop technological capabilities of domestic firms.

The O advantages of domestic firms will have increased from the previous stage, wherever national government policies have generated a virtuous circle of created asset accumulation. These O advantages will exist due to the development of support industries clustered around primary industries, and production will move towards semi-skilled and moderately knowledge-intensive consumer goods. Outward direct investment emerges at this stage. This may be either of a market seeking or trade-related type in adjacent territories, or of a strategic asset seeking type in developed countries. The former will be characteristically undertaken in countries that are either lower in their IDP than the home country, or, when the acquisition of created assets is the prime motive, these are likely to be directed towards countries higher up in the path.

The extent to which outward direct investment is undertaken will be influenced by the home country government-induced 'push' factors such as subsidies for exports, and technology development or acquisition (which influence the I advantages of domestic firms), as well as the changing (non-government-induced) L advantages such as relative production costs. However, the rate of outward direct investment growth is likely to be insufficient to offset the rising rate of growth of inward direct investment. As a consequence, during the second stage of development, countries will increase their net inward investment (i.e. their NOI position will worsen), although towards the latter part of the second stage, the growth rates of outward direct investment and inward direct investment will begin to converge.

Stage 3

Countries in Stage 3 are marked by a gradual decrease in the rate of growth of inward direct investment, and an increase in the rate of growth of outward direct investment that results in increasing NOI. The technological capabilities of the country are increasingly geared towards the production of standardized goods. With rising incomes, consumers begin to demand higher quality goods, fuelled in part by the growing competitiveness among the supplying firms. Comparative advantages in labour-intensive activities will deteriorate, domestic wages will rise, and outward direct investment will be directed more to countries at lower stages in their IDP. The original

O advantages of foreign firms also begin to be eroded, as domestic firms acquire their own competitive advantages and compete with them in the same sectors.

The initial O advantages of foreign firms will also begin to change, as the domestic firms compete directly with them in these sectors. This is supported by the growing stock of created assets of the host country due to increased expenditure on education, vocational training and innovatory activities. These will be replaced by new technological, managerial or marketing innovations in order to compete with domestic firms. These O advantages are likely to be based on the possession of intangible knowledge, and the public good nature of such assets will mean that foreign firms will increasingly prefer to exploit them through cross-border hierarchies. Growing L advantages such as an enlarged market and improved domestic innovatory capacity will make for economies of scale, and, with rising wage costs, will encourage more technology-intensive manufacturing as well as higher value added locally. The motives of inward direct investment will shift towards efficiency seeking production and away from import substituting production. In industries where domestic firms have a competitive advantage, there may be some inward direct investment directed towards strategic asset acquiring activities.

Domestic firms' O advantages will have changed too, and will be based less on government-induced action. Partly due to the increase in their multinationality, the character of the O advantages of foreign firms will increasingly reflect their ability to manage and coordinate geographically dispersed assets. At this stage of development, their O advantages based on possession of proprietary assets will be similar to those of firms from developed countries in all except the most technology-intensive sectors. There will be increased outward direct investment directed to Stage 1 and 2 countries, both as market seeking investment and as export platforms, as prior domestic L advantages in resource-intensive production are eroded. Outward direct investment will also occur in Stage 3 and 4 countries, partly as a market seeking strategy, but also to acquire strategic assets to protect or upgrade the O advantages of the investing firms.

The role of government-induced O advantages is likely to be less significant in Stage 3, as those of FDI-induced O advantages take on more importance. Although the significance of location-bound created assets will rise relative to those of natural assets, government policies will continue to be directed to reducing structural market imperfections in resource-intensive industries. Thus governments may attempt to attract inward direct investment in those sectors in which the comparative O advantages of enterprises are the weakest, but the comparative advantages of location-bound assets are the strongest. At the same time, they might seek to encourage their country's own enterprises to invest abroad in those sectors in which the O advantages are the strongest, and the comparative L advantages are the weakest. Structural adjustment will be required if the country is to move to the next stage of development, with declining industries (such as labour-intensive ones) undertaking direct investment abroad.

Stage 4

Stage 4 is reached when a country's outward direct investment stock exceeds or equals the inward investment stock from foreign-owned firms, and the rate of growth of outward FDI is still rising faster than that of inward FDI. At this stage, domestic firms can now not only effectively compete with foreign-owned firms in domestic sectors in which the home country has developed a competitive advantage, but they are able to penetrate foreign markets as well. Production processes and products will be state of the art, using capital-intensive production techniques as the cost of capital will be lower than that of labour. In other words, the L advantages will be based almost completely on created assets. Inward direct investment into Stage 4 countries is increasingly sequential and directed towards rationalized and asset seeking investment by firms from other Stage 4 countries. The O specific advantages of these firms tend to be more 'transaction' than 'asset' related (Dunning 1993), and to be derived from their multinationality *per se*. Some inward direct investment will originate from countries at lower stages of development, and is likely to be of a market seeking, trade-related and asset seeking nature.

Outward direct investment will continue to grow, as firms seek to maintain their competitive advantage by moving operations which are losing their competitiveness to offshore locations (in countries at lower stages), as well as responding to trade barriers installed by both countries at Stages 4 and 5, as well as countries at lower stages. Firms will have an increasing propensity to internalize the market for their O advantages by engaging in FDI rather than exports. Since the O advantages of countries at this stage are broadly similar, intra-industry production will become relatively more important, and generally follows prior growth in intra-industry trade. However, both intra-industry trade and production will tend to be increasingly conducted *within* multinational enterprises (MNEs).

The role of government is also likely to change in Stage 4. While continuing its supervisory and regulatory function, to reduce market imperfections and maintain competition, it will give more attention to the structural adjustment of its location-bound assets and technological capabilities, e.g. by fostering asset upgrading in infant industries (i.e. promoting a virtuous circle) and phasing out declining industries (i.e. promoting a vicious circle). Put another way, the role of government is now moving towards reducing transaction costs of economic activity and facilitating markets to operate efficiently. At this stage too, because of the increasing competition between countries with similar structures of resources and capabilities, governments begin taking a more strategic posture in their policy formation. Direct intervention is likely to be replaced by measures designed to aid the upgrading of domestic resources and capabilities, and to curb the market distorting behaviour of private economic agents.

Stage 5

As illustrated in Figure 1.1, in Stage 5, the NOI position of a country first falls and later fluctuates around the zero level. At the same time, both inward and outward FDI are likely to continue to increase. This is the scenario which advanced industrial nations are now approaching as the century draws to a close, and it possesses two key features. First, there is an increasing propensity for cross-border transactions to be conducted not through the market but internalized by and within MNEs. Second, as countries converge in the structure of their location-bound assets, their international direct investment positions are likely to become more evenly balanced. It has been suggested elsewhere (Dunning 1993) that these phenomena represent a natural and predictable progress of the internationalization of firms and economies. Thus the nature and scope of activity gradually shifts from arm's length trade between nations producing very different goods and services (Hecksher–Ohlin trade) to trade within hierarchies (or cooperative ventures) between countries producing very similar products.

Unlike previous stages, Stage 5 of the IDP represents a situation in which no single country has an absolute hegemony of created assets. Moreover, the O advantages of MNEs will be less dependent on their country's natural resources but more on their ability to acquire assets and on the ability of firms to organize their advantages efficiently and to exploit the gains of cross-border common governance. Another feature of Stage 5 is that as firms become globalized their nationalities become blurred. As MNEs bridge geographical and political divides and practise a policy of transnational integration, they no longer operate principally with the interests of their home nation in mind, as they trade, source and manufacture in various locations, exploiting created and natural assets wherever it is in their best interests to do so. Increasingly, MNEs, through their arbitraging functions, are behaving like mini-markets. However, the ownership and territorial boundaries of firms becomes obscured[5] as they engage in an increasingly complex web of trans-border cooperative agreements.[6]

The tendency for income levels to converge among the Triad countries has been noted, among others, by Abramovitz (1986), Baumol (1986), Dowrick and Gemmell (1991), and Alam (1992). Indeed, during the 1970s and 1980s, Japan, the EC and EFTA countries have experienced a 'catching up' in their productivity and growth relative to the United States (the 'lead' country); while a range of the newly industrializing countries began to move from Stage 2 to Stage 3 in their IDP.

As a result of these developments, the economic structures of many industrial economies have become increasingly similar. Countries which were once the lead countries in Stage 4 now find themselves joined by others. This tends to reduce their NOI position and pushes them into Stage 5 of the IDP. At the same time, there has also been a 'catching-up' effect among MNEs since the 1970s. Firms that have had relatively low levels of international operations have been internationalizing at faster rates than their more geographically diversified counterparts. These two effects are not unrelated; firms have had to compensate for slowing economic growth in their home country by seeking new markets overseas. Given the similarity in income levels, the factors of production are broadly similar, and, as Cantwell and Randaccio (1990) have shown, firms that are trying to catch up seek to imitate competitors and develop similar O advantages as their competitors in the same industry, *but not necessarily in the same country.*

To take this argument a step further, as income levels, economic structures and patterns of international production among the Triad countries converge, the relative attractions of a particular location will depend less on the availability, quality and price of their natural assets and more on those of their created assets. It has been noted elsewhere that the prosperity of modern industrial economies is increasingly dependent on their capacity to upgrade continually, or make better use of their technological capacity and human resources (Cantwell and Dunning 1991). Since many of these advantages are transferable across national boundaries, it may be predicted that, in the long run, this will lead to a more balanced international investment position, and to an increasing convergence of created asset L advantages.

However, the ability of a country to upgrade its technological and human capabilities is a function of its own location-bound endowments and, in particular, of its natural assets, the characteristics of its markets and the macro-organizational strategies of its government. We believe the role of government in affecting dynamic economic restructuring cannot be overstated. In a myriad of ways, governments can promote new trajectories of economic growth which some countries are better able to cope with than others. This has been amply illustrated by the evolution of Japan's economy compared to that of the United States, especially in the 1980s.

In terms of their gross inward and outward direct investment positions, Stage 5 countries, after an initial burst of new inward direct investment (e.g. as occurred in the United States in the 1980s), may be expected to settle down to a fluctuating equilibrium around a roughly equal amount of inward and outward investment. Inward investment will be of two kinds. The first will come from countries at lower stages of the IDP and will be essentially of the market seeking and knowledge seeking type. The second will be from Stage 4 (or Stage 5) countries whose firms will continue to indulge in rationalized investment among themselves, as well as making outward direct investments in less developed countries, especially in the natural-resource-intensive sectors. In other words, truly rationalized or efficiency seeking MNE activity will occur as plant and product specialization is encouraged in sectors where economies of scale and scope are important.

As the world economy begins to resemble a global village, strategic asset seeking investments may also be expected to rise, and this, too, will lead to increasing convergence among countries as firms seek to improve their O advantages by cross-border mergers and acquisitions (M&As) or strategic alliances. Therefore, in the shorter time frame, inward and outward investment will fluctuate depending on relative innovatory and organizational strength of the participating countries. However as Cantwell has noted,

> The sectoral pattern of innovative activity gradually changes as new industries develop and new technical linkages are forged between sectors. Yet this is a slow process which in general only slightly disturbed the pattern of technological advantages held by firms of the major industrialized countries in the 20 years between the early 1960s and the early 1980s.
>
> (Cantwell 1989, p. 45).

Thus, *pro tem*, at least, it is possible for one country to be a net outward investor compared to another. But over time, according to the extent and speed at which created assets are transferable, the investment gap will again close, leading to a fluctuating investment position around an equilibrium level. It is within this context that the fifth stage will exist.

In other words, an equilibrium of sorts will be perpetuated, but it will not be a stable equilibrium as the relative comparative and competitive advantages of countries and firms are likely to be continually shifting. Hence, along with these fluctuations in relative comparative advantages, when combined with external and internal changes in the domestic economy, gradually the number of countries at Stage 5 will fluctuate.

The acquisition, diffusion and transfer of O advantages will be influenced by the cumulative causation in trade, production and technology, and whether the industry or sector in each of the countries at Stage 5 experiences a 'vicious' or a 'virtuous' circle (Dunning 1988b, Cantwell 1989). In the former case, it may serve to increase technological divergences between countries; in the latter, it may strengthen the technological linkages between them.

In summary, Stage 5 is marked by a gradual convergence of industrial structures among countries and a change in the character of international transactions. MNE activity, in particular, will be directed to efficiency seeking investment with greater emphasis on cross-border alliances, mergers and acquisitions; and the governance and equity position of MNEs will become increasingly *transnational*. The success of countries in accumulating technology, as well as inducing continued economic growth, will depend increasingly on the ability of their firms to coordinate their resources and capabilities at a regional and global level. The economic convergence of industrialized countries on one hand, and high rate of intra-Triad FDI growth on the other, may be expected to foster regional and/or global integration as well as lessening the role of natural assets as a country-specific determinant of FDI. In Stage 5, governments will increasingly assume the role of strategic oligopolists, taking into account the behaviour of other governments in the formation and execution of their own macro-organizational strategies. In this stage too, governments are likely to play a more pro-active role in the fostering of efficient markets, and cooperating with business enterprises to reduce structural adjustment and other transaction costs.

We conclude. Beyond a certain point in the IDP, the absolute size of GNP is no longer a reliable guide of a country's competitiveness; neither, indeed, is its NOI position. This is for two reasons. First the competitiveness of a country is better measured by the rate and character of growth of GNP *vis-à-vis* that of its major competitors. Second, as the motivation of FDI evolves away from being primarily geared to the exploitation of existing O advantages to the acquisition of new O advantages, countries which offer the appropriate location-bound resources for the creation of such advantages may increase their attractiveness to inbound FDI. Investments made to acquire or exploit indigenous competitive advantage, far from representing a weakness of the recipient country, could represent a strength. Certainly, recent evidence seems to suggest that in the Triad at least, inbound and outbound FDI are increasingly complementary to each other, especially at a sectoral level (UNCTAD 1993).

Most of the empirical testing of the basic proposition of the IDP, viz. that there is a systematic relationship between a country's inward and outward investment and its GNP per capita, has used cross-sectional data, and is generally supportive of the proposition.[7] However, new cross-sectional and time series data – some of which are set out in this and later chapters – seem to be pointing to two things. The first is that the shape and position of the IDP probably varies much more between individual countries than it was originally thought. In particular, the economic structure of countries, and the development strategies and macro-organizational policies of governments, appear to be critical in influencing both the role of

MNEs in a country's economy at a given moment of time, and how inward and outward direct investment may help fashion the growth and structure of the economy over time (Dunning 1993). The second is that the underlying nature of the IDP for all countries appears to be undergoing some change, due to a series of events of the global economy, which leads us to revise some of our hypotheses about its trajectory. This issue is taken up in greater detail in Part 2 of this chapter.

Country-specific factors and the IDP

As most of the contributions to this volume will be considering the nature of the interaction between inbound and outbound FDI and the level, composition and growth of the GNP of countries, we will need to write comparatively little at this point about country-specific factors. It may, however, be appropriate to remind ourselves that the IDP was first put forward to illustrate the relevance of the eclectic paradigm of international production in explaining the NOI position of countries, and, indeed, this is one of the main purposes of this volume. It follows, then, that any predictions about the IDP must rest on the contents of the paradigm itself.

Now, as stated earlier, the paradigm avers that a country will attract inbound FDI when (i) foreign firms possess certain O specific advantages over and above those of indigenous firms; (ii) its L bound resources and capabilities favour the deployment of these competitive advantages, relative to those offered by other countries; and (iii) foreign firms perceive that it is to their benefit to internalize the intermediate product markets for these advantages, rather than selling them via the external market, or by a cooperative arrangement, to domestic firms in the host country. Similarly the paradigm hypothesizes that the propensity of a country to be an outward direct investor will rest on the strength and character of the O advantages of its indigenous firms, and the extent to which these might best be exploited by adding value to them in a foreign location, and organized through an MNE hierarchy rather than through a non-equity relationship with a foreign firm.

The eclectic paradigm further suggests some of the ways in which, over time, inbound and outbound investment may affect the trajectory of a country's development path. This it might do by its impact both on the composition and productivity of domestic economic activity, and the ease or difficulty with which a country is able to restructure its resources and capabilities to meet the needs of endogenous and exogenous change. The critical role played by inbound FDI in the upgrading of Singaporean indigenous endowments, and that of outbound FDI in the dynamic restructuring of Japan's post-war development, are two cases in point, although other examples show that FDI does not always have such salutary effects on economic welfare.[8]

Over the past 30 years, there have been a large number of studies on the impact of both outbound and inbound MNE activity on the development and economic restructuring of the countries in which they operate. The overwhelming consensus of these studies is that, for good or bad, this is critically dependent on three main variables, viz. (i) the type of FDI undertaken, (ii) the structure of the indigenous resources and capabilities of the countries concerned, and (iii) the macro-economic and organizational policies pursued by governments.[9] We would then expect the shape and position of the IDP of countries – which traces the interaction between inbound and outbound FDI and advances in the prosperity of those countries – to be determined by the same variables.

We have suggested that one of the characteristics of economic development identified by several writers (e.g. Porter 1990, Ozawa 1992, Narula 1995, Dunning and Narula 1994) is that, as development proceeds, the significance of indigenous assets relative to *natural* assets as a locational attraction to inbound FDI increases. Ozawa (1992), in describing the post-war development of Japan, identifies four distinct stages, viz. those of labour-intensive manufacturing, scale-economies-based production of heavy and chemical industries, assembly-based mass production of consumer durables, and mechatronics-based flexible manufacturing. For his part, Porter (1990) writes about the nature of competitive advantages of a country according to whether they are factor driven, investment driven, innovation driven or wealth driven. While the prosperity of most poor countries is largely resource driven, that of the richest is largely innovation or wealth driven. Naturally, the precise balance of a country's natural and created assets will vary depending on the extent to which it is endowed with the former (cf. Canada with Japan, and Kuwait with Singapore) but as Ohmae (1987) has powerfully shown, even the value of natural resources such as minerals and agricultural products can be dramatically increased by secondary processing and astute marketing, both of which require the input of created assets.

In view of the fact that an increasing number of countries are now at the innovation stage of their IDP – indeed, as we shall suggest later, innovation-led production is changing the trajectory of global economic development - it is not surprising that both outward and inward FDI are being increasingly evaluated by national governments in terms of their perceived contribution to technological capacity and human resource development (Dunning 1994). Governments, too, are becoming aware that, if their FDI is properly to achieve their objectives, they need to provide the location-bound resources and capabilities essential for the efficient creation and deployment of the O specific advantages of both foreign investors and their own MNEs. An appropriate combination of the competitive advantages of firms and countries is likely to make for a *virtuous* cycle of upgrading economic development, with each advantage fostering the other. An inappropriate combination of such advantages – or the lack of one or both – is likely to lead to a vicious cycle to the detriment of economic development.

Structural changes and the IDP

Let us now turn to the main focus of Part 1 of this chapter, which is to consider the ways in which recent technological and organizational changes, as they have impinged upon the governance of both firms and national economies, have affected our thinking about the shape and character of the IDP.

(a) Some shifts in the rationale for FDI

Most of the received literature on MNE-related activity tends to assume that firms engage in FDI in order to exploit best, or organize more efficiently, their existing competitive advantages. Sometimes, these resources and capabilities are combined with foreign location-bound assets to supply domestic or adjacent markets, and sometimes to service more distant markets. In some instances, too, inbound FDI may be used to restructure the existing portfolio of foreign value-added activities by MNEs. Such sequential investment is best thought of as efficiency seeking trans-border activity, as contrasted with market or resource seeking trans-border activity.

In the last decade or more, however, MNE activity has been increasingly motivated by the desire to acquire new competitive advantages, or protect existing advantages. Such strategic asset acquiring FDI has been particularly pronounced within the Triad of advanced industrial countries, and is most dramatically shown by the spate of cross-border mergers and acquisitions (M&As) which have occurred since the mid- and late 1980s.[10] Essentially, such M&As have been (and still are) undertaken by firms for five main reasons: (i) the rising costs of innovation and of entry into unfamiliar markets, (ii) competitive pressures for firms to be more cost effective, (iii) the growing need to tap into complementary technologies and to capture the economies of scale and scope expected from the merger or acquisition, (iv) a desire to protect or advance their global markets, *vis à vis* oligopolistic competitors, and (v) the need to encapsulate the time of the innovating or market entry process.

Such strategic asset acquiring FDI implies that firms may engage in outward FDI from a position of weakness, and that countries may attract inbound FDI because their resources and capabilities offer competitive advantages to foreign MNEs. Thus, part of the contemporary outbound MNE activity directed to the United States is designed to gain access to the technological capabilities of US firms, and their privileged access to US or adjacent (e.g. NAFTA) markets. Such FDI is likely to be determined by a different configuration of O and L advantages than those facing traditional market or resource seeking MNEs.

The effect of strategic asset seeking investment on the IDP is that it is likely to increase the level of outward investment of all countries, but particularly that from medium income and fast growing industrializing nations, as they seek to establish a speedy presence in the most innovatory and dynamic markets of the world. Frequently, firms from developing countries do not have the full range of resources and capabilities to promote a fully blown 'standalone' competitive strategy, and certainly not one which would help them penetrate unfamiliar global markets. Depending on their particular strengths and weaknesses, their liquidity position and the type of assets to which they need access, the mode of foreign involvement by firms is likely to vary between an FDI, a minority joint venture and some form of cooperative alliance. However, *ceteris paribus*, the first of these routes is most likely to be preferred whenever the assets sought are perceived to be critical to protect or advance the core competencies of the investing firm.

As yet, there has been little systematic research into the significance of strategic asset acquiring FDI, relative to that of other kinds.

But, taking inbound FDI in the United States as an example, it is generally agreed by scholars that, although the resurgence of activity by European firms in the 1970s and much of the greenfield investment by Japanese firms in the 1980s reflected the growing O advantages of these firms, relative to those of US firms, many of the transatlantic European M&As in the late 1980s and early 1990s have been geared towards strengthening the O advantages of the investing firms (or diminishing those of their competitors) by buying into US resources and capabilities, and/or markets. One suspects that had it been feasible, there would also have been a substantial amount of M&A activity by US and European firms in Japan during this period.

The presence of strategic asset acquiring FDI is then tending to raise the level of inward investment of industrialized countries – and particularly those which are the leading repositories of advanced created assets. It is also tending to increase the outward investment of these countries – but not to the same extent as inward investment – while raising the outbound FDI by industrializing developing countries, as they seek to aid and accelerate the entry of their firms into global markets. In short, the presence and growth of asset acquiring MNE activity is leading to a flattening out of the NOI position of countries, as compared to that suggested by the traditional version of IDP, viz. at lower levels of GNP the net *inward* investment position will be less, and at high levels of income the NOI position will be lower, than in the absence of such investment.[11] The suggested reshaping of the IDP is portrayed by the dotted line in Figure 1.1.

(b) The emergence of alliance capitalism

Another feature of the last decade has been the growth in non-equity collaborative arrangements of one kind or another. Sometimes, these are being pursued as alternatives to FDI, but, for the most part, they are complementary to it. Increasingly, cross-border *intra*-firm FDI and *inter*-firm cooperative schemes are being perceived as part of a holistic and multi-modal strategy of the leading global players.

It is possible to identify many different kinds of collaborative schemes, but the vast majority fall into two categories. The first take the form of strategic alliances which are specifically intended to gain access (or preclude a competitor from gaining access) to foreign assets or markets. The second embrace a galaxy of international subcontracting relationships, in which inter-firm cooperation goes beyond the production of materials, parts and components, to the design and development of new materials, parts and components. In each case, too, it would seem that the terms of any collaboration are contained less in a formal contract and more by a sense of agreed mission and mutual commitment.

It is the latter characteristic of inter-firm relationships which has led to the term 'alliance' capitalism being coined (Gerlach 1992).[12] Alliance capitalism differs from hierarchical capitalism in that, whereas in the case of the former, the coordination of economic activity is determined primarily by arm's length markets and inter-firm cooperation, in the latter it is decided primarily by arm's length markets and hierarchical *intra*-firm fiat.[13]

While alliance capitalism has long since been a prominent feature of many East Asian economies – most noticeably Japan and South Korea – in the mid-1990s it is spreading – albeit in a modified form – to other parts of the world. This is for three main reasons. The first reflects the lack of experience of hierarchical capitalism by the transition economies of Central and Eastern Europe and China. As these countries struggle to embrace the discipline of free markets, they are finding that the speediest and most effective way to upgrade their natural and created assets is for their newly privatized firms to form cooperative alliances with other domestic, or foreign, firms, rather than to pursue the route of internal economic growth. Second, it reflects the increasing inability of firms to pursue 'stand-alone' strategies in situations in which their core competencies need to be efficiently combined with those of other firms if they – the former – are to be fully effective.

Third, one of the features of the emerging techno-economic paradigm of micro-economic activity, viz. flexible and innovation-led production, is that it requires a symbiotic and continuing relationship between the various participants in the production process, and that this is likely to be most effective if it is based on mutually agreed upon goals and on active and purposeful cooperation, rather than on administrative fiat. Thus, although many firms are currently downsizing the range of their activities in order to concentrate on those central to their core competencies, i.e. becoming *less* hierarchical, they are also concluding new strategic alliances with their critical suppliers and industrial customers along the value chain, and with their competitors across value chains. This they are doing both to leverage more effectively their own special capabilities, and to ensure, by appropriate control procedures, that the goods and services they transact with other firms, and which critically affect these capabilities, are provided at the highest quality and/or the lowest cost.[14]

What are the implications of the advent of alliance capitalism on the international direct investment position of countries and their IDP? Perhaps, the main implication is that such non-equity forms of cross-border production are becoming too important to be ignored in discussing the export and import of resources and capabilities, and the way in which their use is influenced either by hierarchical or by cooperative arrangements involving foreign firms. Here what scant evidence we have[15] suggests that, apart from situations in which inbound and/or outbound FDI is disallowed or regulated by governments, cross-border alliance formation to gain access to new technologies and markets, or to exploit the economies of scale and synergy, tends to involve a two-way exchange of resources and capabilities between firms from advanced industrial countries. By contrast, other kinds of alliances, and especially those which involve firms from both developed and developing countries, are primarily concluded in order to facilitate a transfer of resources and capabilities from the former to the latter countries.[16]

Incorporating such alliances into the IDP would then suggest that inbound transfer MNE activity[17] of the poor or middle income countries would increase, but in the case of the richer countries, one might predict an increase of both inbound and outbound resource transfer. Unfortunately, apart from some data on cross-border inter-firm royalties and fees, it is extremely difficult to quantify either the extent to which alliances *do* transfer resources and capabilities, or the consequence of such transfers on the welfare of the exporting and importing countries. As a subject for further research, the relationships between alliance formation, economic structure and development surely demand some degree of priority.

(c) The role of non-market country-specific differences in explaining the investment development path

In our earlier testing of the hypothesis that a country's outward and inward FDI is systematically related to its stage of development (Dunning 1981, 1986, 1988a), we identified a number of contextual variables which could explain why the shape and position of the IDP differs between countries. *Inter alia*, our research showed that industrial or industrializing countries were likely to generate more outward direct investment at any given level of GNP per head than the natural resource-based economies.[18] At the same time, we made the general assumption that countries – or, more specifically, the governments of countries – pursued market friendly economic strategies, and intervened as little as possible in the organization and allocation of resources within their jurisdiction.

In retrospect, it is clear that, throughout the last three decades, by a bevy of macro-economic and organizational policies, national governments have considerably affected the structure of the IDP of their countries. This they have done by both specific actions to influence the level and composition of inbound and outbound FDI, and by their general economic and social policies, which impact the attractiveness of their location-bound resources and markets to foreign investors. Moreover, notwithstanding the liberalization and deregulation of many markets over the past decade, national governments continue to exercise a powerful influence on a country's international investment position and the profile of its IDP.

Several of the country case studies of this volume confirm this proposition. It is most obviously seen in the case of centrally planned and East Asian economies. But, as revealed by some quite dramatic shifts in the outward and inward FDI position of particular countries – which have often occurred as a direct result of a reorientation in government economic policy – it is no less evident in economies such as the UK, France, Sweden, Greece and Portugal in Europe; Chile, Columbia, Argentina, Jamaica, Mexico and Venezuela in Latin America; China, India, the Philippines, Vietnam and South Korea in Asia; Canada in North America; Morocco, Egypt, Nigeria and South Africa in Africa; and in Iran in the Middle East.

There is already a good deal of evidence that the liberalization and privatization of markets, and the attempts by many governments to increase inbound investment, have led to an increased flow and restructuring of inward investment into many countries, and, *pari passu*, an increased flow of outward investment from other countries.[19] It is also apparent that the role of national governments in affecting the price and quality of location-bound resources within their jurisdictions, and the motivation and capabilities of their own firms to be outward investors, is becoming increasingly significant – and especially in so far as inter-Triad strategic asset and efficiency seeking investment is concerned. Thus, for example, government policies which aim to upgrade the quality of indigenous resources and capabilities to meet the demands of the international market-place are likely to engage in more cross-border transactions (e.g. FDI, trade and cooperative alliances) than those which are designed to promote economic self-reliance.[20]

It follows from the above paragraphs that the relationship between FDI and income levels using cross-sectional country data may well be expected to vary at different points of time because of changes in the role of governments in affecting inward and outward investment. It is also likely to fluctuate according to the direction and character of technological advances and the country from which they originate. Such advances, by their impact on the competitive advantages of firms of a particular nationality, on the cost-effectiveness of the location-bound resources and capabilities of countries, and on the way in which economic activity is organized, are likely to lead to a repositioning of the IDPs of countries. At the same time, longitudinal data show that variations in the trajectory of a country's IDP may occur because of changes in the actions of national governments. In short, then, although we have some ideas about the interaction of the behaviour of governments and inward and outward investment, we need to explore this in a more systematic and rigorous way.

The theory: some concluding remarks

In this chapter, we have suggested that some of the propositions initially put forward to relate the inward and outward direct investment position of countries to their stages of development need reconsideration. Partly, we have argued this is because the *raison d'être* and character of FDI has undergone some important changes. Partly it is because other forms of cross-border involvement – and notably cooperative arrangements – by MNEs need to be incorporated in the analysis; and that the interaction between these other forms and the stages of development may well be different from those of FDI. And partly we have suggested this is because differences in national government policies need to be more explicitly identified as an explanatory variable of the international direct investment of countries, before any satisfactory relationship between outbound and inward investment and economic development can be established.

Lastly, we believe that further attention needs to be given to the form and characteristics of the fifth stage of the IDP, i.e. that in which the outward and inward investment positions – like those of exports and imports – fluctuate around the same level. Here the hypothesis is that the structure of the most advanced industrial economies are both similar and inextricably linked with each other. Although, for a period of time, one nation, through a series of path breaking technological or organizational advances and/or superior macro-economic or macro-organizational policies, might gain a major competitive advantage over other nations, any marked increase in outbound direct investment may well be tempered by a corresponding rise in inbound strategic asset seeking investment and alliance formation. Moreover, due to the increasing ease at which knowledge, information and even organizational techniques can move across national boundaries, any lead by one country is likely to be quite quickly eroded by its competitors, and sometimes, the catching-up process, itself, may be aided and abetted by inbound and outbound FDI and alliance formation.

However, little is known about the mechanism by which this is achieved. Some hints about the dynamic interplay between the O specific advantages of firms and the L specific advantages of countries have been given by Tolentino (1993), Dunning (1993) and Narula (1995); while Ozawa (1992) has explored some of the ways in which inbound and outbound Japanese FDI has affected the structure of Japanese economic development. The conditions under which inward and outward FDI[21] can promote the upgrading of a country's resources and capabilities and advantageously restructure its resource allocation have also been explored by several writers,[22] including Cantwell (1989) and Cantwell and Dunning (1991), who used the concepts of virtuous and vicious cycles to explore the interplay between inward FDI and the competitiveness of a particular industrial sector.

While some of the contributions to this volume take this discussion a little further, much remains to be done. Why, indeed, has inbound FDI promoted advantageous structural economic development in some countries, e.g. Singapore and Thailand, but not in others, e.g. Chile and Nigeria? What determines whether outward direct investment helps a country to upgrade the quality of its indigenous assets, and to promote its dynamic competitive advantage, or, instead, to erode its technological strengths and human resource development? What is the impact of alliance capitalism on both the optimal mode of resource transfer and usage, and on the ways in which these may affect the structure and pace of economic development? It is questions such as these which need the attention of scholars in the years to come.

PART 2: A STATISTICAL EVALUATION

Structural change and the IDP

At the outset it is important to point out that any statistical evaluation of the IDP must necessarily be a tentative one. Any attempt to conduct a thorough empirical analysis of a complex and changing relationship has severe limitations. Given this fact, it is not our intention to develop a rigorous statistical specification and test of the IDP. In fact, our aim is almost exactly the opposite as we wish to demonstrate that a statistical evaluation of the relationship between FDI and economic development cannot be conducted on an aggregate basis across countries, as the IDP represents a paradigm which is idiosyncratic and country specific, and therefore best analysed on a country-by-country basis. We intend merely to argue that the basic relationships postulated by the IDP are still applicable, and how the lacunae regarding the extent and evolution of natural and created assets as well as the changes in the world economy affect the relationships suggested by the IDP.

Structural changes in the world economy

There have been two major developments in the world economy which have impacted the character of the IDP. The first is the introduction of Stage 5, which reflects the catching-up and convergence process of the industrialized economies. As we have discussed in Part 1 of this chapter and elsewhere (Narula 1993, 1995, Dunning and Narula 1994), as countries reach Stage 4 and begin to enter Stage 5, the activities and growth of their MNEs are no longer a function of just the economic conditions of their home country, but the various host countries in which they have subsidiaries. The more globalized the operations of a firm, the greater the extent to which its O advantages are likely to be firm specific, rather than determined by the economic, political and cultural conditions of its home country. Moreover, the O advantages of firms will increasingly be dependent on their ability to acquire and develop *created* assets and their ability to organize these assets efficiently in order to exploit the advantages due to common governance, making the MNE less dependent on its home country's natural resources. As such, O advantages become increasingly firm specific as MNEs become more internationalized. The consequence of this is that the outward direct investment position of a country's firms at this stage is no longer entirely dependent on the economic status and competitiveness of their home country, and increasingly affected by the conditions in the various other countries in which they operate, and therefore, after reaching a certain NOI position, a country's investment position will *not* necessarily be proportional to *its income level or relative stage of development*. To put it another way, we hypothesize that, *ceteris paribus*, a Stage 5 country will continue to experience change in its FDI position regardless of whether its relative stage of development or income levels change. This is readily apparent when examining the NOI position and GDPs of countries like the United States and the UK (see also Chapters 2 and 3), which have either remained at the same relative stage of development or fallen, but continue to experience high growth in both their inward and outward position. Indeed, not only has the share of total worldwide inward investment to industrialized countries increased, but a greater extent of outward investment from these countries is being directed towards other industrialized countries.

Furthermore, the use of GDP as a proxy for development does not take into account the profound changes in the economic structure of the industrialized countries, which have shown a clear trend towards tertiary (i.c. service) sectors. In other words, while their overall economic growth has slowed over the past two decades, there has been considerable structural adjustment between sectors. This has also had an effect on the composition of their inbound and outbound FDI and, because of this, its geographical composition. Since 1980, for example, much of the growth in inward and outward FDI has been directed to the tertiary sector, and has been between industrialized countries (Narula 1995). These changes make a statistical evaluation of the relationship between NOI and GDP of Stage 4 and 5 countries an increasingly difficult exercise through an aggregate, cross-sectional test.

The growth of alternative forms of overseas value-added activity such as strategic alliances needs also to be taken into account, especially in high technology sectors. As suggested in Part 1 of this chapter, strategic alliances have become an important means by which MNEs from industrialized countries have begun to engage in cross-border activities since the 1980s. The evidence suggests that there is an increasing preference for Triad-based MNEs to utilize non-equity-based cooperative agreements in preference to equity-based agreements (such as joint ventures) in their intra-Triad partnering activities in these sectors[23] (Hagedoorn and Narula 1994). Such agreements are naturally not reflected in the FDI data, and since well over 95 per cent of all strategic alliances[24] are intra-Triad in scope (Freeman and Hagedoorn 1994) the use of FDI data for industrialized countries without allowing for the growth of strategic alliances may make the results questionable.

The second consequence of changes in the world economy has been the growing divergence of at least some of the developing economies away from the industrialized economies. The catching-up process described earlier has not occurred among the poorer countries, who have diverged as a group from the wealthier countries and are not exhibiting a tendency to converge in relation to the world leaders (Dowrick and Gemmel 1991, Dowrick 1992, Verspagen 1993), and are in fact 'falling behind'. The effect on the FDI activities of developing countries is that less inward direct investment is from industrialized countries, and those developing countries that are outward investors prefer to invest in the industrialized countries wherever possible to acquire created assets. However, the 'falling-behind' effect is associated primarily with Stage 1 and 2 countries, while a handful of developing countries that are regarded as newly industrializing economies (Stage 3) have been shown to be 'catching up' with the industrialized economies. Indeed, data on FDI flows indicate that the four Asian NICs account for 57.6 per cent of total outward flows from non-oil exporting developing countries between 1980 and 1990, and 83 per cent over 1988–90.

The idiosyncratic nature of countries

Most previous tests of the validity of the IDP have used a cross-sectional study across countries as a surrogate for longitudinal analysis. As the various country studies in this volume will later show, the exact circumstance of each country is unique, and while there are some general similarities between groups of countries, the explanatory power of the 'ideal' IDP based on cross-sectional analysis of a large group of countries is severely limited. This aggregation of countries for a given time period assumes that countries follow a broadly similar investment development path, whereas, in fact, each country follows its own particular path which is determined by three main variables: (i) the extent and nature of its created and natural assets, (ii) its strategy of economic development, and (iii) the role of government. These factors essentially determine the nature and extent of the firm-specific assets of both foreign MNEs and domestic firms operating within its borders.

The character of a country's resource endowments

The extent and nature of a country's natural and created assets are determined by two main issues: (i) its resource structure and (ii) its size.

(i) Resource structure

A country may possess a significant comparative advantage, or an absolute advantage, in primary commodities. Such a country is likely to spawn domestic firms that possess O advantages in the exploitation of such assets. However, especially if such an advantage is a near absolute one, it is likely to be the recipient of considerable inward investment from MNEs that wish to internalize the supply of primary products to their upstream activities located in other countries, and the extent of this inward investment will almost continue to rise as the other L advantages associated with the host country develop. These L advantages include the availability of skilled labour and other infrastructural facilities, and may lead to sequential vertical investment in upstream activities by both domestic firms and MNEs. As a result, a comparative advantage in a natural-resource-based industry may be sustained even when the income levels rise to developed country standards. Such a scenario would result in an NOI position that continues to be negative even when its economy is developed, as for example in Australia. Any outward investment would also tend to be in industries that are either in or related to the primary sector, but would be dwarfed by the increasing extent of inward investment. Such countries would tend to have a much lower (i.e. negative) level of NOI at considerably advanced stages of development.

The *lack* of a natural resource base (i.e. a comparative disadvantage in primary commodities) would, *ceteris paribus*, result in the opposite effect. Inward investment at earlier stages would be muted, and outward investment might begin at an earlier stage to secure the availability of necessary natural resources. Such a country is also more likely to begin strategic asset seeking investment at an earlier stage (e.g. Japan). Overall, these countries would become net outward investors at a considerably earlier stage of development than those well endowed with natural resources.

(ii) Market size

Countries that possess small domestic market size, such as Hong Kong, Singapore and Switzerland, are likely to have not just limited natural resources such as primary commodities, but limited attraction in terms of market size. Thus the lack of economies of scale will inhibit inward foreign investment in earlier stages. As their human capital and infrastructure improves, some inward investment may occur for export processing purposes. The small populations may mean not just small aggregate consumption, but that domestic firms would need to seek overseas markets in order to achieve economies of scale. This not only would result in outward direct investment at earlier stages of development, but also suggests that as income levels rise, domestic investors that were involved in export-oriented production will seek overseas locations to compensate for the shortage of low wage human capital for labour-intensive production. Such countries will reach (and remain at) a positive NOI position at a considerably earlier stage of their development. The opposite scenario would apply for large countries, which would attract larger amounts of inward investment due to the attractions of their large markets, and domestic firms may not have as much incentive to seek overseas markets since economies of scale can be achieved at home.

The dynamics of the natural/created asset evolution are primarily determined by those associated with the economic, social and political environment issues that are generally a direct result of the actions of governments. A statistical analysis of the IDP cannot, given the static nature of a cross-sectional test, capture the dynamic development of created assets. The role of government is even more idiosyncratic and peculiar to each country, and it is exceedingly difficult to translate this into a general variable, or to group countries into distinct groups according to the role of governments in influencing the created/natural asset balance. However, since these issues are dealt with in considerable detail in the country studies throughout the rest of this volume, we will briefly discuss the two main issues that primarily influence the dynamics of created asset development.

Economic system -

The economic orientation of a country may either be outward looking, export oriented (OL–EO) or inward looking, import substituting (IL–IS) (Ozawa 1992). Depending on the orientation of an economy, the use of either (or a hybrid of the two) will substantially affect both economic development and the extent and pattern of FDI, and hence the nature of the path taken by a particular country. An OL–EO regime is likely to achieve faster growth and structural upgrading. Ozawa (1992) argues that an OL–EO regime is a necessary condition for FDI facilitated development. We suggest here that although it is not a necessary condition for growth in the first two stages, the greater the extent of OL–EO policy orientation, the faster the process of structural adjustment and economic growth and the quicker a country's progress through the stages of the IDP. Our earlier discussion of the various stages assumes an OL–EO type of policy regime beyond the second stage, but not for the first two. IL-IS countries would tend to have relatively little inward and outward FDI activity.

The failure of countries to proceed beyond the second stage is associated with the vicious cycle of poverty (VCP). This, when applied in the traditional sense, is explained as follows: low income levels in less developed countries are associated with low savings rates which, in turn, result in low capital investment, thereby keeping income levels low. In the parlance of the eclectic paradigm there is a lack of ownership advantages of domestic firms and location advantages of the country, as well as an inability to develop or acquire these. The O advantages referred to here include financial assets as well as the Oa and Ot types of advantages, whereas the L advantages are those of infrastructure. This cycle can be broken, *inter alia*, through the infusion of capital through FDI, which allows for technological spillovers and financial capital.

Governments and organizations of economic activity

Although the kind of economic system associated with a country broadly determines the path taken by a country, the nature of government policy associated with a particular system can vary between countries with the same economic system and at the same stage of development. There are two main areas of government strategy which directly impinge on the nature of the IDP of a country: macro-economic strategy and macro-organizational strategy (Dunning 1992). The role of governments in determining macro-economic policy is relatively well defined, and is often associated with the economic system. On the other hand, there is considerable variance amongst countries in the role of governments in determining macro-organizational strategy. Macro-organizational strategy primarily influences the structure and organization of economic activity, and the nature of the policies most appropriate at a particular stage should, in an 'ideal' situation, change as the economy evolves, reflecting the nature of market imperfections that the policy is designed to circumvent (Hamalainen 1993). Essentially, in such a best-world scenario, government plays a market facilitating role in which its macro-organizational policy dynamically evolves over time. Increasing economic specialization associated with economic development leads to a growth in market failures and increases the potential benefits of government macro-organizational policy (Durkheim 1964). However, as Hamalainen (1993) points out, governments may also fail, and society is often faced with a choice between imperfect markets and imperfect governments. Given that macro-organizational policy embraces a wide variety of issues,[25] and the fact that there is little agreement on what the optimal involvement of government should be, the macro-organizational policy stance varies widely among countries. The differences between the macro-organizational strategy of countries at the same stage of development influence both the structure of markets and the extent to which economic activity is efficiently conducted, thereby affecting the specialization and economic structure of the country, as well as the extent of FDI activity associated with it.

Evaluating the IDP

As we have earlier indicated, it is not our intention to develop a rigorous specification of the IDP, but merely to examine whether a causal relationship exists between FDI and economic development for 1992, and to illustrate the deviation from the 'ideal' path due to the extent of natural and created assets, as well as those due to structural changes in the world economy. We shall utilize data on

FDI stocks published in UNCTAD (1994). GDP and population data are derived from World Bank (1994). All data are in nominal US dollars. All FDI and GDP figures are normalized by population. Inward FDI per capita is denoted as IWK, outward FDI as OWK, NOI per capita as NOIK, and GDP per capita is denoted as GDPK. In conducting the analysis, we shall also attempt to illustrate that the nature of the relationship varies with the extent of natural and created assets associated with a country.

The extent of natural/created assets is based on a two-fold criteria to allow for differences due to resources intensity as well as differences in country size. High natural asset countries are defined as those countries whose primary exports as a percentage of total exports (PRX) are greater than or equal to 50 per cent or whose area is greater than 1.9 million km^2.[26] Since most developing countries tend to have a comparative advantage in primary commodities, the sample tends to consist largely of developing countries. Although it would be more appropriate to include only those countries which have an absolute advantage in natural resources, rather than those with a comparative advantage, it is exceedingly difficult to find such a measure. Low natural asset countries are assumed to represent countries with a high created asset base, or have a potential to become economies with a created asset base. This group is defined as countries for which PRX ≤ 20 per cent or area is less than 5000 km^2.

Net outward investment

We examine the relationship between NOI and GDP utilizing a quadratic specification. This allows for the fact that the dependent variable changes over time and stages, but it also assumes that the rate of change is more or less constant. Apart from running regressions for the entire sample (ALL) we also do so for a smaller subsample that excludes the most industrialized countries. This has two purposes. First, since we have not developed a specification for the fifth stage of the IDP, by excluding the countries that are most likely to be in Stage 5, we are able to test whether in fact the J-curve initially proposed by Dunning (1981) is still valid for the pre-Stage 5 countries. Second, by excluding the Stage 5 countries we are able to avoid 'stretching' of the IDP due to the cluster of a large number of developing countries at the origin and the spread of the industrialized countries around the X-axis, due to the process of

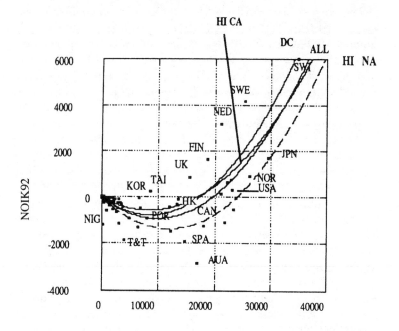

Figure 1.2   NOI and GDP for 1992

convergence and divergence. This would make the second NOI = 0 point further to the right than might actually be the case. The cut-off point for this sample is taken to be the first industrialized country with an NOI > 0. Figure 1.2 shows the plot of NOI per capita against GDP per capita for 1992. We also run regressions for two other subsamples, the created asset countries (HI CA) and the natural asset countries (HI NA). These four curves have been superimposed on Figure 1.2 while the results of these regressions are given in Table 1.1. We have not included the results for 1980 here since these are broadly similar to those for 1992. Nonetheless, there are broad differences in the distribution of the observations for the developing countries and the industrialized countries that are due to the catching-up and falling-behind scenarios due to convergence and divergence which have been evaluated using some simple measures in Table 1.2. In the case of the industrialized countries, which dominate much of the graph, there has been an increasing trend towards a wider distribution along the Y-axis since 1980. The

Table 1.1 Linear regression equations for NOI with GDP based on quadratic relationship

Sample	GDPK	GDPK^2	ADJ.R^2	F-value	N
ALL	−0.1872***	0.957 × 10^{-5}***	0.542	51.69	88
DC	−0.1767***	0.102 × 10^{-4}***	0.418	26.35	73
NA	−0.2292***	0.962 × 10^{-5}***	0.582	36.64	53
CA	−0.1329**	0.789 × 10^{-5}***	0.579	16.33	24

*** Significant at the 1% level. ** Significant at the 2.5% level.

Table 1.2 FDI activity and GDP, 1980 and 1992

	1980 Mean	Standard deviation	Ratio $\frac{ii}{i}$	1992 Mean	Standard deviation	Ratio of $\frac{iv}{iii}$	Ratio of means $\frac{iii}{i}$	Ratio of standard deviations $\frac{iv}{ii}$
	(i)	(ii)		(iii)	(iv)			
All countries								
Inward FDI	246	386	1.6	783	1263	1.6	3.2	3.3
Outward FDI	164	533	3.2	721	1783	2.5	4.4	3.3
NOI	−84	402	−4.8	−62	1076	−17.4	0.7	2.7
GDP	3453	4200	1.2	6231	8717	1.4	1.8	2.1
Industrialized countries								
Inward FDI	749	525	0.7	2671	1746	0.7	3.6	3.3
Outward FDI	837	985	1.2	3562	2717	0.8	4.3	2.8
NOI	87	804	9.2	890	2157	2.4	10.2	2.7
GDP	10919	2167	0.2	22816	4804	0.2	2.1	2.2
Non-industrial countries								
Inward FDI	128	223	1.7	363	574	1.6	2.8	2.6
Outward FDI	6	26	4.2	90	338	3.8	14.8	13.2
NOI	−124	217	−1.7	−273	429	−1.6	2.2	2.0
GDP	1696	2088	1.2	2545	3533	1.4	1.5	1.7
Stage 3 countries								
Inward FDI	556	789	1.4	2694	4414	1.6	4.8	5.6
Outward FDI	40	84	2.1	727	954	1.3	18.2	11.4
NOI	−515	711	−1.4	−1966	3815	−1.9	3.8	5.4
GDP	5402	2975	0.6	11118	3671	0.3	2.1	1.2
Stage 1 and 2 countries								
Inward FDI	97	183	1.9	221	347	1.6	2.3	1.9
Outward FDI	5	26	5.5	12	35	2.8	2.6	1.4
NOI	−94	177	−1.9	−208	335	−1.6	2.2	1.9
GDP	1110	1095	1.0	1285	1182	0.9	1.2	1.1

Note: All values are normalized by population.

mean NOI has become more positive, increasing by a factor of 10.2, while the mean GDP has increased by a factor of just 2.1. Furthermore, the ratio of the standard deviation to the mean of NOI has fallen from 9.2 in 1980 to 2.4 in 1992 for industrialized countries, while this ratio for GDP has remained constant at 0.2. This suggests that convergence phenomena regarding GDP have halted, while the NOI positions of these countries have become increasing similar.

The high growth rate of NOI relative to GDP for the industrialized countries can be contrasted with that of the non-industrial countries (Table 1.2). The mean NOI levels for the non-industrial countries have become more negative but only by a factor of 2.2, whereas their mean GDP levels have increased by a factor of 1.5. The ratio of the standard deviation to the mean of NOI has decreased only slightly, while that of GDP has increased from 1.2 to 1.4 between 1980 and 1992. This suggests there is an increasing variation in the income levels of these countries as a whole, while their NOI positions have remained at the same level of dispersion.

However, as Figure 1.2 illustrates, there seem to be two groups of pre-Stage 4 countries. The majority of developing countries seem to be clustered at the origin, while just a handful of countries are more widely distributed, and roughly correspond to the newly industrializing countries (NICs). If we extract this group, we are able to distinguish between the Stage 1 and 2 countries, and the Stage 3 countries, identified separately in Table 1.2. It is readily apparent that much of the growth associated with the entire sample of non-industrialized countries was primarily associated with the NICs. The mean level of GDP for Stage 1 and 2 countries between 1980 and 1992 has shown only a marginal increase even in nominal terms by a factor of just 1.2, implying that there may even have been a decline in real terms. As for the Stage 3 countries, their GDP growth rate was equivalent to that of the industrial countries. The mean NOI level for Stage 1 and 2 countries doubled over the same period, becoming more negative, while NOI for Stage 3 became more positive, growing by a factor of 3.8.

The change in distribution over time lends support to our earlier comments regarding the changes in the world economy. Nonetheless, there are only minor differences in the regressions between 1980 and 1992, and therefore we shall only present those for the most recent period.

The results of the regressions, set out in Table 1.1 and plotted on Figure 1.2, confirm our hypotheses. By excluding the industrialized countries from our analysis, the results of the regressions seem to be weaker. The curve (labelled as 'DC') provides a better estimation of the true relationship between NOI and GDP for non-industrialized countries.

As Figure 1.2 shows, the results of our regressions also confirm our hypotheses regarding the differences in the 'idealized' IDP due to the differences in the extent of natural and created assets. Countries with above average natural assets tend to demonstrate a lower level of NOI for any given value of GDP relative to the average expected path. Countries with above average created assets, on the other hand, demonstrate a much higher value of NOI relative to the average expected path, and to the natural-asset-type countries. It is interesting to note, however, that although there are differences in NOI for any given level of GDP between the two groups, the difference narrows considerably at higher levels of GDP.

Inward and outward FDI

The effects noted above regarding changes to the extent of NOI are more apparent when examining the two components of NOI separately. As Table 1.2 shows, the mean outward FDI for the industrialized countries increased by a factor of 4.3 between 1980 and 1992 – twice that of the growth of GDP. The ratio of the standard deviation to the mean has also fallen, implying that the level of outward FDI has tended to converge among this group of countries. The mean inward FDI has also increased by a factor of 3.6, but the level of disparity has remained constant.

For pre-Stage 4 countries, outward FDI grew faster than inward FDI between 1980 and 1992, but even in 1992 the extent of outward investment remained at very low levels. It is interesting to note that the ratio of the standard deviation to the mean for outward FDI for developing countries has fallen from 5.5 to 2.8, implying that a larger number of developing countries have begun to engage in outward FDI since 1980. The Stage 3 countries, on the other hand, have showed an 18-fold increase in their outward investment levels, and a fall in the ratio of the standard deviation to the mean from 2.1 to 1.3. Inward investment into the NICs also grew twice as rapidly as that into other developing countries. Thus, as expected, the Stage 3 countries have demonstrated growth of both inward and outward FDI at a much higher pace than both the developing countries as well as the industrialized ones. Their GDP has grown at the same rate as that of the industrialized countries, and twice as

Table 1.3 Log–linear regression equations for inward and outward FDI against GDP

Independent variable	Sample	Constant	LOGGDPK	ADJ.R^2	F-value	N
LOGOWK	ALL	−11.866***	1.9487***	0.866	342.58	54
LOGOWK	NA	−10.812***	1.8199***	0.809	115.63	28
LOGOWK	CA	−14.572***	2.2457***	0.768	57.35	18
LOGIWK	ALL	−3.7024***	1.1626***	0.746	256.85	88
LOGIWK	NA	−4.2996***	1.2751***	0.705	127.39	54
LOGIWK	CA	−4.166***	1.176***	0.755	68.87	23

*** Significant at the 1% level. ** Significant at the 2.5% level.

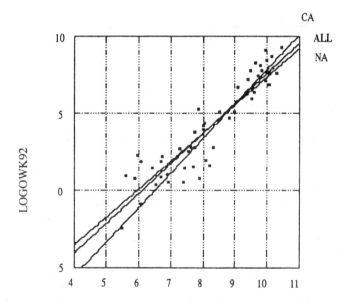

Figure 1.3 Outward FDI and GDP, 1992 (log–linear)

fast as the developing countries. The ratio of the standard deviation to the mean of GDP for the NICs is almost the same as that for the industrialized countries, implying that, as a group, their levels of GDP have converged.

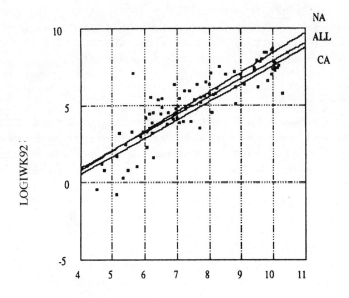

Figure 1.4 Inward FDI and GDP, 1992 (log–linear)

In running regressions for gross inward and outward direct investment, we have utilized a log–linear specification as originally suggested by Dunning (1981). We have done so for three samples – all countries (ALL), the natural asset countries (NA) and the created asset countries (CA), and the results are set out in Table 1.3 and graphed against the data in log form on Figures 1.3 and 1.4. Since a large number of developing countries have no outward investment, there is a considerable loss of sample size when outward direct investment per capita (OWK) is logged. As a result of this, the estimated value of the intercept is inaccurate. In the case of inward direct investment per capita (IWK), although theoretically a constant term is not required, since there is no country for which GDP = 0, it is necessary to include one. It is therefore not meaningful to reconvert the data back into linear form. Nonetheless, it is significant to note that the intercept terms for IWK equations are considerably lower than for OWK, which confirms that in fact inward FDI tends to precede outward FDI.

As Table 1.3 shows, the results are highly significant for all six regressions at the 1 per cent level, with R^2 values greater than 0.7 in all cases. In the case of inward FDI, as hypothesized, created asset countries demonstrate a lower rate of growth of inward FDI than do natural asset countries, while created asset countries have a higher slope for outward FDI than do natural asset countries.

CONCLUSIONS

The current version of the IDP, in introducing dynamic aspects to its framework, represents a paradigm that encapsulates complex phenomena which are exceedingly averse to aggregation. The relationship between FDI and economic development requires the comparison of two phenomena at different levels of economic analysis. While FDI is primarily a micro-economic or firm-specific activity, economic development is a macro-economic or country-specific phenomenon (Gray 1982). The examination of FDI as a country-specific variable requires the assumption that the activities of domestic and foreign MNEs can be aggregated in terms of their motivation, both within industrial sectors and across industrial sectors. Such aggregation can only be justified in countries where the nature, mode and motivation of MNE activity are relatively homogeneous, and the extent of their value adding activities remains at relatively low levels, such as in the lesser developed countries. However, as MNEs become more globalized and engage in more complex investment activity the importance of firm-specific factors in determining the FDI profile of a country becomes increasingly significant. This increasing complexity, together with the differences in measuring FDI between countries, makes any such analysis a hazardous one.

In addition, some of the data reviewed confirm that there have been profound changes in the world economy as a whole, as well as among particular groups of countries and within these countries. The process of catching up and falling behind has resulted in a polarization of countries into three distinct groups. The first group consists of the industrialized countries, which have been shown to have a convergence within the group of income levels, but considerable growth in income levels in the past 15 years. On average, their NOI positions have become increasingly positive, while their levels of gross inward and outward FDI are tending to converge. The second group consists of a handful of economies that can be regarded as being in Stage 3, which are exhibiting high growth in income levels and have become larger net outward investors since the 1980s. Their income levels also show signs of converging as a group, as well as with the industrialized countries. More significantly from our point of view, however, is the fact that their inward and outward FDI has been growing at a rate that outstrips even that of the industrialized countries. The third group consists of the Stage 1 and 2 countries which have experienced a divergence of income levels away from those of the industrialized countries as well as from the Stage 3 countries. Income levels have grown only marginally even in nominal terms, although the extent of FDI activity associated with these countries continues to grow faster than their domestic economies. Nonetheless, their NOI position has become increasingly negative, and both their inward and outward FDI positions have grown at a slower pace than that of either of the other two groups.

Nonetheless, the data reviewed in this chapter indicate that, despite the limitations associated with a static analysis of a dynamic phenomena, changes in the world economy as well as the large differences between countries, there continues to be a relatively strong causal relationship between FDI activity and economic development. Furthermore, we have also been able to examine, albeit simplistically, the hypotheses regarding how the extent of natural/created assets determines the shape of the IDP. Countries that are relatively well endowed in natural assets have a higher growth rate of inward FDI, but a much lower growth rate of outward FDI, than countries that do not have a strong natural asset position as well as those countries with a strong created asset position. In terms of the traditional J-relationship between NOI and development, the J-curve continues to be valid for pre-Stage 5 countries. Natural-asset-type countries tend to have a considerably higher NOI position relative to the created asset countries at any given income level.

Both Parts 1 and 2 of this chapter have sought to show that cross-sectional analysis is not an appropriate tool to capture the dynamic character of the IDP. This requires an oversimplification of complex economic activity into a few general and aggregated variables, an exercise which cannot be undertaken without great caution. For instance, if we restrict ourselves to using GDP as a single indicator of development, the process of economic restructuring as well as the growth of the technological competitiveness of countries are not taken into account. Likewise, the growth of strategic alliances as an alternative mode of international value-added activity and the growth of the activities of governments in the organization of economic activity cannot be usefully included in an aggregate analysis across countries.

For this and other reasons the following chapters examine some of the critical country-specific variables likely to determine both the gross inward and outward investment positions at a given level of income, and the shape of their IDP as they move through the various stages of economic development. A final chapter seeks to relate these differences to the more general statistical relationship which we have shown to exist between a country's international investment position and its gross domestic product per capita.

NOTES

1 See Kumar and McLeod (1981).
2 Earlier called 'cycle'.
3 Or the right to their use.
4 *Natural assets* consists of the 'fruits of the earth' and the stock of unskilled labour. *Created assets* are those derived from the upgrading of natural assets. The latter assets may be tangible or intangible, and include capital and technology as well as those pertaining to skilled labour, such as technological, managerial and organizational expertise. For further details, see Dunning (1994) and Narula (1995).
5 See the article by Reich (1990) for a succinct discussion on this issue.
6 See Gugler (1991).
7 For a review of the various empirical studies, see Narula (1993).
8 Cited, for example, in Dunning (1993), Chapters 11–19.
9 As reviewed, for example, in Dunning (1993).
10 Acquisitions accounted for 83.2 per cent of the outlays by foreign direct investors in the United States between 1986 and 1992 (Fahim-Nader and Bargas 1993).
11 Put another way, in their search for created assets and markets which they perceive necessary to advance their objectives, both firms and countries are acquiring these resources and capabilities by buying out (or investing in) foreign firms, in addition to being bought out (or invested in) by foreign firms. The extent to which these routes are complements to, or substitutes for, each other has not been explored in the literature. For an examination of the consequences of alliance capitalism for theorizing about the determinants of international production, see Dunning (1995).
12 Also called 'collective' capitalism (Lazonick 1992) and the 'new' capitalism (Best 1990).
13 What one writer (Maister 1993) has referred to as a 'farmer' rather than a 'hunter' organizational management style.
14 Other motives for strategic outsourcing include the need to capture the

specialized professional capabilities of suppliers, to shorten cycle times, and to respond better to customers. Examples of firms engaging in 'close' control procurement strategies include Marks and Spencer, Nike and Honda (Quinn and Hilmer 1994).

15 Notably from the work of John Hagedoorn and his colleagues at MERIT. For recent contributions see Hagedoorn and Schakenraad (1991, 1992, 1994) and Hagedoorn (1992, 1993).

16 For example, host governments may compel foreign firms to conclude cooperative arrangements with indigenous firms if they wish to produce within their boundaries, and/or force domestic firms to conclude such arrangements with foreign firms if they wish to transfer their O advantages abroad.

17 It is also worth recalling that the greater part of non-equity technology and organizational transference between countries is undertaken by MNEs.

18 Primarily because the *created* to *natural* asset ratio of the former countries was higher.

19 See especially Contractor (1990).

20 This proposition is explored in more detail in Dunning (1992, 1994).

21 Thus to quite a large extent the US net inward investment position in the 1960s has been eroded by the catching up of many European countries; while the seemingly invincible economic prowess of Japan in several sectors is now being challenged by the United States and Europe.

22 For a review of these, see Dunning (1993), especially the writers mentioned in Chapter 10. See also Dunning (1994).

23 Freeman and Hagedoorn (1994) suggest that between 1980 and 1989, almost 70 per cent of strategic technology partnering agreements between Triad firms and developing country firms were equity based, while for intra-Triad agreements, it was less than 50 per cent.

24 These data only cover strategic technology partnering for the period 1980-9.

25 See Dunning (1992, 1993).

26 These data are both derived from the World Bank (1994).

REFERENCES

Abramovitz, M. (1986) 'Catching up, forging ahead, and falling behind', *Journal of Economic History*, XLVI, 385–406.

Alam, M. S. (1992) 'Convergence in developed countries: an empirical investigation', *Weltwirtschaftliches Archiv*, *128*, 189–200.

Baumol, W. (1986) 'Productivity growth, convergence, and welfare: what the long-run data show', *American Economic Review*, 76, 1072–85.

Best, M. (1990) *The New Competition: Institutions of Restructuring*, Cambridge, MA: Harvard University Press.

Cantwell, J. (1989) *Technological Innovation and Multinational Corporations*, Oxford: Basil Blackwell.

Cantwell, J. A. and Dunning, J. H. (1991) 'Multinationals, technology and the competitiveness of European industries', *Aussenwirtschaft*, *46*, 45–65.

Cantwell, J. and Randaccio, F. (1990) 'The growth of multinationals and the catching up effect', *Economic Notes*, *19*, 1–23.

Contractor, F. (1990) 'Ownership patterns of US joint ventures abroad and the liberalization of foreign government regulation in the 1980s: evidence from the benchmark surveys', *Journal of International Business Studies*, *21*, 55–73.

Dowrick, S. (1992) 'Technological catch up and diverging incomes: patterns of economic growth 1960–88', *The Economic Journal*, *102*, 600–10.

Dowrick, S and Gemmell, N. (1991) 'Industrialization, catching up and economic growth: a comparative study across the world's capitalist economies', *Economic Journal*, *101*, 263–75.

Dunning, J. H. (1981) 'Explaining the international direct investment position of countries: towards a dynamic or developmental approach', *Weltwirtschaftliches Archiv*, *119*, 30–64.

―――― (1986) 'The investment development cycle revisited', *Weltwirtshaftliches Archiv*, *122*, 667–77.

―――― (1988a) *Explaining International Production*, London: Unwin Hyman.

―――― (1988b) *Multinationals, Technology and Competitiveness*, London: Unwin Hyman.

―――― (1992) 'The global economy, domestic governance, strategies and transnational corporations: interactions and policy recommendations', *Transnational Corporations 1*, December, 7–45.

―――― (1993) *Multinational Enterprises and the Global Economy*, Wokingham, England, and Reading, MA: Addison-Wesley.

―――― (1994) 'Reevaluating the benefits of foreign direct investment', *Transnational Corporations 3*, February, 23–52.

―――― (1995) 'Reappraising the eclectic paradigm in an age of alliance capitalism', *Journal of International Business Studies* 26(3).

Dunning, J. H. and Narula, R. (1994) 'Transpacific FDI and the investment development path: the record assessed', *University of South Carolina Essays in International Business*, No. 10, May.

Durkheim, E. (1964) *The Division of Labour in Society*, New York: The Free Press.

Fahim-Nader, M. and Bargas, S. E. (1993) 'US business enterprises acquired or established by foreign direct investors in 1992', *Survey of Current Business*, May, 113–23.

Freeman, C. and Hagedoorn, J. (1994) 'Catching up or falling behind: patterns in international interfirm technology partnering', *World Development*, *22*, 771–780.

Gerlach, M. L. (1992) *Alliance Capitalism: The Social Organization of Japanese Business*, Oxford: Oxford University Press.

Gray, H. P. (1982) 'Macroeconomic theories of foreign direct investment: an assessment,' in A. Rugman (ed.) *New Theories of the Multinational Enterprise*, London: Croom Helm.

Gugler, P. (1991) *Les Alliances Strategiques Transnationales*, Fribourg: Editions Universitaires.

Hagedoorn, J. (1992) 'Organizational modes of inter-firm cooperation and technology transfer', *Technovation*, *10*, 17–30.

The investment development path revisited   41

——— (1993) 'Understanding the rationale of strategic technology part-nering: inter-organizational modes of cooperation and sectoral differ-ences', *Strategic Management Journal*, *14*, 371–85.
Hagedoorn, J. and Narula, R. (1994) *Choosing Modes of Governance for Strategic Technology Partnering: International and Sectoral Differ-ences*, MERIT Working Paper Series No. 94-025.
Hagedoorn, J. and Schakenraad, J. (1991) 'The internationalization of the economy, global strategies and strategic technology alliances', *Nouvelles de la Science et des Technologies*, *9*, 29–41.
——— (1992) 'Leading companies in networks of strategic alliances in information technologies', *Research Policy*, *21*, 163–90.
——— (1994) 'The effects of strategic technology alliances on company performance', *Strategic Management Journal*, *15*, 291–309.
Hamalainen, T. (1993) *The Evolving Role of Government in Economic Organization*, mimeo, Newark: Rutgers University.
Kumar, K. and McLeod, M. (eds) (1981) *Multinationals from Developing Countries*, Lexington, MA: D. C. Heath.
Lazonick, W. (1992) 'Business organization and competitive advantage: capitalist transformation in the twentieth century', in Dosi, G., Gianetti, R. and Toninelli, P. A. (eds) *Technology and Enterprise in a Historical Perspective*, Oxford: Clarendon Press, 119–63.
Maister, D. H. (1993) *Managing the Professional Service Firm*, New York: Free Press/Macmillan.
Narula, R. (1993) *An Examination of the Evolution and Interdependence of Foreign Direct Investment and Economic Structure: The Case of Indus-trialized Countries*, Ph.D. Thesis, Newark: Rutgers University.
——— (1995) *Multinational Investment and Economic Structure*, London: Routledge.
Ohmae, K. (1987) *The Borderless World*, New York: The Free Press.
Ozawa, T. (1992) 'FDI and economic development', *Transnational Cor-porations*, *1*, 27–54.
Porter, M. E. (1990) *The Competitive Advantage of Nations*, New York: The Free Press.
Quinn, J. B. and Hilmer, F. G. (1994) 'Strategic outsourcing', *Sloan Management Review*, *35*, Summer, 43–55.
Reich, R. (1990) 'Who is us?', *Harvard Business Review*, January-Febru-ary, 53–64.
Tolentino, P. (1993) *Technological Innovation and Third World Multina-tionals*, London: Routledge.
UNCTAD (1993)   *World Investment Report 1993*, New York: United Nations.
UNCTAD (1994) *World Investment Report 1994*, Geneva: United Nations.
Verspagen, B. (1993) *Uneven Growth Between Interdependent Economies*, Avebury: Aldershot.
World Bank (1994) *World Development Report 1994*, Oxford: Oxford University Press.

Chapter 2

The United Kingdom
A *par excellence* two-way direct investor

Jeremy Clegg

INTRODUCTION

The United Kingdom is, in at least one way, a unique country for examination in the context of the investment development path (IDP). As the first country to industrialise, the UK was in the position of being the first outward investor of the industrial period. In this respect the UK might be thought of as having enjoyed international first-mover advantages in terms of its comparative foreign direct investment position. It was in the UK that the sudden acceleration of technical and economic development began in the second half of the eighteenth century, transforming the British economy from a traditional agrarian to an industrial structure, based on capital equipment and manufacturing. From around 1830 to the early twentieth century the Industrial Revolution spread throughout Europe and the United States. The diffusion of this process has continued world-wide, throughout the twentieth century, and particularly since the end of the Second World War. It is precisely this perpetuation that has generated continuing large-scale adjustments in international trade and investment patterns, not least on the part of the UK.

The resources on which the economic transformation in the UK was based were coal, iron, water transport, financial capital, a newly created urban working class drawn from the agricultural workforce, and an equally new transport infrastructure constructed around the steam engine – the fundamental innovation of the Industrial Revolution. Such were the founding natural and created assets at the start of the period of industrial history pertinent to the UK's international investment path. The crucial early role of ownership assets that are primarily a function of the structure of the home economy is underlined by Dunning and Narula (1994). Of course, the UK did not possess only the assets noted above. It also benefited from a crucial measure of entrepreneurship, enabling these resources to be exploited and generated in a way that was unprecedented in scale and scope. Without the supply of entrepreneurship the IDP development of a country cannot be determined (Buckley and Casson, 1991). One can also invoke the importance of legal protection of intellectual property and firm-specific advantages in general, but formally proving their importance for the UK's IDP development is another matter. Certainly, had the UK not contained an adequate entrepreneurial class, a European neighbour would surely have industrialized first and seized industrial primacy, going on to its own particular colonial expansion. However, this leading role fell to the UK.

Because international business developed along colonial lines, the early outward investment of the colonial powers was in the less developed economies of the world, rather than in other developed nations. Therefore, like other colonists, the UK began its IDP evolution from a net positive position. The pattern of colonial expansion was driven more by economic motives rather than political or strategic demands, i.e. there was no central planning in the proliferation of international ties. The benefits of FDI are evident even at this early stage – the competitiveness of UK firms is enhanced through the fact that they can select the best resources and locations on a world scale, rather than face the constraints of the home economy. The trading and mining companies largely determined the initial pattern of development, with the UK government bringing up the rear in terms of politics. In this way, the firms involved in early international business were able to select quite freely the foreign locations in which they did business, typically in order to secure supplies of natural resources to cater for the demand of the home market.

Therefore, for much of the nineteenth and twentieth centuries, the operations of MNEs were concentrated in the less developed and developing countries in their role as colonies, with an early emphasis on natural-resource-orientated investment. However, this picture has changed substantially since the inception of the cycle, with not only the emergence of a greater diversity of countries from which multinationals spring (home or source countries), but also an increasing range of countries which receive the affiliates of foreign firms (host countries).

The post-war period has witnessed the rapid growth of multi-national activity between developed countries. The developed countries, represented principally by the membership of the OECD, are now the centre of gravity for world foreign direct investment (FDI) and multinational activity. Through the 1980s, the developed countries accounted for 97 per cent of world outflows of FDI and 75 per cent of inflows. In particular, within the developed economies, the countries of the 'Triad' (the European Union, the United States and Japan) accounted for 81 per cent of world FDI outflows and 71 per cent of world inflows (UNCTAD, 1993). Inevitably, this chapter will focus on the role of UK FDI in the context of the developed countries, because the historical data and contemporary information for the developing countries are especially thin. However, as noted above, this group of countries occupies an important place in the history of multinational endeavour.

In the modern period particular regions, notably Asia and the Pacific and Central and Eastern Europe respectively, have demonstrated major growth as host countries (with the ascent of home-grown multinational enterprise) and clear potential for growth in multinational activity. The list of host countries has recently been extended and deepened by the liberalisation of markets in Central and Eastern Europe, from which foreign multinational activity had been barred or strictly controlled for much of the twentieth century. While MNEs span mainly the developed and the advanced newly industrialising economies (NIEs), this opening up of Central and Eastern Europe offers additional scope for higher levels of geographical diversification. Unfortunately, it follows that the time series and cross-section data are very poor for multinational activity in these additional countries.

The role of politics in the pattern of FDI is quite a conspicuous one. The pursuit of market integration in the EU might be seen as simply a recognition of the intensification of economic relations between developed countries, but it certainly has a political and strategic dimension. All such developments will have their impact on the UK's ownership, locational and internalisation (OLI) configuration and the scope and pattern of FDI. Theory argues that OLI status depends on country (or region), industry and firm-specific factors (Dunning and Narula, 1994). As a mature FDI donor and recipient nation, the interaction of these influences will be particularly complicated. Unlike a nation new to foreign investment, the UK cannot be treated as a *tabula rasa*. A clean slate is the preferred starting point for any theoretical account of the evolution of FDI (e.g. see Buckley and Casson, 1991) as well as for empirical research. Ideally, accurate data on the entire historical period of foreign involvement (at least since the dawn of the industrial age) would be required for maximum information. It is plain that these are not available, so the OLI configuration and the IDP evolution of the UK will be connected by resonances from the ancient past as well as from the more contemporary period. The focus of this chapter is on the competitiveness of the UK and its firms. These are explored through observation of the country and regional trends in a measure constructed to investigate the evolution of the UK's net outward investment (NOI),[1] in the context of the IDP framework. Also using this measure, the broad industrial shifts in the UK's investment status, and its financial components, are studied. These offer some insight into how industrial and firm-level performance contribute to the UK's aggregate NOI position.

THE UNITED KINGDOM'S IDP POSITION IN THE TWENTIETH CENTURY

Regular quantitative data on the UK's FDI were not collected until the beginning of the 1960s (see Buckley and Pearce, 1991). Prior to this estimates were produced only sporadically, principally by individual researchers. In a review of the recent historical development of FDI, a paper by Dunning (1983) presented estimated statistics on the stock of accumulated FDI by country of origin and by recipient country or area since 1914. Updating these figures to 1991 for the UK enables Table 2.1 to be constructed. This table presents both the NOI (at current prices) and the time trend of the IDP coefficient of the UK. This coefficient is a proxy for the stage attained within the IDP framework, and is based on the UK's NOI relative to GDP.[2] The index based on this coefficient enables the tracing of the development of the UK's position, within the context of the IDP.

The UK is classifiable as a Stage 5 economy over the full period considered in the table. Clearly the IDP coefficient of the UK has followed a declining trend throughout. This is a first indicator of the receding international competitive position of the UK. There are two possible explanations of declining national competitiveness. The first is where there is a reduction in locational advantages. However, this would result in more outward FDI, and a decrease in

Table 2.1 The aggregate FDI position of the United Kingdom, US $M (current prices), and investment development path coefficient, 1914–92

	Outward	Inward	Outward/inward	NOI	IDP coefficient
1914	6500	200	32.50	6300	56.72
1938	10500	700	15.00	9800	40.41
1960	10800	5000	2.16	5800	8.05
1971	23700	13400	1.77	10300	7.28
1980	80729	63014	1.28	17715	3.29
1985	90010	56143	1.60	33867	7.31
1990	213944	201594	1.06	12350	1.26
1991	229834	213268	1.08	16567	1.63
1992	287243	232243	1.24	55001	5.23

Notes: FDI data from 1960 onwards are known to include estimates for all industries. FDI data for 1992 are provisional. The IDP coefficient is calculated as NOI divided by GDP, and is expressed as a percentage to improve intelligibility.

Source: See Appendix.

inward FDI; that is, a signature contrary to that actually observed. The second way in which national competitiveness can be lost is where home firms' net ownership advantages have diminished. The steepness of the long-term decline in the IDP coefficient strongly attests to the relative descent of UK ownership advantages. As other countries have industrialized, they have revealed comparative advantage through nascent ownership strengths, which have increasingly enabled them to compete against UK MNEs abroad, and against UK firms operating within the UK.

The dramatic decline in the IDP position in the period 1938-60 almost certainly owes much to the UK's foreign asset depletion started in the 1940s on account of the Second World War. However, consistent with the UK's stage of development classification as a Stage 5 country, there are deviations from the emerging long-term equilibrium. Two mini-peaks are in evidence in the table: in 1985 and in 1991. As the UK's IDP coefficient comes to approximate a lower equilibrium value, such wiggles are theoretically expected to assume a greater proportionate importance. These ephemeral deviations arise when created assets, such as innovatory or organisational prowess, temporarily rise in one country relative to another. The reason why such imbalances become short lived in Stage 5 is because of the intensity of cross-FDI, which acts as an equilibrating conduit or mechanism.

This is bound up with the prediction that, in the polar stage in the development of a country's IDP position, there is no longer any clear trend. The explanation for this offered within the IDP framework is that inbound and outbound FDI increasingly become complementary to each other, as witnessed by the growth of intra-industry FDI. The growing convergence between countries in Stage 5 is reflected in the similarity of industrial structures, while the motives for cross-border activity become progressively symmetrical, increasingly comprising efficiency seeking and strategic asset seeking. The evaporation of basic inequalities between the advanced countries, which account for the majority of FDI, acts against the possibility of long-term sustainable trends in the IDP position. Broadly defined technological gaps between countries in Stage 5 are at historical minima, and are therefore of such short duration that they result in oscillations in the IDP position, being no longer able to sustain lasting trends.

Some key predictions are made for the development of FDI in Stage 5 of an economy's development, which centre on the country pattern and the industry pattern of development. These are scrutinised in this chapter, to assess the applicability of the concept of the IDP to the UK experience. In addition, to investigate the changing financial sourcing of the growth (or decline) in the UK's NOI, some tabular analysis of the components of FDI flows is included.

THE COMPETITIVENESS OF UK INDUSTRY

It is well known from the theory of international business that the competitiveness ascribed to a country cannot be measured by trade in goods, services or technology, or multinational involvement alone (Dunning, 1977; 1993). In order to assess better the competitive profile of development of the UK, it is necessary to turn to some alternative statistics. Table 2.2 presents the available universe estimate data for technology licensing, which began in 1965. The most relevant figures are those that relate to non-affiliated transactions, i.e. those relating to firms that do not have a foreign direct investment relationship with each other. These figures give a guide to the underlying technology-based competitiveness of UK industry. While changes in overall competitiveness may be picked up through oscillations in the IDP index, the technological balance of trade should mirror the relative competitiveness of UK technology.

At no time within the period 1965-93 did the UK have a deficit in non-affiliated technology trade. In all years the ratio of receipts to payments remained clearly above unity. Furthermore, the overall trend is upwards. There is, however, some marked variation over time, with peaks arising in 1979 and 1982. Exchange rate movements mày be partly responsible, particularly in the instance of the decline in the ratio of receipts to payments around the mid-1980s, when the value of sterling fell to a record low against the US dollar.

Royalty transactions reflect receipts and payments governed by licensing contracts. These contracts will have a duration of several years, during which time monies transferred will typically be linked to the sales values, or number of units of output, generated by licensees. While both non-affiliate and affiliate contracts specify the terms and conditions on the basis of which payments are made, there are good reasons for believing that affiliate contracts generate royalty flows more loosely linked to technology traded. This is because of the exigencies of transfer price manipulation, where amounts transferred may be up-valued or down-valued depending on the financial needs of the multinational firm as a

Table 2.2 Technological and mineral royalty transactions' trade
performance for the UK, 1965–94

| | Receipts/payments | | |
	Non-affiliated	Affiliated	Total
1965	1.67	0.60	1.06
1966	1.96	0.62	1.18
1967	1.62	0.64	1.05
1968	1.71	0.61	1.08
1969	1.55	0.59	0.98
1970	1.75	0.60	1.07
1971	1.77	0.57	1.07
1972	1.87	0.58	1.10
1973	2.03	0.60	1.17
1974	2.04	0.58	1.13
1975	1.99	0.50	1.02
1976	2.47	0.57	1.26
1977	2.73	0.53	1.22
1978	2.94	0.53	1.19
1979	4.86	0.53	1.20
1980	4.63	0.53	1.16
1981	4.66	0.57	1.21
1982	5.50	0.60	1.21
1983	4.45	0.71	1.28
1984	3.13	0.68	1.05
1985	2.79	0.74	1.13
1986	2.33	0.73	0.95
1987	1.85	0.71	0.92
1988	4.55	0.72	1.05
1989	3.65	0.72	1.01
1990	3.03	0.65	0.86
1991	3.23	0.92	1.12
1992	3.37	1.12	1.34
1993	3.02	1.14	1.32

Notes: Figures up to 1983 inclusive exclude the oil industry, but include it
thereafter. Figures for all years exclude banking and insurance. From 1988 the
data are estimated in order to exclude transactions in printed matter, sound
recording and performing rights.
Source: See Appendix.

whole. Even so, the picture, while not so favourable as for affiliate
transactions, is one of a clearly rising trend. In 1965 the UK's
affiliated receipts were 60 per cent of its payments, but by 1993
receipts exceeded payments by 14 per cent.

There is nothing in these statistics to suggest a decline in the UK's
technological prowess. Of course, it is perfectly possible that an

increased proclivity to market technology abroad (employ the external market) has substituted for UK outward investment. In fact there is a weak negative correlation between the ratio of non-affiliated receipts to payments, and the annual estimates of the UK's IDP coefficient (for total industry). However, this correlation becomes even weaker, and loses significance, when the technological ratio is related to the IDP index in the industrial sector alone, i.e. the sector with which it should be expected to have the strongest relationship, either complementary or substituting. There may be a lag structure in the relationship, for instance a rise in UK technological competitiveness might correlate most with the NOI 3 to 5 years later. What can be said with certainty is that UK firms do not appear to have lost ground in terms of technology receipts.

Can this be linked to the IDP measure, in particular to government or FDI-induced changes in competitiveness? The licensing statistics begin at a time (1965) when the UK had a substantial negative NOI with the United States. This partly accounts for the low ratio (0.6) of affiliated receipts to payments at the start of the period. The UK affiliates of US firms were heavily technologically dependent on their US parents. The rise in non-affiliate technological trade performance is entirely consistent with spillover and competitiveness benefits arising from this inward investment. It is less easy to ascribe the changes to government policy, other than that of the adoption and maintenance of a liberal stance towards FDI.

Furthermore, the clear upward trend in affiliate-related technological trade performance is suggestive of either or both of the possibilities that UK affiliates of foreign MNEs have become less technologically dependent, or that UK parents have enhanced their technological exports to affiliates abroad. Both of these possibilities suggest a relative strengthening somewhere in the UK technological base. From this discussion, it seems most likely that the UK's competitiveness is not only inextricably linked to FDI, but that FDI has acted in some way as to promote competitiveness.

The competitiveness of the UK in terms of locational advantages is also worthy of discussion. In historical terms, the comparative advantage of the UK in the manufacturing sector, at least in the period 1870-1935, appears to have been in unskilled-labour-intensive, capital-neutral and human-capital-scarce commodities (Crafts and Thomas, 1986). The thesis put forward is that while the UK was well placed for initial industrialisation and leadership in terms of natural resources and the stock of labour, this industrial structure later became a handicap. When industrial production developed to require higher skills and capital intensity the UK was found to be lacking. This resulted in an underlying comparative disadvantage as a production base for technology-intensive products, which rely particularly on higher labour skills and capital-biased production.[3] The attractiveness of the UK as a production base in the modern period may still reflect this pattern of specialisation.

THE DEVELOPMENT OF THE UNITED KINGDOM'S IDP POSITION BY REGION AND COUNTRY

In the last 30 years perhaps the most significant policy changes affecting UK industry have been the decision to enter the European Community (EC, now re-designated as the European Union, or EU) and the privatisation of formerly state sector enterprise. Forces for non-FDI-induced change in the OLI configuration include the effects of government policy and the economic system of a country (Dunning and Narula, 1994). The study of the impact of market integration commands a literature of its own, as does that on deregulation and liberalisation. However, within the context of the investment development path, the entry of the UK into the EC qualifies as a non-FDI-induced change in the OLI condition of the UK, being endogenous to countries but exogenous to firms.[4] The framework set out by Dunning and Narula details the various impacts that FDI and non-FDI-induced changes may exert upon the OLI configuration.

Owing to the complexity of the dynamic structure of impacts it is reasonable to look for some manifestations of both intra- and inter-temporal (static and dynamic) effects of the OLI advantages in the IDP coefficient. These stand as indicators of the competitive position of the UK, as a location, of its firms, and of the disposition to internalise markets. While there has been no policy in the UK specifically directed at FDI, there have been, and still are, regional and structural policies, as well as local government incentives that are employed to attract investment. Regarding FDI abroad, the UK did practise exchange control, which was generally felt not to have made a lot of difference to FDI abroad, particularly that by established MNEs. The study of the UK's FDI by Boatwright and Renton (1975) found that dummy variables for foreign exchange controls introduced in 1965 and 1966 were insignificant, with no effect on either the real or financial components of FDI. In short, it should be expected that the effect of such controls be imperceptible for developed countries with substantial multinational activity, testifying to the efficiency of established MNEs in avoiding these sorts of restrictions.

Partner countries of the UK have engaged in policy specifically directed towards controlling FDI, e.g. regulations against FDI in key industries by Japan in the 1950s and 1960s. Other policy factors are more general (such as demand management policies), or very difficult to identify formally, such as much exchange rate policy since the end of the Bretton Woods Regime. The short-lived UK membership of the EU's exchange rate mechanism (ERM) would nevertheless count as a policy. In terms of international trade policy the IDP sees Stage 5 economies behaving as international strategic oligopolists. With the continual reduction in tariff rates under successive GATT negotiations, this strategic game is played out primarily through the use of non-tariff barriers. Another important strategy is that of forming, deepening and extending integrated markets between groups of countries, to gain efficiency and to increase world market power. Many of the arguments made out for UK participation in the EC and the EU are couched in terms of the dangers of not being included. It therefore is very much to be expected that membership of the EU will have had significant impacts on the UK's IDP coefficient.

There are strong reasons for believing that internalisation is enjoying secular growth. As Dunning and Narula (1994) argue, from Stage 4 of the IDP onwards, the operations of firms abroad will increasingly be internalised as FDI. This view is corroborated by the literature on market integration regarding the responses of firms to trade barriers between the countries within the integrating areas (e.g. Dunning and Robson, 1988; UNCTC, 1990; UNTCMD, 1993). Consequently, the UK's NOI should be indicative of the relative O and L advantages of UK industry.

International merger and acquisition activities are particularly strong indicators of the desire for internalised control of assets. Wherever FDI positions increase particularly sharply, and above trend, this not only suggests new entry rather than expansionary investment, but also international acquisition rather than organic growth. This pattern of behaviour is encountered below on many occasions, particularly around the period associated with the boom in international mergers and acquisitions. It is consistent with firms acquiring strategic positions, rather than investing from a situation of classic superiority in ownership assets, where investors are driven by the need to gain competitiveness through gaining control of key assets. To this extent, bursts of FDI may not reflect current net ownership advantages.

The UK and the developed regions

The IDP approach suggests that one of the characteristics of Stage 4 and 5 countries' FDI patterns should be an intensification in cross-investment between the developed market economies (DMEs). This appears to be borne out by the gross FDI data used to derive the NOI and IDP index. The long-term theory of the IDP would suggest that the UK's NOI should oscillate rather than lead upwards or downwards. The overall impression is one of a modestly declining trend in the IDP coefficient, but this is increasingly overshadowed by swings. On inspection, these swings are especially marked at the bilateral level, and at the industry level. It should be noted that, owing to the laggardly incorporation of key sectors in the official surveys of FDI, the geographical analysis of the UK data from 1962 to 1981 excludes FDI by oil companies, banks and insurance companies, and FDI in the miscellaneous category (mainly property). From 1984 only miscellaneous is excluded. As a result there is some distortion owing to the impact of the exclusion of these sectors arising from industry composition differences between UK inward and outward FDI.

(a) The UK and Europe, and the impact of market integration

The impact of EU membership on the UK's IDP index can be explored through the theoretical effects of internal tariff elimination (Mark I integration) and internal non-tariff barrier reduction (Mark II integration). Tariff removal is transparent and has the universal effect within a common market of relaxing the import-substituting motive for FDI and of encouraging investment strategies that are regionally integrated. Non-tariff barrier removal also encourages integrated production. However, because the latter is less transparent, and concerns government policy, it is liable to be implemented to differing extents and at different rates by member countries. The effect may therefore be to generate asymmetries between countries in terms of market access.

Focusing on the regions themselves, the record suggests some substantial adjustments in the position of the UK IDP coefficient *vis-à-vis* the EU, set out in Table 2.3. It appears that the UK has had a positive IDP position with respect to the EU (here defined as EU(12) throughout) since the first official surveys began – until 1991. The positive regional IDP position progressively increased until the mid-1970s, then monotonically decreased, becoming negative in 1991. There is little suggestion of an acceleration in the growth of the UK's IDP coefficient with the EU in the run up to initial membership; although both gross outward and inward FDI with the EU did fall in 1974, this was probably due to the oil crisis.

An intra-temporal explanation might be that UK firms reacted in the 1970s to investment opportunities to serve a tariff-free EU market by locating production within continental Europe. From an overview of the gross FDI data, it transpires that the decline subsequent to 1978 is attributable mainly to an attenuation of outward UK FDI. While this possibly implicates shortcomings in UK firms' relative ownership advantages, it could be indicative of UK manufacturing firms choosing to service the EU market using exports from the UK, in response to the programme of tariff elimination following UK accession.

The growth of UK FDI to the rest of the EU has fallen behind that of EU FDI in the UK. This much is evident since 1978. Given the evidence from Table 2.2 that overall technological trade performance has not declined, it is possible that UK membership of the EU has acted to decrease outward import-substituting FDI more than it has encouraged integrated pan-European investment. However, there is no direct proof that UK firms' technological standing has been sustained against European firms in particular. In terms of the OLI framework, the prime factors in the development of the UK-EU IDP coefficient would be that locational advantages of production within the UK have risen for EU firms, coupled with the decline in UK firms' net ownership advantages, probably concentrated in areas other than classic scientific technology.

In its approach to the Single European Market, which can be dated from the mid-1980s, the UK has also exhibited distinctive behaviour. UK market liberalisation, particularly seen in the privatisation of former state monopolies coupled with deregulation, has generally preceded that in the continental EU. As monopoly is a trade barrier, and state monopoly is especially insurmountable, this policy stance facilitated market access in the UK without symmetric

Table 2.3 The UK's aggregate IDP position with the major regions of the world, 1962–91

Regions	1962	1965	1968	1971	1974	1978	1981	1984	1987	1991
Western Europe	0.55	0.69	0.89	0.99	1.18	1.60	0.82	1.16	0.47	-1.33
EU(12)	0.91	1.07	1.31	1.41	1.64	1.72	1.29	1.21	1.11	-0.13
Non-EU(12) former EFTA	-0.37	-0.39	-0.45	-0.45	-0.52	-0.15	-0.52	-0.10	-0.75	-1.24
Other Western Europe	0.01	0.01	0.03	0.02	0.06	0.04	0.04	0.05	0.10	0.04
North America	-1.05	-1.74	-1.75	-2.17	-2.14	-1.36	-0.22	3.47	1.37	0.97
Other developed countries	3.10	3.43	3.82	3.16	3.38	2.34	1.83	3.14	1.01	-0.23
Rest of the world	4.28	3.74	3.56	2.95	2.20	2.17	2.11	3.68	2.61	3.06
Africa	1.44	1.12	1.10	1.03	0.88	0.84	0.75	0.72	0.40	0.31
Asia	1.89	1.69	1.48	1.20	0.87	0.86	0.82	0.51	1.05	1.01
Caribbean, Central and South America	0.93	1.00	0.96	0.78	0.44	0.49	0.59	1.52	1.21	1.69
Other countries	0.02	0.03	0.02	-0.06	0.02	-0.02	-0.05	-0.06	-0.06	0.05
World	6.88	6.13	6.52	4.93	4.61	4.76	4.54	11.45	4.46	2.46

Notes: Oil companies, banks and insurance companies are excluded from 1962 to 1981. Miscellaneous FDI (mainly property) is excluded throughout. Inward data for 1962–71 for Africa include countries not specified within 'Other countries' or the major regions. The IDP coefficient is calculated as NOI divided by GDP, and is expressed as a percentage to improve intelligibility.

Source: See Appendix.

access in partner countries. The lead of government policy in this respect in the UK may therefore be partly responsible for the move into a negative bilateral IDP position with the EU. The relative locational advantages of the UK have risen in the eyes of EU investors. UK liberalisation may have allowed inward market-seeking FDI, and FDI orientated at servicing the wider EU market. Often one motive is the desire of firms accustomed to little competition to learn directly from a market which has proceeded furthest down the route of liberalisation, as an investment for the future. While UK gross inward FDI from the EU increased in the service sector by an average of 130 per cent (in current price terms) in the period 1987–91,[5] inward investment increased by 1140 per cent in the 'Other Services' category.

The OLI configuration with respect to the non-EU/former EFTA countries has been very consistent. The IDP position of the UK with EFTA countries has been unambiguously negative throughout (Table 2.3). For EFTA firms, the UK is most likely being viewed as a production base, initially in order to cater for a large home market, and latterly (in anticipation of Mark II integration in the EU) as a base within the EU. These locational advantages do not apply in reverse for UK firms in EFTA, and as a result UK outward FDI is relatively low. The development of the gross investment stocks show that up to 1984 the growth of outward and inward FDI roughly kept pace. Between 1984 and 1991 inward FDI from EFTA rose dramatically, while UK outward FDI stagnated.

The tentative conclusions are that UK membership of the EU has impacted on UK firms and on the UK, mainly by affecting the relative locational advantages of the UK as a production base. This may be a reflection of the desire to serve the UK domestic market, but it could be a response to lower UK wage costs. A competitive response has been elicited on the part of UK firms, but there is no early evidence of positive dynamic impacts on UK ownership advantages to date from increased inward FDI.

The impact of initial membership of the EU, but especially of Mark II integration, has been to reduce the value of the UK's NOI. Gross FDI inflows since the mid-1980s have risen sharply from both the rest of the EU and from EFTA. The UK therefore appears to be acting as a production platform within Europe, even for European firms, and as an attractive host market. In the latter case, it seems probable that UK firms' ownership competitiveness has declined to some extent. This issue is discussed further below, in the context of individual EU partner countries.

(b) The UK and North America, and other regions of the world

The progress of the UK's IDP index with the North American continent is dominated by its relationship with the United States, which is discussed in greater detail later. However, it is clear from Table 2.3 that there have been some far-ranging adjustments in the UK's OLI configuration with respect to North America. There has been a shift from a substantial net negative IDP position to an equally substantial net positive, and then back down again, within a 30 year period.

While the UK's positive IDP position with Asia[6] has remained fairly stable, the picture with Africa is one of decline. The contrast is explained by the deteriorating relative locational advantages of producing within Africa, while production within Asia has remained attractive, and production within the UK has been pursued increasingly by Asian firms. Inward investment from Asia has not been established long enough that any dynamic impacts can be discerned. However, the UK's locational advantages can be presumed to be similar for Asian firms as they have been for Japanese firms.

In Stage 5 it should be expected that countries will invest most intensively in other countries of similar levels of development. Certainly this is reflected in the lower levels of FDI by the UK in the less developed regions of the world. The declining trend in the UK's IDP index with Africa reflects poor host market size and growth and obsolescing historical links with UK firms. So long drawn to the Commonwealth, UK firms have now largely reorientated themselves towards the advanced developed countries. The UK's positive IDP coefficient with Asia went through a trough in 1981, but rose again, probably in response to the growing locational attractiveness of South-East Asian countries as production-base hosts. The positive IDP coefficient with the Caribbean, Central and South America is indicative of an oscillating equilibrium. To close the regional analysis, the UK IDP position with the rest of the world[7] has a generally static trend, with oscillations reflecting the variation of the outward FDI stock with world macroeconomic activity and the ebb and flow of FDI to individual regions.

The UK's bilateral IDP positions with the developed countries

(a) Europe

The UK's long-term IDP position began the twentieth century as across-the-board positive against the rest of the world, and each partner country. Table 2.4 presents the UK's bilateral aggregate IDP coefficient positions for European countries. At the beginning of the period, 1962, the UK has a negative IDP position with just three countries, two of which are barely negative (Sweden and The Netherlands) plus Switzerland. By 1991 the UK recorded a negative IDP position with seven European countries. Four of the five EFTA countries were in this category. This general pattern is consistent with the long-term decline in the UK's overall IDP coefficient, owing to diminished across-the-board ownership advantages. The UK retains considerable attraction for foreign investors because, with just about every partner country, both gross outward and inward FDI have risen, only inward FDI has risen further.

The Netherlands is a case in point. It has become responsible for the UK's largest negative NOI. France is in second place. Both UK outward and inward FDI with The Netherlands have risen rapidly since 1981, outward FDI by 372 per cent, but inward FDI has risen by 1175 per cent. The strong UK IDP position in the Federal Republic of Germany throughout the post-war period has almost evaporated though, as is the case for France, both gross outward and inward FDI have been growing vigorously.

The impact of market integration has been the intensification of gross FDI flows within the EU. The UK has shared fully in this, but the net inclination has been for the UK's IDP position to emerge lower. The most notable exception is Spain, where the UK has significantly expanded its NOI, as it has also in Italy. It seems likely that UK firms enjoy net ownership advantages with Spanish firms, and that the host country has locational advantages in the form of lower wage costs.

The data in Table 2.4 confirm that the typical bilateral IDP position of the UK has declined between 1962 and 1991. What we have seen to date is an asymptotic descent in the aggregate IDP coefficient, coupled with a commensurate averaging-down of the UK's bilateral positions with individual countries. The theory, when applied to this long-run development, suggests that the initial primacy of UK firms' ownership advantages has followed a sectoral

Table 2.4 The UK's aggregate IDP position with selected European countries, 1962–91

Countries	1962	1965	1968	1971	1974	1978	1981	1984	1987	1990	1991
European Union (12)											
BLEU	0.19	0.15	0.22	0.19	0.14	0.18	0.07	0.17	0.11	-0.01	0.06
Denmark	0.01	0.03	0.03	0.01	0.01	0.04	0.00	0.06	0.02	0.01	-0.01
France	0.18	0.21	0.30	0.29	0.33	0.20	0.19	0.03	0.14	-0.10	-0.33
FRG	0.21	0.27	0.35	0.43	0.60	0.71	0.35	0.60	0.54	0.00	0.09
Greece	0.00	0.01	0.01	0.01	0.01	0.01	0.01	0.02	0.02	0.03	0.03
Irish Republic	0.23	0.25	0.27	0.30	0.34	0.30	0.26	0.23	0.28	0.18	0.27
Italy	0.07	0.06	0.10	0.03	0.10	0.09	0.12	0.13	0.22	0.27	0.31
Netherlands	-0.16	-0.11	-0.16	-0.05	-0.11	-0.02	0.14	-0.23	-0.63	-1.07	-1.29
Portugal	0.09	0.09	0.06	0.06	0.06	0.04	0.04	0.04	0.10	0.16	0.15
Spain	0.09	0.10	0.14	0.14	0.17	0.16	0.12	0.15	0.31	0.58	0.60
Non EU(12) former EFTA											
Austria	0.01	0.01	0.01	0.02	0.09	0.08	0.02	0.06	0.03	0.04	0.04
Finland	0.00	0.00	-0.01	-0.02	-0.05	-0.03	0.01	-0.03	-0.02	-0.06	-0.06
Norway	0.03	0.02	0.02	0.02	-0.01	0.02	0.02	0.06	-0.01	-0.04	-0.02
Sweden	-0.05	-0.03	-0.07	-0.06	-0.09	-0.08	-0.12	-0.04	-0.15	-0.41	-0.42
Switzerland	-0.36	-0.39	-0.41	-0.40	-0.46	-0.11	-0.37	-0.14	-0.59	-0.74	-0.78

Notes: Oil companies, banks and insurance companies are excluded from 1962 to 1981. Miscellaneous FDI (mainly property) is excluded throughout. The IDP coefficient is calculated as NOI divided by GDP, and is expressed as a percentage to improve intelligibility.

Source: See Appendix.

decline, and that the locational advantages of the UK, which at one time were almost unassailable across manufacturing industry, have become of mixed quality for the newer breed of activities. Without such pronounced ownership and locational advantages in key stages of manufacturing activity there has grown a greater diversity in the country pattern of the IDP coefficient. Countries which historically (at least during the industrial period) could never aspire to be net investors in the UK are easily able to move to such a position. In this sense the unit of analysis of the IDP coefficient is no longer the aggregate curve, but that of shorter-term cycles with partner countries.[8] What determines these cycles, and how they relate to the tenets of the IDP, is what shall concern us in the discussion below. What is evident through the tabular analysis is that the absolute level of dispersion in the bilateral IDP positions has increased consistently. This is because of the multinationalisation of world industry, and the fact that over time FDI becomes a bigger percentage of GDP as firms increasingly interpenetrate each others' home industry.

(b) European countries outside the European Union

Countries outside the European Union, even the countries of EFTA, have an incentive to service the EU market from within. Although tariff barriers might not form an obstacle, strategic considerations argue for production within the integrating market – to gain experience and improve competitiveness within the single largest market in Europe. These considerations impart locational advantages to countries within the integrating area. Of the five countries selected in this category, two began as net donors of investment and were joined by two more in the interim. Only with Austria does the UK maintain a positive IDP position.

The experiences of Switzerland and Sweden bear a number of similarities. By 1991 the UK's IDP position with both has become more strongly negative than in 1962, though more so with Switzerland. Again, while UK firms have increased their gross investment in both countries, the UK has received a greater inflow within the same period.

In the context of rising gross flows of FDI between the UK and other European countries, the most tenable argument is that UK locational advantages have risen for at least two reasons within the EU: the fast liberalisation of key industries, and generally lower wage costs. Coupled with these, the advantages of internalisation rise within an integrating market because of the need for greater corporate integration and a higher intensity of information (and learning) flows, which are less amenable to non-affiliate contracts. UK ownership advantages may have declined, though not primarily in respect of marketable technology generation.[9]

There appears to be a tendency for those countries in which the UK invests most intensively to be those from which the UK receives most FDI. Were this pattern to be repeated at the industry level, it could be appropriate to advocate some form of rivalistic investment strategy on behalf of UK and foreign firms. What is clear, however, is that the observed pattern agrees with the prediction that Stage 5 countries will invest in their immediate neighbours in terms of development in the IDP framework. The rest of the EU does appear to be investing heavily in the UK. This raises questions over the possibility of FDI-induced competitive impacts on UK industry and native UK firms. This cannot be answered within the current time frame for European FDI in the UK, but some guidance is sought below from the experience of longer-term investors in the UK.

(c) Other developed countries

The UK's IDP position with the United States has undergone the greatest transformation, shown in Table 2.5. There is a sporadic burst of FDI beginning after 1981, as might be expected for Stage 5 countries. As a result, the post-war net negative standing of the UK with the United States became reversed during the early 1980s and is often attributed to the recognition by UK firms of the attractiveness of the market size in the United States, and the geographical diversification benefits that such expansion confers. It is worth noting that UK gross outward FDI continued to rise through the 1980s, only levelling off (but barely declining) when sterling stood at an all-time low against the dollar in 1984-5. Another interesting aspect is that the growth of UK gross FDI in the United States was mirrored by US FDI in the UK. Both took off at the same time. Between 1981 and 1991 US FDI in the UK increased by 167 per cent, while UK FDI in the United States increased by 244 per cent.[10] This testifies to the feverish pace of mergers and acquisitions in the 1980s, which, overall, left the UK ahead in terms of FDI.

Over the 30 years from the early 1960s to 1990, there has been almost a complete cycle in the UK bilateral IDP position with the

Table 2.5 The UK's aggregate IDP position with selected developed countries outside Europe, 1962–91

Countries	1962	1965	1968	1971	1974	1978	1981	1984	1987	1990	1991
North America											
Canada	1.10	0.84	1.04	0.69	0.64	0.37	0.40	1.30	0.42	0.38	0.38
USA	−2.14	−2.58	−2.79	−2.86	−2.79	−1.73	−0.62	2.17	0.94	0.32	0.59
Other developed countries											
Australia	1.78	1.96	2.19	1.92	2.21	1.45	1.26	2.28	0.73	0.39	0.14
Japan	0.03	0.03	0.02	0.00	0.07	0.08	−0.05	−0.05	−0.25	−0.74	−0.67
New Zealand	0.37	0.38	0.31	0.26	0.21	−0.01	0.11	0.20	0.17	−0.04	−0.03
South Africa	0.92	1.03	1.25	0.94	0.89	−0.20	0.51	0.72	0.37	0.32	0.33

Notes: Oil companies, banks and insurance companies are excluded from 1962 to 1981. Miscellaneous FDI (mainly property) is excluded throughout. The IDP coefficient is calculated as NOI divided by GDP, and is expressed as a percentage to improve intelligibility.

Source: See Appendix.

United States. This can be interpreted as the presence of an oscillating equilibrium, apt to occur between Stage 5 foreign investors, where OLI advantages (here mainly L and I advantages) tip one way then another (Dunning and Narula, 1994). Clearly, there is some indication that UK firms' ownership advantages have caught up with those of US firms, through being capable of investing on US home territory. Buckley (1981), studying European takeovers in the United States between 1976 and 1979, found these to be primarily horizontal in nature. This was supported by the observation that entry into the US market was characteristically in industrial areas that were closely related to parent firms' main business in terms of technology. Apart from FDI associated with conglomerate activity, UK firms' technological ownership advantages would seem to be competitive relative to those of many US firms.

Could this turnaround in the UK's FDI prowess *vis-à-vis* the United States be caused by a bilateral cycle induced by US FDI in the UK? The long period of UK net inward FDI with the United States, in theory, could have led to FDI-induced changes in the UK's location-bound competitive advantages, spawning enhanced UK firms' O advantages (an inter-temporal pro-competitive impact). If this is the case, the periodicity appears to be at least 30 years for a full cycle (i.e. the bilateral IDP index passing through zero twice), and at least half that for a reversal of the IDP coefficient. The conversion of the UK NOI suggests that some competitive effects are genuinely transferred, via the impact of inward FDI on the OLI configuration, take root and are retransferable at a future date. Of course, while a case could be made out that a country-level analysis of the IDP position reflects competitive abilities specific to the transferor, the impact on ownership advantages should in principle be reusable in any country.

If mini-cycles are increasingly to be expected, then there should be evidence of countries being kicked into a new cycle following episodes of inward FDI. The UK and the United States would appear to be a case in point. Because both are Stage 5 countries with mature industry structures in place, the likelihood of an identifiable cycle is greater. This is because the transmission of the spillover impacts of inward FDI is accelerated. When inward FDI involves, in effect, the creation of a completely new industrial base (e.g. FDI into a Stage 2 country) the bilateral IDP position of the investing country will move more sedately to a lower equilibrium, and perhaps not complete a cycle. Governments can have a key role in generating thrusts of FDI through the effect of their domestic industrial policy. The fact that the US telecommunications industry was the first to liberalise gave US firms knowledge of how to operate in competitive markets. While US industry was initially too powerful for large-scale inward FDI to occur, when the UK market was liberalised, US firms were in the forefront to invest. As a result, all the big telecommunications investors in the UK are from the United States, echoing a pattern first encountered in UK manufacturing industry in the 1950s.

The issue of bilateral FDI cycles has been treated most notably in the oligopolistic reaction literature. Graham (1974; 1978) found evidence of retaliation by European firms through defensive FDI into the United States, using industry-level data. Here cycles will have a much shorter period, and are essentially involved in building up intra-industry FDI in order to contain rivalry. Rivalry may have a part to play in explaining the bunching of gross cross-flows seen already in the data in this chapter. This would work mainly through the effect on the internalisation incentives (via external market imperfections) and the need to internalise production in foreign locations to make credible threats against rivals. However, the cross-hauling of FDI is mainly a response to underlying locational conditions well documented in the literature. For instance, there is the fact that countries at similar stages of development, such as Stage 5 countries, will invest most heavily in each other because their firms' market knowledge is mutually applicable and the factor intensity of production is similar.

While there is no longer any basic asymmetry between the UK and the United States, a significant gap has opened up with Japan (Table 2.5). The UK's modest IDP position with Japan up to the mid- to late 1970s has been replaced by a spectacular swing to net negative. By 1990-1 the UK's stance with Japan was a scaled-down version of its position with the United States during the 1960s and 1970s. Japanese government control over inward FDI during the 25 years since the end of the Second World War will undoubtedly have materially affected the level of inward FDI, especially at a time when Japanese industry craved foreign technology. This has led to a very weak direct foothold in Japan by foreign MNEs, compared with what could have been attained over a full 50 year period free of regulation. The UK's OLI status relative to Japan will have been affected, as will that of other investing nations. Added to this, the bilateral IDP position of Japan relative to all countries is likely to be shifted up, as a result of the fact that Japan is a relatively resource-lacking economy.

The Japanese motives for production within the UK include those of catering for a large domestic market and of securing a low-cost production base within the EU, in the face of regional protectionism. In complete contrast to the United States, the current status of the UK's IDP coefficient with Japan is the outcome of a very modest rise in UK real gross outward FDI into Japan, coupled with a substantial rise in Japanese gross inward investment into the UK. For the future, this invites the question of whether the UK will experience a full cycle with Japan and, in particular, whether any upgrading of UK L advantages through Japanese inward FDI-induced changes will result in sufficient upgrading of UK O advantages to result in raised FDI in Japan. To date, little aggregate evidence exists in terms of UK FDI in Japan, but the periodicity of the US cycle would suggest a trough to peak lag of about 10-15 years, which would place the UK backlash in around 2005-10.

The growth of UK gross outward FDI has stagnated somewhat in real terms in the traditional Commonwealth hosts of Canada, Australia and New Zealand. This has possibly occurred as a side effect of UK firms reorienting themselves towards the European market. However, this levelling is not true of inward FDI. The first two of these countries have been resolutely building up their multinational presence in the UK.

(d) UK membership of the European Union and bilateral country IDP positions

Both the regional and country pattern of the UK's IDP supports the belief that the UK has been viewed as a favourable production location. This is not linked solely to the UK's membership of the EU, as inward FDI into the UK by non-EU countries has pre-dated UK accession. Because the growth of FDI is linked to market size and market growth, it is natural for FDI growth to follow the same periodicity as the short-term business cycle (of 3-7 years). However, a number of aspects of the UK's FDI flows appear to be in some way related to membership of the EU, as is the fact that, notwithstanding macroeconomic cycles, the UK's IDP position and OLI configuration emerge in a modified state after each swing. It is one of the great merits of the IDP approach that it dispenses with the ebb and flow of cyclical components, because it is based on NOI. Of course, changes in the NOI are related to economic cycles: it is during expansionary phases that differentials in the OLI configuration of countries become manifest in the differential growth of gross outward and inward FDI.

The impact of EU membership during Mark I integration appears to have been greater for UK outward than UK inward FDI. Outward FDI rose significantly to the rest of the EU (especially to the Federal Republic of Germany and France) between 1971 and 1974, possibly indicating a strategic FDI response to the reduction of tariff barriers on trade. This first flush of FDI had noticeably turned downwards by 1978, and had receded by 1981. EU countries then invested strongly in the UK, with the big acceleration in UK gross inward FDI dating very clearly from around 1981–4. UK gross outward FDI also leapt into the rest of the EU at the same time. This appears to be part of a Europeanisation of FDI, as UK outward FDI also rose to non-EU Europe. This may reflect an episode of macroeconomic cyclical expansion, but after 1984 its effect is to leave the UK with a more pronounced negative IDP coefficient with EFTA.

There was a perceptible impact from the first enlargement of the EU (in 1973) on gross UK inward FDI from non-EU countries. In 1971–4 Switzerland and Sweden both increased their holdings in the UK. Switzerland in 1981–4 and Sweden in 1984–7 then began to build sharply on this, with the increases levelling off in 1990–1. UK gross outward FDI to European countries outside the EU actually matched the increases to EU countries.

While UK FDI abroad tends to rise in concert with inward FDI, the net effect tends to be a reduction in the IDP position. The leading exception is that of the UK and the United States. In the context of all the evidence of this chapter, the overall pattern suggests that the leading factor driving the declining IDP index of the UK is the inexorable long-term catching up of other developed countries, via their firms' accreting ownership advantages. In the shorter term (during the short-term cycles) the locational advantages of the UK appear to be persuasive. There is a progression towards more multinational production on a general basis because of the rising need for direct presence within national markets, as the segmentation of markets falls via tariff reduction and economic integration.

The increasing intensity of intra-EU FDI is distinctive in that it comes earlier than inward FDI from non-EU countries (with the exception of US FDI in the UK). Most inward FDI from non-EU countries came in a second wave in the mid-1980s, and it would seem likely that this was a strategic response to the earlier pan-European FDI. This favours the belief that competitive responses by EU firms have been accelerated by market integration. Gross inward FDI from the developed countries of the rest of the world took off somewhat later, around 1984–7. It can be argued that US firms are able to react faster either because of familiarity with the UK market, or because FDI has been expansionary rather than new entry.

It is worth noting the apparent low explanatory power of exchange rate variations in determining the timing of FDI. While exchange rate variations may explain the refinancing flows of an existing FDI stock (best seen in quarterly or annual changes in FDI), they do not seem to account for new FDI flows. The big peak evident in these data for UK merger and takeover FDI in the United States seems little related to the effects of the sterling exchange rate against the dollar.

THE EVOLUTION OF THE UNITED KINGDOM'S IDP POSITION BY INDUSTRY AND SECTOR

The discussion in this section focuses on the recent time trends of the UK's IDP coefficient, but from a complementary angle. The raw data employed are for annual stock levels, but are here rendered into IDP coefficients for industry groups. The data selected are annual estimates since 1973 which, while they do not provide the disaggregation of the (nominally) triennial census, nevertheless do allow the tracking of a clearer time path.

The time trend of the UK's aggregate IDP coefficient (since 1965) is presented in Table 2.6, in which one sees a high degree of variance year on year. As has been seen above, while the UK continues to be a net outward investor, its overall IDP position has declined steadily in real terms since the 1960s. This decline is punctuated by a steep rise in the early 1980s. As was discussed earlier, this would seem to have much to do with the UK's position relative to the United States.

The finer annual detail of the aggregate IDP index reveals the inevitable year on year fluctuations. The data agree broadly with the pattern already noticed in Table 2.1, and on this larger scale it is even more apparent that in 1991 the IDP position again strengthened. When this trend is broken down by broad industry some marked divergence in fortunes emerges. The leading positive IDP

Table 2.6 The UK's aggregate annual IDP position and IDP position by industry group, 1965–91

	Banking	Other financial institutions	Industrial and commercial	Total
1965	–	–	–	8.97
1966	–	–	–	10.09
1967	–	–	–	10.04
1968	–	–	–	9.22
1969	–	–	–	11.01
1970	–	–	–	6.88
1971	–	–	–	6.40
1972	–	–	–	8.89
1973	0.50	1.47	4.80	6.80
1974	0.44	2.21	4.99	7.66
1975	0.36	2.34	6.43	9.16
1976	0.28	2.05	4.49	6.80
1977	0.27	2.03	4.74	7.00
1978	0.32	1.78	3.61	5.56
1979	0.21	1.40	2.09	3.43
1980	0.12	1.67	4.98	6.43
1981	−0.08	1.84	6.31	7.72
1982	−0.34	1.92	6.23	7.39
1983	−0.71	2.27	10.42	11.51
1984	−0.81	2.05	7.02	7.73
1985	−0.22	1.96	7.06	8.12
1986	−0.60	1.00	6.42	5.90
1987	−0.92	0.85	7.86	6.53
1988	−0.69	0.65	6.48	5.12
1989	−1.04	−0.09	3.87	1.35
1990	−1.18	0.34	3.95	1.71
1991	−1.16	0.65	7.44	5.64

Notes: Industrial and commercial companies includes oil companies and persons. Deviations in the estimates of the IDP for some years compared with those in previous tables arise because of differences between sources. The IDP coefficient is calculated as NOI divided by GDP, and is expressed as a percentage to improve intelligibility.
Source: See Appendix.

position is recorded by the industrial sector.[11] The peak in the total curve for 1983 derives entirely from this sector and is undoubtedly related to the peak of acquisition activity in the United States in that year, already noted. Other financial institutions (covering insurance, etc.) record a trend that declines slightly over the period, but the most dramatic development is the switch in the UK's IDP position in banking, to net inward investor in 1981. This resulted from an increase in gross inward FDI rather than an increase in gross outward FDI. The inference is that either the ownership advantages of foreign banks had risen, or the inward locational advantages of the UK in these service industries had risen appreciably. The latter construction is the most tenable as banks seeking to enhance their competitiveness will choose to locate in London, because of its prominence as an international financial centre. The UK's locational advantages are a magnet for the growing population of banks seeking an international positioning.

THE COMPOSITION OF FDI FLOWS IN THE UNITED KINGDOM'S IDP POSITION

The firm-level characteristics of size, degree of international involvement and experience, management and organisation strategies, and innovatory capacity are all recognised influences on the FDI behaviour of firms. It is predicted that, over time, ownership advantages become progressively firm specific, less a function of the home economic structure and more one of the foreign locational choices made by MNEs. Part of the argument is that the nationalities of firms becomes blurred in Stage 5 of the IDP. The way that firms change their behaviour can be glimpsed, even in aggregate data, by looking at how they choose to finance foreign operations, which is strongly linked to size and maturity. The components of FDI can give some insight here. For instance, net reinvested earnings would be expected to increase as a component of NOI growth abroad, as MNEs (and their affiliates) become established. The level of dependence on the home economy, for finance at least, might be seen to decline for a Stage 5 country.

Annual flows of FDI are, in principle, the first differences in the FDI stock. In practice, valuation adjustments to the stock figures following surveys, and factors such as exchange rate movements, mean that FDI flows do not align perfectly with stock value changes. Although reinvested earnings are attributed to the home economy and are then notionally returned to affiliates abroad as direct investment outflows, they in fact indicate financial independence on the part of foreign affiliates. UK FDI flow data distinguish the key components in the financing of FDI flows, and so provide a window on the behavioural changes underlying the larger picture evident in the statistics on FDI stocks. The data here are essentially balance of payments figures, in which the convention is to record outward FDI flows prefixed with a minus sign, while FDI inflows are attributed a positive sign. This convention is retained in studying the components of the change in the UK's IDP position in Table 2.7. The IDP approach posits that, with increasing maturity, foreign

Table 2.7 Components of annual NOI flows in the UK's IDP position, 1962–91

	Unremitted profits of subsidiaries	Net acquisition of share and loan capital	Change in inter-company accounts	Change in branch indebtedness
1962	−0.13	−0.05	0.06	−0.15
1963	−0.09	−0.04	0.02	−0.14
1964	−0.20	−0.04	−0.03	−0.03
1965	−0.14	−0.01	−0.14	−0.02
1966	−0.24	0.06	−0.01	−0.02
1967	−0.23	0.02	−0.04	−0.03
1968	−0.23	−0.11	0.00	−0.11
1969	−0.40	0.03	−0.05	−0.06
1970	−0.27	−0.13	0.06	−0.01
1971	−0.25	−0.13	−0.06	0.04
1972	−0.25	−0.07	−0.13	−0.06
1973	−0.67	−0.29	−0.18	−0.05
1974	−0.71	0.11	−0.09	−0.17
1975	−0.59	−0.06	0.15	−0.01
1976	−0.72	−0.18	−0.06	−0.09
1977	−0.31	−0.17	0.06	0.04
1978	−0.32	−0.45	−0.02	−0.07
1979	−0.20	−0.62	0.15	0.01
1980	−0.41	−0.42	0.47	0.00
1981	−0.54	−0.60	−0.31	0.01
1982	−0.33	−0.24	0.16	0.06
1983	−0.39	−0.45	0.20	0.16
1984	−1.07	−0.62	0.62	−0.10
1985	−0.89	−0.68	−0.34	0.10
1986	−0.99	−1.35	0.01	0.25
1987	−1.22	−0.95	−0.77	0.14
1988	−1.44	−0.96	−0.40	0.24
1989	−1.38	−0.70	0.86	0.00
1990	−1.54	0.50	1.71	0.04
1991	−1.40	0.06	0.90	−0.07

Notes: The balance of payments convention is retained here: that net outflows and inflows are recorded as negative and positive entries respectively.
The IFDP coefficients are for the components of NOI flows. These are divided by GDP, and are expressed as a percentage to improve intelligibility.
Source: See Appendix.

affiliates will become more proactive in generating their own ownership advantages (rather than simply employing those of the parent). This is part of the prediction of the IDP approach that the importance of created relative to natural assets in the competitive process rises over the course of the investment path. It is a well-known phenomenon that the proportion of unremitted profits (reinvested earnings) rises with the age of the affiliate. Interpreted within the context of the IDP, increased reinvested earnings as a means of financing FDI growth would suggest that foreign affiliates are becoming less dependent on their parent firm. As a Stage 5 (and positive NOI) foreign investing economy, the net reinvested earnings standing of the UK should be expected to be increasingly negative, i.e. for there to be rising reinvestment abroad relative to reinvestment within the UK. In Table 2.7, the development over 30 years since the early 1960s does indeed bear out these expectations. Although attributed to the UK by convention, this growth of net unremitted profits is an index of the extent to which, on balance, the UK's investment status lies in the hands of affiliates abroad.

The continued growth in the financing of UK NOI from affiliate-generated funds appears to have been at least partly offset by a decline in the net acquisition of share and loan capital (i.e. net attributable to UK firms) since the mid-1980s, when a peak was reached coincident with the boom in UK net acquisitions abroad, noted earlier. This could signal the growth of independent borrowing abroad by UK affiliates, now sufficiently large to raise their own debt finance at cheap rates from third parties. This latter element is unobservable, because it is not attributable to parent firms as FDI. Nevertheless, it would be an indicator of significant behavioural shifts within multinationals. It is perfectly tenable that, notwithstanding the practical merits of estimating an IDP coefficient, the capital under the control of UK ultimate beneficial owners (UBOs) might exceed that of foreign UBOs in the UK. This would imply that, for a Stage 5 economy, net outward MNE activity as a method of international market servicing might substantially exceed that indicated by the IDP coefficient.

The rising importance of MNE integration for changes in the IDP position are evident in the IDP coefficients for the components of the net changes in inter-company accounts. Large net inflows of this source of finance were recorded in the late 1980s, probably as a response to a rise in relative UK interest rates. Although minor in terms of its importance for both gross and NOI the statistical series of net changes in indebtedness by MNEs operating abroad in the form of branches (rather than in that of incorporated foreign affiliates) appeared to follow a similar pattern. These responses by MNEs affecting NOI cannot be counted as underlying changes in the OLI configuration. However, they do testify to the increased ability of MNEs with large internal capital markets to respond to international capital market segmentation. Therefore, it is an example of the maturation of MNEs, and of these firms transcending their county of origin.

A further implication for the IDP arises from the evidence here that the past history of the UK, originally as the dominant, and then as one of a few leading NOI nations, builds a degree of inertia into the IDP position, as measured by the IDP coefficient. It could be argued that the effect of the UK's outstanding stock of net FDI, and the reinvested profits thereof, is to enable the UK to retain the mantle of a great investing nation at a higher level than might be possible based on current prowess. This helps to slow the decline in the UK's path, to the point where no clear trend, either down or up, is apparent.

CONCLUSIONS

This chapter suggests that the concept of the investment development path is a useful one. Although the pattern of interactions is harder to discern for a mature investing nation, such as the UK, some of the predictions of the approach are borne out. For instance, there does appear to be evidence of some long-term periodicity (as distinct from the world business cycle) in the IDP index. The declining trends, as witnessed in Tables 2.1 and 2.6, are overlaid by spasmodic episodes of increasing IDP positions with individual partner countries. The reversal of the UK's NOI position with the United States does support the existence of a country-specific cycle, with a turnaround period of at least 15-20 years (and probably more). This is some indication of a Stage 5 transitory disequilibrium. The question that remains is whether such a cycle will be manifest for UK NOI with Japan.

The UK is an attractive host within the EU. The motives for this inward investment straddle those of market-seeking, wage cost reduction, and the securing of other location-specific advantages. These latter derive from operating within liberalised and deregulated markets, and external locational economies (notably London as an international financial centre). Through market liberalisation, government can make an impact on locational attributes, though the percolation of these impacts into UK firms' ownership advantages cannot be assessed on these early data.

In terms of competitiveness, the UK as a location has its areas of light but also, it might appear, its areas of shade. Taking at face value the UK's sound performance in international technology trade, it is possible to venture the conclusion that the overall secular decline in the UK's IDP index stems from shortcomings in the ownership advantages of firms in respect to the application of technology within the UK. This may be linked to weaknesses in the stock of higher skills within the UK which are necessary for the more technology-intensive production and development of innovative products.

In a world of lowering trade barriers and market integration, there is an incentive to move to increased interpenetration between economies, and ultimately network-orientated investment patterns. This favours rising FDI levels in all host countries. This is reflected in the greatly widened dispersion in the bilateral IDP values seen in this chapter. Against this background, the UK's net ownership advantages appear to have declined *vis-à-vis* its advanced industrial partners in Europe. At the same time, UK firms have become more competitive in the United States. One explanation of this is that UK firms have benefited from prior US FDI in the UK. This might be borne out by an inter-temporal study of the intra-industry intensity of transatlantic FDI.

There are undoubtedly advantages conferred on the UK by its historical priority as a net outward investor. The maturity of its international operations means that the reinvested earnings IDP coefficient is higher than the aggregate IDP coefficient. This buoys up the aggregate path. Another possible consideration is that, to the extent that foreign affiliates tend in general to raise more finance abroad independently as they mature, UK parent firms may have a higher IDP coefficient in respect to the foreign capital that they control rather than that which they own.

Further work can clearly be done. For instance, investigating the intensity of intra-industry FDI as expected in Stage 5. It remains an open question whether the UK's IDP coefficient is asymptotic to zero, or whether it will actually become negative. As has been seen here, the instances of bilateral negative IDP positions with other developed countries have been on the increase. As yet, the data do not suggest any perceptible fall in the UK's NOI position with newly industrialised and industrialising countries. A rise in inward FDI of substance from these countries, i.e. a general change in sign in the NOI position of the UK (and of other existing developed economies), is not ruled out in the IDP approach. Perhaps, in the long period, countries such as the UK might expect a continual whittling down of NOI, as an outcome of the new industrial centres in the world.

NOTES

1   Net outward investment is obtained by subtracting gross inward investment from gross outward investment. The net FDI value obtained may be positive or negative, depending on the country concerned and its stage of development.

2   The IDP coefficient or measure is obtained by dividing the NOI by GDP. The division of one data series by another when both are at current prices, in principle, eradicates inflationary effects (assuming that the appropriate deflators for each are sufficiently close). However, FDI is recorded at book values, and so pre-existing FDI becomes over-deflated using this approach. Alternatives were considered. For instance, the deflation of the first differences of the FDI stock to constant (1985) prices was tried, employing the UK's GDP deflator (IMF, various years). These deflated differences were then recombined to produce an estimate of a constant price series, which was then normalised by GDP at constant prices. While this resulted in an increase in the historical level of the IDP coefficient, it did not materially alter the trend or variation in the index. Consequently, the simplest method was retained, of dividing NOI by GDP, both at current prices.

3   Even before the First World War, the comparative advantage of the United States was found to lie in human-capital-intensive, unskilled-labour-scarce commodities (Crafts and Thomas, 1986).

4   Regarding such policy changes as exogenous to firms may be regarded as naive by political scientists, in that the motive force for many such changes is commercial pressure from producer interest groups (in much the same way as trade protection motives are accepted to be by economists). Government is a variable, but does normally come under some control from within the system. Building this into the IDP framework would naturally make the linkages still more involved.

5   The same percentage increase of roughly 130 per cent is recorded for all industries combined.

6   Asia is defined to include the countries of the Middle East, the Indian subcontinent and the newly industrialised and industrialising countries of South-East Asia.

7   The rest of the world is a summary group covering Africa, Asia, the Caribbean and Central and South America.

8 This point is made by Ozawa in this volume.
9 This was earlier supported by the evaluation of non-affiliate licensing transactions, presented in Table 2.2
10 As was noted, in 1984 oil, banks and insurance were included in the geographical data for the first time. While this will have increased the gross flows, the annual data which included estimates for these industries throughout still record a peak (around 1983), as does the UK's NOI.
11 This sector is defined as industrial and commercial companies, including oil companies and persons.

APPENDIX: MAIN SOURCES OF DATA

National account and exchange rate statistics

International Monetary Fund (various years) *International Financial Statistics*, Washington, DC: IMF.
Mitchell, B. R. (1988) *British Historical Statistics*, Cambridge: Cambridge University Press.

Foreign direct investment

Business Statistics Office, *Business Monitor MA4, 1981 Supplement, Census of Overseas Assets*, 1981, London: HMSO.
Central Statistical Office, *Business Monitor MA4, 1991, Overseas Transactions*, London: HMSO.
——— *Business Monitor M04, 1987, Census of Overseas Assets*, London: HMSO.
——— (various years) *United Kingdom Balance of Payments* (CSO 'Pink Book'), London: HMSO.
Dunning, J. H. (1983) 'Changes in the level and structure of international production: the last one hundred years', Chapter 5 in M. C. Casson (ed.) *The Growth of International Business*, London: George Allen and Unwin. Tables 5.1 and 5.2.

International technology licensing

Business Statistics Office (for years 1974-6) *Business Monitor M4, Overseas Transactions*, London: HMSO.
——— (for years 1977-88) *Business Monitor MA4, Overseas Transactions*, London: HMSO.
Central Statistical Office (for years 1989-93) *United Kingdom Balance of Payments* (CSO 'Pink Book'), London: HMSO.

BIBLIOGRAPHY

Boatwright, B. D. and Renton, G. A. (1975) 'An analysis of United Kingdom inflows and outflows of direct foreign investment', *Review of Economics and Statistics 57*, No. 4: 478–86.

Buckley, P. J. (1981) 'The entry strategy of recent European direct investors in the USA', *Journal of Comparative Corporate Law and Securities Regulation 3*: 169–91.

———— and Casson, M. C. (1991) 'Multinational enterprises in less developed countries: cultural and economic interactions', in P.J. Buckley and J. Clegg, (eds) *Multinational Enterprises in Less Developed Countries*, London: Macmillan.

———— and Pearce, R. D. (1991) *International Aspects of UK Economic Activities*, Reviews of United Kingdom Statistical Sources, The Royal Statistical Society and the Economic and Social Research Council, London: Chapman and Hall.

Crafts, N. F. R. and Thomas, M. (1986) 'Comparative advantage in UK manufacturing trade, 1910-1935, *Economic Journal 96*, September: 629–43.

Dunning, J. H. (1977) 'Trade, location of economic activity and the multinational enterprise: a search for and eclectic approach', in B. Ohlin, P.-O. Hesselborn, and P. M. Wijkman. (eds) *The International Allocation of Economic Activity*, London: Macmillan.

———— (1983) 'Changes in the level and structure of international production: the last one hundred years', in M. C. Casson (ed.) *The Growth of International Business*, London: George Allen and Unwin.

———— (1988) 'The investment development cycle and Third World multinationals', Chapter 5 in J. H. Dunning *Explaining International Production*, London: Unwin Hyman.

———— (1993) *Multinational Enterprises and the Global Economy*, Wokingham, Berks.: Addison-Wesley.

———— and Narula, R. (1994) *Transpacific Foreign Direct Investment and the Investment Development Path: The Record Assessed*, Essays in International Business, No. 10, May 1994.

———— and Robson, P. (1988) 'Multinational corporate integration and regional economic integration', in J. H. Dunning and P. Robson, (eds) *Multinationals and the European Community*, Oxford: Blackwell: 1–23.

Graham, E. M. (1974) *Oligopolistic imitation and European direct investment in the United States*, Unpublished DBA dissertation, Harvard Graduate School of Business.

———— (1978) 'Transnational investment by multinational firms: a rivalistic phenomenon', *Journal of Post Keynesian Economics 1*, No. 1: 82–99.

United Nations Conference on Trade and Development (UNCTAD) (1993) *World Investment Report 1993: Transnational Corporations and Integrated International Production*. Programme on Transnational Corporations, New York: United Nations.

United Nations Centre on Transnational Corporations (UNCTC) (1990) *Regional Economic Integration and Transnational Corporations in the*

1990s: Europe 1992, North America, and Developing Countries, UNCTC Current Studies, Series A, No. 15, New York: United Nations.

United Nations Transnational Corporations and Management Division (UNTCMD) (1993) *From the Common Market to EC 92: Regional Economic Integration in the European Community and Transnational Corporations*, Department of Economic and Social Development, New York: United Nations.

United States Department of Commerce (1989) *Foreign Direct Investment in the United States: US Business Enterprises Acquired or Established by Foreign Direct Investors*, 1980-86, July.

Chapter 3

The United States
Some musings on its investment development path

Edward M. Graham

INTRODUCTION

The United States is one of the most interesting of nations in terms of the evolution of its investment development path (IDP) during the almost fifty years since the end of World War II. During the first half of this period, the United States established itself by a wide margin as the leading home nation to direct investment and, indeed, it was the international spread of US business firms that motivated the development of what has become the field of research in foreign direct investment. Such basic terms as 'multinational enterprise' and 'transnational corporation' were coined largely to describe large American firms that had extended their operations internationally during this period. In the mid- to late 1970s, when it was in fashion to link multinational firms to 'neoimperialism', American-based multinationals became the target of a wide range of critics who saw these firms as ubiquitously dominating the world economy to the detriment of civilized society.

During the 1980s, however, the trend of the net direct investment position of the United States went into reverse, as large amounts of foreign direct investment began to flow into the US economy at rates faster than the US direct investment abroad flowed out. This was the result of the international spread of activities of scores of firms that were not based in the United States. It was perhaps no accident that, as the source nations of FDI became increasingly diverse, criticism of the multinational enterprise (MNE) became muted to the point where, by now, foreign direct investment by MNEs is almost universally held in high esteem. By the late 1980s the United States was still the largest home nation to direct investment, but it had become the largest host nation as well. As Figure 3.1 clearly shows,

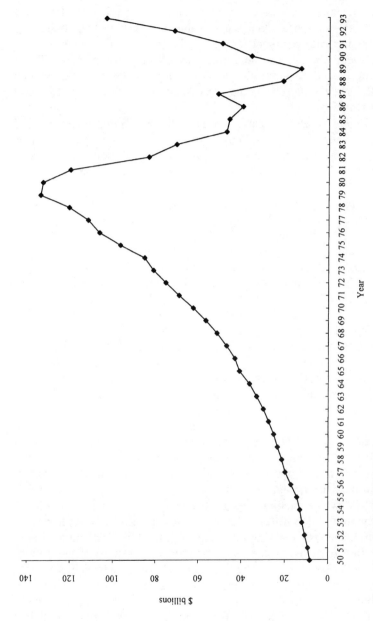

Figure 3.1 Net US FDI position

by the end of the decade, on an historic cost basis, direct investment in the United States was just about equal in magnitude to US direct investment abroad. On a market value basis as calculated by the US Commerce Department, however, the value of the latter did still substantially exceed the former, by as much as perhaps 50 per cent. Nonetheless, the rate at which direct investment flowed into the United States during the second half of the 1980s was little short of stunning.

Figure 3.1 also indicates that during the 1990s to date, the trend of the US net direct investment position reversed itself again, as flows of foreign direct investment into the United States decelerated sharply following 1990 and flows of US direct investment abroad began to grow rapidly. Thus, by the end of 1993 the United States was once again substantially a net outward direct investor nation, even on an historic cost basis.

It is very tempting to claim that the steady rise in the net outward direct investment position of the United States from 1950 through 1979, as indicated in Figure 3.1, was the result of 'le défi americain', i.e. the internalization in multinational operations of technological and managerial competencies of US firms (i.e. superior 'O' advantages held by these firms) that so intrigued and simultaneously annoyed Europeans during the 1960s and 1970s. By this same interpretation, the reversal of this rise during the 1980s came about as a consequence of the decline of these competencies relative to those of non-US rivals, especially ones based in Europe and Japan. Also consistent with such a story would be a 'renaissance' in US industry that many observers see as currently on-going. By this account, the reversal of the decline of the US net direct investment position should be interpreted as the result of US firms upgrading their 'O' advantages by means of successfully 'downsizing' and otherwise rationalizing their operations and simultaneously upgrading their technological competencies.

The whole picture thus presented is quite consistent with the Dunning and Narula depiction of the advanced industrial nations simultaneously entering into Stage 5 of the IDP. The United States, having been the 'leader' nation when the most advanced nations were at Stage 4 of their development, plays a somewhat unique role in the convergence that occurs during Stage 5. This is because convergence results from other nations' firms 'catching up' in terms of the quality of their 'created assets' (technology and managerial prowess) to their US rivals. Hence, in a relative sense, the quality of such assets of US firms would be declining even if in an absolute sense these assets were being continuously upgraded. As we have just seen, the evidence of the 1980s, at first glance, is quite consistent with such a decline, albeit that the limited evidence of the 1990s suggests the possibility of a reversal in the decline.

The remainder of this chapter is divided into three sections. The next section takes a more detailed look at the available information regarding the flows of direct investment out of and into the United States during the past fifty years. One immediate result of this examination is that certain of the hypotheses just introduced regarding the Stage 5 trajectory of the US IDP path must be nuanced. The following section attempts to interpret further the trajectory of this path in light of issues posed by Dunning and Narula in the introductory chapter of this volume. One theme that emerges is that while, overall, the Dunning and Narula hypotheses regarding Stage 5 are supported, some of the nuances uncovered suggest the need for further refinement of these hypotheses. At the end of the chapter an attempt is made to draw whatever conclusions might be warranted, at this time, about the validity of the Stage 5 hypothesis.

THE US IDP IN SOME DETAIL

It does not in fact take much plombing to uncover that the story outlined in the introductory section above, i.e. that of the early post-war dominance of US industry, followed by a period of decline, followed by a period of renaissance, is too simple to explain fully the US IDP. The first inkling comes from Figure 3.2, which shows the evolution of the gross outward and inward direct investment positions as well as the net positions of the United States for 1950–1993.

Perhaps the first thing that should be noted is that both these series are affected by changes in baseline that follow from the benchmark surveys periodically performed by the Bureau of Economic Analysis, the agency within the US Commerce Department that compiles the direct investment data. Thus, for example, the data show a decline in the outward investment position of the United States occurring between 1981 and 1982. This, however, is the result of a one-time downward adjustment of the series following the 1982 benchmark survey of US direct investment abroad. Likewise, an apparent jump in foreign direct investment in the United States in 1980 is the result of recalibration of the inward series following the

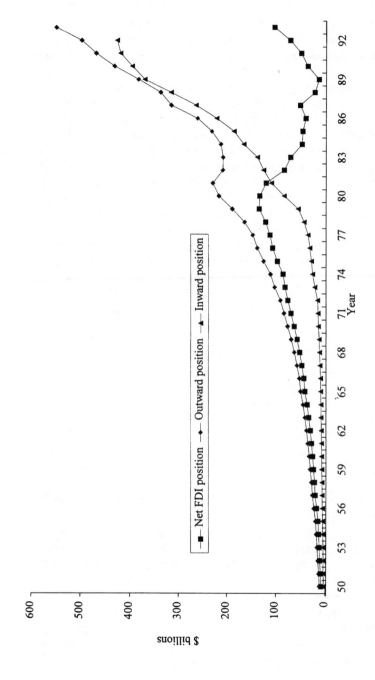

Figure 3.2 Net gross inward and outward FDI position

1980 benchmark survey of foreign direct investment in the United States.

It should also be noted that both series are reported at historical cost, resulting in early investment being understated in terms of current value relative to later investment because the effects of inflation are not taken into account. The benchmark adjustment would suggest that the net outward direct investment position of the United States for years prior to 1981 was somewhat overstated, because both outward flows were somewhat overestimated and inward flows somewhat underestimated during these years. Alas, we have no clue as to exactly when the discrepancies occurred. But the historical cost basis tends to cause the current value of old investment to be understated relative to that of new investment and, because of the preponderance of outward over inward direct investment prior to the past decade and a half, the net outward investment position of the United States on a current cost (rather than historical cost) basis is likely understated.

These statistical factors aside, one aspect of Figure 3.2 particularly stands out, notably that US direct investment abroad and foreign direct investment in the United States have both grown steadily and enormously over the past four decades. The latter lags the former, and this lag would still be evident even if the inward and outward flows prior to 1981 were to be adjusted to reflect the discrepancies noted just above. The lag is surely consistent with some story of a post-World War II lead by US firms in industrial technology (and other O advantages of US firms) over their non-US rivals and a subsequent closing of the gap by these rivals. But the overall picture, it would seem, is also one of a long term continuous international expansion of activities by many firms, both US and non-US in origin. The much discussed 'globalization' of business thus appears to be a very real phenomenon driving the statistics. What must be asked is whether globalization has a life of its own that is not adequately addressed in terms of those factors driving the investment development paths of individual nations. Is the totality of globalization in some sense greater than the sum of its components?

Figure 3.3 indicates the US direct investment position in the manufacturing sector only. Roughly the same patterns are observed as in the overall direct investment position. However, in manufacturing, the reversal of the trend from a rise to a decline in the net position begins a little sooner (1979) for the manufacturing position

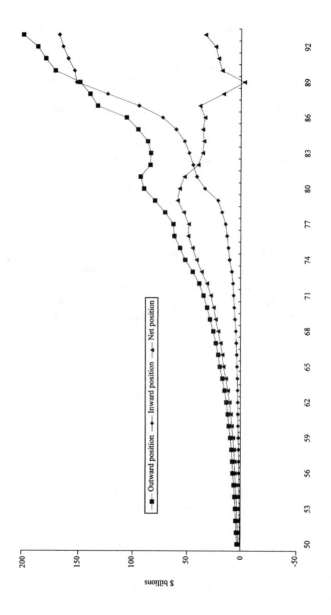

Figure 3.3 US manufacturing FDI position

than for the overall position (1980). Also, the ensuing decline, until 1987, is a little flatter for manufacturing than for all industries. But during the years 1987–1989, the US net direct investment position in manufacturing drops much more precipitously than does the overall position. This doubtlessly is due to the rash of takeovers of US firms by foreign investors that occurred during those years (see Graham and Krugman 1995). This takeover activity both began and ended quite abruptly and one important issue to be considered in the section following is to what extent the takeovers were consistent with the Dunning and Narula notion of strategic asset acquiring FDI.

Following 1989, it must be noted, the US net manufacturing position again reverses, such that the net outward position begins to grow, just as does the net position for all industries. This is, of course, consistent with a 'renaissance' in the US manufacturing sector.

Some additional insight into the trajectory of the US investment development path can be gleaned from examination of the components of the changes in this path. The yearly changes in the direct investment position for the United States (i.e. the net flows, both inward and outward) are the sum of capital flows and valuation adjustments, and the published data break down capital flows into three categories ('accounts' in the terminology of the US Commerce Department): new equity flows, changes in inter-firm debt (i.e. debt between affiliate and parent), and changes in retained earnings.

Figure 3.4 indicates the breakdown of FDI flows *to* the United States by account. Three things become immediately clear. First, new equity flows to the United States, perhaps the best measure of the spread into the United States of new activity by non-US-based multinationals, reach a peak in 1989 and, after two years of small declines, fall substantially beginning in 1992. Second, however, in 1992 and 1993 these flows remain substantial and, indeed, they are well above the levels of 1985 and earlier years, even after allowing for inflation. Third, the deceleration in the rise in FDI in the United States following 1989 is driven as much by reductions in retained earnings of affiliates of foreign firms in the United States in 1990, 1991 and 1992 as by reductions in new equity flows.

These former – reductions in retained earnings which, for balance of payments purposes, count as negative inward FDI flows – are in turn driven by net negative earnings of these affiliates (see Table 3.1). These in turn reflect doubtlessly start-up and turnaround costs of enterprises newly established or acquired in the United States.

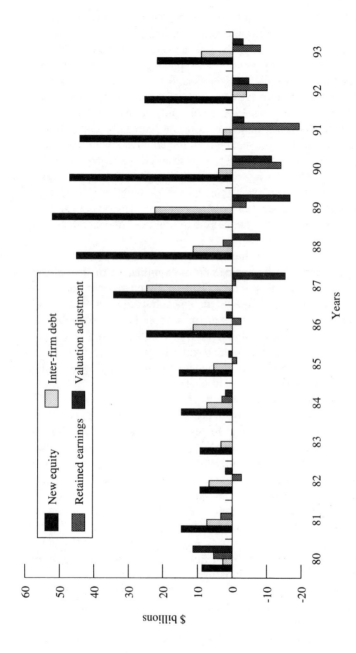

Figure 3.4 FDI flows to the United States by component

But, also, the losses associated with these costs, and the associated efforts of non-US multinational firms to put their new US affiliates in order, might also contribute to reduced flows of new equity into the United States. Some of this reduction in fact is the consequence of the sale of assets acquired by foreign investors back to US investors, as the former attempt to rationalize their US operations and to weed out unprofitable lines of business or ones that do not fit into the overall strategic plans of the firm[1]. Indeed, in some cases, e.g. the holdings of Maxwell, foreign-controlled assets in the United States are reverting to domestic control as the result of liquidation of operations that have gone bankrupt. One might expect new equity flows to recover as foreign direct investors in the United States succeed in putting their US houses in order. This latter, in fact, seems already to be happening; losses by US affiliates of foreign firms tapered significantly following the recession year of 1991.

One hypothesis is that the whole situation in the early 1990s with respect to foreign direct investment in the United States might be likened to a group of persons who have eaten a very large meal, some of whom as a consequence have come down with indigestion. Some of these persons indeed have eaten so much that they regurgitate their food; others simply restrain from eating for a time. However, all will almost surely recover fully with time, and eventually the banquet will resume. The decline in FDI in the United States of the early 1990s, if this hypothesis is correct, is more probably a lull rather than a break in trend.

But another hypothesis is that actual or anticipated governmental policy actions in response to the FDI boom of the late 1980s have had some 'chilling effect' on the rate of direct investment in the United States. Especially during the late 1980s, there arose some furore in US policy circles over what was perceived as the 'selling of America' to foreign-based (and, most particularly, Japanese-

Table 3.1 Earnings before interest and tax of US affiliates of foreign firms, 1989–1993 ($ billions)

1989	1990	1991	1992	1993
−0.5	−5.2	−12.0	−4.8	−1.0

Source: US Dept of Commerce, Bureau of Economic Analysis, 'Foreign Direct Investment in the United States: Detail for Historical-Cost Position and Related Capital and Income Flows, 1993', Survey of Current Business, August 1994, Table 2, and earlier tables.

based) multinationals. A number of restrictive measures were proposed and one of these, the Exon–Florio amendment to the Omnibus Trade and Competitiveness Act of 1988, was actually passed into law.[2] This law gives the US President the right to review and block takeovers of US firms if these threaten to impair the national security. Potentially, the law gives the US government very wide reaching powers to intervene in foreign direct investments achieved via mergers and takeovers, which was the dominant mode of direct investment into the United States during the 1980s. In fact, the law has been used rather sparingly; any chilling effect that might be attributed to its existence would have to be based on the law's potential reach, not its actual history.

This furore by and large died down during the early 1990s but a 'policy residue' remains. Much of this 'residue' takes the form of laws and policies that impose some sort of discriminatory standard on foreign firm participation in the United States in certain instances, e.g. (and most especially) technology consortia.[3] Overall it is very difficult to determine how much of the decline in direct investment activity in the United States following 1990 has been due to a policy-induced 'chilling effect' and how much of it is due to 'indigestion'. Time will help to sort these issues out.

The situation with respect to flows of outward US direct investment by account is more complicated, as indicated in Figure 3.5. These flows have been published in detailed form (i.e. broken down by account) by the US Commerce Department only since 1982, and hence we must limit our examination to the years 1982 and later. Several things stand out from this examination. During the 1980s, there was almost no direct investment equity flow from the United States to the rest of the world. The increases in the outward direct investment position during this time occur largely as the result of increases in retained earnings: 1982 saw a large drop in this investment position caused by a downward valuation adjustment, as already noted, following the 1982 benchmark; there were also smaller downward valuation adjustments during 1983 and 1984, but the remainder of the decade saw significant upward valuation adjustments. Also, during the years 1982–1984, inter-firm debt from parent to affiliate was reduced; this doubtlessly was a response to the very high rates of interest that prevailed in the United States during those years. Beginning in 1990, equity flows out of the United States picked up, and there appears to be a weak upward trend in these during the years 1990–1993.

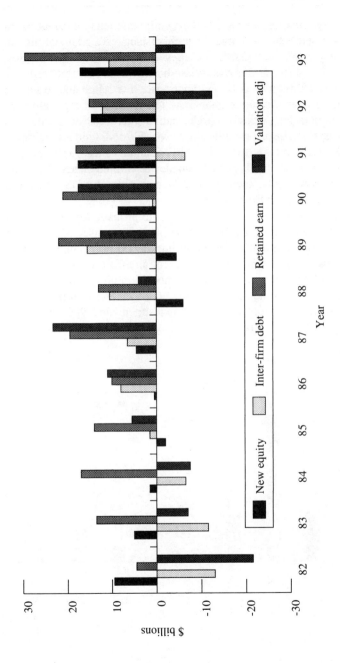

Figure 3.5 FDI flows from the United States by component

Legend: New equity | Inter-firm debt | Retained earn | Valuation adj

Y-axis: $ billions (30, 20, 10, 0, -10, -20, -30)

X-axis: Year (82, 83, 84, 85, 86, 87, 88, 89, 90, 91, 92, 93)

Exactly what to make of all this is not completely clear. It is not wholly baseless to claim that the numbers suggest a near stalling out of the expansion of overseas activities of US firms during the 1980s, followed by a rise in this expansion during the 1990s. But while the first part of this story is not without base, it is rebuttable. Retained earnings are one means of financing the expansion of an established business activity. A plausible alternative interpretation of the data would be that already-established US-based MNEs did enlarge their overseas activities during the 1980s, financing these with retained earnings or other funds raised outside the United States. It would seem, however, that there was little new entry by US firms into overseas markets during that time.

What is clear is that the 1990s, to date at least, represent something of a new era for US multinationals in the sense that any lapse in their expansion that occurred during the 1980s has ended during the 1990s. Figures 3.6 and 3.7 represent an effort to examine what, if any, shifts have occurred in the composition of US outward direct investment during the 1990s. Figure 3.6 indicates by destination the 1989 stock of US outward direct investment and the cumulative 1990–93 flows of outward equity investment, each depicted as a

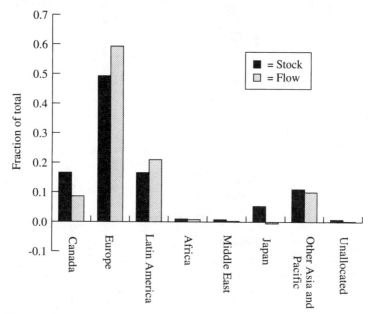

Figure 3.6   1989 stock and 1990–1993 flow by region

fraction of the total ('total' being the total stock in 1989 and the total cumulative flows 1990–1993, respectively). What can be seen is that, by this measure, Canada, the Middle East, Japan and 'unallocated' received proportionately less of recent flows than of earlier flows (where the 1989 stock share indicates percentage of earlier flows to any given area) whereas Europe, Latin America, and 'other Asia and Pacific' (i.e. Asia and Pacific less Japan) all received proportionately more of the flows. That there would be some adjustment in the destination of US outward direct investment is to be expected; one would in fact expect considerable amounts of this investment to be flowing to those Stage 3 nations that had entered into periods of rapid growth. Thus, what is surprising about the shift in shares is that the direct investment flowing to the Asia/Pacific area is not greater than it actually is. Also, the increase in the share of US direct investment flowing to Europe is not surprising in light of the Dunning and Narula hypotheses regarding investment behaviour among Stage 5 nations, but by these same hypotheses we would expect a much larger share going to Japan. We shall return to these matters in the next section.

Figure 3.7 depicts shifts in the share of US outward direct investment by sector. As can be seen, relatively greater shares of this direct investment are flowing into the manufacturing sector and into the sectors labelled 'other services' and 'other industries' in 1990-1993 than in earlier years; the share going into banking remains virtually constant, while the shares going into petroleum, wholesale trade, and other financial services (this category includes all financial services *except* banking and insurance) are declining. The observed shifts are consistent with a story of a US 'renaissance' in the manufacturing sector. They also reflect a growing share globally of FDI flowing into the services sector: the decline in the shares of wholesale trade and other financial services (both sub-sectors of the services sector) are more than offset by the increases in shares of 'other services' and 'other industries'. This is true at least if we assume that the lattermost category consists mostly of service-related activities; one of the major components of this category is insurance, and it is a fair assumption that this component accounts for much of the observed growth of this category. Available data do not allow verification of this assumption, however.

Other factors that might have contributed to the resurgence of US direct investment abroad include all of the following:

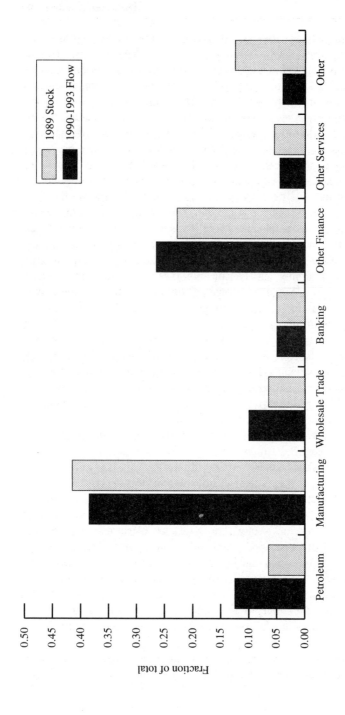

Figure 3.7 1989 stock and 1990–1993 flow: US direct investment abroad by industry

1 A resurgence of competitiveness of US firms following major adjustments in corporate strategy occurred during the 1980s, and especially in the second half of that decade. These adjustments were occasioned at least in part by the response of US firms to the competitive challenges posed by foreign competition, not least of all to foreign-controlled firms that entered the US market by means of direct investment. The strategic adjustments included such steps as 'downsizing' (i.e. reduction of bloated staffs and increased use of contracting from outside suppliers for inputs, including most especially services, that could be more efficiently produced external to the firm than internally),[4] new emphasis on product innovation, adoption of 'lean' production techniques, and the joining of strategic alliances.

2 Tied to this resurgence, there seems to have been a spate of 'strategic asset seeking' and 'knowledge seeking' acquisitions, especially in Europe, by US-based firms seeking to bolster O advantages. Merger and acquisition activity was quite high in Europe in the very late 1980s and early 1990s, and this might help account for Europe receiving a high share of US direct investment in recent years. Such acquisitions as General Motors' 50 per cent interest in the SAAB motor vehicle interests of SAAB Scania come to mind. By means of this acquisition, GM acquired both needed production capacity and technology and know-how needed to upgrade its product worldwide.

3 The effects of US government policy were probably of some importance. The effects of this policy upon direct investment by US firms are, however, even more difficult to analyse than the effects of government policy upon inward direct investment. A number of considerations can, however, be raised. For example, the breakup of American Telephone and Telegraph (AT&T) in the early 1980s and the partial deregulation of the US telecommunications industry both removed legal impediments imposed by the US government on overseas activities by AT&T and by the so-called 'baby bells' (the regional telecommunications firms that were spun off from AT&T), and these firms began aggressively to seek overseas opportunities beginning in the late 1980s and into the 1990s. At the same time, the greater competition in the US telecommunications industry that followed the breakup and deregulation doubtlessly motivated these firms to upgrade their O advantages. Also, the terms of the AT&T breakup resulted in certain types of activities (e.g.

value-added services) being declared by the US judge presiding over the case as off-limits to the successor firms within the United States. Many of these firms subsequently sought to develop competencies in these activities via participation in them in overseas markets. They did this partly in anticipation of additional deregulation in the United States in the future that might enable them eventually to enter these lines of business at home.[5] Thus, overseas investments by the AT&T successor firms (including AT&T itself) have enabled them to develop O advantages abroad that government policy prevented them from developing at home.

Beginning during the Reagan administration in the United States and continuing through the Bush and Clinton administrations, the US government embarked on a number of activities that could be termed 'industrial policy'. (This was true in spite of ideological abhorrence of such policies by the Reagan and Bush administrations, which nonetheless justified them on grounds of national security.) The earliest activities included mostly ones that were supported by the Defense Advanced Research Projects Agency (DARPA), now simply the Advanced Research Projects Agency (ARPA), such as the SEMATECH consortium to improve the manufacturing capabilities of US semiconductor manufacturers (the earliest of the major industrial policy ventures). Later, the 1988 Omnibus Trade and Competitiveness Act created the Advanced Technology Program and the Manufacturing Extension Program. Some analysts believe that these programs, created largely to bolster the development of so-called 'dual-use' technologies (those destined largely for civilian markets but with military applications), have contributed substantially to the technological competitiveness of US firms. Other analysts, however, are sceptical. It is pointed out, for example, that the total funding of all such activities is but a small fraction of total research and development expenditure in the United States and that the scale of projects actually undertaken has been typically quite modest. This last continues to be the case even under the Clinton administration, which came into office promising to expand significantly US government support of technology. Exactly what has been the impact of these programs upon the competitiveness of US firms has not been rigorously analysed, and in 1995 there were indications that the Republican-dominated Congress might be prepared to reduce or terminate them.

Some aspects of US government policy (as well as policies of state and local governments), however, seem at variance with increased competitiveness of US firms. By many measures, the current quality of publicly provided education in the United States has deteriorated since the 1950s and 1960s. Education specialists worry about evidence that US public education is not as effective as that of certain other nations, e.g. Japan and many Western European nations, especially at primary and secondary levels. This might suggest the possibility of human resource deficiencies in the United States. To date, however, the excellence of US universities seems largely to compensate for deficiencies at the lower levels of the education system. Also, the role of foreign-born students who received primary, secondary, and even undergraduate educations in their home countries but who are graduates of US postgraduate university programmes and who remain in the United States plays a significant role in the maintenance of the US human resource base. Nonetheless, the possibility of serious deterioration of this base is not wholly to be dismissed.

Some portions of the physical infrastructure of the United States are in visible decline (including highways and railways). Many analysts believe that there will consequently be adverse effects upon the competitiveness of US firms relative to international rivals. However, other portions of the infrastructure (e.g. that of telecommunications services) that have in recent times been enormously upgraded, and these may be more important to the competitiveness of US firms in high technology sectors than the traditional infrastructure.

All things considered, it is virtually impossible to assess what is the impact of US government policies on US outward direct investment. This is because it is difficult, at best, to assess what effects these policies have had on the competitiveness of US firms. One suspects that the impact is rather substantial in certain sectors (e.g. certainly telecommunications and perhaps semiconductors) but that the impact has not been very great on other sectors. But these are issues that bear additional analysis.

IS THE US IDP CONSISTENT WITH THE STAGE 5 HYPOTHESIS?

The overall answer to this question is 'yes'. The net international direct investment position of the United States during the 1980s as a percentage of total outward investment dropped sharply, consistent with the hypothesis. This was the consequence of non-US firms that had previously maintained relatively lower levels of international operations than their US rivals internationalizing at a more rapid rate than these rivals. Worldwide, at least in those industries that could loosely be classified as 'global', firms from many countries have been seeking to imitate their most effective rivals, irrespective of their home nations (see Cantwell and Sanna-Randaccio 1990) and this has generally motivated a more rapid expansion of European and Asian-based firms into the United States than expansion of US-based firms into Europe or Asia during the 1980s. Also, there is considerable evidence that at least some percentage of the takeovers of US firms by foreign firms that were rife during the 1980s were driven by 'knowledge seeking' or 'strategic asset seeking' motivations, consistent with the hypothesis. All of this is consistent with the notion of other advanced nations converging upon the leader (the United States), 'in the structure of their location-bound assets'.

But, during the 1980s, there was significant evidence of erosion of the competitiveness of US firms in a number of important industries that may not be entirely explained by this type of convergence. US firms in these industries were becoming, in some cases, bloated, bureaucratic and slow moving in an environment that demanded an increasing capability continually to upgrade their technological capabilities. Also, many US firms were deficient relative to their international rivals in terms of abilities effectively to manage human resources. However, with the passing of time, competition from abroad has in many instances forced US firms out of their complacency and one manifestation has been 'knowledge seeking' acquisition abroad by these firms. This is slightly contrary to Dunning and Narula's notion that Stage 5 countries are primarily *recipients* of FDI generated by 'knowledge seeking' acquisition by firms from countries in lower stages of development. To be sure, as just noted, some portion of the inward FDI into the United States was also of this variety. But the point is that the United States, the first country arguably to reach Stage 5, was *both* a source of and a host to knowledge seeking FDI. But this is a mere quibble with the Stage 5 hypothesis, posed to suggest that some of the theoretical detail might need fine tuning to meet reality.

The really important issue is whether, as Dunning and Narula predict, there exists a 'fluctuating equilibrium' in the US direct investment position. They argue that in terms of their inward and outward direct investment positions, Stage 5 countries, after an initial burst of new inward direct investment (e.g. as occurred in the US in the 1980s), may be expected to settle down to a fluctuating equilibrium around a roughly equal amount of inward and outward investment.

Has this been actually happening with respect to the United States? Otherwise put, is there evidence of such a 'fluctuating equilibrium'?[6] Figure 3.8 represents a first effort to find such an equilibrium if it exists. In the exhibit, the net international direct investment position of the United States is depicted as a (decimal) fraction of the stock of US direct investment abroad (US DIA). Thus, the value 0.0 indicates that outward and inward direct investment stocks are in balance. As can be seen, something of a fluctuating equilibrium in fact seems to have existed for almost thirty years, from 1950 to about 1979, but this occurred before any country, including the United States, presumably had reached Stage 5. This equilibrium, if it existed at all, certainly preceded the predicted 'burst of new inward direct investment' which, as is so evident from the exhibit, occurred after 1979. Thus, the mean value of this early equilibrium is not anywhere near 0, as Stage 5 demands. The question is, is there a fluctuating equilibrium in recent times?

I would submit that, from the evidence of the exhibit, it is difficult at this time to ascertain such an equilibrium. This is meant to be a purely neutral statement, i.e. the predicted equilibrium might be in the process of asserting itself, but it might not be. One characteristic of such an equilibrium would be that the net direct investment position would sometimes be positive (US direct investment abroad would exceed FDI in the United States) and sometimes negative. In fact, the US position has never been negative and, as noted earlier, after approaching zero in 1989, it has moved away from balance ever since. But not much time has passed since 1989, and the recent trend towards a growing, positive position could reverse in due course. Only time will tell.

The bottom line, I believe, is that the Stage 5 hypothesis, when applied to the United States, remains somewhat speculative. It must be emphasised too that the United States is the number one test case for the hypothesis. If the fluctuating equilibrium does establish itself, the hypothesis will clearly be strengthened. If not, some rethinking clearly will be in order.

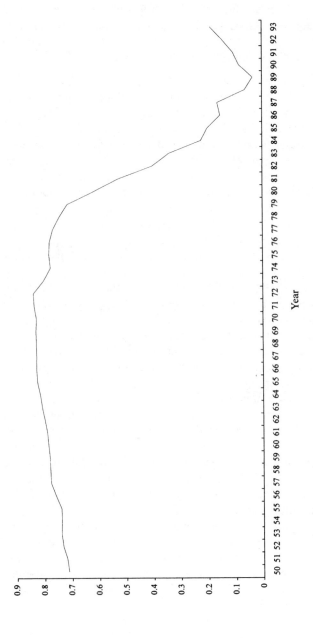

Figure 3.8   US net direct investment position as fraction of US direct investment abroad

Table 3.2 Net FDI flows from and to the United States, five and ten year back moving averages, 1986–1993 ($ billions)

Ending year	1986	1987	1988	1989	1990	1991	1992	1993
5 year back moving average	−80.2	−32.2	−49.0	−34.0	−10.0	9.7	20.4	82.2
10 year back moving average					−84.0	−34.0	1.2	56.5

Source: Calculated from US Department of Commerce data.

A POSTSCRIPT

John Dunning, in his capacity as coeditor of the volume, has pointed out to me that the fluctuating equilibrium might not necessarily be around a zero net FDI position, this position reflecting the stocks of inward and outward FDI, but rather around some stock equilibrium determined as an initial condition when a country moves into Stage 5. This would imply that over some medium length period (Dunning suggests three to five years), net FDI flows would be zero. Redefined thusly, however, the United States still has not experienced such a 'fluctuating equilibrium', as is demonstrated in Table 3.2.

The bottom line, in my view, remains the same. The fluctuating equilibrium might be in the process of asserting itself, but then it might not be. With respect to its direct investment situation, the United States is still adjusting to shocks that occurred during the 1980s, as described earlier in this chapter. A perturbed system, even if it eventually settles into an equilibrium, does so often with a considerable lag during which the system behaviour can appear inconsistent with the existence of an equilibrium, as is well known from the behaviour of systems governed even by simple linear differential equations. Thus, again, I would submit, with respect to whether the United States is moving towards a fluctuating equilibrium, only time will tell.

NOTES

1 Sales of assets of foreign direct investments to domestic investors result in a negative flow of equity investment into the United States.
2 Various proposed measures that failed to pass are discussed in the various editions of Graham and Krugman (1989, 1991, 1995). The

Exxon–Florio measure is discussed in all three editions. See also Graham and Ebert (1991) for a more complete discussion of the legislative history of Exon–Florio and analysis of the earliest cases subjected to review under this measure.

3 On these, see Warner and Rugman (1994).

4 This suggests something of the reverse of the Coase/Williamson story of firm growth to achieve economies of internalization.

5 Indeed, at the time of this writing, legislation that would permit this has been passed by the US Senate.

6 One problem is that Dunning and Narula never precisely describe this equilibrium. Does 'fluctuating equilibrium' mean that the equilibrium itself is constantly shifting, perhaps due to variance in some underlying parameter, but that it reverts to a stationary mean (or even to a mean that follows a predictable process)? Or, are they saying that the actual investment position varies around a stationary equilibrium? Their description of the equilibrium in their chapter of this book seems to fit the second interpretation better, where the equilibrium would be zero.

BIBLIOGRAPHY

Cantwell, J. and Sanna-Randaccio, F. (1990) 'The growth of multinationals and the catching up effect', *Economic Notes*, 19, pp. 1-23.

Graham, E. and Ebert, M. (1991) 'Foreign direct investment and US national security: fixing Exxon–Florio', *The World Economy*, 14, 3, pp. 245–268.

Graham, E. and Krugman, P. (1995) *Foreign Direct Investment in the United States*, Washington, DC: Institute for International Economics (earlier editions 1989 and 1991).

Warner, M. and Rugman, A. (1994) 'Competitiveness: an emerging strategy of discrimination in US antitrust and R&D policy', *Law and Policy in International Business*, 25, pp. 945–982.

Chapter 4

Sweden
A latecomer to industrialization

*Ivo Zander and Udo Zander**

INTRODUCTION

Sweden's comparatively late development from a rural economy into an advanced industrial nation provides an interesting illustration of the investment development path (IDP) framework. The initial sources of Sweden's competitive advantages were strongly associated with the existence of abundant natural resources, in particular copper and iron ore and vast forests. Foreign capital, expertise and direct investments related to mining and metal production were attracted into Sweden, thus supporting the advancement of industrial activity in the Swedish economy.

While foreign influences became an important part of early Swedish industrial activity, the new ideas and technologies were rapidly assimilated and improved in the Swedish context. Around the turn of the century, increasingly advanced and firm-specific skills started shifting industrial activity towards the mechanical engineering industries. A number of Swedish MNEs were born before the First World War, and rapidly expanded their operations outside the home market. The growth of foreign sales and manufacturing operations, combined with increasingly restrictive policies towards foreign ownership in Swedish industry, soon created a net outflow of foreign direct investment (FDI) from Sweden.

Although there is limited systematic information on the early development of the Swedish IDP, both inward and outward flows of foreign direct investment appear to have picked up just before the turn of the century. It also appears that the number of foreign-owned establishments in Sweden exceeded the number of Swedish-owned establishments abroad before the turn of the century,[1] and that the inward and outward flows became more balanced some time in the

Table 4.1 Swedish outward and inward foreign direct investment, 1955–1993 (billion SEK, current prices[1])

Year	Outward FDI	Inward FDI	Outward–Inward FDI	Three-year average	Outward FDI/GDP (%)	Inward FDI/GDP (%)	GDP (MSEK)
1955	137				0.3		50,755
1956	135				0.2		55,164
1957	191				0.3		58,919
1958	171				0.3		62,242
1959	357				0.5		66,307
1960	288	134	154		0.4	0.2	72,128
1961	346	167	179	147	0.4	0.2	78,466
1962	430	322	108	−25	0.5	0.4	85,097
1963	391	754	−363	44	0.4	0.8	92,106
1964	747	360	387	81	0.7	0.4	102,716
1965	538	320	218	229	0.5	0.3	113,032
1966	735	654	81	197	0.6	0.5	122,952
1967	877	584	293	3	0.7	0.4	133,458
1968	673	1,039	−366	358	0.5	0.7	141,621
1969	1,696	550	1,146	365	1.1	0.4	153,798
1970	1,093	779	314	701	0.6	0.5	172,226
1971	1,255	611	644	794	0.7	0.3	186,215
1972	1,903	478	1,425	986	0.9	0.2	203,758
1973	1,503	615	888	1,356	0.7	0.3	226,744
1974	2,430	674	1,756	1,462	0.9	0.3	256,127
1975	2,303	562	1,741	2,130	0.8	0.2	300,785
1976	3,476	583	2,893	2,769	1.0	0.2	340,197
1977	4,315	643	3,672	2,927	1.2	0.2	370,016
1978	3,005	788	2,217	2,869	0.7	0.2	412,450
1979	3,506	787	2,719	2,382	0.8	0.2	462,307

Year						
1980	3,796	1,586	2,210	3,322	0.7	0.3	528,076
1981	6,411	1,374	5,037	4,788	1.1	0.2	581,685
1982	8,918	1,800	7,118	7,281	1.4	0.3	636,015
1983	11,995	2,308	9,687	9,688	1.7	0.3	712,310
1984	15,052	2,793	12,259	11,668	1.9	0.4	797,333
1985	19,939	6,881	13,058	13,748	2.3	0.8	866,601
1986[2]	21,812	5,885	15,927	15,653	2.3	0.6	947,263
1987	20,123	2,150	17,973	20,205	2.0	0.2	1,023,602
1988	32,277	5,563	26,714	32,902	2.9	0.5	1,114,502
1989	65,683	11,664	54,019	51,500	5.3	0.9	1,232,602
1990	85,778	12,010	73,768	44,028	6.3	0.9	1,359,879
1991	42,478	38,180	4,298	27,920	2.9	2.6	1,447,327
1992	7,104	1,409	5,695	2,239	0.5	0.1	1,441,723
1993	15,703	18,980	-3,277		1.1	1.3	1,442,181

Notes: 1 One SEK equals about 0.14 US dollars.
 2 Figures include reinvested profits from 1986 onward, and are continuously revised by the Central Bank (Riksbanken).

Source: Riksbankens Årsbok (1961, 1964, 1967, 1970, 1975), Sveriges Riksbank, Förvaltningsberättelse (1980,1985), Sveriges Riksbank, Statistisk Årsbok (1989, 1993), Central Bureau of Statistics, Department of National Accounting.

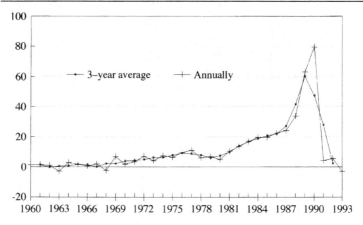

Figure 4.1   Sweden's investment development path 1960–1993
(outward–inward investment, billion SEK, 1991 prices)
Note: 1 SEK equals about 0.14 US dollars.

interwar period. A more accurate picture of Sweden's IDP can be
drawn from the 1950s and onward (Figure 4.1, Table 4.1).[2] Overall,
in the postwar period the flow of outward FDI exceeded the inward
flow. However, there was a notable change in the early 1990s, when
the net flow of FDI turned negative. This development indicates that
outward and inward FDI are becoming more closely balanced, and
that the Swedish economy might be entering Stage 5 of the IDP.

The following sections expand on the historical development of
the Swedish economy and present the main characteristics of its
different stages of economic development. Particular focus is placed
on the patterns of overall industrial activity, the sources of competitive advantage, patterns of outward and inward foreign direct
investment, and the role of government in affecting economic
activity. Although economic development did not proceed in dis-
tinctly separable stages, the presentation starts with the period
before 1914. It is followed by two sections illustrating the development in the periods 1918-1938 and after 1946.

THE NATURAL RESOURCES FOUNDATION –
INDUSTRIAL ACTIVITY BEFORE 1914

Swedish economic development for a long time was slower than in
other Western European countries, and the transformation into an
industrial society was helped by being in the right place at the right

time (see Heckscher, 1932, 1950; Söderberg, 1946; Jörberg, 1970; Larsson and Olsson, 1992).[3] Sweden possessed an abundance of natural resources which were in high demand during the Industrial Revolution but also were of limited availability in other European countries. Also, industrial development was supported by some favourable events, by which growing industries were able to replace declining ones in a relatively continuous process.

Swedish copper mining started in the 9th century (in the Bergslagen region in central Sweden). Iron mining followed in the 12th century, which is also when the first Swedish blast furnaces were developed. Swedish copper production started on a large scale in the 17th century, and was intimately associated with the need to finance Sweden's military activities on the European continent. Copper production peaked in the 1650s, during which time Sweden's share of world production was estimated at between 30 and 70 per cent. The Swedish government played an active role in managing the copper resources, aspiring to limit copper production and support high prices. In fact, the number of copper coins in the Swedish economy reflected this policy – when foreign demand for the metal weakened, an increasing amount of copper coins would be issued domestically.

Swedish copper production started declining in the beginning of the 18th century, and eventually came to lose its significance altogether. However, by the time of its decline it had already started to be replaced by iron production, which was favoured by several circumstances. Sweden possessed an abundant supply of pure and high-quality iron ore, and had the necessary wood supplies for the dominating production process based on charcoal. As forests were being depleted in Great Britain, and no other European country could provide an equal combination of iron ore deposits and forest resources, Sweden became within a short time the dominant supplier of high-quality iron in Europe. At the beginning of the 18th century, Sweden's share of world production was estimated to be 30-35 per cent, and more than 80 per cent of British iron imports came from Sweden.

Sweden's superior position in the iron industry was partly based on the need for charcoal in the production process, and the introduction of the Cort process in the 1780s, which allowed the use of fossil fuels, changed conditions dramatically. As pit coal deposits were lacking in Sweden, competition based on the new and cheaper production methods was basically out of the question, and gave rise to Swedish producers' concentration on high-quality, upgraded products. Nevertheless, as demands for all kinds of iron products continued to surge during the industrialization of Europe, Sweden's production of iron continued growing, although its overall position relative to other countries was greatly diminished.[4]

Interestingly, Sweden did not export iron ore prior to the development of an indigenous iron industry. Extraction of iron ore and exports of timber and iron products were, similar to what had been experienced in the copper industry, highly regulated. The introduction of the Thomas–Gilchrist method in 1876, however, removed much of Sweden's advantage from pure and high-quality iron ore deposits in central Sweden. As the new method allowed the use of high-phosphorus iron ore in the production process, it made possible the exploitation of the abundant resources of phosphorus iron ore in northern Sweden. Starting in the 1890s, successive exploitation of the Luossavaara–Kiirunavaara and Gellivaara mines created a very strong position for the Swedish mining industry. Grängesberg, a company established in 1883, had controlled large deposits of low-phosphorus ores in central Sweden and was also to take on a leading role in the exploitation of the northern mines.[5] In the 1910s, iron ore had come to represent some 15 per cent of Sweden's total exports.

Although there was an abundance of forests in Sweden, the lumber industries initially showed a relatively slow growth. Partly, this was the result of the demand for wood and charcoal from the mining and iron industries,[6] but also because Great Britain had placed prohibitive import duties on foreign timber in the course of the Napoleonic wars.[7] As most of the British import restrictions had been abolished by 1849, and the introduction of steam power reduced the need for locating production close to hydro power resources, the Swedish saw-mill industry began to develop. Experiencing its most important growth period between 1850 and 1870, the expansion of saw-mill production continued until the turn of this century.[8] By about this time, much of the primeval forests had been taken out, and the stock of old, high-quality forests was declining.

As the saw-mill industry stagnated about the turn of the century, further growth became associated with pulp production. Emerging in the 1870s, the Swedish pulp industry was aided by some fortuitous circumstances. For sawing purposes, spruce had less value than pine, but for pulp production the reverse was initially true. The sulfite pulp industry was entirely confined to spruce, and demand thus increased where Swedish supply was the most plentiful. As the subsequently introduced sulfate process could employ both spruce and pine, it also became possible to exploit the timber of smaller dimensions which had been left by the saw-mill industry. The real breakthrough in terms of production appears to have taken place in the 1890s, when both the sulfite and sulfate production processes had become more fully developed (Samuelsson, 1985).[9]

A very significant feature of Swedish industrial activity before the First World War was the introduction of several revolutionary inventions around the turn of the century (Appendix 4.1). These inventions were to become instrumental in transforming the raw-material-based economy, and promoted the subsequent development of an unusual number of large industrial firms (Gustavson, 1986). As the inventions were strongly associated with the development of more advanced engineering skills, they were also instrumental in the internationalization of Swedish firms.

Indigenous inventions such as dynamite, three-phase electrical current, the lighthouse, and the spherical ball bearing promoted the growth of firms like Nitro Nobel, ASEA, AGA and SKF. Other inventions, such as the safety match and match manufacturing machinery, electric arc welding, and the adjustable wrench figure prominently in Sweden's technological history, furthering the expansion of the firms Swedish Match, ESAB and Bahco. In many cases, inventions were significant improvements of ideas which had been picked up elsewhere. This was particularly the case with the separator and the telephone and telephone switches, which became the fundamental products of Alfa Laval and Ericsson.

Sources of competitive advantage before 1914

Although specialized industrial skills were gradually built up in the fields of mining, copper and iron production, as well as in the saw-mill and pulp and paper industries, much of the international positions of Swedish firms was based on the existence of abundant natural resources.

One important aspect of Sweden's early industrial development was the inflow of foreign expertise, which became prominent in the 16th century and onward (Heckscher, 1935; see also Sölvell, 1994). In particular, immigrants were attracted by abundant natural resources which could be exploited through the introduction of new production techniques. Finnish immigrants, settling in the central and northern parts of Sweden, became involved in the exploitation of the Swedish iron ore and forest deposits. The copper industry was reformed by the Dutch immigrant Silentz and the Germans Kock-Cronström, and tar production techniques were improved by the Dutch immigrant van Swinderen. Louis de Geer became instrumental in transforming the Swedish metals industry, bringing in a large number of his highly skilled countrymen, the Walloons, in the early 17th century.[10] The Walloons introduced new methods of iron production, ranging from the construction of furnaces to the forging process.

Influences from foreign immigrants were also significant in the field of mechanical engineering. The first Swedish mechanical engineering workshop was set up in 1809 by the British engineer S. Owen. His work with steam engines (used in, for example, threshing machines, rolling mills and steamships) spawned more than 20 mechanical workshops in the early 19th century. The second mechanical workshop in Sweden was established in 1822 and run with the help of British workers and foremen. This workshop later became instrumental in the development of Swedish steam engines for both steamships (1829) and locomotives (1878). The first part of the 19th century saw the establishment of several additional work-shops, which among other things became engaged in steam engines for ships and railways, shipbuilding and railway equipment (see Appendix 4.2).

Certainly, a large part of the technological influences were also imported through the foreign travels and international education or employment of Swedish engineers (Carlsson, 1986; Ahlström, 1993). Other influences came in the form of standardized information embodied in foreign licences and patents. The refinement of these ideas and indigenous development required the establishment of internal drawing departments, and resulted in the establishment of the first research laboratories in Sweden.[11] Thus, structured in-house research and development was introduced as a new and increasingly important aspect of Swedish industrial activity.

While foreign ideas and technology figured prominently in the early phases of Swedish industrialization, it might be noted that foreign capital also played an important role. The trading houses, sometimes established by immigrants such as the Dickson and Hall families in Gothenburg or the Finlay and Jennings families in Stockholm, supplied much of the capital and also became involved in ownership of the forest products industries. For its part the

Swedish government was responsible for much of the foreign borrowing for the construction of railways which started in the 1850s (most of the financing was obtained from France, Great Britain and Germany). This released some of the limited internal capital for the development of other industries.

Gradually, domestic banks became a much needed source of capital. In particular, two banks, Stockholms Enskilda Bank (founded by A.O. Wallenberg in 1856) and Stockholms Handelsbank (1871), created increasingly close linkages with the emerging pulp and paper and mechanical engineering firms (Olsson, 1986; Glete, 1987). The Stockholms Enskilda Bank and the Wallenberg family perhaps more than any other group became actively involved in industry. Taking a long-term view on industrial development, it supplied financial stability and management resources to firms in the Swedish pulp and paper industry and later in the mechanical engineering industries. As the expansion of Swedish industry led to the accumulation of domestic industrial capital the imports of foreign capital ceased around 1910.

Flows of outward and inward FDI before 1914

Initially, Swedish exports of iron, timber, and also manufactured products were channelled through trading houses. Because the inputs to the raw-material-intensive industries could be found within Sweden, there seems to have been limited push for outward foreign direct investment. One of the pioneering firms in establishing more extensive foreign sales channels, the steel products producer Sandvik, started using foreign agents in the 1870s. There were also some investments in foreign manufacturing before the turn of the century, including Wicanders Korkfabriker (cork and linoleum products, investment in Finland, 1871), Alfa Laval (separators, the United States, 1883), Nobel (explosives, Germany, 1886), ASEA (electrical equipment, Finland, 1897, and Norway, 1898) and Perstorp (chemicals, Norway, 1898). SKF established manufacturing operations in Great Britain in 1911. However, the establishment of more substantial foreign sales and manufacturing operations took off after the First World War (SOU 1975: 50).

Initially, the flow of inward FDI appears to have been limited, and it was primarily directed towards the exploitation of natural resources. The Falu copper mine was partly owned by German interests in the 14th century, but until the mid-19th century most of the foreign ownership was associated with immigrants who had set up their own businesses in Sweden. During the 1860s and 1870s, however, foreign interests to an increasing extent had started acquiring land, forests and mines. The largest acquisition took place in 1872, when a British consortium acquired Klotenverken in Dalecarlia, involving forests, mines, iron works and blast furnaces. Having also acquired railways, the successor Trafikaktiebolaget Grängesberg-Oxelösund (TGO) became Sweden's largest company when limited liability companies were introduced in 1896. Other foreign-owned companies were Åmmebergs Zinkgruvor (acquired by the Belgian zinc works Vieille Montagne in 1857) and Gällivareverken (acquired by British interests in 1864), both involved in mining operations.

Most of the inward FDI that followed until the First World War related to the mining, quarrying and forestry industries (Nordlund, 1989). Increasing tariff protection and the breaking of the Interstate Treaty between Sweden and Norway in 1897 supported inward direct investment in both natural resources and manufactured products. The majority of the foreign investors were based in Denmark, Norway, Great Britain and Germany, and they preferred to set up majority-owned subsidiaries. At the turn of the century, 20 per cent of the iron ore industry and more than 75 per cent of other mining activities were owned by foreign interests. In total, foreign-owned investments accounted for almost 7 per cent of Swedish employment.

Government policy and intervention before 1914

Industrial growth was deliberately encouraged by the Swedish kings as early as the mid-17th century through imports of industrial know-how and the immigration of entrepreneurs and industrialists. The immigrants invested both knowledge and capital on the basis of 'privileges', or a monopoly contract. Many of the privileges were awarded in the mining and metals industries, in which privileges had been granted to Swedish businesses since at least the 1340s.

Government's further promotion of industry was primarily related to the early regulation of copper and iron production (e.g. through the establishment of the Mines Authority, 1630-1649), and also to the accumulation of capital for the construction of Swedish railways. Although several trade associations and training institutes were established to support advancements in iron production, mining and forestry, these associations are likely to have emerged mostly as a result of industry initiatives. Some of the more important associations and training institutes were the Swedish Iron Masters' Association (Jernkontoret, established in 1747), the Falu Mining School (1820), the Filipstad Mining School (1830) and the Forestry Institute (Skogsinstitutet, 1820).

The development of more advanced and specialized technical skills was supported by the establishment of two technical institutes in Stockholm (1826) and Gothenburg (1829), both of which later received university status (the Royal Institute of Technology in Stockholm in 1876, and the Chalmers Institute of Technology in Gothenburg in 1882). These two institutes were to become important suppliers of engineers for a wide range of Swedish industries. Another achievement which would prove significant for the development of more advanced industries in later periods was the establishment of compulsory popular education in 1842 and the foundation of a series of technical secondary schools in the mid-19th century.

THE MATURING OF SWEDISH INDUSTRY 1918-1938

Although the transition from a basically agrarian and natural-resource-based economy was slow, there are indications that the decades around the turn of the century provided the starting point for the industrialization of Sweden.[12] In the first two decades after the turn of the century, Swedish industrial activity became more diversified, although many of the newly established firms and industries would be closely connected to existing ones (Sölvell, Zander and Porter, 1991). In particular, forestry products became significantly less important, while pulp and paper, iron ore and mechanical engineering products came more to the forefront.

One critical component of sustained industrial development in Sweden were the numerous mechanical engineering shops which had been established in the 19th century. These engineering shops supplied the increasing need for machines and engines for the iron and pulp and paper industries, and were to become intimately associated with the development of the Swedish shipping and shipyard industries. In many respects, cross-fertilization was mutual, as the mechanical engineering industries could take advantage of high-quality iron and steel products supplied by the iron industry.

The Swedish shipping and shipyard industries were stimulated by growing exports of iron, sawn timber, and pulp and paper products, and also by overall demand created by increased world trade.[13] The shipyard industry (including the firms Eriksberg, Götaverken, Arendal, Lindholmen, Kockums and Uddevallavarvet) benefited significantly from the skills developed in the many mechanical workshops. The workshops provided steam and later diesel engines, and also a wide range of metal constructions. By the 1920s, Sweden had become a leading shipbuilding nation, accounting for some 5-6 per cent of world production (half of the production was exported).

The shipyard industry created a favourable environment for the development of related products and services. The welding equipment firm ESAB, which had been established in 1904, developed increasingly sophisticated welding techniques for the construction of ships. Cranes of various constructions, marine turbines and refrigeration systems also clustered around the shipyard industry. In addition, the shipyards supported the Swedish steel industry as they became important buyers of various steel manufactures.

In a similar way, the mining, iron and steel, and pulp and paper industries promoted the development of a power generation and power distribution industry. Underground mining required explosives and the manufacture of drill steels and rock drilling machines which could cope with the hard rocks that occur predominantly throughout Sweden. The development of rock drilling machinery led to the accumulation of skills in pneumatic and later hydraulic equipment, which became prevalent among Swedish firms. Improved efficiency in underground mining also required the introduction of electrical power generators and electrical engines, which replaced the older lever systems after the turn of the century. Energy-intensive processes in the iron and steel and pulp and paper industries promoted the exploitation of hydro-electric power and furthered the development of techniques to distribute electricity over long distances.

While a large number of Swedish firms based on significant inventions had appeared around the turn of the century, there are also examples of firms which emerged as a response to growing domestic demand and expanded in the interwar period. Thus, Saab-Scania and Volvo gradually developed international positions in heavy trucks, which were particularly suited for timber haulage, and later in passenger cars and aircraft.[14] Electrolux, exploiting a patent on absorption refrigeration, and Swedish Match, creating a worldwide network of sales subsidiaries and monopolies, also expanded into international markets. A large number of small and medium-sized firms appeared in the wake of the larger firms, particularly in the interwar period (Dahmén, 1985). Many of these firms were manufacturers of specialized components, e.g. automotive parts and electrical equipment.

Sources of competitive advantage 1918-1938

The diversification of Swedish industry after the turn of the century was associated less with natural resources and more with the development of upgraded skills and firm-specific resources. Gradually, a pool of workers and engineers knowledgeable in precision mechanical engineering became available throughout a range of new industries.[15] While technical departments appear to have been established in many firms in the 19th century, the interwar period saw the development of formalized research and development departments among major Swedish firms (Ahlström, 1993). Increasingly, in-house R&D and firm-specific knowledge became the basis for further international expansion. With few exceptions, the technological activity of Swedish firms was concentrated at home,[16] and a majority of all newly introduced technologies appear to have had their origin in Sweden (Zander, 1994).

As a complement to in-house technological activity, industry associations provided to an increasing extent an opportunity to carry out joint research programmes and continued to disseminate new technological findings among the associated firms. For example, the Royal Swedish Academy of Engineering Sciences (Ingenjörsvetenskapsakademien, IVA), the Wood Pulp Research Association (Pappersmassekontoret) and the Swedish Institute for Metals Research (Metallurgiska Institutet) were all established between 1917 and 1920.

Flows of FDI and the role of government 1918-1938

As foreign markets rapidly became important for the sale of specialized products and equipment, exports from Sweden were soon joined by FDI. Although it is difficult to establish the exact time when Swedish outward FDI came to exceed the inward flows, it appears that it happened some time during the interwar period. At this time, many Swedish firms had consolidated their positions as producers of technologically advanced products, and were able to make concerted efforts to expand out of the limited Swedish home market.

Swedish firms investing abroad were primarily seeking new markets for further growth opportunities (SOU 1975: 50; Lundström, 1986), and their foreign activities predominantly reflected ambitions to exploit firm-specific skills by providing services and adaptation of products according to local market needs. With a few exceptions, including a limited number of firms in the pulp and paper and textile industries, access to raw materials or low-cost labour appears to have been of secondary consideration in the FDI decisions of Swedish firms.[17]

For many Swedish MNEs, the 1920s and 1930s were the most important periods of internationalization (some of the firms which developed rapidly during this period were AGA, Alfa Laval, ASEA, Ericsson, SKF and Swedish Match), although some important firms also experienced considerable development after the Second World War (e.g. Atlas Copco, Electrolux and Volvo). Many of the foreign investments took the form of sales subsidiaries, some of which later developed more extensive manufacturing capabilities. Foreign subsidiaries were predominantly established in Europe, in particular in Germany, France and Great Britain. Also, in the interwar period investments picked up in Latin America and the United States, which came to account for a growing but limited share of all foreign establishments.

As indicated, some Swedish firms had established foreign manufacturing operations very early on, but most firms started foreign manufacturing somewhat later. For example, ESAB established manufacturing operations in various European countries during the 1920s, while Sandvik and Atlas Copco did not start producing abroad until the late 1930s (Johanson and Wiedersheim-Paul, 1975). In some cases, pressures from host country governments were important drivers of the internationalization of manufacturing operations. Also, fear of losing foreign sales in an increasingly protectionist world supported the transfer of manufacturing technology to foreign units just before the Second World War.[18]

While the outward flow of FDI picked up substantially in the interwar period, the inward flow experienced a less favourable development. In the period immediately before the First World War, German interests had started to acquire large parts of the mining fields in central Sweden. As foreign ownership became an increasingly debated issue, it resulted in a new law which was passed in 1916, prohibiting foreigners and foreign firms to acquire or exploit Swedish mineral resources.[19] While the new regulations significantly reduced foreign-owned investments in natural resources, they also provided an effective obstacle to major acquisitions of Swedish firms by foreign-based firms.

In the interwar period, partly as a result of changing legislation, there was a marked decline in the number of foreign-owned establishments focusing on natural resources, and a shift towards market-seeking investments in the food, mechanical engineering and chemical industries.[20] Some of the more important foreign firms which established operations in Sweden included Philips (1923), IBM (1928), GKN (1930) and ITT (1938). These companies were to remain among the most important foreign-owned employers in the postwar period. There was also a shift from manufacturing operations in favour of the establishment of sales subsidiaries. Partly, this was related to the increasing interest among US firms to establish operations in Sweden.

Overall, the foreign-owned firms' share of Swedish employment was reduced from about 7 per cent at the turn of the century to just above 4 per cent in 1929, and it was to remain at this level until 1938. In terms of the share of total Swedish production, foreign ownership was particularly prominent in products like bottle glass, margarine, chocolate and confectionery, detergents, paints and varnishes, and certain electrical products. The pattern indicates the strong relative influence by firms from Denmark, Germany and the United States.

THE INTERNATIONALIZATION OF INDUSTRIAL ACTIVITY AFTER 1946

As Swedish industry emerged intact from the Second World War, it was in a favourable position to supply the growing needs for industrial products throughout Europe. Many Swedish firms were able to consolidate their international positions in the immediate postwar period, involving the establishment of an increasing number of foreign sales and manufacturing units. The importance of foreign sales in Swedish MNEs continued to grow throughout the postwar period (Swedenborg, 1979), and as a result a large number of these firms had achieved more than 80 per cent of total sales in foreign countries by the late 1980s (Swedenborg, Johansson-Grahn and Kinnwall, 1988; Andersson, 1993).

Over time, however, some Swedish industries have been restructured owing to foreign competition. In particular, Swedish natural-resource-based industries such as mining and steel retained and somewhat improved their positions in the first two decades after the war, but experienced significant decline during the 1970s.[21] Similarly, with a growing demand for ships after the Second World War, Swedish shipyards sustained their position among the world leaders until the mid-1970s. At this time, new low-cost entrants from Japan, Korea and Spain had come in to take on a more prominent role in the industry.

As some of the traditional Swedish industries declined, industrial activity became more concentrated in other directions. In particular, increasingly advanced and complex engineering products (including transportation equipment, power generation and telecommunications) and pulp and paper came to account for a significant proportion of Swedish industrial production. Also, the postwar period saw the development of the medical instrument and pharmaceutical industries, in which Swedish firms were able to create strong international positions in selected niches.

A few new Swedish firms were able to build international positions on the basis of major inventions, including Tetra Pak (liquid packaging machinery), Gambro (artificial kidneys), IKEA (furniture retailing) and Inter Innovation (automatic teller machines). There was also new business formation within the established MNEs, frequently based on follow-up inventions within or connected to established areas of technological activity (Wallmark and McQueen, 1986). These 'second hits' sustained international expansion and investments through the transfer of manufacturing technology to foreign countries (Zander, 1991).

In the postwar period, many of the established MNEs consolidated their domestic industries through mergers and acquisitions.[22] This went hand in hand with increased research and development expenditure and the economies of scale developed by those firms which internationalized their operations most forcefully. Firms like ESAB and Electrolux all assumed dominant roles in their respective industries. In other cases, two or three leading Swedish manufacturers survived. For example, Saab-Scania and Volvo remained competitors in cars, buses and heavy trucks, SCA, Stora and

MoDo competed in pulp and paper, and Sandvik and Fagersta Secoroc remained active in the manufacture of rock drills. Efforts to consolidate the domestic industry also spilled over to international markets. The 1970s and 1980s saw a major change in the mode of foreign expansion among Swedish MNEs, as much of their internationalization efforts became based on foreign acquisitions (Swedenborg, 1982; Forsgren, 1989; Andersson, 1993).[23] It appears that a majority of the foreign acquisitions were related to existing or closely related products and technologies. Most of the acquisitions targeted either direct competitors or firms in existing businesses who could provide access to new markets. Few of the acquisitions involved unrelated technologies or new customers, and most involved smaller firms (Forsgren and Larsson, 1984).

Towards the end of the 1980s, foreign acquisition programmes took on even more substantial proportions, as some Swedish MNEs became involved in industrial restructuring at an international level. In 1988, ASEA merged its core operations with Brown Boveri in Switzerland to form ABB. A few months later, ABB announced a major alliance with Westinghouse in the United States. With the acquisition of the US firm Combustion Engineering in 1989, ABB formed the world's largest electro-technical group. Also, Volvo had developed but never realized plans of merging operations with Renault in France, and Tetra Pak acquired Alfa Laval in 1991, forming the Tetra Laval Group.

Sources of competitive advantage in recent years

Throughout the postwar period, the sources of competitive advantage were increasingly associated with improved firm-specific capabilities. In particular, the development of more advanced industrial products has been accompanied by increasing R&D expenditure. In the early 1960s, Swedish R&D expenditure amounted to 1.7 per cent of its GDP, while it had increased to 2.3 per cent in 1981, 2.6 per cent in 1985, and slightly more than 3.0 per cent in 1991.[24] Most of the R&D was (and is) carried out by the large MNEs, which came to rely heavily on in-house development (Swedenborg, 1992).[25] Only a small fraction of their total R&D expenditure seems to have been related to the purchasing of licences, patents and other know-how (Granstrand, 1981; Vahlne & Hörnell, 1986).[26]

The growth of Swedish MNEs also created new sources of competitive advantage which were intimately linked to the increased presence in foreign markets (SOU 1981: 43; SOU 1983: 17). When foreign sales expanded, the firms gained benefits from diversifying their sales internationally. As foreign sales were increasingly supported by the transfer of manufacturing technology to foreign units, it was also possible to provide better service to local customers and to respond more effectively to new local business opportunities. Other potential benefits which came with internationalization were the possibility to shift production to the most favourable locations in terms of labour costs and exchange rates, and the ability to improve financial operations through the establishment of foreign-based financial intermediaries.[27]

Also, over time the international growth of Swedish MNEs created a secondary source of firm-specific advantages which derived from R&D in foreign countries. The share of foreign R&D in Swedish MNEs increased gradually from the 1960s onward, and had reached an average of about 30 per cent in the period 1985-1990 (see Appendix 4.3). A large part of the increase appears to have followed the general growth in foreign direct investment and the need to support increasingly sophisticated foreign manufacturing operations. However, during the 1970s and 1980s increased foreign technological activity was related to the more frequent use of foreign acquisitions. These acquisitions added new technological capabilities which for various reasons were kept and further developed by the foreign units.[28]

Following the overall pattern of foreign sales and manufacturing operations, most of the more recent foreign R&D of Swedish MNEs was carried out in advanced industrialized countries (Håkanson, 1981; Håkanson and Nobel, 1993; Zander, 1994). Over the entire postwar period, the two most important sources of foreign-developed technology have been Germany and the United States. Other countries accounting for a relatively large proportion of foreign technological activity include Switzerland, Great Britain and Italy. In contrast, Japan only accounted for a very small share of all foreign technological development in Swedish MNEs.[29]

Flows of outward and inward FDI after 1946

In the decades following the Second World War, Swedish firms continued their foreign expansion. As the inward flow of FDI increased more slowly than the outward flow, the period was to show a significant net outflow of FDI from Sweden. It was not until the early 1990s that the net flow of FDI would show the first signs of once again becoming more balanced.

As many of the industrial products of the Swedish MNEs required services and modifications according to local demand, the postwar period saw a continuous expansion of foreign assembly and manufacturing subsidiaries. The setting up and expansion of foreign manufacturing operations increased gradually but significantly throughout the 1960s and 1970s (Lund, 1967; SOU 1975: 50; Swedenborg 1979, 1982, 1985; Swedenborg, Johansson-Grahn and Kinnwall, 1988; Ghauri, 1990). As the trend continued in the 1980s, among both established MNEs and those that were less internationally experienced, the share of foreign manufacturing exceeded 60 per cent in several important firms by the late 1980s (Andersson, 1993). As production in foreign subsidiaries expanded, so did their share of total sales.

Most of the manufacturing units of Swedish MNEs were established in Europe, followed by North America, Latin America and a group of countries including South Africa, Australia, New Zealand and Japan. Manufacturing investments in Africa and Asian countries were of very limited significance. Following the creation of the EEC in 1957, many Swedish firms decided to set up manufacturing in the European Community to support sales (a free trade agreement did not come into effect until 1972 while full free trade, with the exception of agriculture, was implemented in 1984). However, interest in the United States for exports and foreign manufacturing increased significantly during the late 1970s and early 1980s. As a result, the United States increased its share of total foreign manufacturing employment from 9 per cent in 1978 to 19 per cent in 1986.[30] In the period 1986-1990, the average annual outward flow of Swedish FDI was around $7 billion.[31]

Inward FDI continued to develop at a rather sluggish pace in the postwar period (Johansson, 1968; Samuelsson, 1977). While investments in natural resources had been reduced by the restrictive laws of 1916, foreign-owned investments increasingly related to textiles, food products, mechanical engineering and chemicals. Establishments by major firms involved Unilever (1946), Nestlé (1955) and Litton (1959). In the early 1960s, about 30 per cent of all employees worked in companies with US parents, 25 per cent in companies with Scandinavian parents, and 15 per cent in companies with British parents. Foreign-owned firms thereby accounted for about 4.5 per cent of total Swedish industrial employment.

In the 1970s, the most important sources of new investment were the United States, Great Britain, The Netherlands, Germany and Denmark. While there was increasing use of acquisitions as a means of establishment, the overall impact on the Swedish economy remained relatively limited. Foreign-owned firms had come to account for 5 per cent of total employment in Swedish industry, which was quite modest in an international comparison.[32] In 1983, the share of foreign employees had reached 7 per cent, most of the increase being accounted for by the chemical and food industries (Vahlne, 1985).[33]

The profile of foreign-owned subsidiaries in Sweden indicates that some were established to exploit technology developed outside Sweden, while others might have sought to benefit from the created assets which had evolved in Sweden since the turn of the century. Of approximately 160 firms which were majority owned by foreign companies in 1970, slightly less than half were engaged in chemicals (in particular paint, pharmaceuticals, detergents, consumer chemical products and printing), petroleum and rubber production, textiles and food products. With the exception of narrow niches (such as chemicals for the pulp and paper industry), these are areas which have not figured prominently in Swedish industrial activity.

The remaining firms were, however, engaged in traditional sectors of the Swedish economy, such as in the mechanical engineering sector (metals, machinery, electro-equipment, and instruments). In particular Swedish skills in precision mechanical engineering and technological niches sometimes seem to have attracted foreign firms. For example, IBM was established in Sweden in 1928 and developed substantial operations around electro-mechanical equipment such as printers. Nestlé acquired the food producer Findus (1962) which had developed substantial knowledge in freezing technology. Also, in the 1980s enhanced FDI activity among Finnish firms spilled over into Sweden. Major acquisitions were made in office equipment and forestry-related equipment. In the late 1970s, foreign-owned firms accounted for 5-6 per cent of total industrial R&D expenditure in Sweden.[34]

Although the net FDI flow had been positive throughout most of the postwar period, and in spite of a law introduced in 1982 requiring authorization of foreign acquisitions of shares in Swedish firms, the late 1980s saw a significant increase in the amount of FDI into Sweden. In the period 1986-1990, the annual average FDI inflow was about $1 billion.[35] In particular, the creation of ABB through a merger between Swedish ASEA and Brown Boveri in 1988 significantly increased the proportion of foreign ownership in Swedish industry (the major part of ASEA became a wholly owned subsidiary of the Swiss-based ABB). Also, increased foreign acquisition activity among Finnish firms increased further the presence of foreign-owned firms in Sweden.

By 1991, foreign-owned subsidiaries accounted for 10 per cent of total Swedish employment.[36] As before, their presence continued to be particularly strong in chemicals, food, mechanical engineering, and wholesale and retailing. Also, and interesting in a historical perspective, the share of foreign-owned employment had increased in the minerals industry in the late 1980s and early 1990s. As many establishments took the form of acquisitions of technologically advanced firms, the foreign-owned share of Swedish R&D expenditure increased to 15 per cent. However, a large part of the increase was attributable to the formation of the Swedish–Swiss ABB.[37]

There was a particularly marked shift in 1993 and 1994 during which inward FDI exceeded the outward flow. Part of the change was explained by a few major acquisitions by foreign-owned firms,[38] and by the reduction of a large number of foreign acquisitions which were made by Swedish multinationals in the 1980s. Also, political indications that Sweden was increasingly in favour of joining the European Community, liberalization of legislation on acquisitions by foreign-owned firms, and a weak Swedish currency might have contributed to enhanced interest among foreign firms to invest in Sweden.[39]

The role of government after 1946

After the Second World War, Swedish industry was in a relatively favourable position to meet a surging demand for raw materials and industrial products in Europe. The international positions of Swedish firms were further strengthened by a significant devaluation in 1949. The devaluation made the Swedish krona undervalued for almost two decades, and promoted the export-dependent iron and steel and pulp and paper industries. It also supported growth throughout a range of Swedish manufacturing industries with an international focus.

In the 1950s and 1960s, Swedish industrial policy adhered to the principles of non-intervention, while macro-economic strategy was to keep down interest rates to stimulate growth in manufacturing.[40]

The creation of investment funds, by which profits could be written off against funds to be used in the future, created a favourable tax situation among the larger Swedish firms (see Bergström, 1982). There was a firm belief in privately owned and managed firms, and government did not assume any greater ownership in industry. In the mid-1960s, publicly owned manufacturing companies accounted for less than 5 per cent of total industrial employment. However, an important and indirect form of industrial policy was the solidaristic wage policy, which became particularly pronounced in the 1960s. The policy was aimed at reducing wage differentials across various industrial sectors and occupations, and thus promoted the expansion of internationally successful industries at the expense of less competitive ones. Increased pressure for wage increases in the mid-1960s and 1970s became a significant input into the restructuring process.

As the effects of the 1949 devaluation diminished and other European countries recovered from the war, many traditional Swedish industries fell into difficulties in the 1970s. As the overall growth rate of the Swedish economy declined, government's ambitions to restore the overall competitiveness of Swedish industry initially focused on adjustments of the exchange rate.[41] Three devaluations in 1976 and 1977 amounted to an overall depreciation of some 20 per cent (additional depreciations were undertaken in 1981 and 1982, amounting to a total of 25 per cent, followed by a depreciation of some 15-20 per cent in 1993).

A more active industrial policy was also implemented, involving the Ministry of Industry which was established in 1967. The stated goal of the ministry was to manage the transition of Swedish industry into more advanced industries, but government increasingly found itself involved in the long-term support of the ailing mining, steel and shipbuilding industries (Bosworth and Rivlin, 1987; Svenskt näringsliv och industripolitik, 1991).[42] Temporary, sectoral support became increasingly common in the mid-1970s, and peaked in 1982-1983.[43] While direct support to industry was back at the levels of the mid-1970s by 1987 and was to be further reduced in the 1990s,[44] government had increased its ownership in industry and accounted for about 9 per cent of total industrial employment.

Increasingly, the Swedish government took on a more subtle role in its efforts to promote innovation and industrial activity. In 1968, the National Board for Technical Development (STU) was formed to support technical research projects, co-operative research and industrial development. It was later complemented by the Industrial Development Fund, aimed at supporting long-term and more high-risk development projects. In 1989, government had come to account for 11 per cent of all industrial R&D.[45] Other measures to promote R&D included tax incentives allowing firms to make an extra deduction of their R&D costs from profits before tax (1973, redesigned in 1981 and abolished in 1982), and the introduction of 'renewal funds' which were exempted from taxation if used for R&D work, vocational training of employees, or the support of higher education (1984). These measures were in line with a shift in policy to stress research and development, industrial renewal, and education as the most important policy components.[46]

During the 1980s and early 1990s, the Swedish government also introduced policies to deregulate financial markets,[47] strengthen anti-trust legislation, and to privatize state-owned companies. Also, legislation was enacted to prohibit discriminatory rules on acquisitions by foreign-owned firms and company by-laws on share ownership (see OECD, 1993). All major parties started supporting the idea of joining the European Community in the late 1980s, resulting in a formal application for membership in 1991. A referendum in 1994 ended in a close vote in favour of joining the Community. Much of the necessary adjustments of Swedish laws had by then already been made, and the decision most probably increased the propensity to invest in Sweden both among foreign and Swedish firms.[48]

CONCLUSIONS

The development of the Swedish economy overall compares favourably with the predictions of the IDP framework, although it displays some facets which might be particular to the Swedish context. While early competitive advantages depended on natural resources and limited the need for outward foreign investments, improved engineering skills and the subsequent development of firm-specific advantages in advanced industrial products led to a significant increase in outward FDI after the turn of the century. Several Swedish firms evolved and set up foreign sales and manufacturing units outside Sweden before the First World War, and FDI activity was further enhanced in particular after the Second World War.

Although the outward FDI flows seem to have caught up with

inward flows before the Second World War, it might be emphasised that FDI into Sweden was legally restricted. Of particular note was the 1916 restriction on foreign ownership in industries based on the extraction of natural resources, which was later adopted by firms in other industries as well. Although foreign-owned firms were able to acquire non-voting and minority equity, the obstacles to major acquisitions by foreign firms put a general restriction on the flow of FDI into Sweden.[49]

The development of inward FDI was further influenced by several distinctive characteristics of Sweden and its institutional framework. In terms of population and economic activity in general, Sweden is a small country and does not provide the necessary market size for most import substituting operations.[50] While trade barriers were reduced in the postwar period, the limited size of the local market and relatively high transportation costs to the European markets sustained the reluctance to invest among foreign-owned firms. As for institutional considerations, non-membership of the European Community for a long time probably reduced Sweden's attractiveness as a site for production aimed at exporting to other European countries. Rapid increases in relative wages in Swedish industry in the 1960s and 1970s promoted outward rather than inward flows of FDI.

While inward FDI remained modest throughout the postwar period, liberalization of legislation in the 1990s led to a marked increase in acquisition activity among foreign-owned firms. A weak Swedish currency and signals that Sweden was to enter the European Community might have contributed to the enhanced interest among foreign firms to invest in Sweden. Overall, the net flow of FDI became more balanced in the early 1990s. This was not primarily the effect of other countries catching up in their economic development, but rather the result of MNE activity. While some foreign-owned firms expanded their sales in the Swedish market, others acquired major competitors in an attempt to restructure their industries on an international scale.

It is possible that the flows of outward and inward FDI are becoming more closely balanced, and that Sweden is about to enter Stage 5 of the IDP. A large proportion of Swedish MNEs with a high dependence on international sales and investment points to a long-term net outflow of direct investment, while acquisitions by foreign-owned firms might lead to periods of net inflows. Essentially, the balance will be affected by the ability of Swedish MNEs to maintain and upgrade their firm-specific advantages. Continuous development of new products and services will lead to additional investments in foreign countries, but might also reduce the probability of international takeovers by foreign-owned firms.

A notable feature of the Swedish economy is the absence of Swedish investments in developing countries. As Sweden already possessed abundant natural resources and rapidly developed advanced industrial products, economic activity from the outset focused on industrialized countries. In particular, much of the trade and FDI activity of Swedish firms was directed towards European countries.[51] FDI in the United States and Latin America increased gradually after the First World War, although their relative importance was to remain limited. MNE activity in Japan and the Asian countries was insignificant throughout the postwar period. Likewise, inward FDI was dominated almost entirely by highly industrialized countries. At the turn of the century, the most important sources of FDI were Denmark, Norway, Great Britain and Germany, while investments from the United States became more common in the interwar period. In the postwar period, Dutch, Swiss and Finnish firms were added to the list of the most important foreign-owned investors in Sweden.

Perhaps the most intriguing aspect of the development of the Swedish economy is how it has managed the transition into an advanced and diversified economy. The leap from a rural economy based on natural resources to an industrialized country initially seems to have been supported by importing ideas and basic technologies as well as foreign direct investments, and by the rise of entrepreneurship manifested in a wave of establishments of small firms at the turn of the century.

In many cases, new ideas and technologies were imported through immigration or by the active acquisition and assimilation of foreign inventions by Swedish engineers and business managers. In some industries, like iron and steel, industry associations became actively involved in the dissemination of new products and manufacturing technologies among the Swedish firms. The exploitation and further development of the imported technologies had a foundation in the establishment of popular education in 1842 and a number of technical institutes which were set up in the early and mid-19th century. In particular, a growing number of skilled workers in the field of mechanical engineering provided a general pool of resources which could be exploited throughout a range of Swedish industries.

As Swedish economic activity initially clustered around the mining, iron and steel and forestry industries, it is perhaps not surprising that metal manufactures and pulp and paper products gradually took on a more prominent role in the economy. The basic industries also favoured the development of a number of related technologies, such as explosives, rock drills and rock drilling equipment. Generally, new industries and firms seemed to be firmly linked to the existing ones, as illustrated by the growth of the shipyard, power generation and distribution, and transportation industries and the many specialized suppliers which emerged in their wake.

However, the rapid introduction of new technologies required more than imported technologies, improved technical skills and linkages to established industries. By the turn of the century Sweden had already built up a critical mass of entrepreneurial activity, which was supported by risk capital provided by a growing number of domestic banks. Frequently, new technological opportunities resulted in the establishment of a large number of firms and experimentation with various technical solutions and designs. While failure was common among the newly started ventures, there are indications that the survival and international growth of a few, future MNEs was based on strong industrial ambitions and a long-term view and commitment to the development of certain industries among owners. This mentality is particularly displayed by the Wallenberg family and the Stockholms Enskilda Bank, who became important financiers and were also actively involved in the restructuring of firms which fell into economic difficulties.

Throughout the interwar and postwar periods, the introduction of new technologies became more of a Swedish affair, and the sources of competitive advantage were increasingly associated with firm-specific capabilities and formal R&D departments. New and improved technologies were the basis for international expansion, and resulted in the establishment of large networks of foreign sales and manufacturing subsidiaries. In addition to the advantages which are associated with multinational operations, internationalization and foreign acquisitions over time created a secondary source of firm-specific advantages through the expansion of R&D activity in foreign markets.

This reflects a further step in the remarkable internationalization of trade in goods, services and manufacturing that Swedish firms have witnessed in the postwar period. The expansion of foreign

R&D in Swedish MNEs could increasingly lead to a situation where the firms contribute to both outward and inward flows of technological capabilities in the Swedish economy. However, there are reasons to believe that the historical and in many cases still dominating role of home country technical units will make technology flow more easily from the home country to foreign units than the other way round.[52] If this is true, the openness of the Swedish economy to inward FDI and foreign inventions could prove crucial for the assimilation and further development of technology which was so successful in the early part of the century.

NOTES

*   The authors would like to thank Professor Örjan Sölvell for his helpful comments and suggestions.

1   As indicated by Nordlund (1989), SOU (1975: 50) and Swedenborg (1979).

2   The data were collected from the Swedish Central Bank, and are based on permissions granted for outward and inward FDI (permission might not in all cases have resulted in actual investments). The data cover funds that are used for stock purchases or the granting of long-term loans which are not of a portfolio type.

3   Sweden's agricultural population represented 90 per cent of the total in the 16th century, and was reduced to 70-75 per cent in 1870 and about 50 per cent in 1910.

4   The Swedish iron industry became subject to a series of innovations emanating in Europe, requiring continuous restructuring and a pronounced focus on high-quality products (see Ruist, 1985). The assimilation and dissemination of new ideas were frequently associated with the Swedish Iron Masters' Association (Jernkontoret), which had been established in 1747.

5   The northern mines were brought under common ownership by Grängesberg in 1904, creating LKAB (which became 100 per cent owned by the Swedish state in 1957).

6   In the 1850s, the use of wood resources for iron ore extraction and iron production was 4-5 times greater than Swedish timber exports.

7   Also, there was competition from Norway, which was in a better position to export to Great Britain and other European countries. Norwegian competitiveness later deteriorated, partly because forest resources became depleted (some Norwegian firms subsequently invested in Swedish saw-mills), partly because of a relatively low capital intensity.

8   In the late 19th century, sawn timber had come to account for about 45 per cent of total Swedish exports.

9   Growing 10-fold in the 20 years before the Second World War (in the 1930s, Sweden's world market share in pulp production was 15 per

cent), the Swedish pulp industry was also to become the backbone of the Swedish paper industry, which assumed a dominant role in Europe in the decades following the Second World War.

10 Louis de Geer also became involved in the production of brass, paper and textiles, and in shipbuilding.

11 In several cases, Swedish inventions became important for sustaining technological progress. The first paper-making machines were imported from Britain and Germany in the 1810s and 1840s, but major improvements of pulp production techniques related to the discoveries of the Swedes C. D. Ekman (introducing the sulfite method in 1872) and S. Lewenhaupt (improving the already established sulfate method). In the iron industry, much of the technological impulses came from abroad, but Swedish engineers from time to time were able to make significant contributions. Having acquired a British patent in 1856, F. Göransson introduced the Bessemer method for high-quality steel production in the 1860s. One of the first research laboratories was run by Gustaf de Laval, who had imported and improved separator technology in the 1870s.

12 In the 1870s, the iron, steel and mining industries employed about a quarter of the industrial labour force, while the timber products industry employed about a fifth. Industry's share of gross domestic product had increased to a point where it exceeded agriculture's contribution in the mid-1890s.

13 By the 1850s, Sweden had the world's largest fleet of steamships, and the number of ships and tonnage were increased more than five-fold over the following two decades.

14 Volvo was established as a subsidiary of the ball bearing manufacturer SKF.

15 From the interwar period and onward, precision mechanical engineering was used in the development of high-quality cameras (Hasselblad), electro-mechanical products (Original Odhner, later Facit), fishing reels (ABU), liquid packaging machinery (Tetra Pak), textile machinery (IRO), and teller-operated cash dispensers (Inter Innovation). Substantial knowledge was also built up in areas like cooling (Findus, Frigoscandia) and logistical and transportation systems.

16 One notable exception was Alfa Laval, a producer of separators and dairy equipment, which had become very much dependent on research and development in the US subsidiary already at the turn of the century.

17 Pulp and paper firms made limited investments in North America, while textile firms located operations in Portugal and Finland. Gränges, a company active in mining and metal manufacturing, was involved in foreign mines (notably the LAMCO-project in Liberia).

18 For example, this type of technology transfer took place in the separator manufacturer Alfa Laval (see Wohlert, 1981; Gårdlund and Fritz, 1983).

19 The law stipulated that no more than two-fifths of the share capital or no more than one-fifth of the voting stock could be acquired by foreigners and foreign firms. Permission to exceed these limits could be granted only by the Swedish state. The law was amended and further

reinforced in 1973, when it was made possible to control foreign acquisitions of Swedish firms which were not directly associated with natural resources. In the late 1970s, about 80 per cent of all Swedish firms had introduced restrictions on foreign ownership according to the 1916 law.

20 Other explanations for the shift towards more advanced products, such as the abolition of the pharmacists' monopoly on production and efforts among foreign firms to break the development of local cartels, are discussed by Nordlund (1989).

21 At the beginning of the 1950s, Sweden controlled 60 per cent of the European iron ore market. This share was reduced to 15 per cent in the mid-1970s when open-pit mining was introduced in other countries.

22 During the transformation of Swedish industry, the emergence of new industries had attracted entry from a large number of firms (this was the case in, for example, separators, ball bearings, rock drills, railway equipment, marine diesel engines, turbines, household appliances, aircraft and cars). For example, Alfa Laval at the turn of the century had more than 15 domestic competitors in separators, and SKF had nine domestic competitors in ball bearings (including Nordiska Kullagerak-tiebolaget and Stockholms Kullager). Sandvik had several domestic rivals in rock drills, amounting to more than 10 even in the 1960s. ASEA and Electrolux had several competitors in various industry segments (e.g. electrical motors, power transmission and household appliances), and ESAB had three Swedish rivals in welding equipment (ASEA, Hägglunds and AGA).

23 In the 1980s, acquisitions had come to account for 70 per cent of all foreign establishments. Lindvall (1991) shows that international acquisitions by major Swedish firms in the period 1978-1982 were primarily made in Europe (40 per cent), the United States (29 per cent) and the Scandinavian countries (15 per cent). Data from a larger sample of Swedish MNEs indicate that the United States accounted for 15 per cent of the acquisitions in the period 1974-1978 (Jagrén and Bergholm, 1985; as in the previous case, percentages relate to the number of acquisitions).

24 Science and Technology Policies in Sweden (1986) and Svenskt näringsliv och näringspolitik (1994).

25 The R&D intensity of Swedish MNEs, measured as total R&D expenditure over total sales, increased from 1.8 per cent in 1965 to 2.3 per cent in 1974 and 4.2 per cent in 1986.

26 Internationally, the most important sources of externally purchased technology were the industrialized countries, in particular the United States, the Nordic countries, Germany and Great Britain. Långtidsutredningen (1995) indicates that in the 1970s and 1980s R&D performed by consultants or external R&D organizations did not account for more than 10 per cent of total R&D expenditure among Swedish firms.

27 The internationalization of the finance function is described by Åhlander (1990).

28 Foreign technological activity was quite significant in some firms. For

example, firms like ABB (previously ASEA), ESAB, SKF and Esselte (office equipment) reached shares of foreign technological activity of between 50 and 85 per cent in the late 1980s. Other firms, predominantly in the iron and steel industry, maintained almost all of their technological activity in Sweden.

29 As to the scanning for new technology through minority-owned ventures and strategic alliances, evidence on the activities of Swedish MNEs is scarce. The number of minority-owned ventures increased from about 40 in 1965 to some 130 in 1978 (Swedenborg, 1979). However, the growth rate decreased towards the end of the period and there was a decline in the number of employees they represented. Also, minority-owned ventures were particularly well represented in the developing countries. This indicates that market access or local government requirements could have been a more important motive for establishing minority-owned ventures than the search for new technological capabilities.

30 The development was part of the worldwide focus on the United States as a host country for FDI in the 1980s. In the mid-1980s, more than 50 per cent of all foreign production of Swedish MNEs was undertaken in the European Community, while overall 80 per cent was located in the industrialized countries (Hedlund and Zander, 1986; Swedenborg, 1992).

31 See Table 4.1 and UN (1992). In the concluding years of the 1980s, European countries once again became the most important recipients of Swedish FDI. In the period 1981–1985, the United States had accounted for about 30 per cent of all outward FDI, while the European Community accounted for about 40 per cent. The corresponding figures for the period 1986–1990 were 15 per cent and 70 per cent (Isaksson, 1993; UN, 1992; also, see Appendix 4.4).

32 Figures presented by Samuelsson (1977) indicate that foreign-owned subsidiaries accounted for 52 per cent of total employment in Canada, 24 per cent in Australia, 22 per cent in West Germany, 19 per cent in The Netherlands, 15 per cent in France and 10 per cent in Great Britain. The equivalent figures for the United States and Japan were 2.5 per cent and 2.0 per cent respectively.

33 The share of total industrial employment accounted for by foreign-owned firms was particularly high in petroleum products, chemicals, instruments and rubber products. At a more detailed level, foreign-owned subsidiaries accounted for a majority of Swedish production in petroleum products, iron alloys, plastic raw materials, frozen food, computer equipment and TV sets. Substantial shares of production were also obtained in paint, auto parts, carpets, elevators and communication equipment.

34 SOU (1982: 15) and Vahlne (1985). Overall, the foreign-owned firms in Sweden displayed a relatively high share of white collar employees, indicating that sales rather than local manufacturing was the most common mode of operation. Also, import and export ratios further indicate a relatively large proportion of wholesaling and retailing units. The foreign-owned firms tended not to be as research intensive as Swedish MNEs, although they had an edge over purely domestic

Swedish firms. However, a small group of newly established foreign-owned units were particularly R&D intensive, and the group of foreign-owned units which carried out R&D were almost as R&D intensive as Swedish MNEs.

35 See Table 4.1 and UN (1992).

36 Svenskt näringsliv och näringspolitik (1994).

37 According to some estimates, the formation of ABB increased the foreign-owned share of total Swedish R&D expenditure from 8 per cent to 18 per cent between 1987 and 1988 (Svenskt näringsliv och näringspolitik, 1992/93).

38 In 1994, Singer & Friedlander acquired the Swedish brokerage firm Carnegie for 1.2 billion SEK, and AKZO acquired the Swedish chemical conglomerate Nobel Industrier.

39 The restrictions on acquisitions by foreign-owned firms were abolished in 1992 and clauses in corporate by laws on restricted shares were abolished in 1993.

40 Other components of what has been dubbed the 'old industrial policy model' included an active labour market policy to stimulate mobility between stagnating and growing industries, and redistribution of wealth through taxes and public sector growth (Eliasson, 1986; also, see Lindbeck, 1990).

41 There had also been a rather dramatic expansion of the public sector during the 1960s, which together with the decline of the mining, iron and steel, and shipyard industries severely strained the Swedish economy (see e.g. Dahmén, 1992; Eliasson, 1986).

42 Also, government assumed ownership in parts of the textile industry.

43 A common solution to the problem of industrial restructuring was to merge companies, gradually reducing employment and overcapacity. Two examples are the creation of Svenska Varv AB in the shipyard industry in 1977 (later Celsius Industrier), and the creation of the steel manufacturer SSAB in 1978 (involving the three large producers Domnarvet, Oxelösund and NJA). Other companies in which government held a majority share of ownership were LKAB (mining, acquired in 1957), ASSI and NCB (forestry and pulp), and Procordia (diversified).

44 Svenskt näringsliv och näringspolitik (1994).

45 Svensk industri och industripolitik (1989). Government-supported, long-term research programmes included space technology (1972), energy research (1975) and custom design circuits and information technology (1983).

46 See e.g. Svenskt näringsliv och näringspolitik (1991).

47 Regulations imposed by the Central Bank concerning lending and deposit rates were abolished in 1985, and foreign banks were able to obtain licences to operate in Sweden in 1986 (in 1991, foreign brokerage firms and co-operative mortgage institutions could establish branches in Sweden on equal terms with domestic firms). The exchange control regulations which had been introduced in 1939 were gradually lifted and had by and large been abolished by 1989.

48 According to a survey by Braunerhjelm (1990), uncertainty about

Sweden's membership of the European Community created a bias among Swedish firms to locate new investments in the European countries.

49 It has been suggested that Sweden has upheld a long-standing tradition of openness towards foreign trade, which would have reduced the need among foreign firms to establish local production in order to circumvent tariffs. On this account, however, evidence is rather mixed. Having adopted mercantilism for extended periods of time, a short period of liberalization during the latter half of the 19th century was followed by a period of customs protection for a wide range of products, including industrial goods (trade liberalization was achieved through Sweden's accession to the Cobden-Chevalier treaty, which was in effect in 1860-1895). Protection through various forms of customs continued until the Second World War. The creation of EFTA in 1960 (including Austria, Denmark, Great Britain, Norway, Portugal, Sweden, Switzerland and later Finland) and Sweden's free trade agreements with the EEC in 1973 and 1977 have reduced trade barriers only over the past three decades.

50 The population was 2.3 million in 1800, about 4 million in 1870, and had grown to 8.5 million in 1990.

51 See Ohlsson (1969), Larsson and Olsson (1992), Dahmén (1992) and Swedenborg (1992). While early exports from Sweden focused on Great Britain and Germany (before the First World War, the two countries together accounted for more than 50 per cent of Swedish exports), Swedish trade and economic activity was to become increasingly diversified across Europe.

52 See Håkanson and Zander (1986) and Zander (1994). 'Not-invented-here' syndromes and strong technical pride in the home units are some of the factors that might prevent learning from technological advancements in foreign units.

Appendix 4.1 Major Swedish firms established around the turn of the
century

Firm	Established	Major products
Atlas Copco[1]	1873/1898	Railways, steel constructions, rock drilling equipment
Ericsson[2]	1876	Telephones, switches
Bofors[3]	1880s	Artillery
ASEA[4]	1883	Power generating and distribution equipment, electrical motors
Alfa Laval[6]	1883	Separators, dairy equipment
Bahco	1887	Adjustable wrench, hand tools
Scania-Vabis[6]	1891/1900	Motor vehicles
Swedish Match[7]	1892	Safety matches, match manufacturing equipment
Stal-Laval[8]	1893/1913	Steam turbines
C.E. Johansson	1901	Measuring pieces, instruments
AGA	1904	Lighthouses, gases
ESAB	1904	Welding equipment and consumables
SKF	1907	Ball and roller bearings

Notes: 1 The earlier name was Atlas Diesel (after a merger between AB
Atlas, later Nya AB Atlas, and AB Diesels Motorer in 1917).
2 The company was established as L.M. Ericsson.
3 Bofors was already founded in 1646 as a smithy, but was
transformed into a modern engineering firm in the 1880s.
4 ASEA was created in 1890 in a merger between Elektriska
Aktiebolaget and Wenström & Granströms Elektriska Kraftbolag.
5 The company was named Separator until 1963.
6 VABIS was established in 1891 and Scania in 1900. The two
companies merged in 1911.
7 The forerunner of Swedish Match, which was created through a
series of mergers in the 1910s, dates back to 1845.
8 De Laval Ångturbin was established in 1893 and Svenska
Turbinfabriks AB LjungStröm in 1913. Stal-Laval was created in a
merger in 1959.

Appendix 4.2 Early mechanical engineering workshops in Sweden

Firm	Established	Major fields
Motala	1822	Shipbuilding, marine engines, railway equipment, farming equipment
Jonsereds	1832	Textiles, chain-saws, heavy cranes
Munktells	1832	Steam locomotives, pulp machinery, rifles, construction vehicles, farming equipment
Keiller (Götaverken)	1841	Marine engines, shipbuilding, railway equipment, pulp machinery
Kockums	1844	Marine engines, shipbuilding, railway equipment, logging machinery
Lindholmen	1844	Marine engines, shipbuilding, farming equipment
Bolinders	1845	Steam engines, diesel engines, marine equipment, wood processing equipment
Trollhättan (NOHAB)	1847	Marine engines, railway equipment, aircraft engines, aircraft, turbines
Eriksberg	1853	Marine engines, shipbuilding

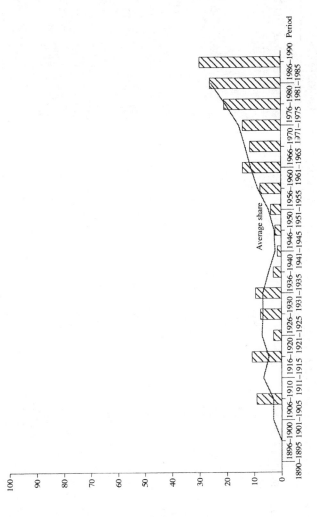

Figure 4.3 The share of foreign technological activity in major Swedish MNEs, 1890–1990 (measured as the share of US patents originating in foreign units)

Source: Zander (1994)

Appendix 4.4 Flows of outward and inward foreign direct investment in Sweden, 1955–1988 (MSEK, current prices)

Year	Outward FDI	Western Europe[1]	North America (USA)[2]	Inward FDI	Western Europe[1]	North America (USA)[2]
1955	137	57	12			
1956	135	44	20			
1957	191	79	46			
1958	171	59	18			
1959	357	194	63			
1960	288	110	9	134	101	33
1961	346	132	12	167	98	68
1962	430	288	52	322	294	27
1963	391	241	10	754	393	355
1964	747	505	80	360	192	156
1965	538	331	47	320	207	113
1966	735	407	145	654	321	333
1967	877	532	124	584	212	362
1968	673	397	93	1,039	364	672
1969	1,696	799	562	550	239	301
1970	1,093	610	184	779	497	263
1971	1,255	598[3]	250 (86)	611	284[3]	— (263)
1972	1,903	1,190	324 (121)	478	200	— (230)
1973	1,503	915	185 (140)	615	348	— (230)
1974	2,430	1,326	452 (397)	674	288	— (327)
1975	2,303	1,414	291 (269)	562	433	— (107)

Year								
1976	3,476	2,036[4]	576	(529)	583	395[4]	171	(121)
1977	4,315	2,460	639	(557)	643	470	94	(94)
1978	3,005	1,488	585	(576)	788	502	205	(204)
1979	3,506	1,568	1,061	(988)	787	590	118	(118)
1980	3,796	1,587	1,304	(1,194)	1,586	1,110	417	(404)
1981	6,411	3,173[5]	—	(1,862)	1,374	1,043[5]	—	(273)
1982	8,918	4,575	—	(2,498)	1,800	1,176	—	(392)
1983	11,995	7,385	—	(2,348)	2,308	1,517	—	(547)
1984	15,052	8,384	—	(4,222)	2,793	2,179	—	(379)
1985	19,939	7,602	—	(6,188)	6,881	5,229	—	(1,496)
1986[6]	21,812	9,192	11,253	(11,202)	5,885	4,641	992	(993)
1987	20,205	15,014	4,297	(4,041)	2,198	1,474	33	(29)
1988	32,405	29,315	2,083	(2,132)	5,671	4,813	347	(345)

Notes:
1 Includes EFTA and the European Community 1955–1970.
2 Figures within parentheses indicate figures for the United States.
3 Figures on outward flows for 1971–1975 include West Germany, Great Britain, France, Norway, Denmark, Finland, Belgium, Ireland, Switzerland and The Netherlands. Figures on inward flows for 1971–1975 are for the same countries but exclude Belgium.
4 Figures on outward flows for 1976–1980 include West Germany, Great Britain, France, Norway, Denmark, Finland, Belgium, The Netherlands, Luxembourg and Italy. Figures on inward flows for 1976–1980 are for the same countries but exclude Luxembourg and Italy and include Switzerland.
5 Figures on outward flows for 1891–1985 include West Germany, Great Britain, France, Norway, Denmark, Finland, Belgium, The Netherlands, Switzerland, Italy and Spain. Figures on inward flows for 1981–1985 are for the same countries but exclude Belgium, Italy and Spain and include Luxembourg.
6 Figures for the period 1986–1988 collected from World Investment Directory (1992). Figures on both outward and inward flows for 1986–1988 include the European Community and EFTA countries.

Sources: Riksbankens Årsbok (1961, 1964, 1967, 1970, 1975) and Sveriges Riksbank, Förvaltningsberättelse (1980, 1985).

138   Sweden

REFERENCES

Åhlander, K. (1990) *Aspects of Modern Treasury Management – Organization and External Financial Activities in Swedish MNCs*, Doctoral Dissertation, Stockholm: Institute of International Business.

Ahlström, G. (1993) 'Industrial research and technical proficiency – Swedish industry in the early 20th century', Lund Papers in Economic History, No. 23, Lund: Lund University.

Andersson, T. (1993) 'Utlandsinvesteringar och policy-implikationer', in *SOU 1993: 16*, Stockholm: Norstedts. (Foreign investments and policy implications)

Bergström, V. (1982) *Studies in Swedish Post-War Industrial Investments*, Uppsala: Acta Universitatis Upsaliensis, Studia Oeconomica Upsaliensia 7.

Bosworth, B. P. and Rivlin, A. M. (eds) (1987) *The Swedish Economy*, Washington, DC: The Brookings Institution.

Braunerhjelm, P. (1990) *Svenska industriföretag inför EG 1992 – Förväntningar och planer*, Stockholm: IUI/Överstyrelsen för civil beredskap. (Swedish industrial firms facing the European Community 1992 – expectations and plans)

Carlsson, S. (1986) 'A century's captains of industry', *Scandinaviska Enskilda Banken Quarterly Review*, No. 2.

Dahmén, E. (1985) 'Mellankrigstiden – industri i omvandling', in *Sveriges industri*, Stockholm: Sveriges Industriförbund. (The interwar period – industrial transformation)

—— (1992) 'Den industriella utvecklingen after andra världskriget', in *Sveriges industri*, Stockholm: Industriförbundet. (Industrial development after the Second World War)

Eliasson, G. (1986) 'Is the Swedish welfare state in trouble? A new policy model', *Scandinavian–Canadian Studies*, Vol. 2, 1986.

Forsgren, M. (1989) 'Foreign acquisition: internationalization or network interdependency?', in L. Hallén and J. Johanson (eds) *Networks of Relationships in International Industrial Marketing*, Greenwich, CT: JAI Press.

Forsgren, M. and Larsson, A. (1984) 'Foreign acquisitions and the balance of power in transnational enterprises: the Swedish case', Working Paper No. 2, Center for International Business Studies, Uppsala University.

Gårdlund, T. and Fritz, M. (1983) *Ett världsföretag växer fram – Alfa-Laval 100 år.* (The growth of a world company – Alfa-Laval 100 years)

Ghauri, P. N. (1990) 'Emergence of new structures in Swedish multinationals', in S. B. Prasad (ed.) *Advances in International Comparative Management*, Greenwich: CT JAI Press.

Glete, J. (1987) *Ägande och industriell omvandling – Ägargrupper, skogsindustri, verkstadsindustri 1850-1950*, Stockholm: SNS Förlag. (Ownership and industrial transformation – groups of owners, the forestry and mechanical engineering industries 1850-1950)

Granstrand, O. (1981) 'The role of technology trade in Swedish companies', RP 81/3, Stockholm: Institute of International Business.

Sweden 139

Gustavson, C. G. (1986) *The Small Giant – Sweden Enters the Industrial Era*, Ohio University Press.

Håkanson, L. (1981) 'Organization and evolution of foreign R&D in Swedish multinationals', *Geografiska Annaler*, 63B, pp. 47–56.

Håkanson, L. and Nobel, R. (1993) 'Foreign research and development in Swedish multinationals', *Research Policy*, 22, pp. 373–396.

Håkanson, L. and Zander, U. (1986) *Managing International Research & Development*, Stockholm: Mekan.

Heckscher, E. F. (1932) *Sveriges ekonomiska utveckling i fågelperspektiv*, särtryck ur Tidskriften Ekonomen. (Sweden's economic development from a bird's-eye view)

—— (1935) *Sveriges ekonomiska historia från Gustav Vasa*, Stockholm: Albert Bonniers Förlag. (Sweden's economic development from Gustav Vasa)

—— (1950) *Survey of Sweden's Economic Evolution in Economic Conditions and Banking Problems*, Stockholm: The Swedish Banks Association.

Hedlund, G. and Zander, I. (1986) 'Swedish MNCs' strategies for Europe – preliminary report for the Penelope project', Stockholm: Institute of International Business.

Isaksson, M. (1993) 'De svenska direktinvesteringarna i ett internationellt perspektiv', in *SOU 1993: 16*, Stockholm: Norstedts. (Swedish international investments in an international perspective)

Jagrén, L. and Bergholm, F. (1985) 'Det utlandsinvesterande företaget – En empirisk studie', in G. Eliasson *et al. De svenska storföretagen – En studie av internationaliseringens konsekvenser för den svenska ekonomin*, Stockholm: Industriens Utredningsinstitut. (Firms investing in foreign countries – an empirical study)

Johanson, J. and Wiedersheim-Paul, F. (1975) 'The internationalization of the firm – four Swedish cases', *Journal of Management Studies*, October, pp. 305–322.

Johansson, H. (1968) *Utländsk företagsetablering i Sverige*, Uddevalla. (Foreign-owned establishments in Sweden)

Jörberg, L. (1970) 'The industrial revolution in Scandinavia 1850–1914', in C.M. Cipolla (ed.) *Volume IV: 1700-1914 The Emergence of Industrial Societies*, The Fontana Economic History of Europe.

Långtidsutredningen (1995) *Svenskt näringslivs teknologiska specialisering*, bilaga 11, Stockholm: Finansdepartementet. (Technological specialization in Swedish industry)

Larsson, M. and Olsson, U. (1992) 'Industrialiseringens sekel', in *Sveriges industri*, Stockholm: Industriförbundet. (The century of industrialization)

Lindbeck, A. (1990) 'The Swedish Experience', Seminar Paper No. 482, Institute for International Economic Studies, Stockholm University.

Lindvall, J. (1991) *Svenska industriföretags internationella företagsförvärv – Inriktning och utfall*, University of Uppsala: Department of Business Studies. (Foreign acquisitions by Swedish industrial firms – focus and outcome)

Lund, H. (1967) 'Svenska företags investeringar i utlandet', in *Sveriges industri*, Stockholm: Industriförbundet. (Foreign investments by Swedish firms)

Lundström, R. (1986) 'Swedish multinational growth before 1930', in P. Hertner and G. Jones (eds) *Multinationals: Theory and History*, Aldershot: Gower Publishing.

Nordlund, S. (1989) *Upptäckten av Sverige – Utländska direktinvesteringar i Sverige 1895-1945*, Umeå Studies in Economic History 12, Umeå University. (The discovery of Sweden – foreign direct investments in Sweden 1895-1945, summary in English)

OECD (1993) *Reviews on Foreign Direct Investment – Sweden*, Paris.

Ohlsson, L. (1969) *Utrikeshandeln och den ekonomiska tillväxten i Sverige 1871-1966*, Stockholm: IUI. (Foreign trade and economic growth in Sweden 1871-1966)

Olsson, U. (1986) *Bank, familj och företagande – Stockholms Enskilda Bank 1946-1971*. (Banks, family and business – the Stockholms Enskilda Bank 1946-1971)

Ruist, E. (1985) 'Metallindustri', in *Sveriges industri*, Stockholm: Sveriges Industriförbund. (Metallurgical industry)

Samuelsson, H.-F. (1977) *Utländska direkta investeringar i Sverige – En ekonometrisk analys av bestämningsfaktorerna*, Stockholm: Industriens Utredningsinstitut. (Foreign direct investments in Sweden – an econometric analysis, summary in English)

Samuelsson, K. (1985) 'Industrisamhällets framväxt 1850 till 1914', in *Sveriges industri*, Stockholm: Sveriges Industriförbund. (The emergence of industrial society 1850 to 1914)

Science and Technology Policies in Sweden (1986), Stockholm: Norstedts.

Söderberg, T. (1946) *Det svenska näringslivets stora omvandling*, Studentföreningen Verdandis småskrifter, nr. 484, Stockholm: Albert Bonniers Förlag. (The great transformation of the Swedish economy)

Sölvell, Ö. (1994) 'Sveriges framtid finns i historiska ''Hollywoods''', in MTC-Kontakten, Jubilenmstidskrift, Stockholm, MTC. (Sweden's future lies in historical 'Hollywoods')

Sölvell, Ö., Zander, I. and Porter, M. E. (1991) *Advantage Sweden*, Stockholm: Norstedts.

SOU 1975: 50, *Internationella koncerner i industriländer – Samhällsekonomiska aspekter*. (International groups in industrialized countries – economic aspects).

SOU 1981: 43, *De Internationella investeringarnas effekter – Några fallstudier*. (The effects of international investments – some case studies)

SOU 1982: 15, *Internationella företag i svensk ekonomi – En jämförelse mellan svenska multinationella, utlandsägda och nationella företag*. (International companies in Swedish industry – a comparison between Swedish multinationals, foreign-owned multinationals and domestic firms)

SOU 1983: 17, *Näringspolitiska effekter av internationella investeringgar – Betänkande från directinvesteringskommitté*. (Economic policy effects from international investments)

Svensk industri och industripolitik (1988, 1989), Industridepartementet.

Svenskt näringsliv och näringspolitik (1991, 1992/93, 1994), Industridepartementet and NUTEK.

Swedenborg, B. (1979) *The Multinational Operations of Swedish Firms – An Analysis of Determinants and Effects*, Stockholm: The Industrial Institute for Economic and Social Research.

——— (1982) *Svensk industri i utlandet – En analys av drivkrafter och effekter*, Stockholm: Industriens Utredningsinstitut. (The multinational operations of Swedish firms – an analysis of determinants and effects)

——— (1985) 'Sweden', in J.H. Dunning (ed.) *Multinational Enterprises, Economic Structure and International Competitiveness*, Chichester: John Wiley.

——— (1992) 'Svenska multinationella företag', in *Sveriges industri*, Stockholm: Industriförbundet. (Swedish multinational firms)

Swedenborg, B., Johansson-Grahn, G. & Kinnwall, M. (1988) *Den svenska industrins utlandsinvesteringar 1960 1980*, Stockholm: IUI. (Swedish foreign direct investments 1960–1980).

Vahlne, J.-E. (1985) 'Multinationella företag i svensk industri', in *Sveriges industri*, Stockholm: Sveriges Industriförbund. (Multinational firms in Swedish industry)

Vahlne, J.-E. and Hörnell, E. (1986) *Multinationals: The Swedish Case*, London: Croom Helm.

Wallmark, T. and McQueen D. (1986) *100 viktiga svenska innovationer under tiden 1945–1980*, Lund: Studentlitteratur. (100 important Swedish innovations 1945–1980)

Wohlert, K. (1981) *Framväxten av svenska multinationella företag – En fallstudie mot bakgrund av direktinvesteringsteorier Alfa-Laval och separatorindustrin 1876–1914*, Uppsala: Almqvist & Wiksell International. (The growth of Swedish multinational firms – Alfa Laval and the separator industry 1876–1914, summary in English)

United Nations World Investment Directory (1992), Vol. 3, New York: United Nations, Transnational Corporations and Management Division.

Zander, I. (1994) *The Tortoise Evolution of the Multinational Corporation – Foreign Technological Activity in Swedish Multinational Firms 1890-1990*, Doctoral Dissertation, Stockholm: Institute of International Business.

Zander, U. (1991) *Exploiting a Technological Edge – Voluntary and Involuntary Dissemination of Technology*, Doctoral Dissertation, Stockholm: Institute of International Business.

Chapter 5

Japan
The macro-IDP, meso-IDPs and the technology development path (TDP)

Terutomo Ozawa

Private people who want to make a fortune, never think of retiring to the remote and poor provinces of the country, but resort either to the capital, or to some of the great commercial towns. They know that where little wealth circulates, there is little to be got; but that *where a great deal is in motion, some share of it may fall to them*. The same maxims which would in this manner direct the common sense of [individuals] . . . should make a whole nation regard the *riches of its neighbours as a probable cause and occasion for itself to acquire riches*. A nation that would enrich itself by foreign trade, is certainly most likely to do so when its neighbours are all rich and industrious (italics added).

Adam Smith, *An Inquiry into the Nature and Causes of the Wealth of Nations* (1776)

JAPAN: THE CLIMBER OF THE INDUSTRIAL HIERARCHY

A hierarchical world and the ladder (stages) of development

John Dunning's 'investment development path (IDP)' theory (1981) and its latest version (Dunning and Narula 1994) are implicitly built on the notion that the global economy is necessarily *hierarchical* in terms of the various stages of economic development in which its diverse constituent nations are situated. When a number of nations with lower per capita income experience net negative investment positions, there are naturally a certain number of nations with higher per capita income whose net positive investment positions correspond in value.

What does such a path demonstrate? The IDP essentially traces out the net cross-border flows of industrial knowledge, the flows that are internalised in foreign direct investment (FDI) and that restructure and upgrade the global economy, although there is also the non-equity type of knowledge transfers such as licensing, turn-key operations, and the like. In this respect, the IDP can thus be interpreted as *a cross-border learning curve* exhibited by a nation that successfully moves up the stages of development by acquiring industrial knowledge from its more advanced 'neighbours'. A move from the 'U-shaped' (i.e. negative NOI) portion to the 'wiggle' section of the IDP indicates an *equilibration in knowledge dissemination*: that is, a *narrowing* of the industrial technology gap between the advanced and the catching-up countries.

In general, it should be expected that *the smaller the technological gap, the greater a catching-up nation's capability of absorbing technology and skills (both technical and organizational), and the more involved its government is in promoting locally controlled industries, the flatter, and the shorter, the U-shaped portion of the IDP*. In fact, the U-shaped segment may entirely disappear if inward FDI is restricted by the government but non-equity (externalised) channels of knowledge absorption are used instead. Thus, the IDP curve conceptualised by Dunning is an idealised pattern based on free-market exchanges of knowledge among countries.

This way of interpreting the IDP is useful in analysing the experiences of Japan as a latecomer to the scene of modern industrialisation. The Japanese government actively orchestrated the catching-up strategy of its industry on a rather nationalistic basis; it minimized inward FDI, through which foreign interests directly control the ownership of local productive capacities, but instead encouraged the maximum use of licensing and other non-equity forms of acquiring advanced industrial knowledge from the West. Furthermore, Japanese industry itself had a well-developed capacity to seek, assimilate, and even improve on, state-of-the-art technology from the West, as will be discussed below. Hence, the Japanese experience does not trace out the typical pattern of the IDP. Yet, if other forms of knowledge acquisition are taken into account, the main idea of knowledge transfers and equilibration propounded in the IDP paradigm still holds and can be attested to in the context of Japan's catching-up development.

In analysing the Japanese experience, furthermore, it is important to keep in mind that the process of industrialisation is *not* a smooth, continuous and simultaneous expansion of all the segments of domestic industry, but *a sequence of stages* in each of which a certain industrial sector serves as the main engine (the 'leading' sector) for structural upgrading. In this regard, my view jibes with what W. W. Rostow (1960) emphasised:

> At any period of time, the rate of growth in the sectors will vary greatly; and it is possible to isolate empirically *certain leading sectors, at early stages of their evolution, whose rapid rate of expansion plays an essential direct and indirect role in maintaining the overall momentum of the economy.* For some purposes it is useful to characterise an economy in terms of its leading sectors; and a part of the technical basis for the stages of growth lies in the *changing* sequence of leading sectors. In essence it is the fact that sectors tend to have a rapid growth-phase, early in their life, that makes it possible and useful to regard economic history as *a sequence of stages rather than merely as a continuum, within which nature never makes a jump* (italics added).
>
> (Rostow 1960, p. 14)

As we will see below, the idea that a successful process of development is punctuated by stages in a step-like fashion gives an important analytical supplement to Dunning's IDP.

'Flying-geese' paradigm and meso-IDPs

The stage idea is also explicit in the so-called 'flying-geese' paradigm of industrial development expounded by Kaname Akamatsu (1961, 1962) and elaborated on by others.[1] In fact, the flying-geese paradigm places the sequential pattern of development in a global context in which the economic development of a latecomer nation is interpreted as a derived process, a process that involves *interactions* with much richer 'neighbours' (in the Smithian sense) through trade, FDI and other forms of economic engagement. As Akamatsu (1962) put it, 'It is impossible to study the economic growth of the developing countries in modern times without considering the mutual interactions between these economies and those of the advanced countries' (p. 1). The interactive form of development is in line with the IDP which is, as interpreted above, *a locus of cross-border interactive learning (emulation) and teaching (leadership).*

Akamatsu's original work focused on how a given manufacturing industry (textiles) developed in a follower-goose country (as Japan used to be). Figure 5.1(a) depicts what he identified as the 'funda-mental' flying-geese formation, *the sequential triple-step appear-ance of imports, domestic production and exports over a long span of time* (as long as half a century), each with a wave-like trend

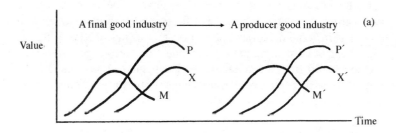

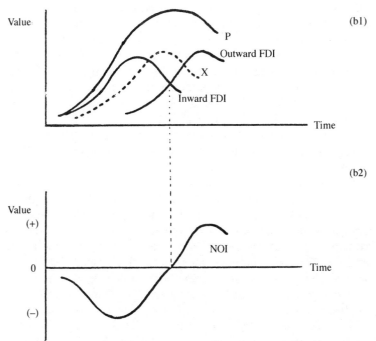

Figure 5.1   Flying-geese (FG) paradigm and the meso-IDP:
(a) Akamatsu's 'fundamental' FG pattern of industrial growth; (b1) MNE-facilitated FG pattern of industrial growth; (b2) meso-IDP (in a particular industry)

curve, a curve initially rising, then cresting and eventually declining (hence, a pattern homologous to a flying formation of wild geese). Each set of triple waves (imports -> domestic production -> exports) occurs first in the industrial growth of a final good (a 'consumer good') and then in that of a producer good (a 'capital good') with a considerable time lag in the developmental sequence between the two vertically related sectors. He found these similar patterns in cotton yarn, cotton fabrics and cotton textile machinery. What he illustrated is a changing pattern of trade competitiveness over time, a gradual shift from a comparatively disadvantaged position (i.e. the import phase in the beginning) eventually to a comparatively advantaged one (the exporting phase).

In fact, the developmental full-cycle process of some of the Japanese industries he examined took more than a half century, a rather prolonged time period by today's standards. For example, the imports of cotton yarn began right after the Meiji Restoration of 1868 (the official beginning of Japan as a modern state), but it was not until around 1887 (20 years later) that domestic production began to exceed imports, finally leading to the export phase, which in turn reached its peak at the turn of this century. On the other hand, the imports of capital goods (spinning and weaving machinery) started around 1883, but their domestic production and exports became significant only around 1903 and finally reached their respective peaks in 1939 (Akamatsu 1962).

Why did it take so long for Japan to develop a vertically integrated cotton textile industry (inclusive of textile machinery)? Two important reasons are conceivable. First, in those days, FDI in textiles – that is, MNEs in cotton yarns, fabrics and textile machinery – was rather rare, since the textile industry (especially its downstream segments) then had a highly competitive market structure devoid of strong oligopolistic market power and without much extra organisational capacity to operate across national borders. The advanced Western countries – and their relatively small-sized textile manufacturers – were still interested in retaining and jealously guarding the textile industry at home, a dominant industrial employer at that time, although it was declining as a proportion of GDP in the face of emergent heavy industries such as electric machinery, chemicals and automobiles at the turn of this century. (It is, indeed, in the latter types of industry that MNEs in manufacturing began to emerge as the firms' size increased and their products became differentiated.)

More importantly, furthermore, the Japanese government in those days was pursuing an infant-industry strategy, bent on developing domestic industries of its own through all sorts of subsidies and protective measures. In short, the two sets of flying-geese formations (one for final goods, the other for producer goods) thus exhibited rather prolonged secular curves, basically mirroring Japan's self-reliant (or anti-inward-FDI) stance of industrialisation and the unavailability of MNEs, at that time, in textiles and textile machinery which could bring about industrialisation practically 'overnight' (complete transfers of textile production facilities).

Nowadays, in sharp contrast, the governments of developing countries are interested in a much more speedy pace of industrial transformation by attracting MNEs as 'instant' transplanters of industrialisation. The result is a considerably speeded-up (sharply accelerated) appearance for the flying-geese formation of industrial development in a highly *time-compressed* fashion for both final goods and upstream producer goods.

One such possibility (what may be called an MNE/host-accelerated flying-geese pattern of industrial growth) is illustrated in Figure 5.1(b1). Time compression occurs especially when the MNEs' and host governments' strategic decisions coincide in establishing, as quickly as possible, vertically integrated local production (of final goods as well as producer goods) and in turning it into an export industry for the purpose of earning foreign exchange.

The conventional wisdom of FDI holds that the firm will first export to a particular overseas market, and then once a sufficient volume of sales is secured through exports, it will gingerly switch to local production – first, through licensing and then through FDI. These days, however, some MNEs may decide to set up local production from the very start without first exploring an overseas market via exports. In this case, local production necessarily precludes the import curve in the host country. In addition, the government of a developing host country is likely to impose, as is often the case, both *export and local content requirements*. If such an effort to domesticate/localise MNE-initiated ventures on the part of the host country is successful, both an export curve and a production curve for some (if not all) producer goods will appear almost simultaneously in the early stages of industrial growth without much time lag after the appearance of the local production curve for a final good. In other words, in the context of the flying-geese paradigm of catching-up development, MNEs thus act as a compressor of the intertemporal length of Akamatsu's 'fundamental' pattern of industrial growth.

Suppose that a developing country has a potential comparative advantage in a labour-intensive light industry, say, apparel, and that it can attract MNEs in apparel to develop and exploit such comparative advantage. As illustrated in Figure 5.1(b1), the domestic productive capacity for apparel (a curve P) will thus be developed by inward FDI (a curve labelled Inward FDI). These inward investments are likely to be highly export oriented, although the domestic demand for apparel will also rise as local labour is fully employed by such export-led development policy. In fact, if such a policy for export-led, labour-driven development is successful, local wages will inevitably rise and even shortages of low-skilled labour will occur (as experienced in early-postwar Japan and the Asian newly industrialising economies or NIEs). In the end, then, the country will lose a comparative advantage in labour-intensive, low-skilled industries, thereby making the initial policy for labour-driven development no longer suitable.

The rising incomes, however, will in turn contribute to an increase in domestic savings (hence, the availability of funds needed), enabling the country to have a more capital-intensive, sophisticated industry whose products can also be demanded at home because of an increased domestic purchasing power. This self-altering process is the ineluctable result of labour-driven industrialisation, as it is posited in, and explained by, the 'principle of increasing factor incongruity', a principle based on the 'Smithian vent-for-surplus' theory and the 'Stolper-Samuelson factor-price-magnification' effect (Ozawa 1992). To paraphrase the Schumpeterian notion of 'creative destruction', this self-upgrading process may be called 'structural creative destruction'.

As local wages rise, the host country starts to lose comparative advantages in labour-intensive industries. Consequently, inward FDI (of the labour-seeking type) begins to decline and eventually disappear, while outward FDI will appear in order to transplant the now comparatively disadvantaged activities onto lower-labour-cost countries in a manner that develops or augments the latter's comparative advantage.[2] (Indeed, this is exactly what has happened in the Asian NIEs – and is about to happen in four members of the Association of South East Asian Nations or ASEAN-4: Thailand, Malaysia, the Philippines and Indonesia, especially Thailand. The Asian NIEs are, in fact, the major manufacturing investors in the

ASEAN-4 countries' labour-intensive industries, notably apparel and sundries. Even the ASEAN-4 are now investing in China and Vietnam where wages are still lower than at home.) As shown in Figure 5.1(b2), this sequential process of FDI – first inward and then outward – can be depicted as a *meso*-IDP, an IDP distinct from Dunning's IDP, which can now be contrasted as a *macro*-IDP. This concept of the meso-IDP is useful to demonstrate the *positive* net outward investment positions of the Asian NIEs in labour-intensive industries (notably, apparel and sundries), even though their macro-IDPs are still in the 'below-parity' or 'negative NOI' zone (i.e. at the bottom of the U-shaped portion of their macro-IDPs).

Assuming that a catching-up country develops step by step in line with its compatible factor endowments and its prevailing level of technological sophistication, a series of the meso-IDP curves are expected to appear, as illustrated in Figure 5.2(a). If this happens, they will trace out Dunning's macro-IDP as an *envelope* curve. This envelope curve will not stay flat but will turn up in a U-shaped path. For, since such a successfully catching-up country is moving up the ladder of industrialisation from low value-added, low-technology industries to higher value-added, higher-technology ones over time, the level of industrial knowledge accumulated in the process rises steadily and eventually becomes on a par with the advanced world. That is to say, as the knowledge gap narrows, the rate of outward FDI (cross-border knowledge dissemination) becomes greater than that of inward FDI (cross-border knowledge absorption). This is also reflected in the fact that each successive wave of the meso-IDPs (say, from textiles to metal products to automobiles) necessarily becomes larger and larger, because higher value-added manufacturing is more knowledge intensive as well as capital intensive; hence, both inward and outward FDI will grow in value.

The series of meso-IDPs illustrated in Figure 5.2(a) assume a stylised hypothetical situation in which both MNEs and the host country are interacting freely in an idealised fashion without any impediments to FDI flows, inward and outward. In contrast, if a catching-up country inhibits inward FDI but promotes outward FDI, such an asymmetry will be equally reflected in the shapes of the meso-IDP curves: while the net negative portions (the U-shaped portions) of all the meso-IDP curves disappear, their positive portions alone can be observed (Figure 5.2b). Indeed, as will be detailed below, this modified model of the meso-IDP fits nicely to

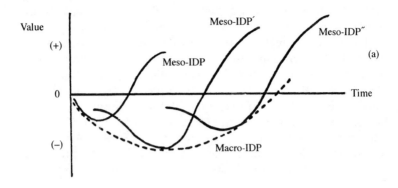

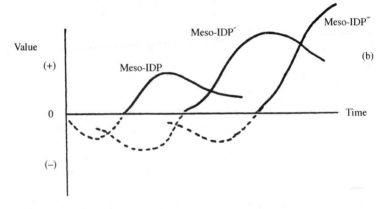

Figure 5.2   Structural upgrading and meso-IDPs: (a) a macro-IDP as an envelope curve of meso-IDPs; (b) 'distorted (inward-FDI-inhibiting)' meso-IDP

the experiences of the Japanese economy after World War II, since Japan – early on, intentionally at the policy level, and later, at the market structural level – came to establish *an inward-FDI-inhibiting, but outward-FDI-fostering regime* (although it is currently making efforts to redress such FDI imbalance).

A GREAT CATCH-UP: THE JAPANESE EXPERIENCE

Japanese industry has gone through various stages of development very rapidly and successfully. In fact, incessant *stages-delineated* industrial upgrading has been its major hallmark, especially in the post-war period. As I have emphasised elsewhere (1979, 1985, 1992), the nature, direction and magnitude of Japan's technology absorptive efforts and its inward and outward FDI have been both policy and market coordinated in a mutually reinforcing manner as Japan climbed the ladder of industrialisation stage by stage.

Japan adopted a highly orchestrated industrial development policy aimed at building up industries in as self-reliant a manner as practical; hence it emphasised absorption of advanced Western technologies mostly under licensing agreements and without foreign ownership cum managerial control (Ozawa 1974). Consequently, as already mentioned earlier, Japan did not exhibit the typical pattern of IDP à la Dunning and Narula. Inward FDI was kept to a minimum, while technological absorption in unbundled form (i.e. licensing) was promoted. Consequently, ever since the end of World War II, Japan's net outward FDI has never been negative (its NOI shows only positive values as indicated in Appendix Table 5.1).

Pre-World War II experience

It is worth noting, however, that in the pre-war years, especially from the start of this century to the mid-1930s, Japan did exhibit for a short while a negative U-shaped net outward investment path. The very first wave of inward FDI occurred at the turn of the century. In 1899 the Japanese Civil and Commercial Codes were substantially liberalised to accommodate the new rights of foreign investors in Japan (including guarantees for industrial property rights), a revision that ushered in what Mark Mason (1992) calls 'an unusually tolerant period in Japan's treatment of foreign investment' – up until 1930.

As soon as the unequal commercial treaties of the mid-1800s with the West went through their first phase of revision, Japan began to erect high tariff walls for the purpose of fostering domestic industries. Partly because of this, many American (e.g. Western Electric, B.F. Goodrich Rubber, GE, Ford, GM, Victor Talking Machine and Otis Elevator) and European firms (English Electric, Dunlop Rubber, I G Farben and Siemens) were then induced to set up production in Japan (Mason 1992).

Interestingly enough, the very first inward FDI in modern Japan took the form of a joint venture, Nippon Electric Company (NEC)

(Arisawa 1967). It was 54 per cent owned by Western Electric and 46 per cent locally owned. The following description of this venture reveals some interesting features of Japan's efforts to acquire Western technology:

> [Western Electric] was established to manufacture telephones just three years after the 1876 invention of that device by Alexander Graham Bell in Boston. The manufacturing arm of the Bell System from 1881, Western Electric quickly followed its parent organization into numerous foreign markets . . .
>
> The Japanese authorities, who recognized the usefulness of telephones almost immediately, initially encouraged their manufacture in Japan independent of foreign involvement. Japan's Ministry of Industry first imported the telephone less than twenty months after Bell's invention. The Osaka Police Department put the telephone to use in Japan shortly thereafter, and, before long, the principal government ministries in Tokyo operated phones for limited office purposes. At the factory of the Ministry of Industry, engineers tried with crude lathes and other limited equipment to *replicate the imported sets*. By 1885, government workers had managed to produce 252 telephone sets based on the imported models. Still, the quality and technical sophistication of these devices continued to lag behind the latest examples from the West, and their manufacture could not keep pace with demand. Smaller Japanese firms such as Oki & Company also tried to match foreign phone makers, but proved little more successful in terms of quality or volume.
>
> Apparently dissatisfied with the results of these early efforts, the authorities chose to rely more on foreign producers to meet domestic needs. As a first stop, Dr Oi Saitaro of the Ministry of Communications (MOC) was *dispatched to the United States and Europe* in 1888 to *report back* on the state of foreign telephone companies and the systems they had established. During his visit, Oi met with top managers at Western Electric among other firms, and, upon his return to Japan the following year, recommended that his government adopt some of the American company's telephone systems (italics added).

> (Mason 1992, pp. 27–28)

Indeed, this episode best *typifies* the Japanese pattern of knowledge absorption from the West throughout its history of modernisation. First of all, (1) the tradition of reverse engineering and reproduction (i.e. stripping down an imported manufacture to find out how it is made and how it works, as seen in the fact that 'engineers tried . . . to replicate the imported sets'); (2) the frequent dispatching of experts or study missions to the West for field research (as was the case with Saitaro who was 'dispatched to the United States and Europe'); and (3) the active role of government (and its various agencies) as a scanner/locator and experimenter of state-of-the-art foreign technologies ('Japan's Ministry of Industry first imported the telephone less than twenty months after Bell's invention') – and a promoter (and often a negotiating partner) of absorption and adoption once some foreign technologies were found promising and critical.

The brief period (1899–1930) of an inward FDI boom, however, came to an end with the rise of militarism in Japan. In the meantime, Japan's outward FDI began to take place in its newly acquired colonies such as Formosa (Taiwan), Korea and Manchukuo in the 1930s. It was part of Japan's imperial expansion designed to secure military advantages in such strategic industries as mining, transportation, communication, and some sectors of heavy and chemical industries. Because Japan regarded those territories as its own, overseas investment in them was treated basically the same as domestic investment except that economic development in the territories was more closely planned and controlled as part of Japan's colonial management. Be that as it may, the rise in outward FDI must have caused an abrupt change in Japan's net outward investment position from negative to positive by the start of World War II.[3]

Post-World War II experience: technology development path (TDP)

It was after World War II that Japan was able to devote practically all its national energy and resources (since it no longer needed to spend for military purposes) to catch up with the advanced West in industrial endeavours by making best use of its huge technology gap vis-à-vis the West, a gap that had widened during the war. Luckily, Japan could concentrate on industrial efforts under the benign tutelage of the United States in the context of the deepening Cold War. The United States largely tolerated Japan's protectionism which enabled the latter to build up industries by importing technol-

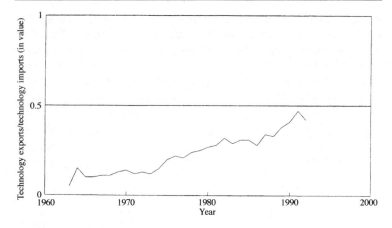

Figure 5.3   Japan's balance of technology trade as a technology development path (TDP)
Source: Appendix Table 5.2.

ogy mostly through licensing agreements and restricting inward FDI to a minimum.

As a result, Japan's learning curve took the form of what may be called a 'technology development path' (TDP) via licensing rather than that of an IDP. In fact, if we measure the ratio of Japanese exports of technology to imports of technology (or net technology exports), a negative 'net technology receipt' pattern – akin to a negative NOI pattern – can be observed, as shown in Figure 5.3 (see also Appendix Table 5.2).

It is interesting to note that the ratio is still below parity (a ratio of one), but that it has been steadily increasing (from 0.05 in 1963 to 0.42 in 1992), indicating Japan's rising level of technological capacity. In 1992, Japan paid royalties and fees for industrial technology amounting to $4.7 billion, 34 times the amount ($136 million) it paid in 1963, partly reflecting the growth of its capacity to absorb and make use of imported technology. On the other hand, in 1992 Japan received about $2 billion, as much as 285 times the amount ($7 million) it received back in 1963, another clear indication of the enormous technological progress it had made over the previous 30 years. All this attests to the fact that Japan has not become merely dependent on imported technology; rather, *because of* imported technology it was able to raise its own technology development capacity. This is because imported technology was looked at as a 'raw material', just like any other raw material, to be processed, assimilated, synthesised with local industrial knowledge, transformed into 'finished technologies', and exported back to the world (Ozawa 1985).

Yet the above aggregate statistics miss the vital changes that have occurred (1) in its relations *vis-à-vis* technology trade partners, and (2) in different industrial sectors as Japan climbed the ladder of industrialisation stage by stage, each stage led by a certain growth industry.

For example, as may well be expected, Japan has been exporting a substantial amount of technology to the developing countries practically without importing in return. In fact, Asian countries are Japan's largest customer for technology sales, accounting for 47 per cent (in 1991).[4] Some industrial technologies have begun to be imported from other Asian countries in the recent past, but such imports are still insignificant in value. Japan thus runs a totally one-sided surplus in technology trade with the developing countries. Another interesting picture emerges when one looks at Japan's technology trade with four other major advanced countries: the United States, the United Kingdom, Germany and France (Figure 5.4). Japan began to experience a surplus in technology trade with

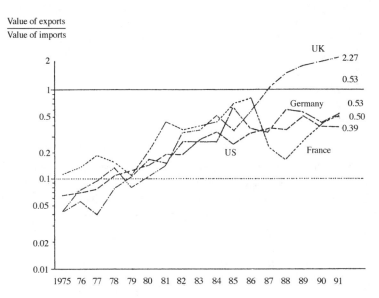

Figure 5.4 Japan's technology trade with other major countries
Source: Japan's Science and Technology Agency (1993) p. 141.

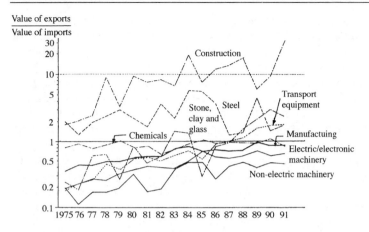

Figure 5.5   Japan's balance of technology trade by manufacturing
industry
Source: Japan's Science and Technology Agency (1993), p. 141.

the United Kingdom in 1987, with technology export receipts more
than twice the payments in 1991. (This means that Japan is already
in the 'wiggle' stage of TDP *vis-à-vis* the U K!) Japan still registers
technology trade deficits *vis-à-vis* the other three countries, but such
deficits have been declining (e.g. Japan's technology export receipts
were only about 4 per cent of its technology import payments *vis-à-
vis* Germany in 1975, but they grew to 53 per cent in 1991).

Similarly, disaggregation of Japan's technology trade balance by
industry reveals the differences in the sectoral patterns of such trade
balance (Figure 5.5). Japan's top net technology exporter is the
construction industry, followed by the steel industry, the stone,
clay and glass industry, and the automobile industry. Their appear-
ances as net technology exporters occurred in that order. The
chemical industry is near parity, oscillating around the balance
line. Indeed, these curves may be called 'meso-TDPs'. As will be
discussed below, the differences in the timing of the appearance of
surpluses are reflective of the progressive stages of structural
upgrading Japan has gone through.

STAGES OF STRUCTURAL UPGRADING, KNOWLEDGE
INTENSIFICATION AND FDI

Japan's catching-up development in the post-war period has been
both focused on the present and forward looking. It made the best

use of the prevailing economic conditions at a particular point in time, although it *constantly* endeavoured to move into and build *higher-income-elastic and technologically dynamic (higher-productivity)* industries. Early on, being abundant in labour and scarce in capital, Japan initially stressed light industry, notably textiles and sundries, so as to produce competitive exportable products in order to earn precious foreign exchange. Textiles were Japan's number one (most comparatively advantaged) exports back in the 1950s. Yet, whatever foreign exchange Japan earned was channelled first into the modernisation of heavy and chemical industries which Japan had already developed before the war. Consequently, steel came to replace textiles as Japan's leading exports before the start of the 1970s. But in the early 1970s Japan started to de-emphasise heavy and chemical industrialisation and targeted the development of higher value-added, components-intensive, assembly-based industries, notably automobiles and electronics. Most recently, moreover, Japan has been moving into high-technology, innovation-driven industries.

These series of industrial upgrading and competitiveness developments can be chronologically divided into four sequential stages of industrialisation (Ozawa 1991a, 1992, 1993):

Stage I   Expansion and reliance of labour-intensive ('Heckscher–Ohlin') manufacturing in textiles, sundries and other light industry goods as the leading export sector (1950 to the mid-1960s).

Stage II   Scale-economies-based modernisation of heavy and chemical ('undifferentiated Smithian') industries such as steel, aluminium, shipbuilding, petrochemicals and synthetic fibres as the leading growth sector (the late 1950s to the early 1970s).

Stage III Assembly-based, subcontracting-dependent (components-intensive) mass production of consumer durables ('differentiated Smithian' industries), such as automobiles and electric/electronics goods as the dominant sector (the late 1960s to the present).

Stage IV   Mechatronics-based, computer-aided flexible manufacturing of highly research and development (R&D) intensive ('Schumpeterian') goods, such as high-definition televisions, new materials, fine chemicals and advanced microchips (the mid-1980s onwards).

The transition from one phase to another has certainly not been clear cut but has overlapped in the above chronological approximations. Nor have any earlier (now comparatively disadvantaged) industries, say textiles, steel and shipbuilding, disappeared from Japan's industrial base; although their relative importance (output as a proportion of GDP) has declined, they still remain an integral part of Japan's manufacturing base. In fact, the recently arrived era of Schumpeterian industries is instrumental in revitalising the earlier-stage industries by way of introducing, say, 'super-fibres', 'super-metals', and 'super-ships'. For example, Japan's textile industry now enjoys (1994) a surprisingly high value-added ratio of 40 per cent.[5] Thus, Japanese firms remaining in the 'old' industries are surviving because of their technological upgrading, often benefiting from technological spillovers from the budding Schumpeterian industries.

Labour-driven development and the macro-motivated type of FDI

Although it may now be hard to imagine, Japan was a poor, low-wage Asian economy in the early postwar period. Japan initially did pursue labour-driven, export-oriented development as a way of creating local employment and exporting low-wage manufactures in order to earn badly needed foreign exchange. Indeed, back in the 1950s Japan started out as a low-cost subcontractor for the United States' 'big five' apparel makers: Regal Accessories, Republic Cellini (Hy Katz), Marlene, Spartan Mayro and CBS (Jack Clark), all southern US manufacturers who produced low-end products in Japan (Bonacich and Waller 1994). And in those days, most of the textiles imported into the United States were from Japan:

> The Far East was to the southern United States what the South was to the Northeast: an opportunity to cut costs. The early apparel importers worked almost exclusively with the large Japanese trading companies, especially Mitsui. *US importers would take sample products they had either brought or made themselves and have them made in Japan at a lower price.* As one source put it, 'We taught them how to make the garments, about thread tension, how to pack a carton, etc.' (italics added)
>
> (Bonacich and Waller 1994, p. 81)

Japan's labour-driven industrialisation in the 1950s, however, soon led to shortages of low-skilled workers and to wage increases, as predicted by the principle of increasing factor incongruity mentioned earlier. By the mid-1960s, for example, the ratio of job offers to job seekers in the under 19 years' old category (i.e. least-skilled workers) had come to exceed parity and reached 2 in 1966 and more than 5 in 1970 (Ozawa 1979, p. 79). Many factors contributed to this development, but most importantly, rising incomes and Japan's traditional system of corporate promotion based on educational background encouraged an ever-increasing number of young people to seek higher education.

As a consequence, labour-intensive manufacturing such as apparel had to be transplanted from Japan to neighbouring locations, such as Taiwan, Hong Kong and South Korea, where low-wage labour was then in abundant supply. The majority of Japanese overseas ventures thus transplanted were small and medium sized rather than large – and might even be considered 'immature' or 'aberrant' by Western standards at that time. The first phase of Japan's postwar outward FDI can be characterized as follows:

> given the influence of the peculiar macro-economic forces on the Japanese economy, the more competitive the industry (that is, the less technologically sophisticated the product and the smaller the firm-specific advantage), the greater the need so far for the Japanese [labour-intensive] manufacturing sector to resort to overseas production in developing countries – a phenomenon not envisioned in the prevailing monopolistic theory of direct foreign investment.
>
> (Ozawa 1979, p. 10)

Thus, this rather unique (at that time) macro-motivated 'elementary' type of FDI emerged as Japan ended the stage of labour-driven industrialisation and exporting.

Heavy and chemical industrialisation and FDI (first, resource-seeking and later, house-cleaning type)

While Japan was still in the labour-driven phase, it made incessant efforts to modernise and expand the heavy and chemical industries it had already built before World War II. It eagerly absorbed state-of-the-art technologies from the West throughout the 1950s and 1960s. During the period from 1952 to 1973, for example, the electric/electronic and non-electric machinery industries registered no less than 6,050 technology import contracts (licensing agreements), accounting for 44.1 per cent of the total, the chemical industry recorded 2,009 contracts or 14.6 per cent, and the steel and metal industries 1,252 contracts or 9.1 per cent – all together amounting to more than two-thirds (67.8 per cent) of the total secured by Japanese industry. Over the same period, Japan paid a total of $6.4 billion for technology imports.[6] Interestingly, *the amount of royalties and fees paid for technology imports has been much larger (about four times) every year than the amount of inward FDI.* In 1970, for example, $433 million of royalty payments as against $113 million of inward FDI; in 1975, $704 million as against $207 million; in 1980, $1,154 million as against $252 million, and so forth (see Appendix Tables 5.1 and 5.2). This clearly attests to the fact that throughout the postwar period Japan had an excellent capacity to absorb the latest technology mainly because of the already well-founded industrial base handed down from the pre-war era, especially in the heavy and chemical industries.

As a result of successful heavy and chemical industrialisation (mostly in the 1960s), Japan soon emerged as the world's leading producer and exporter of resource- and energy-intensive goods (such as steel, aluminium, ships, heavy machinery and chemicals). Indeed, Japan's steel industry emerged as a major net technology exporter in the early 1970s, next to the construction industry whose technological achievements were accomplished partly as a by-product of an enormous reconstruction and expansion of Japan's physical public infrastructure (highways, ports, warehouses, office buildings and residential dwellings) during the high-growth period of 1950–1974, as we saw in Figure 5.5. Since these industries are highly resource intensive, securing resource supplies from overseas became of paramount importance for resource-indigent Japan.

Early on, Japan relied on trade for importing vital resources but soon began to secure the supply sources by FDI. The resource-seeking type of FDI took two basic forms: (1) the 'invest and import' approach in which equity ownership, mostly partial, of foreign resources is sought in order to ensure import supplies; and (2) the 'loan and import' approach in which direct loans are extended in exchange for long-term supply contracts (Ozawa 1982). These investments involved large amounts of investment for minerals and energy resources such as iron and copper ores, bauxite, oil and natural gas. They were actively made especially in the early 1970s and immediately after the 1974 oil crisis, although Japanese industry had initiated such investment projects as early as the mid-1950s – usually with the majority of funds provided by the Japanese government.

The headlong rush to build up heavy and chemical industries in a small island economy soon led to the malignancies of pollution, congestion and ecological destruction, as they used industrial space extensively and were pollution prone. The high capital–labour ratio required in these industries also led to a continuous rise in wages, further weakening the labour-intensive sectors, a phenomenon akin to the so-called 'Dutch disease'.

The sheer impracticality of continuing the expansion of such resource-intensive and pollution-generating industries at home compelled Japanese industry to transplant abroad resource-processing activities such as ore smelting. Hence, what may be called a 'house-cleaning' type of FDI came to emerge in the 1970s. In addition, at the start of the 1970s a concerted national drive was launched towards less resource-consuming, more pollution-controlling and more knowledge-intensive industries – in other words, toward those industries with the great potentials of high growth elasticity and technological innovation.

Components-intensive, assembly-based manufacturing and FDI (first, trade-conflict-skirting, but later, rationalising, type)

Automobiles and auto-parts had long been targeted by the Japanese government as one of the most promising industries in which both higher labour productivity and technological progress were possible and whose products were highly income elastic. In fact, as early as 1948 the 'Basic Automobile Industry Policy' was announced for the purpose of laying a foundation for the modernisation of the auto industry, and in 1956 the 'Machine Industry Law' selected auto-parts as one of the 17 industries for promotion, which qualified for special funding from the Japan Development Bank.[7]

In addition to automobiles, another components-intensive, assembly-based industry that successfully emerged in Japan in the 1970s was consumer electronics. Both automobiles and consumer electronics came to capitalise very adroitly on Japan's dual industrial structure in which numerous small and medium-sized enterprises coexisted alongside a limited number of large-scale firms; the former specialised at the relatively labour-intensive end, while the latter operated at the relatively capital-intensive, scale-based end of vertically integrated manufacturing. This multi-layered structure proved to be serendipitously instrumental in producing the *networks* of cooperative subcontracting arrangements necessary for the vertically multi-layered assembly operations of automobiles and consumer electronics, which required myriad subassemblies, parts, components and accessories. In fact, the multi-layered industrial structure – composed of manufacturers of different sizes and different levels of technological sophistication ranging from large, modern cooperations down to very small, family-managed 'cottage-type' shops – is an *ideal* industrial structure for assembly-based industries.

It was also in Japan's auto industry (at Toyota Motor Co., to be exact) that a new manufacturing paradigm, 'lean' or 'flexible' production, originated as a superior alternative to Fordist mass production (Womack, Jones and Roos 1990). This technological progress came to be reflected in rising technology exports in the transport equipment (mostly, automobile) industry, as we saw in Figure 5.5.

But the very success of building up the efficient, large-scale (hence exploitative of scale/scope economies) hierarchies of assembly operations in highly differentiated automobiles and electronics goods, along with increased R&D and technological accumulation (which is reflected in rising technology exports), resulted in Japan's export drive and its ever-expanding trade surpluses. These developments in turn quickly led to trade conflicts and the sharp appreciation of the yen.

To circumvent protectionism, Japanese producers of automobiles and electronics goods began to replace their exports with local assembly operations in the Western markets, initially in North America, and then in Europe. At the same time, they also started to produce fairly standardised (hence, relatively low value-added) parts and components, or those that can be cost-effectively produced locally, both in low-wage developing countries, especially in Asia, and in high-wage Western countries – in the latter, with the installation of labour-cost-reducing and labour-quality-augmenting automation equipment mostly shipped from Japan. Thus, a network of Japanese overseas ventures began to *straddle* the advanced host countries and the developing host countries simultaneously. From the former they extract monopolistic ('Schumpeterian') rents and from the latter, monopsonistic ('Ricardian') rents. This is essentially a *transpositioning, across national borders, of the dual or multilayered structure that was originated domestically in those high-income-elastic industries* (Ozawa 1993).

Most recently, these assembly-based FDIs are going beyond the trade-conflict-skirting phase to reach a new phase of rationalised cross-border production and marketing. More and more sophisticated components are produced at home and supplied to the overseas manufacturing outposts. Similarly, low-end products (models) are assigned to production and marketing in the developing host countries, especially in Asia; some are increasingly imported back into Japan. Here, we can discern a *more refined or more sharply delineated and specialised form of trade* within an industry (i.e. intra-industry) or more appropriately within a firm (i.e. intra-firm trade) and within a production process (i.e. *inter-process trade*), a *new* form of trade made possible by the rationalisation-seeking type of FDI.

In the third wave of Japan's outward FDI, Japan also started to recycle overseas its huge financial surpluses generated from both high net domestic savings and net exports. Japanese banks and other financial institutions, awash with cash, eagerly financed their own advances as well as those of other Japanese MNEs (Ozawa and Hine 1993). All of a sudden, the list of the world's 10 largest banks, ranked in terms of assets, began to be monopolised by Japanese banks. In 1989, nine Japanese banks came to rank among the top 10.

Flexible production and the 'strategically networking (alliance-seeking)' phase of investment

In this latest and still incipient phase of structural upgrading of home and global operations, revolutionary changes have already occurred – and continue to unfold – in Japan's manufacturing system (supply side) and its consumption behaviour (demand side). On the supply side, Japanese industry has metamorphosed into an ever-more-efficient system characterised by computer-integrated manufacturing (CIM) and continues to push for new flexibility.

On the demand side, Japanese consumers are beginning to partake in the benefits of a strong yen as the domestic markets are deregulated and become more open to imports. In fact, the home markets are emerging as the major marketing outlets for Japan's own overseas ventures, which were once motivated to secure overseas markets. Moreover, Japanese entrepreneurs are nowadays innovating *inward* – first for domestic consumers, and then, when a new product has been successfully test-marketed at home, it is exported overseas and eventually produced overseas. Japan has, thus, become a major initiator of the product cycles of many new products (especially in consumer electronics). More and more product and process innovations are trickling down from Japan into overseas markets, on a par with the United States on which the product cycle theory of trade and FDI (Vernon 1966) was originally modelled.

Japan has come a long way and now stands on an equal – even superior in some areas – footing with the West to interact in terms of sophisticated technologies and demand conditions. Japanese firms thus possess a common capacity to engage in inter-corporate alliances as equal partners who can offer unique corporate assets. Consequently, they are increasingly engaged in numerous forms of strategic alliances with the most advanced Western firms (Ozawa 1994). Perhaps the most popularly known is the tripartite mega-alliance to design and produce 256-megabit dynamic random access memory chips, an alliance among the electronics giants from the United States, Japan, and Germany: IBM Corp., Toshiba Corp. and Siemens AG.

As a way of recapitulation, the preceding discussions are schematically summarised in Figure 5.6. It illustrates the links between the series of structural upgrading in Japan and its corresponding waves of outward FDI. Table 5.1 also sheds supplementary light on the structural characteristics of Japan's industrial dynamism discussed above. The interconnectedness of compositional changes in Japan's industrial structure, exports and FDI is discernible in the table. Light industries are represented by food, beverages, tobacco, textiles, apparel and leather products; heavy and chemical industries by chemicals, petroleum, coal products, basic and fabricated metal products; and components-intensive, assembly-based industries by machinery and transport equipment.

It is worth stressing that the waves of outward FDI shown in Figure 5.6 reveal *only* the *positive* ('above-parity') NOI portions of the meso-IDPs, since the negative ('below-parity') NOI portions have been substituted by the meso-TDPs in the Japanese case, a feature that matches the stylised pattern demonstrated earlier in Figure 5.2.b.

CONCLUSIONS

Dunning's IDP paradigm provides a thought-provoking framework to examine the Japanese experience, especially because the case of Japan seems so 'deviant' from the 'norm' set forth in the macro-IDP pattern. Yet if the IDP is interpreted as it is in this chapter, as a locus

Stages of industrial upgrading

   I   Labour-driven industrialisation
   II Heavy and chemical industrialisation
   III Assembly-based manufacturing
   IV Innovation-driven flexible manufacturing

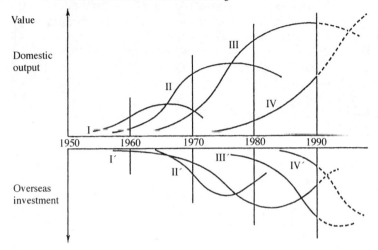

Phases of overseas investment

   I'   Low-wage-labour-seeking investment
   II' Resource-seeking and house-cleaning investment
   III' Assembly-transplanting investment
   IV' Strategically networking (alliance-seeking) investment

Figure 5.6 Japan's structural upgrading and outward FDI
Source: Ozawa (1993), p. 132.

of the cross-border learning curve, the Japanese case can fit into it
nicely, especially when it is supplemented by the TDP.

However, to fully understand how Japan's economic development
and its interactions with the West – and hence, with their MNEs –
have proceeded since the end of World War II, the stages perspective adopted is critical. In fact, the essential process of economic
development, particularly when it occurs relatively smoothly and
efficiently in an accelerated manner as it did in Japan, involves a
ratchet-like upscaling of the industrial structure stage by stage, each
stage being *compatible* with the prevailing factor endowments and
overall technological sophistication at home. In addition, inflows of
advanced technology (via licensing or FDI) become practically an
endogenous variable of economic growth in the context of an open-

Table 5.1 Structural changes in industry, exports and FDI (in percentages)

	Food, beverages and tobacco	Textiles, apparel and leather	Chemicals, petroleum and coal prod.	Basic and fabricated metal prod.	Machinery and transport equipment	Other manufac.
A Changes in industrial structure						
1955	42.5	11.9	7.2	10.7	7.3	20.3
1970	17.4	7.6	14.0	16.6	22.8	21.4
1980	14.4	6.1	13.8	16.3	31.1	18.4
1990	9.1	3.5	13.7	12.4	45.7	15.6
B Changes in exports						
1955	6.2	37.3	5.1	19.2	n.a.	n.a.
1970	3.4	12.5	6.4	19.7	46.3	11.8
1980	1.2	4.8	5.3	16.5	62.7	9.5
1990	0.6	2.5	5.5	6.8	74.9	9.6
C Changes in FDI						
First surge (1969–1973)	5.0	23.8	18.9	14.7	22.9	14.7
Second surge (1978–1985)	4.3	5.2	16.6	25.2	38.2	10.5
Third surge (1986–1989)	5.2	2.6	11.2	9.8	50.5	20.7

Sources: Changes in industrial structure are computed from data from the Economic Planning Agency, as reproduced in Pilat (1994, p. 282); changes in exports are from a table in Pilat (1994, p. 74); and changes in FDI from a table in Ozawa (1993, p. 136).

economy, interactive, derived process of development, given the internal capacity to absorb technology from abroad.[8] Similarly, outward FDI serves as a resource *reallocative* mechanism to assist structural upgrading at home, another endogenous variable of economic growth. In fact, this hints at a *new* growth theory, the theory of economic development which explicitly recognises the existence of MNEs as the generators/disseminators of industrial knowledge across national borders – that is, as *endogenous* variables within the system of global capitalism.

The Asian NIEs and the new NIEs (ASEAN-4) – and now the 'new' new NIEs (China, Vietnam and India) – have moulded their developmental strategies along the line of MNE-facilitated development in order to 'swing-up', so to speak, the U shaped portion of the IDP curve, meso and macro alike. But they, too, are moving up the ladder of structural upgrading stage by stage – from the bottom rung of labour-driven industrialisation to the next rung of heavy and chemical industrialisation and, then, on to that of assembly-based manufacturing, thereby generating the waves of the meso-IDPs in the process – a pattern analogous to a formation of flying geese. Japan seems to have been a role model for other East and South East Asian countries to emulate in their drive to economic modernisation. Indeed, this is one key driving force for the current flying-geese formation of tandem economic development in Pacific Asia.

NOTES

1 Akamatsu originally conceived the idea of the flying-geese paradigm back in the early 1930s by publishing a number of articles written in Japanese for *Shogyo Keizai Ronso*, Nagoya. Kiyoshi Kojima (1958, 1975, 1990), Akamatsu's chief protégé, has been most active in studying the interactive path of FDI-enhanced trade and economic growth involving both an advanced home country (a 'lead' goose) and the developing host countries ('follower' geese) by introducing the concept of pro-trade FDI (comparative advantage augmentation). This author also worked with Kojima in elaborating on the mechanisms of dynamic comparative advantage (Kojima and Ozawa 1984a, 1984b, 1985). Ozawa linked FDI specifically to the flying-geese framework of analysis by emphasising the role of TNCs as 'inter-stage arbitrageurs of economic development' (Ozawa 1991b, 1992, 1993). Early on, other scholars provided some empirical evidence for the existence of flying-geese patterns in a variety of industries, but their analyses were focused mainly on trade and not so much on FDI and the role of MNEs as a major linkage provider (*inter alia*, Rapp 1967, Ikema 1970, Matsumura 1975, Shinohara 1982, Yamazawa 1990).

2 As noted above, this trade augmentation process is stressed by Kiyoshi Kojima (1975).
3 Unfortunately, I have not been able to find reliable data on the exact values of Japan's inward and outward FDI in those earlier years.
4 Science and Technology Agency (1993), p. 348.
5 *Nikkei Weekly*, Nov. 7, 1994, p. 6.
6 Computed from Science and Technology Agency (1974).
7 For an analysis of the automobile industry in Japan, see, for example, Mutoh (1988).
8 One of my graduate students, Sergio Castello, emphasises this point in his Ph.D. dissertation (tentatively entitled 'Globalisation of small economies as strategic behaviours'), work in progress at Colorado State University.

Appendix Table 5.1 Japan's outward and inward FDI and GDP

	Outward FDI (in million dollars)	Inward FDI	NOI	GDP (in billion yen)	Population (in thousands)	GDP per capita (in thousand yen)
1961	104	47	57	19,337	95,180	203
1962	62	46	16	21,943	96,090	228
1963	125	88	37	25,113	97,080	258
1964	44	70	−26	29,541	98,110	301
1965	105	51	54	32,866	99,210	331
1966	101	43	62	38,170	99,980	382
1967	137	37	100	44,731	101,150	442
1968	228	93	135	52,975	102,290	518
1969	230	56	174	62,229	103,490	601
1970	397	113	284	73,345	104,670	701
1971	417	210	207	80,701	106,100	761
1972	852	165	687	92,394	107,760	859
1973	2,200	−28	2,228	112,498	109,100	1,031
1974	1,839	213	1,626	134,244	110,570	1,214
1975	1,976	207	1,769	148,327	111,940	1,325
1976	1,871	89	1,782	166,573	113,090	1,473
1977	1,725	31	1,694	185,622	114,170	1,626
1978	2,584	10	2,574	204,404	115,190	1,775
1979	2,665	290	2,375	221,547	116,160	1,907

Appendix Table 5.1 (continued)

	Outward FDI (in million dollars)	Inward FDI	NOI	GDP (in billion yen)	Population (in thousands)	GDP per capita (in thousand yen)
1980	2,993	252	2,741	240,176	117,060	2,052
1981	4,804	151	4,653	257,963	117,900	2,188
1982	4,448	492	3,956	270,601	118,730	2,278
1983	4,198	403	3,795	281,767	119,540	2,357
1984	5,660	14	5,646	300,543	120,310	2,498
1985	7,592	705	6,887	320,419	121,050	2,647
1986	15,196	440	14,756	334,609	121,670	2,750
1987	23,769	463	23,306	348,425	122,260	2,850
1988	35,669	-289	35,958	371,429	122,780	3,025
1989	49,119	-286	49,405	395,844	123,260	3,212
1990	44,904	1,124	43,780	426,559	123,610	3,451
1991	23,617	2,202	21,415	451,998	124,040	3,644

Sources: Outward and inward investment is from the Bank of Japan, *Kokusai Shushi Tokei Geppo* (Monthly Statistics of Balance of International Payments), various issues; gross domestic product from the Bank of Japan, *Economic Statistical Annual*, various issues; and population from Economic Planning Agency, *Keizai Hakusho* (White Paper on the Economy), 1992.

Appendix Table 5.2 Japan's technology trade (in million dollars)

Year	Imports (A)	Exports (B)	B/A
1963	136	7	0.05
1964	156	15	0.15
1965	166	17	0.10
1966	192	19	0.10
1967	239	27	0.11
1968	314	34	0.11
1969	368	46	0.13
1970	433	59	0.14
1971	488	60	0.12
1972	572	74	0.13
1973	715	88	0.12
1974	718	108	0.15
1975	704	143	0.20
1976	796	174	0.22
1977	891	185	0.21
1978	851	204	0.24
1979	1,022	258	0.25
1980	1,154	308	0.27
1981	1,535	432	0.28
1982	1,851	590	0.32
1983	2,047	587	0.29
1984	2,400	734	0.31
1985	2,560	784	0.31
1986	2,502	700	0.28
1987	2,601	882	0.34
1988	3,136	1,024	0.33
1989	3,692	1,398	0.38
1990	4,484	1,841	0.41
1991	4,272	2,021	0.47
1992	4,691	1,992	0.42

Source: compiled from various issues of Science and Technology Agency, *Kagaku Gijutsu Hakusho* (White Paper on Science and Technology), Tokyo: Finance Ministry Printing Office.

BIBLIOGRAPHY

Akamatsu, K. (1961) 'A theory of unbalanced growth in the world economy', *Weltwirtschaftliches Archiv* 86, No. 2: 196–215.

―――― (1962) 'A historical pattern of economic growth in developing countries', *The Developing Economies 1*, preliminary issue (March–August): 1–23.

Arisawa, H. (ed.) (1967) *Nihon Sanggyo Hyakunenshi* (100-year History of Japanese Industry), Vol. 1., Tokyo: Nihon Keizaisha.

Bonacich, E. and Waller, D. (1994) 'Mapping a global industry: apparel production in the Pacific rim triangle', in E. Bonacich *et al.* (eds) *Global Production: the Apparel Industry in the Pacific Rim*, Philadelphia: Temple University Press: 21–41.

Dunning, J. H. (1981) 'Explaining the international direct investment position of countries: toward a dynamic or developmental approach', *Weltwirtschaftliches Archiv* 11, No. 1: 30–64.

―――― and Narula, R. (1994) *Transpacific Foreign Direct Investment and the Investment Development Path: The Record Assessed*, South Carolina Essays in International Business, No. 10 (May).

Ikema, M. (1970) *Import Dependence in the Australian Economy*, unpublished Ph.D. thesis, Australian National University.

Kojima, K. (1958) 'Shihon chikuseki to kokusai bungyo (capital accumulation and international division of labour)', in K. Kojima (ed.) *Keizaiseisaku to Kokusai Boeki* (Economic Policy and International Trade), Tokyo: Shunjusha: 443–496.

―――― (1975) 'International trade and foreign investment: substitutes or complements', *Hitotsubashi Journal of Economics* 16, No. 1 (June): 1–12.

―――― (1985) *Nihon-no Kaigai Chokusets Toshi* (Japanese Direct Investment Abroad: An Economic Analysis), Tokyo: Bunshindo.

―――― (1990) *Japanese Direct Investment Abroad*, Tokyo: International Christian University, Monograph Series 1.

―――― and Ozawa, T. (1984a) 'Micro and macro economic models of direct foreign investment', *Hitotsubashi Journal of Economics* 25 , No. 1 (June): 1–20.

―――― (1984b) *Japan's General Trading Companies: Merchants of Economic Development*, Paris: OECD.

―――― (1985) 'Toward a theory of industrial restructuring and dynamic comparative advantage', *Hitotsubashi Journal of Economics* 26 , No. 2: 135–145.

Mason, M. (1992) *American Multinationals and Japan: The Political Economy of Japanese Capital Controls, 1899–1980*, Cambridge, MA: Harvard University Press.

Matsumura, S. (1975) *Nihon Sen'i Sangyo no Hatten to Tenbo* (Japan's Textile Industry: Growth and Prospects), Tokyo: Chiseido.

Mutoh, H. (1988) 'The automotive industry', in R. Komiya, M. Okuno, and K. Suzumura (eds) *Industrial Policy of Japan*, Tokyo: Academic Press: 307–331.

Ozawa, T. (1974) *Japan's Technological Challenge to the West, 1950–1974: Motivation and Accomplishment*, Cambridge, MA: MIT Press.

―――― (1979) *Multinationalism, Japanese-Style: The Political Economy of Outward Dependency*, Princeton, NJ: Princeton University Press.

―――― (1982) 'A newer type of foreign investment in third world resource development', *Rivista Internazionale di Sienze Economiche e Commerciali* 29, No. 12 (December): 1133–1151.

—— (1985) 'Macroeconomic factors affecting Japan's technology inflows and outflows', in N. Rosenberg and C. Frischtak (eds) *International Technology Transfer: Concepts, Measures, and Comparisons*, New York: Praeger, 222–254.

—— (1991a) 'Japanese multinationals and 1992', in B. Burgenmeier and J.L. Mucchielli (eds) *Multinationals and Europe 1992: Strategies for the Future*, London & New York: Routledge: 135–154.

—— (1991b) 'The dynamics of Pacific Rim industrialization: how Mexico can join the Asian flock of "flying geese"', in R. Roett (ed.) *Mexico's External Relations in the 1990s*, Boulder & London: Rienner: 129–154.

—— (1992) 'Foreign direct investment and economic development', *Transnational Corporations* 1, No. 1 (February): 27–54.

—— (1993) 'Foreign direct investment and structural transformation: Japan as a recycler of market and industry', *Business & the Contemporary World* 5 , No. 2: 129–150.

—— (1994) 'Technical alliances of Japanese firms: an industrial restructuring account of the latest phase of capitalist development', in J. Niosi (ed.) *New Technology Policy, Technical Alliances, and Social Innovations*, London: Pinter: 150–169.

—— and Hine, S. (1993) 'A strategic shift from international to multinational banking: a macro-developmental paradigm of Japanese banks *qua* multinationals', *Banca Nazionale del Lavoro Quarterly Review*, No. 186 (September): 251–274.

Pilat, D. (1994) *The Economics of Rapid Growth: The Experience of Japan and Korea*, Aldershot, Hants: Edward Elgar.

Rapp, W. V. (1967) 'Theory of changing trade patterns under economic growth', *Yale Economic Essays*, Fall: 69–135.

Rostow, W. W. (1960) *The Stages of Economic Growth: A Non-communist Manifesto*, Cambridge: Cambridge University Press.

Science and Technology Agency (1974) *Kagaku Gijutsu Hakusho* (White Paper on Science and Technology), Tokyo: Finance Ministry Printing Office.

—— (1993) *Kagaku Gijutsu Yoran* (Statistics on Science and Technology), Tokyo: Finance Ministry Printing Office.

—— (1994) *Kagaku Gijutsu Hakusho* (White Paper on Science and Technology), Tokyo: Finance Ministry Printing Office.

Shinohara, M. (1982) *Industrial Growth, Trade, and Dynamic Patterns in the Japanese Economy*, Tokyo: University of Tokyo Press.

Smith, A. (1776) *An Inquiry into the Nature and Causes of the Wealth of Nations*, London: Routledge, republished New York: E.P. Dutton, 1908.

Vernon, R. (1966) 'International investment and international trade in the product cycle', *Quarterly Journal of Economics* 80, No. 2: 190–207.

Womack, J.P., Jones, D.T. and Roos, D. (1990) *The Machine That Changed The World*, New York: Macmillan.

Yamazawa, I. (1990) *Economic Development and International Trade: the Japanese Model*, Honolulu: East-West Center.

Chapter 6

New Zealand
The development of a resource-rich economy

Michèle Akoorie

INTRODUCTION

The objective of this chapter, simply stated, is to apply the concept of the investment development path (IDP) to New Zealand. New Zealand is currently in the latter phases of Stage 3, but, as might be expected from an economy that is resource rich, continues to have a large negative net outward investment position, given the high levels of inward foreign direct investment (FDI). Nonetheless, outward FDI has been seen to increase in importance in the past decade or so. Table 6.1 shows the growth in inward direct investment (expressed as a percentage of GDP). The corresponding growth in outward direct investment in this period suggests that New Zealand may be rapidly moving towards the latter stages in the IDP. However, more recent data showing that the growth of outward FDI is complemented by corresponding increases in the amount of inward investment suggest that New Zealand is following the pattern characteristic of resource-rich countries, where inward investment will always be higher than outward investment.

The analytical framework used here has been derived from Dunning and Narula (1994). The framework suggests that there are two catalysts for change which will affect a country's propensity to invest abroad or attract outward direct investment. These catalysts are, first, non-FDI-induced change that is exogenous to firms but endogenous to countries. These changes reflect changes in government policy thus determining the way in which markets and resources are organized. Second, FDI-induced change refers to changes in the strategies of multinational firms which influence the nature of OLI in that period and lead to changes in the configuration of the OLI in consecutive periods.

Table 6.1 Inward and outward FDI, New Zealand 1963–1993

Years	I/GDP	O/GDP	Net FDI/GDP
1963–1965	0.94	0.05	0.88
1966–1968	0.69	0.62	0.66
1969–1971	1.25	0.12	1.22
1972–1974	1.11	0.11	0.99
1975–1977	2.04	0.24	1.79
1978–1980	2.79	0.57	2.21
1981–1983	3.15	2.83	0.32
1984–1986	4.27	1.72	2.54
1987–1989	3.96	6.45	−2.28
1990–1992	21.90	20.36	1.54
1993*	39.31	−19.08	1.13

Notes: GDP at constant 1982/1983 prices.
Source: Calculated from Balance of Payments Statistics New Zealand, 1963–1993.
* 1993 only

Static changes (whether FDI or non-FDI induced) during a particular time affect the operations of firms *during* that period. However, dynamic changes refer to changes that may occur during a particular period which affect the *subsequent* operations of firms. Thus, for each period it is the interactions between static and dynamic changes and interactions between government policy (non-FDI changes) and the strategies of MNEs (FDI) which determine the relative configurations of OLI during the next stage of the cycle. By using a longitudinal approach, the development of the investment path in relation to industry structure can be explained more clearly. Longitudinal studies will identify the changes *within* a given period that will affect the strategies of firms in a *subsequent* period.

The remainder of the chapter is structured in the following manner. The IDP of New Zealand is examined in four periods. The first period provides the background of the development of the New Zealand economy to about 1938. The country-specific advantages for New Zealand in the early phase of FDI investment are briefly identified. The second period from 1938 to the late 1960s is equivalent to Stage 2 of the IDP. In this phase the non-FDI influence of government policy is significant in influencing the strategies of MNEs. The third period, from about 1970 to 1984, shows how FDI influences become more important as determinants of change in the OLI configuration of firms. The fourth period, from

1984 until 1994, examines how shifts in government policy have influenced the growth in the rate of both inward and outward investment. The changing dynamics within this period have accelerated the rate and progress of the IDP. A summary and conclusions on the applicability of the IDP to New Zealand conclude the chapter.

1870–1938: OUTWARD LOOKING, EXPORT ORIENTED

A long-term perspective on the world economy from the 1880s suggests that during this period there was significant economic integration between foreign direct investors from 'mother countries' and their colonial interests. The motivation for this investment was to provide raw materials for the growing industrial output of the countries of Europe and Great Britain. Subsistence agricultural systems in many colonies in the tropical zones of Africa and Asia were replaced by plantation crops producing export commodities. The success of these agricultural activities depended on effective organisation (provided by expatriate managers), stable administrative systems, an efficient physical infrastructure and good communications systems, all of which were provided, with varying degrees of competence, by the colonising powers.

The development of the pastoral base of the New Zealand economy fitted into this colonial system of integration from the mid-1860s onwards, with some distinct variations on the colonial model. These variants were, first, New Zealand was located in a temperate agricultural zone, where the pastoral base of the economy had potential for development, and second, FDI (in the frozen meat industry) occurred at a very early stage, from the 1880s onwards. The third variant was the role played by the colonial government in encouraging the development of agricultural processing industries, through the establishment of research and regulatory institutions.

1938–1967: EXPORT ORIENTED, IMPORT SUBSTITUTING

External dependency

By 1920 the pattern of New Zealand's economic structure was established. The economy was highly dependent on income derived from the exports of a pastoral economy, such as wool, frozen meat and dairy products (Fisher 1932). The returns to producers depended on the prices received for agricultural products in one principal market, Britain. Investment in productive capacity was dependent on growth in demand while returns to farmers depended on the margin between cost of production and prices received. The location advantages emphasised, on the input side, factor cost and quality, and on the output side, market size, growth and accessibility.

The Depression of the 1930s confirmed the instability of the economy with its high degree of dependence on exports of primary commodities (Simkin 1951). The effects of falling prices for export commodities were distributed evenly in the economy, since the service and manufacturing sectors of the economy depended on income generated from farm receipts. The instability of the economy was compounded by the effects of government borrowing for economic and structural development. From 1840 to 1887 New Zealand imported capital and built the basis for foreign debt. From 1887 to 1934 further borrowing was needed to finance the interest payable on previous loans (Rosenberg 1961).

Government from the mid-1930s onwards increasingly exerted its influence over the economy. The policies developed were, like earlier policies, pragmatic and piecemeal in character. Gradually, a pattern of insulation was established which emphasised stability rather than expansion. The underlying assumption of government policy was that the economic future of the country depended on the export of primary products (Hawke 1985). Despite the variations in export prices, increasing demand induced by wartime shortages, and the bulk purchasing arrangements between the British and New Zealand governments until 1954, confirmed the apparent long term viability of the export sector. The long term trend of increasing incomes until the 1970s also seemed to confirm the wisdom of policies that supported the agricultural sector of the economy. (GDP per capita at constant 1982/1983 prices increased from $NZ 17,068 in 1962 to $NZ 29,204 in 1976. From 1977 to 1979, however, GDP per capita actually declined.)

Government intervention in the international trade sector occurred in two major ways. First, the marketing of dairy products, meat and wool was brought under the control of Agricultural Producer Boards, with control shared between farmers and government. Initially, the function of the Producer Boards was to establish price stabilisation mechanisms for commodity prices but their role was equally if not more importantly to defend and expand markets.

The Agricultural Producer Boards had access to preferential

government funding. The development of O advantages of the New Zealand Dairy Board was encouraged through government intervention since the Board operated on behalf of dairy cooperatives who controlled the output. The Board also internalized the international marketing and financial functions of the dairy industry: the Dairy Board was increasingly involved in organising international trade. The O advantages of the dairy industry were also developed through government support in funding government departments and research institutes. In the dairy industry much of the technology was specific to New Zealand's production conditions and the role of the private sector in R&D was relatively minor. The relatively high level of education of farmers encouraged the absorption of this investment. Estimates of total spending on agricultural technology over the last fifty years suggest that it had generated an annual average rate of return of approximately 30 per cent. This in turn led to very high total factor productivity in agriculture (Bollard 1993).

The OLI configuration of the agricultural industry in New Zealand was influenced by a significant degree of government intervention. This is most evident through government activities in regulating and controlling the operations of firms. By intervening in the marketing and pricing arrangements the government had direct influence over both domestic and foreign producers. Overseas producers could not directly participate in the dairy industry unless they were land owners, since farmers owned the dairy cooperatives. In the meat industry domestic and foreign processors were subject to quotas, as well as output and pricing controls. However, in certain sectors such as frozen meat processing which required extensive capital investment, foreign investment was encouraged. Government policy, however, supported the use of regulations to ensure that domestic companies were not to be unduly disadvantaged relative to foreign investors.

From 1938 the government set up a system of import licensing and exchange controls. This represented a decision, supported by popular sentiment, that the direction of the economy should be determined less by events overseas and more by the choice of New Zealanders (Sutch 1966). One of the initiating events was the decline in official reserves, occasioned by the government's use of central bank credit to maintain dairy farmers' incomes and finance housing programmes. Import licensing was introduced as a crisis measure but soon became presented as a desirable new policy

(Hawke 1981). Throughout the period of import licensing, the justification for its use was that it would foster the development of domestic industries. Import licensing and exchange controls thus became important for sheltering industrial profits and jobs although this was not their original intention.

Until 1964 there were no statutory regulations governing inward FDI in New Zealand. Successive governments in the postwar era had adopted an essentially passive attitude towards inward FDI. Government departmental reports favoured inflows of FDI if it was accompanied by technical knowledge (Deane 1967). The Overseas Takeover Regulations (1964) established the threshold for approvals at 25 per cent. Restrictions on farmland acquisition by overseas interests were introduced, except approvals for acquisitions that would benefit the development of agricultural industries. The general requirements established a more selective approach to overseas investment that emphasised access to technology not available locally, the development of export markets, the balance of payments effects and the cost of servicing investments.

The alternative to using inward FDI to upgrade local manufacturing would have been to use loan capital and import overseas technology. However appropriate macro-organizational policies would have been needed to create the human capital base capable of absorbing technology innovation. New Zealand had achieved high levels of universal education, though compulsory secondary schooling was only introduced in 1944. However, the majority of the population did not have any form of tertiary educational qualifications, since the tight labour market rendered it almost unnecessary. The education system, based on the British system, was geared towards the preparation of a small, eligible minority for undergraduate university education (Dunstall 1981). Government research institutes emphasising agricultural science carried out postgraduate activity. Macro-organisational policies were not therefore geared towards the development of an indigenous manufacturing base for the economy.

The quantitative restrictions placed on imports during this period encouraged foreign firms to establish local production units, in a market which they had previously serviced through exports. Government policy favoured import substitution as a means of reducing dependency on imports and to develop the basis of an industrialised economy. Import substitution and small market size encouraged the formation of high cost units of suboptimal size, creating inefficiencies, since import substitution favoured the exchange of high cost (small scale) local production for (low cost) more efficiently produced imports. Import substitution also enabled foreign firms to build up oligopolistic positions in certain industry sectors, since there was no specific monopoly legislation to prevent this. However, price controls and legislation against restrictive trade practices were used to moderate the effects of industry dominance.

Industry structure

The industry structure that developed in the postwar period can be classified into four major categories. The first category consisted of the processing industries associated with the agricultural sector. Processing technologies were developed indigenously to cover a wide range of activities, including yarn spinning, carpet weaving, high and medium density fibre board production, fruit and vegetable processing, butter making and dairy food technology. These processing technologies were developed and used by a wide range of organisations, a few large private ones, producer boards and farmer cooperatives. In this sector there were generally low levels of foreign ownership except for the meat freezing industry. By the mid-1950s foreign-owned firms accounted for nearly 50 per cent of New Zealand's total frozen meat exports (Roche 1993a).

The second category included other resource-based industries such as fishing, wood processing (using the extensive exotic wood plantings of *Pinus radiata* that had been established with state support during the 1930s), electricity generation and tanning of leathers. The incentives to develop modern extraction methods in these sectors were limited. Market potential was unknown and processing was complicated. In these sectors technological development was slow and indigenous technologies did not emerge. Development took place only by importing technologies or joint ventures (as with fishing) or by exporting the unprocessed materials for further processing by ultimate end users.

The third major category was the small but diverse manufacturing sector, built on the base of a fabricating economy, established mainly in the nineteenth century. Most firms were locally owned with limited vertical or inter-industry integration. A wide range of intermediate and consumer goods were produced on a small scale at relatively high cost for a geographically dispersed local market and protected by trade barriers from foreign import penetration (Bollard

1993). Industrial technology was either derivative or dated or both, since firms had little incentive to acquire overseas technologies nor ready access to such technology. The average size of industrial firms was therefore small; firms employing more than 100 people accounted for under 4 per cent of the total establishments over the period 1925–1964. More than half of the industrial establishments employed ten people or less (Hawke 1981).

The subsidiary operations of MNEs formed the fourth major grouping category. Import restrictions prompted the establishment of most MNE subsidiaries in New Zealand since the introduction of quantitative restrictions on imports (Deane 1970). Those companies principally affected by import controls were electrical machinery and chemical companies, particularly pharmaceutical and paint companies. A substantial increase in the flow of inward FDI occurred in the 1950s following the reinforcement of import controls. Industry categories included consumer goods, chemicals, metal products and machinery, with Australian and British investment predominating. The only significant period for the establishment of US manufacturing operations was before the 1950s. Deane (1975) suggests that the prevailing licensing system in the postwar period was heavily biased in favour of sources from within the Commonwealth, especially Britain. Evidence from the late 1950s suggests that more foreign manufacturing firms were established in New Zealand in the 1950s than in any preceding comparable period.

Foreign-owned firms were generally larger in scale than New Zealand-owned firms. Over 50 per cent of the 147 foreign-owned firms surveyed by Deane (1970) employed over 200 people. Value of gross output and value added per person varied across the range of surveyed industries, but certainly in paint, pharmaceutical and other chemicals, where New Zealand firms possessed few O advantages, the value added was consistently higher than for New Zealand manufacturing. The inherent problems associated with small size and high costs of local production affected both the export behaviour of subsidiary firms and their capacity to utilise parent technologies and manufacturing methods. The principal reason for the establishment of foreign firms in New Zealand was the exploitation of existing O advantages rather than the acquisition of advantages. This is consistent with research findings in other countries during the same period (Dunning and Narula 1994).

The growth of FDI

From 1938 until the late 1950s New Zealand was in Stage 2 of the IDP, characterised by rising inward investment, accompanied by low or negligible outward investment. The role of FDI-induced changes in changing the configuration of the OLI variables in this period may be summarised as follows. Foreign subsidiaries exploited existing O advantages in the domestic market. The competitive advantages over local firms were the availability of technical assistance, internalisation capabilities through sourcing components and the ability to access both foreign and domestic sources of capital. The L advantages offered to foreign firms were no different from those offered to domestic firms in manufacturing. Foreign firms were certainly disadvantaged compared with domestic firms in their inability to access some L specific assets, such as natural resources. This can be viewed as an economic benefit foregone, evidenced by the slow rate of technological development and economic contribution of nascent industries such as wood technology, leather and fishing.

Horizontal integration, through the acquisition of competitor firms, was a natural consequence of small market size where the potential to make profits from exporting was limited. Industrial concentration was evident in many industries, such as tobacco, carpet making and packaging (Deane 1970). In these industries the increased volume of business required to allow the use of large scale methods of production was achieved by the acquisition of smaller units and subsequent rationalisation. In the absence of macro-organizational policies of government in the education and training of a technically competent managerial cadre, it is evident from the higher percentage of professional and technical staff employed by foreign firms compared with local firms that foreign investment in manufacturing created the nucleus of a skills base in manufacturing in New Zealand.

Government protection policies in the traditional agricultural industries, apart from the meat industry, favoured domestic over overseas producers by restricting access to resources. Government policy had also emphasised the indigenous development of created assets through public funding of agricultural technology. The competitive advantages of the New Zealand Dairy Board in marketing and organisational structures were protected from foreign investment through statutory legislation.

1967–1984: NEW FORMS OF EXPORT ORIENTATION, IMPORT SUBSTITUTION

The incentive to diversify the basis of the economy in the 1960s was prompted by several changes in the economic environment. These changes had a direct impact on the New Zealand economy, since the effect of declines in export receipts for the major commodity products led to a decline in farm income and consequently domestic demand. The full impact of these changes had, during the 1970s, been mitigated by subsidy and stabilization policies, financed by external borrowing. Rigidities in the economic structure, resulting from decades of regulatory controls, made structural adjustment to accommodate external realities difficult (Douglas and Callen 1987).

One change in the external environment was the increased self-sufficiency of agricultural production in Britain, culminating in New Zealand's acceptance of quotas on the import of dairy products in 1961. This development preceded the entry of Britain into the EC in 1973, with the important proviso that New Zealand's agricultural exports were a special case although subject to declining quotas which were to be renegotiated regularly (Monetary and Economic Council 1970). Even if access to the British market had continued at the pre-1960 levels, the changes in the market demand and food distribution patterns in Britain throughout the 1970s suggested that the future of bulk processed products from New Zealand was uncertain (Condliffe 1969).

Administrative controls on export output from New Zealand were the political manifestations of a more general global shift in the pattern of world trade. New Zealand's trade patterns, with a high dependence on agricultural products, were characteristic of world trade patterns of the nineteenth century. Postwar trade had grown most strongly in manufactured goods, while the percentage share of agriculture in world trade was declining compared with both manufacturing and services (Crocombe et al. 1991). The policy responses by New Zealand's government during the 1960s regarding this situation were related to increasing exports as a means of correcting persistent balance of payments deficits, rather than increasing import restrictions, or the unpalatable alternative of internal retrenchment. While the trend from the 1950s to the 1970s was towards a positive trade balance, it was generally outweighed by a deficit on invisible items so the current account balance was generally in deficit. This was addressed through three primary means. First, government policy placed an increasing emphasis on manufactured exports. This was to be achieved through the introduction of export incentive schemes. The policies favoured domestic firms since 40 per cent of foreign firms operating in New Zealand were restricted from exporting (Deane 1970). Those who were not subjected to restrictions generally had low exporting levels. Producing for a small domestic market and protected by import barriers, foreign subsidiaries in New Zealand were simply not competitive on world markets. Second, taxation incentives were introduced to encourage the export potential of 'new' products such as deer (venison and velvet), wine, cashgora, thoroughbred stock, kiwi fruits and soft fruits. Third, government policy favoured geographical diversification of export markets.[1] Producer Boards were encouraged to expand their existing range of markets, create new markets as well as emphasising higher value-added products. Within the traditional agricultural industries, dairy technology developed to include dried milk derivatives (for industrial and consumer use). Technology development was geared towards the use of milk-based products as a food ingredient as well as its traditional use as a consumer product. The response in the meat industry was more conservative, since the industry was preoccupied in upgrading its plants to meet EEC hygiene requirements, which were conveniently disguised import restrictions (Roche 1993a).

There was some relaxation of import restrictions for domestic firms in the sense that increased licence allocations were linked to export performance. The continuation of import licensing together with export incentives effectively disguised the underlying problem, which was the continual misallocation of resources. The preliminary steps towards the establishment of a free trade arrangement with Australia were taken by concluding the New Zealand Australia Free Trade Agreement (NAFTA). This agreement provided for a preferential trading arrangement of a very limited range of products between New Zealand and Australia.[2]

Evidence from survey findings suggests that changes in government policy were effective in stimulating structural change (Le Heron 1980) by encouraging initial export efforts. However, since firms were insulated against the full cost of exporting, this suggests that without export promotion, exporting might only be a transient activity, as later research showed (Akoorie and Enderwick 1992). Most firms in this study had been exporting for less than five years. Nevertheless, some fast rates of growth in exports of manufactured goods were achieved in the late 1960s and early 1970s stimulated by the devaluation of the New Zealand dollar. However, increased rates of protection to Australian industries following the oil crisis of 1973 meant that the proportion of New Zealand industry that exported actually declined in the mid-1970s. Between 1971/1972 and 1975/1976 manufactured exports increased from 6 per cent to 12 per cent of total, of which one-quarter consisted of locally produced aluminium (using hydro-electric power at the Tiwai Point smelter).

There were several reasons why the reallocation of resources in the economy was a relatively slow process. First, coordination between the government and private sector occurred through negotiations and consensus. This process of indicative planning led to the establishment of several sector councils, one of which was the New Zealand Planning Council. The role of the Council was to inject more concern for long range planning into the routines of government administration (Report of the Task Force 1976). However, the Council was concerned with a wide range of issues including equity and social matters and economic issues. Attention to longer term issues gave way to a more readily achievable consensus on output targets for existing sectors.

Second, the impetus for a commitment to a change of direction was not sustained when foreign exchange was plentiful in the early 1970s, so that the need for a more coordinated approach to export promotion was less pressing. The effects of rising oil prices on the economy meant that consensus on the future direction of the economy was difficult to achieve when the total economy was expanding less rapidly than had been customary over a long period (Hawke 1981). From the 1970s onwards, however, there was a significant change in the composition of New Zealand's economic base, which reflected declining rates of investment in agriculture. This was the result of the increasing importance accorded to the industrial sector, while doubts grew over the long term prospects of farming. In 1936 the share of agriculture in the composition of GDP was about 36 per cent. By 1976/1977 this had shrunk to less than half this value. The share of manufacturing had increased only marginally, while the share of services in the composition of GDP had increased to more than 50 per cent of the total. The share of the non-traded sector (since it included the government sector) was considerable. By 1981 Australia was the principal destination for New Zealand's manufactured goods, taking 39.4 per cent of the total (BIE 1983).

The growth of inward FDI

From the 1970s onwards the amount of inward investment gradually increased from $NZ 130 million in 1970 to $NZ 343 million in 1980. These changes reflect the underlying shifts that were occurring in the economic structure during the period 1967–1984.

The increasing amount of inward investment can be explained by the increased demand in the New Zealand market for consumer durables of more technological complexity and the importation of advanced overseas technology in a series of large scale public sector energy projects in industries such as synthetic fuels, fertiliser production, oil refining, electricity generation, aluminium and steel production. The objective of government policy in the case of fuels was to make New Zealand self-sufficient in energy sources, a response to the oil crises of the 1970s. The resulting large scale development projects also had a strong political connotation since they could be used for boosting employment in politically attractive constituencies. Since most of these projects were in non-tradable sectors the potential for technology spin-offs was not immediately apparent. However, integration of local construction firms in large project development did have the effect of stimulating the O advantages of engineering and construction firms that were later utilised in outward FDI infrastructural development projects in the Pacific and South East Asia area (Crocombe *et al.* 1991). Similarly, the sale of state-owned assets in the energy sector to Fletcher Challenge Ltd, a domestic industrial conglomerate, enabled that firm to acquire O advantages that were subsequently used in the expansion of energy interests in the production of industrial methanol.

During this period, Australia became an increasingly important source of direct investment for New Zealand, equalling from 1971 the investment flows from Britain, while the proportion of investment from North America and other countries also increased. The source of investment flows became increasingly global rather than regional (BIE 1983).

Government policy in the development of regional trade arrangements with Australia and export incentives encouraged outward investment by New Zealand firms, in the manufacturing sector. Investment by both Australia and New Zealand in each other's pastoral-based production sectors was insignificant, since both countries produced a similar range of commodities. A memorandum of understanding in the Closer Economic Relations (CER) agreement formalised an arrangement that the two countries would continue to protect these respective sectors. Their relative importance fluctuated between 4 per cent and 8 per cent over the period 1969–1970 and 1979–1980. The share of manufacturing in the total level of Australian FDI in New Zealand generally exceeded 50 per cent, while the share of Australian investment in services was around 35 to 40 per cent with the levels of investment in services increasing relative to manufacturing by 1980 (BIE 1983).

Inflows of FDI to New Zealand (relative to total investment and as a proportion of GDP) has accounted for a smaller proportion of capital formation than it has in Australia, with inward FDI in New Zealand having averaged 9.0 per cent of private investment and 5.7 per cent of total investment from 1951 to 1982. By contrast foreign investment in Australia averaged 11.5 per cent of private investment and 7.3 per cent of total investment over the same period (Vautier 1984).

Further analysis by industry sector shows the sectoral differences between patterns of investment by Australian and New Zealand firms. Investment by Australian firms in New Zealand industries over the period 1969 to 1980 showed that 62.9 per cent of the total investment over the period was in manufacturing and 41.6 per cent was in services (BIE 1983). No significant investment occurred in the primary sector while within the manufacturing sector investment fluctuated over the period. Net inflows were negative in six out of twelve industries listed under the manufacturing classification (Vautier 1984).

This suggests that for Australian firms an important motivation for investing in New Zealand was to exploit the L advantages of the market. This is supported by empirical evidence from a BIE survey of Australian firms. For firms investing in the pre-1970 period (from 1938) their principal motivation was to take advantage of the expected growth in the host market. From 1970 onwards the frequency with which firms cited L advantages declined in favour of the exploitation of patents and know-how developed in Australia, which was a principal motive of nearly 40 per cent of firms. This is consistent with the post-1970 pattern in New Zealand of the gradual opening up of the economy. Internalisation factors are consistent with the pattern of vertical integration shown in the establishment of wholesale and retail affiliates in New Zealand (BIE 1983). This finding supports the process of the IDP, that firms will undertake investment in industries in which they have an O advantage in countries that are lower down on the IDP. Australia as a Stage 4 country had O advantages in manufacturing compared with New Zealand.

By contrast, the motivations cited for New Zealand firms in Australia support the suggestion that in the initial stages of outward investment, firms will seek to invest in countries that are higher up on the IDP, to *acquire* O specific advantages. This is supported by evidence from a survey of motivations of New Zealand firms to invest in Australia (Vautier 1984). Australian operations by New Zealand firms were dominated by investment in distribution (especially wholesaling) followed by manufacturing and finance, insurance and business services. The motivations cited suggested that the development of skills, knowledge and benefits of exposure to an overseas market stressed the importance of acquiring O advantages. Australia had the L advantage of a larger market with access to lower cost inputs, enabling a firm to achieve production efficiencies through economies of scale. The underlying reasons for investment in distribution suggest that internalisation factors were also a significant motivation for expansion. Control of marketing would be improved since firms could obtain market information and product knowledge, which could not be gained through distribution by an agent.

1984–1994: AN OUTWARD-LOOKING, EXPORT-ORIENTED ECONOMY

Structural change and adjustment

A New Zealand economic survey by the OECD in 1980 showed that the performance of the New Zealand economy had deteriorated, compared with other economies of the OECD, since 1960. The average real rate of growth of GDP in the 1960s was 4 per cent per annum. This was well below the figure of 5.5 per cent a year for the OECD as a whole. In the 1970s the figures were 2.5 and 3.5 respectively. The average growth rate disguises considerable variations on a year-to-year basis. In the 1960s the growth rate varied from over 6 per cent in 1963–1964 and 1965–1966 to −0.4 per cent in 1967–1968. In the 1970s it varied from 7.2 per cent in 1973–1974 to −2.7 per cent in 1977–1978. Not only was the New Zealand economy performing poorly compared with other OECD economies, but its growth rates also compared unfavourably with the growth rates being experienced by the newly industrialising economies of South East Asia.

The underlying causes were structural. Government intervention to compensate for market imperfections effectively prevented firms from making structural adjustments to accommodate changing external circumstances. The remedies applied since 1960 were largely palliative. Since 1945 industrial development had been supported by a high level of protection coupled with demand management policies that successfully aimed at a very high level of employment (OECD 1980). The OECD report also pointed to the controlled nature of the economy in which wage fixing and price controls enabled domestic inflation to be held at moderate levels. The social consensus in New Zealand emphasised security and stability and in the affluent 1970s an equitable distribution of income rather than economic growth was a politically desirable objective. The economy was in very poor condition, as the OECD report indicated:

> The rural exporting sector lost ground in relative terms, domestic manufacturing acquired a high cost structure that was uncompetitive internationally, the exchange rate became progressively overvalued and over a period of almost twenty years, the tertiary sector absorbed a high proportion of the increase in the labour force.
>
> (OECD 1980, p. 19)

Non-agricultural production accounted for about 89 per cent of GDP of which manufacturing accounted for 23 per cent and service industries accounted for 66 per cent. A considerable shift had occurred in the distribution of exports, away from traditional agricultural products. Non-agricultural products comprised less than 7 per cent of the total in 1958–1959, but by 1981 accounted for over 32 per cent of total exports. This figure, however, disguises the contribution made by resource-based products. Other primary commodities such as forest products, fishing and fruit contributed to 14.5 per cent of this total in 1981, whereas manufacturing exports contributed to only 17.3 per cent of the total (BIE 1983). Inward FDI was occurring in the forestry and fishing sector. Processed timber products rather than logs and timber were becoming more important relative to logs and sawn timber.

The new economic policy introduced by the Labour government from 1984 included regulatory reforms and economic liberalisation

(Bollard 1987). Internally, these reforms involved deregulation in the finance and transport industries, the removal of entry licensing in manufacturing and other services, the abolition of price controls and the easing of controls over merger acquisition and trade practices. Subsidies to the agricultural sector were eliminated and corporate and personal tax structures were reformed. Concessions for favoured forms of investment such as research and development were withdrawn. With the passing of the State Owned Enterprises Act (1986) the government signalled its intention to restructure state-owned enterprises, removing their monopoly rights and opening the way for future privatisation.[3]

Macro-economic reform emphasised anti-inflationary measures. Government policy was to fund its deficit fully through internal borrowing. The independence of the New Zealand Reserve Bank was established with agreed targets for inflation. The policy objectives were identified as creating a stable economy with low inflation rates and sound macroeconomic policy which would be attractive to foreign investors. The process of structural reform and the opening up of the economy subjected business to new competitive pressures (New Zealand Planning Council 1988, Baird et al. 1990). Industry deregulation meant easier entry and exit for firms, which induced the erosion of monopoly rents, caused considerable merger and acquisition activities, and generally created more competitive pressures to perform (Bollard 1993). In the primary production areas, Producer Boards retained control of overseas marketing in dairy products, kiwi fruits, apples and pears. Publicly funded research institutions were restructured to reduce the crowding effect on private spending on research and development. A significant effect of trade liberalisation is that it led to more technology imports (with some displacement of local technology), more intra-industry trade and industrial integration.

In the area of macro-organisational reform, government policy was to facilitate the workings of factor markets, in particular the labour market. The Employment Contracts Act in 1986 (following the abolition of compulsory unionism) changed the practice of nationwide collective wage determination in favour of individual or site-wide agreements. In other areas of reform, initiatives were introduced for improved labour performance at the firm level, such as the application of Japanese management practices in motor vehicle assembly. Pressures on the labour market created labour shortages since the demand for technologically skilled labour had not been matched by reform in the education sector. Implementation of the policy objectives of supplying a technologically skilled workforce was difficult.[4]

Reforms of significance in the external trade sector included the termination of import licensing, the reduction of tariffs, the floating of the exchange rate and the removal of capital controls. The timetable for completion of the CER free trade agreement with Australia was accelerated and in 1987 agreement was reached on the progressive elimination of restrictions on investment in services, although in Australia prohibitions on investment in certain sectors such as banking remained, which was not the case in New Zealand.

From the perspective of inward and outward investment to New Zealand, the relaxation of controls led to a significant increase in both inflows and outflows of capital. Although approvals for overseas investment were still required from the Overseas Investment Commission, raising the approvals threshold to $NZ 10 million, removing restrictions on overseas media ownership as well as farmland ownership effectively eliminated many restrictions which had been applied to investment in 'sensitive' areas of the economy.[5]

Inward FDI

The fluctuating levels of investment in the early periods of reform reflect a degree of uncertainty and commitment of government and opposition to carry out structural reform with its attendant socially undesirable consequences of increased long term unemployment and dependency on the state for welfare assistance. As illustrated in Table 6.2 inward investment flows declined from $NZ 364 million in 1983 to $NZ 205 million in 1984, but recovered in 1985 and 1986, only to fall back again in 1987 and 1988. Policy changes since 1984 have led to some considerable changes within the inward and outward investment patterns.

Table 6.3 shows the trends in origins of inward FDI between 1987 and 1993. This table shows that over a seven-year period, investment from the United States and Canada (in terms of value) is almost as great as investment from Australia (the values for the United States, however, are distorted by a single acquisition in 1991, namely the purchase of Telecom NZ). In terms of the number of projects, Australia is still the most important source of investment for New Zealand. The greater geographic dispersion of inward investment is shown by the increasing number of investments

Table 6.2 Foreign direct investment, New Zealand: 1971–1984

Year	Inward ($NZ million)	Outward ($NZ million)	Net (I–O)
1971	101	10	91
1972	111	7	104
1973	119	9	110
1974	146	11	135
1975	149	15	134
1976	191	23	168
1977	184	28	156
1978	234	40	194
1979	255	52	205
1980	270	81	189
1981	304	102	202
1982	311	279	32
1983	311	257	54
1984	341	335	6

Note: Calculated on three-year moving average basis.
Source: Statistics New Zealand: Direct Investment Statistics.

from other countries (excluding other EC countries). This grouping includes other Asian countries. In this category, the HPAEs (High Performing Asian Economies) have extended their investment interests to New Zealand. These countries include Taiwan, South Korea and Singapore. The most significant single country in this category is Singapore.

The number of enterprises in New Zealand with foreign ownership had not changed significantly between 1986 and 1991, averaging 2.5 per cent over the period. However, the percentage of businesses with significant foreign equity (greater than 25 per cent) has increased steadily over the period since 1987, accounting for 77.1 per cent of all foreign-controlled businesses since 1991 (Enderwick and Akoorie 1994). The increasing importance of FDI in New Zealand's economy is also shown by the ratios of FDI to GDP and to domestic capital formation. As a percentage of gross fixed capital formation FDI has averaged around 5 per cent between 1980 and 1989. Over the years 1990 to 1991 this percentage increased to more than 20 per cent. The exceptionally large inflows to New Zealand are, however, the results of several specific transactions such as the privatisation of former state-owned assets. Broad estimates of New Zealand's total stock of inward FDI show that New Zealand's share of world stock of inward FDI actually declined

Table 6.3 Net NDI inflows to New Zealand: country of origin ($NZ million)

Year	Australia	UK	USA/ Canada	Japan	Other EC	Asia	ROW	Total
1987	−40	96	343	−23	12	−6	19	402
1988	114	170	−70	19	29	−86	60	238
1989	343	306	79	−31	75	−27	−19	725
1990	1,237	735	271	379	16	110	75	2,824
1991	−728	−537	3,716	107	150	160	64	2,932
1992	879	761	−796	11	167	394	109	2,026
1993*	2,952	729	536	−30	−85	459	−161	4,398
1987/1993 Total	4,745 35.1%	2,260 16.7%	4,079 30.1%	432 3.2%	364 2.7%	1,504 11.1%	147 1.1%	13,545 100%

Note: *Provisional
Sources: Statistics New Zealand, New Zealand Treasury.

Table 6.4 Sectoral patterns of inward investment, New Zealand.
Overseas Investment Commision applications (acquisitions and business
commencements) 1991–1993

% by sector ($NZ million)	1991	1992	1993
Agriculture	431	671	249
Mining	114	41	252
Total primary $m	545	712	501
% Total	8.2%	10.4%	5.3%
Manufacturing	1,673	608	3,035
Total	25.3%	8.9%	32.3%
Construction	105	261	1,824
Wholesale/retail	847	790	581
Transport/storage	648	48	748
Financial services	994	4,080	536
Communications	1,550	299	299
Total tertiary	4,394	5,539	5,873
Total	66.4%	80.8%	62.4%

Note: These figures do not correspond with FDI inflows compiled by Statistics
New Zealand. The OIC figures relate only to approvals given (up to the amount
for which approval is requested). They also include transactions where there
is no beneficial change in ownership; transactions which do not proceed;
transactions between two offshore parties (i.e. where there is no net inflow of
funds to New Zealand). OIC figures made no allowance for disinvestment or
remittance of earnings from existing investments. (Treasury, New Zealand)
Source: OIC (year ending 31 March).

from 0.5 per cent in 1980 to 0.3 per cent in 1991. By contrast,
Australia's share of world stock of inward FDI grew from 2.9 per
cent to 7.3 per cent over the same period.

The sectoral patterns of inward FDI are shown in Table 6.4.
Foreign involvement is particularly high in mining and quarrying,
manufacturing, transport, storage, communication and business and
financial services. The sectoral patterns of investment can be further
divided into two main types, resource-based investments and non-
resource-based investments.

(a) Resource-based investments: acquiring L advantages

Between 1985 and 1991 the foreign-owned percentage of agricultural services, hunting, forestry and fishing increased by 18.2 per
cent but the investment took place in larger (in terms of number of

employees) enterprises. There are two main reasons for the increasing investment in New Zealand's forestry resources. First, access to domestic forestry investment possibilities for New Zealand and foreign investors was limited in the 1980s while the future ownership of substantial state-owned resources in forestry was debated. The response of New Zealand producers was to expand into alternative sources of supply. In the late 1980s the government opted to privatise the state exotic forests, which led to substantial international investment. Second, global estimates of forestry resources and use suggested that Northern Hemisphere users such as the United States, Canada and China had been experiencing a wood deficit, while producer countries such as New Zealand, South Africa, Chile, Japan, Brazil and the CIS had a wood surplus.[6] Investment in the forestry industry preceded state forest asset sales with joint ventures in New Zealand processing and medium density fibre plants being established with Japanese partners. While foreign technology and capital have been important in establishing further value-added activities in New Zealand, the relatively higher proportion of unprocessed timber to wood products exported from New Zealand reflects the incentives for investors to exploit resources in New Zealand and carry out processing within the destination markets.

The major international forestry companies operating in New Zealand in 1991 were International Paper, Oji Paper, Sanyo, Kokusaka Pulp and ITT Rayonier (Roche 1993b). Fletcher Challenge Ltd, a New Zealand based company, ranked sixth in the world industry rankings in 1991 and eighty-fifth in the top 100 transnational corporations ranked by foreign assets in 1992 (UNCTAD 1994). In 1994, International Paper had a 40 per cent share of one of New Zealand's three major forestry companies, Carter Holt Harvey (OIC 1993). For the year ending 1993, forestry investment in New Zealand was $NZ 77 million, accounting for 19.6 per cent of total applications by foreign investors.

New Zealand's tourism receipts in 1993 reached $NZ 3.5 billion from 1.25 million visitors per annum. Tourism numbers increased by 13.1 per cent in 1993, substantially more than the OECD average increase of 3.8 per cent (New Zealand Tourism Board 1994). Before 1984 the state had a dominant role in the industry through its ownership of the Tourist Hotel Corporation which subsidised hotel investment in inaccessible areas. The state retains an advisory and regulatory role in the development of the industry, but the industry structure and pattern of development are still highly fragmented.

Private investment in recreational facilities has been encouraged by the relaxation of controls on ownership of rural land.

(b) Non-resource-based investments

In 1990 the total value of foreign purchased privatised assets was $NZ 6.6 billion. The sales of former state-owned assets from 1986 involved the relinquishment of state ownership in a range of commercial enterprises including NZ Steel, Post Bank, Shipping Corporation, Government Printing, State Insurance, Maui Gas and Synfuel, Tourist Hotel Corporation, New Zealand Railways Corporation, Telecom New Zealand, the Bank of New Zealand and cutting rights for New Zealand Forestry Corporation forests (Ebashi 1993). Most of the foreign-owned investment relates to the service sector, in particular communications and banking. The privatisation of New Zealand's telecommunications network was accompanied by deregulation in the sector. Bell Atlantic's purchase of the telecommunications network in 1990 resulted in an upgrading of the network through investments in technology and management skills. Subsequently, Telecom New Zealand has undertaken contracts to upgrade telecommunications in countries further down the IDP, such as Indonesia.

Inward FDI in the financial services sector was restricted by government policy and stringent financial regulations on the operations of banks.[7] The financial markets were highly segmented through restrictions on individual activity. Trading banks were subject to a variety of direct controls on interest rates, deposit taking, and sectoral directions and limits on lending were determined by regulation. Segmentation resulted in barriers to competition between institutional groups and in addition restrictive entry conditions reduced competition within each segment (Harper 1986). Deregulation and structural changes saw the removal of interest rate controls, the relaxation of entry restrictions into banking and, within the banking system, a review of the state-owned banking activities and the removal of restrictions on foreign ownership. The effects of deregulation were to encourage economies of scope, expansion within sectors and overseas by then domestically owned banks. There was further specialisation in the sector, with the development of merchant banks, facilitating the merger and acquisition activity characteristic of the post-1984 environment. Competitive pressures from multinational and domestic banks encouraged further rationalisation of the sector. Of the eight major banking groups operating in New Zealand, only one is still New Zealand owned. Of the remaining seven banks, five are owned by Australian banks and two are owned by British banks.

The dominance of this sector by Australian banks suggests the existence of O advantages of Australian banks which derive in part from economies of scale and scope obtained across an integrated financial market (New Zealand and Australia). The catch-up in technology in banking required substantial investment of capital and management to undertake the scale of rationalisation required to scale down the branch network operations, and improve profitability.

In the manufacturing sector, activities related to asset acquisitions and commencements in New Zealand for 1993 accounted for only 9.6 per cent of total applications whereas applications for farming activities, including non-traditional activities, accounted for 14.3 per cent of total applications. Agri-business and food processing have been attractive targets for multinational investors; H.J. Heinz acquired the New Zealand operations of Goodman Fielder Wattie, in 1992 (OIC 1992). Integration of Australasian operations to service the growing Asian market in consumer branded foods links the competitive advantages of food multinationals with access to the L advantages of New Zealand, operating as an export platform for Asian markets. Further rationalisation has taken place within the manufacturing sector between Australia and New Zealand following the full integration under CER. There has also been increasing specialisation within subsidiary operations (Bollard 1993).

Outward investment by New Zealand firms

(a) Outward investment by country of destination

Outward FDI by New Zealand firms only began in 1984, owing to controls on capital outflows until that time.[8] Table 6.5 shows the trends in country of destination of New Zealand investment flows from 1990 to 1993. The principal destination of New Zealand's direct investment has in the past been Australia. The economic reforms of the 1980s designed to encourage cost competitiveness in New Zealand favoured industry rationalisation and further specialisation encouraging the relocation of manufacturing facilities to Australia. The negative investment flows to Australia from 1991

Table 6.5 New Zealand, direct investment by country of destination, 1990–1993, net outflows ($NZ million)

Year	Australia	UK	USA/Canada	Japan	Other EC	Asia	ROW	Total
1990	3,402	−361	445	16	−881	689	−143	3,961
1991	−539	2,082	−260	5	1,279	624	−646	2,546
1992	305	−174	78	−6	838	−1,739	1,066	728
1993	−541	−43	−408	11	399	−2,235	123	−2,693
1990–1993	2,627	1,504	−145	26	2,428	−2,301	400	4,542
Four-year total	57.8%	33.1%	−3.1%	0.57%	53.4%	−50.6%	8.8%	100.0%

onwards may be a reflection of the turning tide in New Zealand, as the effects of labour market reforms, low inflation rates and economic recovery have favoured reinvestment by New Zealand firms to service the Australian market (Enderwick and Akoorie 1994). The change in investment flows for Britain and other EC countries is worth noting. The positive investment flows for 1991 for Britain and other EC countries indicate the response of New Zealand firms to the proposed creation of the Single European Market in 1992 to establish operations in Europe. Asia had become an increasingly important destination for New Zealand exports, but it is not a primary destination for investment as Table 6.5 shows. New Zealand firms are generally reluctant to commit significant resources to these new and psychically different markets. Overall, the general trend has been towards a decline in outward investment flows by New Zealand firms, reflecting the improved economic climate for domestic, as opposed to foreign, investment.

(b) Outward FDI by industrial sector

Official data on outward investment by sector are not available from New Zealand sources, although data are available from main recipient countries such as Australia. These data have been used, together with other data from longitudinal studies of outward investment by New Zealand firms, to establish investment patterns (Akoorie 1993). The pattern of investment in Australia over the period 1989 to 1993 shows that there has been an increase in investment in the manufacturing sector (principally food processing) over the period from $A 821 million in 1989 to $A 2,243 million in 1993 (Australian Bureau of Statistics 1989-1993). Investment in the financial services sector, over the same period, peaked at $A 3,553 million in 1991 and has since declined back to below 1989 levels ($A 2,828 million in 1993). A tentative conclusion from these data is that they reflect increasing investment by New Zealand firms in the resource-based sector based on their O specific advantages.

(c) Outward investment: resource sector

From 1984 onwards the size and scale of outward investment by New Zealand firms increased substantially (Akoorie 1993). The initiating group of outward investors were firms in the forestry, pulp and paper sector. The New Zealand Dairy Board (with statutory rights on the export of New Zealand Dairy products) and Goodman Fielder Wattie, a food processing group,[9] were the other resource-based firms engaged in outward FDI.

An examination of the patterns and motivations for investment by the group of forestry firms showed that as first-time investors, their motivations followed the previously identified patterns of market access or resource acquisition (Akoorie 1993). For forestry, the stimulus to outward investment in resources was the uncertainty regarding access to future domestic sources of supply. Access to North American markets, for pulp and paper, was a principal motivation for the acquisition of manufacturing operations in Canada for one firm. The motivations for outward investment in this sector were associated with exploiting existing O advantages, since the firms concerned had vertically integrated in New Zealand and had considerable experience (encouraged by the IS policy of the previous decades) in horizontal integration through acquisition. The L specific factors prompting outward investment in resources were to pre-empt the activities of South American producers in the North American market. Internalisation factors encouraged the expansion of single-resource-based industrial conglomerates into substantial investments in other commodity-based businesses, such as synthetic fuel derivatives.

The Dairy Board is a significant player in world dairy products, accounting for 25 per cent of the small percentage of world dairy products actually traded. The Dairy Board's strategy in the last decade has been to increase the proportion of revenue derived from branded consumer goods (Dobson 1990). Its O specific advantages are both in production efficiencies and technology innovation in consumer and industrial uses for milk-based derivatives. The Board has used outward investments to acquire O advantages in industrial caseins in developed country markets. It has also been exploiting existing O advantages through investment in countries lower down on the IDP. An important aspect of the Dairy Board's investment strategy has been to balance acquisitions between developed and developing country markets. Market potential, as a consequence of changing dietary habits in the South and East Asian markets, has prompted the Board to invest in local production units in newly emerging markets such as Malaysia and South Korea.

(d) Outward investment in non-resource-based sectors

New Zealand based firms in the non-resource-based sectors invested outwards to acquire strategic assets. For financial services firms (banks and insurance) these investments were principally in Britain, Europe and Australia. The aggressive competition in the home market, following deregulation, together with rapid diversification and the lack of experience in managing the integration of global acquisitions, meant that outward investment in this sector was short lived (Akoorie 1993). New Zealand based firms did not have the competitive advantages necessary to survive the depth of competition both domestically and overseas. Retrenchment occurred in the banking sector and following rationalisation activity in the 1990s, foreign-owned banks have dominated the domestic sector. The internationalisation of the financial services sector was completed following the acquisition of two, major New Zealand-owned insurance companies by British interests.

Strategic asset seeking by industrial conglomerates was a key motivation for the expansion of New Zealand based firms in the 1980s (Akoorie 1993). Their strategy in the domestic market was to acquire manufacturing companies with undervalued and often underperforming assets. This strategy was subsequently extended to overseas acquisitions in North America, Britain and Australia. The O advantages of the conglomerates were in the identification and acquisition of suitable targets, not in the subsequent integration of acquisitions into a suitable organisational framework. Consequently, the rapid expansion faltered by 1989 and significant reorganisation and retrenchment took place. New Zealand MNE expansion was hampered by lack of experience and the instability of the financial structures used to undertake expansion.

Indigenous construction and engineering services firms had acquired O advantages through joint venture involvement with overseas firms on the large scale, publicly funded construction projects of the 1980s. These were linked with the competitive advantages firms had developed through adapting technology-based solutions to indigenous activities, such as geothermal engineering. Firms coordinated their O advantages in New Zealand based consortia and acquired further O advantages through experience in overseas projects. The adaptability and small scale of solutions-based engineering and construction was particularly suited to infrastructural developments in South East Asia.[10]

SUMMARY AND CONCLUSIONS

The purpose of this chapter has been to apply the concept of the IDP to a country case study, New Zealand. The longitudinal study of the development of the New Zealand economy has shown that both FDI influences and non-FDI influences have contributed to the development of the economy, but their relative importance has varied over time. In the early period of New Zealand's development, the FDI influences predominated. The strategies of British firms in banking and financial services (which fostered the development of the pastoral industries) and in the meat industry pushed out the frontier of production possibilities for these industries. During this period the role of government was to develop the infrastructure and to balance the interests of the respective groups in a tightly knit homogeneous society. Over time and through investment in infrastructure, education and services, the influence of the state became more powerful. The state therefore invested in creating assets which could be utilised by both domestic and foreign firms. The state also favoured the interests of local settlers over foreign influences by competing with private interests through investment in banks, insurance and financial services. Even as early as the 1920s the state began to exert an influence over the agricultural sector through regulation and by establishing Producer Boards to coordinate its international marketing functions.

From the 1930s onwards, the importance of FDI-influenced change, relative to non-FDI-influenced change, gradually weakened. The export-oriented, outward-oriented stance changed into an inward-oriented import substitution policy. The objectives of government policy were to maintain full employment and to insulate the economy from external shocks. Import substitution policies encouraged the development of manufacturing in order to create an economy that was less dependent on imports and more diversified in its structure. The competitiveness of domestic and foreign firms was therefore affected by their inability to source imports from the most efficient sources of supply. Their ability to upgrade technology and import more capital-intensive machinery was affected by import restrictions applied in varying degrees of severity over the period as well as the exchange controls and controls on capital outflows. The non-FDI influences of government policy therefore affected the OLI configuration of firms. Access to L specific resources was restricted by government policy. The low rates of inward invest-

ment over the period relative to other countries are a reflection of
the inward orientation and restrictive nature of the policies applied.
The results of the long period of inward orientation and the
increasingly unfavourable environment for trade in agricultural
commodities led to a long term decline in New Zealand's growth
rates. The reforms introduced after 1984 forced firms (and the
government) into a period of extensive restructuring. The reorientation of government policy has moved away from directly influencing the strategies of MNEs. A feature of the New Zealand economy
over the last ten years has been that the strategies of both New
Zealand and foreign-based MNEs have increasingly influenced the
directions of the economy. Access to resources such as forestry,
tourism and infrastructure have allowed MNEs to use their competitive advantages to upgrade indigenous resources.

The conclusions that can be drawn from this chapter are as
follows. First, the rate of progress along the IDP for a given country
can either be accelerated by government policy (as in the case of
Japan or the high performing Asian economies) or be inhibited as
has been the case in New Zealand. There is a marked contrast
between the rapid rates of growth and expansion of the economy
between 1870 and 1930 and the decline from 1960–1984 which can
only be partially explained by events in the external economic
environment. The external orientation and outward stance of the
economy from 1984 to 1994 has led to substantially increased
inward investment as well as the emergence of some New Zealand
based MNEs of substantial size within their respective industry
sectors. In this sense these firms have benefited from industry
protection, but their international competitive positions have only
developed since economic liberalisation.

Second, the experience of the New Zealand case study confirms
the dynamic aspects of the IDP. Changes in the OLI configuration of
firms occur as a result of changes which began in a preceding
period. The full extent of the change in configuration may not be
evident until some initiating event occurs, such as a dramatic change
in government policy which affects the inward and outward investment of firms. The conclusions are, however, that a country may
deviate from its expected path on the IDP depending on the
orientation of government policy. This finding is consistent with
the findings for other countries, such as India, in which the role of
government policy has shaped the trajectory of the IDP.

Third, the chapter confirms the importance of created assets in a country even when it has substantial natural resources. The natural resource base of New Zealand, however, is dependent on substantial investment in human capital to derive economic rent from the use of these assets. In the past New Zealand has exported the outputs derived from these created assets in embodied form, yet the potential for the exploitation of technology transferred in disembodied form has been underutilised.

NOTES

1 Through establishing Trade Commissioner posts to help open up 'new' markets. The government also initiated an export drive, assisting manufacturers with market information as well as training in export techniques.
2 The NAFTA agreement was superseded by the Closer Economic Relations agreement (CER) in 1983. The CER agreement provided for eventual free trade in goods between New Zealand and Australia. The timetable for completion was accelerated in 1987.
3 Through the State Owned Enterprises Act 1986. The principal architect of reform was the then Minister of Finance, the Rt Hon. Roger Douglas.
4 This is not to imply that there has been a lack of reform in the education (particularly the tertiary) sector. The school leaving age has been raised to 16 and more school leavers are being encouraged to seek skills qualifications.
5 Approvals were still required from the Overseas Investment Commission (OIC). However, the OIC has adopted a liberal attitude towards investment and has only declined 0.2 per cent of applications referred to it between 1985 and 1990 (Enderwick and Akoorie 1994).
6 *Source*: Tasman Pulp and Paper Ltd, Internal Report.
7 Australian Banks were restricted from operating in New Zealand until the Memorandum on Services Agreement between Australia and New Zealand was concluded in 1987.
8 Although there were some substantial acquisitions by Fletcher Challenge in Canada in 1983, for which special permission was obtained.
9 Their New Zealand operations were acquired by J. H. Heinz in 1992. Goodman Fielder still operates as an Australian-based MNE.
10 Industry coordination through ENEX, a group of engineering consultancy firms, has assisted these firms to develop expertise in bidding for aid-funded development projects.

BIBLIOGRAPHY

Akoorie, M. (1993) 'Patterns of foreign direct investment by large New Zealand firms', *International Business Review*, 2, 2: 169–189.
Akoorie, M. and Enderwick, P. (1992) 'The International Operations of

New Zealand Companies', *Asia Pacific Journal of Management*, 9, 1: 99–117.

Australian Bureau of Statistics, *Foreign Investment Australia*, 1989–1993.

Baird, M., Savage, J. and Petherick, A., (1990) *Responding to Change: What Firms say about Structural Adjustment*, No. 54. New Zealand Institute of Economic Research, Wellington.

Bollard, A. (1987) Introduction in A. Bollard and R. Buckle (eds) *Economic Liberalisation in New Zealand*, Wellington: Allen and Unwin and Port Nicholson Press.

—— (1993) 'New Zealand: technology and development', in H. Soesastro and M. Pangestu (eds) *Technological Challenge in the Asia-Pacific Economy*, Sydney: Allen and Unwin.

Bureau of Industry Economics (1983) *Australian Direct Investment in New Zealand*, Canberra: Australian Government Publishing Service.

Cundliffe, J. (1969) *The Economic Outlook for New Zealand*, Wellington: New Zealand Institute of Economic Research.

Crocombe, G., Enright, M. and Porter, M. (1991) *Upgrading New Zealand's Competitive Advantage*, Auckland: Oxford University Press.

Deane, R. (1967) *Foreign Investment in New Zealand Manufacturing*, unpublished Ph.D. Thesis, Victoria University of Wellington.

—— (1970) *Foreign Investment in New Zealand Manufacturing*, Wellington: Sweet and Maxwell (NZ) Ltd.

—— (1975) 'An economic policy dilemma: the case of foreign investment in New Zealand', in R. Carey (ed.) *Foreign Investment Policy in New Zealand*, New Zealand Institute of Public Administration.

Dobson, W. (1990) 'The competitive strategy of the Dairy Board', *Agribusiness*, 6, 6: 541–558.

Douglas, R. and Callen, L. (1987) *Toward Prosperity*, Auckland: David Bateman.

Dunning, J. (1981) 'Explaining the international direct investment position of countries: towards a dynamic or developmental approach', *Weltwirtschaftliches Archiv*, 118: 30–62.

Dunning, J. and Narula, R. (1994) 'Transpacific foreign direct investment and the investment development path: the record assessed', *Essays in International Business*, 10, University of South Carolina.

Dunstall, G. (1981) 'The social pattern', in W. Oliver with B. Williams (eds) *The Oxford History of New Zealand*, Wellington: The Clarendon Press, Oxford, and Oxford University Press.

Ebashi, M. (1993) *Foreign Direct Investment in New Zealand*, Wellington: New Zealand Institute of Economic Research, No. 37.

Enderwick, P. and Akoorie, M. (1994) 'Internationalisation and the New Zealand economy', in J. Deeks and P. Enderwick (eds) *Business and New Zealand Society*, Auckland: Longman Paul.

Fisher, A. (1932) 'The New Zealand economic problem – a review', *Economic Record*, VIII: 74–87.

Gardner, W. (1981) 'A colonial economy', in W. Oliver with B. Williams (eds) *The Oxford History of New Zealand*, Wellington: The Clarendon Press, Oxford, and Oxford University Press.

Harper, D. (1986) *The Financial Services Industry: Effects of Regulatory*

Reform, Wellington: New Zealand Institute of Economic Research, No. 35.

Hawke, G. (1981) *The Making of New Zealand*, Wellington: VUW Working Papers in Economic History.

—— (1985) *The Making of New Zealand: An Economic History*, Wellington: Cambridge University Press.

Le Heron, R. (1980) 'Export linkage development in manufacturing firms: the example of export promotion in New Zealand', *Economic Geography*, 56, 4: 281–299.

Monetary and Economic Council (1970) *New Zealand and an Enlarged EEC*, Wellington: M & EC Report, 19.

Muir, V. (1953) 'The emergence of state enterprise in New Zealand in the nineteenth century', *Explorations in Entrepreneurial History*, V: 186–197.

New Zealand Planning Council (1988) *Prospects: Economic and sectoral trends*, Wellington.

New Zealand Tourism Board (1994) *Tourism in NZ: Strategy and Progress*, Wellington: NZTB.

Organization for Economic Co-operation and Development (1980) *New Zealand Economic Survey*, Paris: OECD Publications.

—— (1993) *OECD Reviews of Foreign Direct Investment – New Zealand*, Paris: OECD Publications.

Overseas Investment Commission – New Zealand (1987–1993) Decision Sheets on Investment Applications, various years, Wellington: OIC.

Report of the Task Force on Economic and Social Planning (1976) *New Zealand at the Turning Point*, Wellington.

Roche, M. (1993a) 'Internationalisation as company and industry colonisation: the frozen meat industry in New Zealand in the 1900s', *Economic Geographer*, 49, 1: 2–7.

—— (1993b) 'Geography – internationalisation and the condition of forestry in New Zealand', *New Zealand Geographer*, 49, 2: 23–31.

Rosenberg, W. (1961) 'Capital imports and growth – the case of New Zealand – foreign investment in New Zealand, 1840–1958', *The Economic Journal*, LXXI, March, 93–113.

Simkin, C. (1951) *The Instability of a Dependent Economy*, London: Oxford University Press.

Stone, R. (1973) *Makers of Fortune: A Colonial Business Community and its Fall*, Auckland: Auckland University Press and Oxford University Press.

Sutch, W.B. (1966) *The Quest for Security in New Zealand 1840–1966*, Wellington: Oxford University Press.

United Nations Conference of Trade and Development (1994) *World Investment Report: Transnational Corporations, Employment and the Workplace*, New York and Geneva: United Nations.

Vautier, K. (1984) *New Zealand Direct Investment in Australia*, Australia New Zealand Foundation, 1984.

Chapter 7

Spain
A boom from economic integration

*José Manuel Campa and Mauro F. Guillén**

INTRODUCTION

The case of Spain may be taken as representing a group of middle-income countries that, in spite of being early industrializers and having achieved relatively high standards of living, have not moved far in what has been termed the 'investment development path' (Dunning and Narula 1994; Tolentino 1993: 92–119). Dunning and Narula (1994) posit that the relationship between foreign direct investment (FDI), on the one hand, and the ownership, locational and internalization (OLI) advantages of countries and firms, on the other, change according to the country's stage of economic development. In other words, the relative weights and roles of the three elements of the OLI or eclectic approach to international production vary as countries (and their firms) become richer, shift from natural to created assets, and become more embedded in the world economy (Dunning 1979, 1981, 1988; Agarwal 1980). Similarly to the rest of Europe's western and southern fringes (Ireland, Portugal, Italy and Greece), inward FDI in Spain has historically exceeded outward FDI by a wide margin. Presently, there are only timid (and sometimes contradictory) indications that the growth rate of outward FDI is accelerating, and that inflows and outflows are becoming more balanced as more Spanish firms try to exploit their ownership advantages abroad.

Studying the case of Spain is important because during the 1980s it has been one of the most dynamic countries in terms of economic growth and FDI activity, consolidating its position as an attractive host country and as an emerging source of FDI. In 1991, the historical record year, Spain received US$ 10.5 billion in FDI, the fourth largest inflow in the world surpassed only by the United

Table 7.1 Annual flows of inward and outward FDI, 1959–1993

Year	Inward	Outward	In-out	Inward	Outward	In-out
	(current million pesetas)			(% GDP)		
1993	1855609	442843	1412766	3.048	0.727	2.321
1992	1914494	546958	1367536	3.253	0.929	2.324
1991	2300996	676906	1624090	4.197	1.235	2.963
1990	1819851	454814	1365037	3.631	0.907	2.724
1989	1244988	280384	964604	2.764	0.622	2.141
1988	843254	229708	613546	2.100	0.572	1.528
1987	727279	100598	626681	2.012	0.278	1.734
1986	400903	66858	334045	1.240	0.207	1.033
1985	280085	43810	236275	0.993	0.155	0.838
1984	267007	49015	217992	1.046	0.192	0.854
1983	158180	34440	123740	0.702	0.153	0.549
1982	182842	65525	117317	0.927	0.332	0.595
1981	78605	30079	48526	0.461	0.176	0.285
1980	85416	25736	59680	0.563	0.170	0.393
1979	80803	24218	56585	0.612	0.183	0.429
1978	56888	12897	43991	0.504	0.114	0.390
1977	28042	13495	14547	0.304	0.146	0.158
1976	13492	4253	9239	0.186	0.059	0.127
1975	12512	1990	10522	0.207	0.033	0.174
1974	15701	–	–	0.305		–
1973	18787	4257	14530	0.447	0.101	0.346
1972	14101	2614	11487	0.405	0.075	0.330
1971	12335	1720	10615	0.416	0.058	0.358
1970	12482	2507	9975	0.475	0.095	0.379
1969	13103	929	12174	0.550	0.039	0.511
1968	10029	1854	8175	0.482	0.089	0.393
1967	10783	645	10138	0.585	0.035	0.550
1966	7717	582	7135	0.474	0.036	0.439
1965	6956	207	6749	0.496	0.015	0.481
1964	4688	340	4348	0.388	0.028	0.360
1963	2478	161	2317	0.231	0.015	0.216
1962	1378	54	1324	0.151	0.006	0.145
1961	1248	49	1199	0.159	0.006	0.153
1960	2165	10	2155	0.317	0.001	0.315
1959	964	4	960			

Sources: Moreno Moré (1975; 92, 95); Aguilar (1985: 65–66); Ministerio de Comercio (1993: 226–227, 231); Durán Herrera and Muñoz (1984: 381–382).

States, the UK and France. That same year, outward FDI stood at US$ 3.6 billion (see Table 7.1 for annual data in local currency). In 1990 the ratio of outward to inward FDI stocks stood at 0.23, only slightly higher than in 1980 because, despite the high increase in

Table 7.2 Stocks of foreign direct investment (FDI) and number of large firms for selected countries

Country	Outward FDI (% GDP)	Inward FDI (% GDP)	Ratio of outward to inward FDI		Outward FDI increase	Inward FDI increase	Fortune Global 500 firms	
	1990	1990	1980	1990	1980–1990	1980–1990	Industrial	Service
USA	7.8	7.2	2.65	1.09	1.96	4.76	159	136
Japan	6.9	1.2	0.53	5.85	12.22	1.10	135	140
Germany	10.1	8.0	1.18	1.27	3.51	3.27	32	43
France	9.2	7.2	1.04	1.27	4.67	3.83	26	29
Italy	5.1	5.3	0.78	0.97	8.05	6.52	7	15
UK	23.3	20.8	1.28	1.12	2.84	3.24	41	43
Spain	3.1	13.5	0.22	0.23	13.31	12.89	3	14
Ireland	–	11.5	–	–	–	1.33	0	0
Greece	–	21.1	–	–	–	3.10	0	0
Portugal	0.9	10.6	0.23	0.08	3.98	11.05	1	1
South Korea[a]	0.9	2.2	0.12	0.40	15.30	4.76	12	3
Taiwan	8.2	6.2	0.04	1.32	132.90	4.05	1	1
China[b]	0.7	3.8	0.06	0.18	63.82	21.10	–	–
Argentina	–	6.2	–	–	–	1.64	1	0
Mexico	–	11.4	–	–	–	3.10	3	1
Brazil	0.5	7.8	0.04	0.06	3.68	2.12	1	2
Chile	0.6	22.2	0.05	0.03	4.24	6.97	0	0

Notes: [a] Calculations based on outward stock for 1989.
[b] Calculations based on outward stock for 1979 and inward stock for 1981.

Sources: United Nations Conference on Trade and Development, World Investment Report 1993 (New York: United Nations, 1993), pp. 248–250; World Investment Report 1994 (New York: United Nations, 1994), pp. 415–420; Fortune (25 July 1994, and 22 August 1994).

inward and outward flows, both increased at similar rates. In 1990 stocks of FDI were 13 times greater than 10 years earlier. When compared to the other large EU countries, Spain seems to be approaching Italy in terms of the relative importance and growth of outward FDI, and the United Kingdom as far as inward FDI is concerned. As the country developed economically over the last 30 years, Spain has attracted considerably more inward FDI as a percentage of GDP than countries such as Germany, France or Italy, while investing less abroad (Table 7.2).

It is useful to compare the Spanish experience to those of the emerging economies of Europe, East Asia and Latin America that are playing increasingly important roles in FDI. Spain entered the decade of the 1980s with a ratio of inward stock to GDP lower than those for Portugal, Greece, Taiwan and Brazil, equal to Mexico's, and higher than for Ireland, Chile, South Korea or China. Spain's outward stocks in 1980 were much higher than for any of these countries. The Spanish trajectory during the 1980s stands out for the relatively rapid increase both in inward FDI (only China's has been faster, with Portugal's almost as fast), and in outward FDI (though South Korea's and again China's have been faster). The only large emerging economy whose ratio of outward to inward FDI surpassed Spain's 0.23 in 1990 was South Korea's 0.40. Relative to GDP, however, Spain's outward stock in 1990 was three times larger than South Korea's, and its inward stock six times larger. Unlike South Korea, but similarly to Italy, Spain features a much higher number of large service firms than large industrial firms (Table 7.2), which is reflected in the fact that most Spanish outward investment is in services while most of South Korea's is in manufacturing or in trading of South Korean manufactured goods.

In this chapter we first provide a historical summary of FDI patterns in Spain since the dawn of industrialization but focusing on the last 30 years. Attention will be devoted to the role of the government as well as to the economic and political cycle, both domestic and international. Using industry and country-level data, we analyse the locational and ownership factors behind the evolution of inward and outward FDI since the country's entry into the European Union. Finally, we deal with the issues of the creation of assets through R&D, the internalization advantages of Spanish firms, and the future prospects for FDI.

HISTORICAL OVERVIEW

As is true of many other countries, the FDI cycle in Spain has historically been affected by domestic political events and upheavals as well as by domestic and international economic situations. Liberal trade policies in the mid-19th century set the stage for the arrival of French, Belgian and (after 1870) British investments in railways, mining, wineries, banking, insurance and public utilities. The return of protectionism and legal hindrances to foreign investment after 1891 slowed down the inflows. Meanwhile, Spanish investments abroad paled by comparison, with Cuba and Argentina as the major destinations (Tortella 1994: 128–134; Nadal 1975: 25–53, 87–121).

The 1920s witnessed the rise of American, German and French investment in electrical machinery, chemicals, automobiles and telecommunications despite growing restrictions to foreign investment and trade (Campillo 1963). Over this early period of industrialization, Spain attracted foreign investment at increasing rates albeit with many ups and downs dictated by political, financial or economic crises. Most of these early flows of FDI had to do with the exploitation of either natural assets such as mineral deposits and unique agricultural products (wines in particular) or the underdeveloped market for transportation, communication, banking, insurance and basic industrial goods. During the first two decades of the century, Spanish investment abroad was negligible except for the mostly speculative flows during World War I.

The Great Depression was less severe in Spain than elsewhere in Europe or North America, but nonetheless devastating for FDI. The Civil War of 1936–1939 represented a further setback to foreign investment and trade. After the war, the authoritarian government became dominated by a group of populist and staunchly nationalist economic policy-makers who implemented a series of foreign exchange controls and protectionist measures, and encouraged import-substitution investments in industry, while the Allied powers imposed a trade embargo that remained fully in place until the late 1940s. Foreign ownership restriction to a maximum of 25 per cent, the overvaluation of the currency, the intricate system of multiple exchange rates, mounting inflation and economic stagnation provoked capital flight and close to zero inward FDI. The liberalization and stabilization measures of 1959 allowed the pattern of increasingly high inward FDI and a trickle of outward FDI to return.

From liberalization to EU membership, 1959–1986

The liberal economic reforms of 1959 assigned foreign capital several roles: to supplement the meagre level of domestic savings, to generate much-needed hard currency, and to facilitate technology transfers (Varela Parache and Rodríguez de Pablo 1974; Muñoz *et al.* 1978: 45–60). The reformers also introduced changes in the protectionist regime: very steep tariff barriers were substituted for non-tariff barriers to trade. The punitive taxation of imports of industrial and consumer goods in a domestic market of considerable growth potential attracted inward FDI during the 1959–1973 period. For example, in the auto industry the government imposed high tariffs and stringent local content requirement rules but also offered attractive economic and fiscal packages (Hawkesworth 1981). During the 1960s and early 1970s, inward FDI ranged between 0.15 and 0.59 per cent of GDP, while outward FDI stayed under 0.1 per cent of GDP. By the mid-1970s and despite the reduction in foreign activity in Spain, inward investment was still about four times higher than outward investment (Figure 7.1, top panel).

Spanish investments abroad in the 1960s had to do with (1) access to raw materials (uranium, paper pulp, petroleum, various metals, fisheries), (2) the creation of distribution channels for Spanish fish, beverages, and food products, (3) construction and engineering projects, and (4) banking. Manufacturing FDI based on ownership advantages was not significant until the early 1970s. While manufacturing FDI was initially worth 20 per cent of total outward FDI, by the mid-1970s it represented nearly 40 per cent. Firms in the chemical, paper, mechanical, electro-mechanical, textile and beverage industries invested in manufacturing activities abroad (COCINB 1973: 25; Muñoz *et al.* 1978: 352–353). Most analysts agree that the government did little to facilitate outward FDI during this period. Exchange controls were too tight and state subsidies to help create distribution channels abroad were not very effective (Varela Parache 1972; Moreno Moré 1975: 106–107). One destination of intense Spanish outward FDI in the early and mid-1970s was the relatively depressed French department of the Eastern Pyrenees (the historic Roussillon), to the north of one of Spain's most developed industrial regions, Catalonia (Castellvi 1973; Raurich *et*

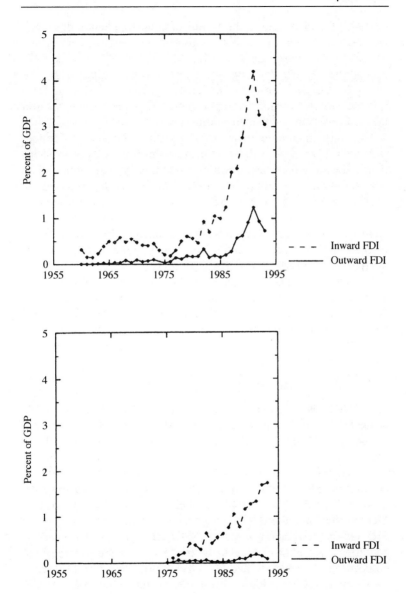

Figure 7.1 Top panel: foreign direct investment in Spain, 1960–1993.
Lower panel: manufacturing direct investment in Spain
Sources: Moreno Moré (1975: 92, 95); Aguilar (1985: 65–66); Ministerio de
Comercio (1993: 226–227, 231); Durán Herrera and Muñoz (1984: 381–382).

al. 1973). Catalan firms in the textile, clothing, appliance, chemical, beverage and food processing industries invested there to secure access to the European Common Market given that the 1970 Preferential Agreement with Spain failed to reduce tariffs significantly for labour-intensive manufactured goods. This specific location was selected for its geographical proximity and relatively lower labour costs than in other European areas.

The world economic crisis of 1973 and the transition to democracy after 1975 slowed down FDI in Spain. But by the late 1970s both outward and inward flows resumed their upward trend albeit with significant annual ups and downs until the mid-1980s (see top panel in Figure 7.1) due to the second oil shock, the 1981 world recession, and the initial uncertainty over the socialist electoral victory in 1982. In 1985 outward and inward flows represented 0.16 and 1.00 per cent of GDP, respectively, more than three times the rates for the early 1970s. This upward trend since the mid-1970s was in part facilitated by changes in governmental regulations. The agencies that had tightly controlled foreign transactions since the 1940s were dismantled as the Ministry of Commerce assumed authority over foreign investment authorization and control (De Erice 1975).[1]

EU membership and the FDI boom

The 1986–1992 period featured economic liberalization in the context of membership of the European Union (EU), rapid economic growth (by 1992 Spain's per capita income was 80 per cent of the UK's), expansion of private enterprises in both manufacturing and services, huge inflows of FDI peaking at 4.2 per cent of GDP in 1991, and the coming of age of outward FDI, towering also in 1991 at 1.2 per cent of GDP (Figure 7.1, top panel). Membership of the EU has meant that both the origin of inward FDI and the destination of outward FDI accounted for by other EU countries have almost doubled to roughly two-thirds of the total compared to between 30 and 50 per cent prior to 1986 (Ministerio de Comercio 1993). Flows from the United States or to Latin America have fallen in relative terms, while destinations such as France, The Netherlands and Portugal have become increasingly popular with Spanish firms. Outside of Europe, Morocco has recently attracted manufacturing investment. Japan remains a minor source or destination of FDI (Portillo 1994).

Most of the momentous surge in outward FDI has been in services, both financial and non-financial (utilities, air transportation, telecommunications). Outward manufacturing FDI as a percentage of GDP trebled since the mid-1970s but has yet to reach the 0.3 per cent mark (see Figure 7.1, lower panel), and the total share of outward manufacturing FDI has fallen from an all-time high of 46 per cent in 1977 to 11 per cent in 1993. Acquisitions have been more common than greenfield operations (Figure 7.2, top panel).

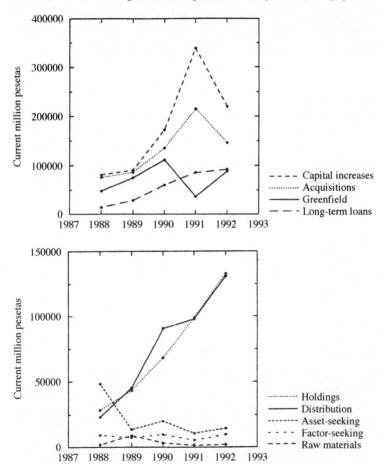

Figure 7.2 Top panel: outward FDI by mode, 1988–1992. Lower panel: outward FDI by goal
Source: Dirección General de Transacciones Exteriores, Ministerio de Economía y Hacienda.

Since 1988 Spanish acquisitions abroad have mostly taken place in
Latin America and the EU, targeting firms in utilities, banking,
plastics and oil and gas (Durán Herrera 1992: 227–228). The goals
sought by outward investments are, in decreasing order of importance, market access through distribution, technological assets,
cheap factors, and, lastly, the procurement of raw materials (Figure 7.2, lower panel). By comparison, between 1975 and 1978
outward factor- or raw-materials-seeking FDI was four times
higher than distribution FDI (Nueno Iniesta *et al.* 1981: 152–153).

Despite the unprecedented volume of outward FDI since 1986,
inward investment stole the show, with much of its fast growth
taking place through acquisitions of Spanish firms (Figure 7.3).
The most active acquirors were firms based in the UK and
France, while the most targeted industries were food, beverages,
chemicals and pharmaceuticals (Durán Herrera 1992: 227). One
important difference with outward FDI referred to the relative
importance and growth of manufacturing investment. Inward manufacturing FDI has increased since the mid-1980s although less
rapidly than total inward FDI (see Figure 7.1, lower panel), and
its share of the total has fluctuated annually between 35 and 65 per
cent. Given that the Spanish economy was becoming less protected,

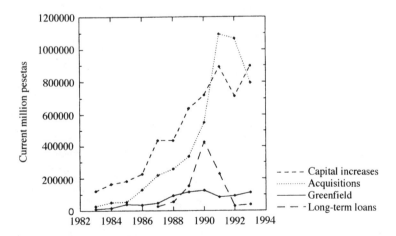

Figure 7.3 Inward FDI by mode, 1983–1993
Note: Data for 1984 refer to January–November only.
Source: Boletín Económico de ICE, several issues.

many of these acquisitions had to do with other kinds of barriers of entry defined at the industry level of analysis, an explanation that we explore further in the following sections.

OUTWARD FOREIGN DIRECT INVESTMENT

This section presents a more detailed analysis of the type of FDI transactions that have taken place; their breakdown by major country of origin and/or destination; and their implications for a better understanding of where the Spanish economy is in the investment development path (IDP). The increase in FDI activity in the last five years occurred both in outward and inward direct investment. Although the annual rate of increase in both types of FDI between 1988 and 1992 has been similar (24 per cent for outward FDI and 23 per cent for inward FDI), inward direct investment started at a much higher level and, as a result, the Spanish capital account has worsened during this period.

The first task of this section is to analyse empirically the relationship between the types of FDI pursued by Spanish companies and the economic conditions in the respective host countries. The IDP has clear predictions not only on the pattern of FDI activity a country will follow through its process of economic development, but also on the pattern of its FDI flows in terms of the host countries, the economic purpose of the investment and the mode in which the investment is most likely to take place. We will use detailed data on Spanish FDI activity during the period 1988 to 1992 to contrast those implications empirically. We will first analyse Spanish outward FDI activity in each country according to its economic purpose. Later we will analyse the differences across industries in the mode FDI activity takes place.

The level of development of the host country is a major predictor of the type of inward investment. A less developed country does not have a high level of created assets and its comparative advantage lies in its endowment of natural assets (such as raw materials, or cheap factors of production). As a country develops, both its stock of created assets and its stock of capital increase. The increase in the stock of capital raises the marginal productivity of natural assets and the relative price of these assets. This process causes a shift in inward FDI from seeking natural assets towards pursuing created assets. We therefore expect a country's per capita income to be negatively related to the percentage of factor-seeking FDI into the country and positively related to the percentage of asset-seeking investment.

The existence in the host country of created assets not currently available in the home country induces asset-seeking FDI. The amount of created assets in a country is positively correlated with the country's level of development and its level of scientific activity. We expect countries with higher levels of scientific activity to have a relatively higher level of asset-seeking inward FDI. We use two measures of scientific activity as proxies for the existing level of created assets in the host country. The number of scientists and engineers in the country measures the amount of inputs a country devotes to R&D activity while the number of patents in force in each country is a measure of the country's R&D output.[2]

Existing trade flows will also determine the purpose of FDI activity. Companies are more likely to invest in foreign marketing and distribution for their products in countries that represent an important present and/or potential market for them. Therefore, we expect the current level of trade flows between the host country and Spain to be a positive predictor of the percentage of inward FDI that is for distribution activities.[3] We also expect certain countries to have a higher probability of being served without distribution activities. Factors favouring this effect will be geographical proximity to Spain and high levels of international trade.[4]

The data compiled by the Spanish Economic Ministry distinguish FDI transactions according to their economic purpose. Investors are required to classify their investment within one of the following categories: marketing and distribution, production using Spanish technology, production without using Spanish technology, sourcing of raw materials, joint ventures, holdings, and others. We grouped these investments according to the IDP framework as follows: marketing and distribution are defined as investments in distribution; those investments with the purpose of sourcing raw materials and of manufacturing overseas using Spanish technology are factor-seeking investments; and an investment is defined as asset seeking when its purpose is production without using Spanish technology or the establishment of an overseas joint venture.[5]

The lower panel of Figure 7.2 describes the breakdown of outward FDI according to these different economic purposes. Investments in distribution have grown throughout this period signalling the increase in export orientation of Spanish companies. The other two types of foreign investment present a much smaller amount of overall FDI activity and their levels have remained practically constant. Financial investments in the form of holdings and other financial transactions accounted for approximately 40 per cent of the total outward investment flow during this period (see Figure 7.2). Financial investments are very sensitive to short-run fluctuations in returns and to regulatory differences across countries. As such, they are hard to analyse in the context of the investment development framework. Therefore, we will restrict our analysis to the other four types of investment.

Table 7.3 shows the results of correlating the percentage of total Spanish outward FDI flows to each host country that is asset seeking, factor seeking or in distribution with the independent variables defined above.[6] The first three columns report the results of regressions for which the dependent variable is the annual outward FDI flow by purpose to each host country as a percentage of total Spanish FDI to that country. In the last three columns the dependent variable was defined as the ratio of the annual value of each type of Spanish FDI into the host country divided by that country's GDP. The goal is not to understand the country variables that determine the *amount* of FDI the country receives for each purpose but to determine what country characteristics make it more likely to be a destination of a certain *type* of FDI, i.e. the percentage of Spanish FDI in the country that has a given economic purpose.

The first column of Table 7.3 confirms the hypothesis that Spain's outward investment in search of created assets will be more likely in those countries with a comparative advantage in those assets. The results show both per capita income (GDPCAP) and the number of scientists (SCI) in the host country to be a positive and significant influence on the percentage of Spanish FDI that is asset seeking. We also ran this specification substituting the input measure of scientific activity by an output measure (the number of granted patents in the host country) and the results were similar. Both the level of development and the level of scientific activity are positive predictors of the relative importance of asset-seeking investments.

The results for investments in distribution and factor-seeking investments are also partly consistent with the theory. Investments in distribution are relatively larger for those countries with which Spain has a higher level of international trade (SPTRADE). We also find the existing stock of Spanish FDI in those countries (SFDIGDP) to be negatively correlated with the importance of distribution activities. Factor-seeking investments are likely to occur in

Table 7.3: Total outward FDI by purpose and country of destination [a]

	PASSTSK	PMRKTSK	PFCTRSK	PASSTGDP	PMRKTGDP	PFCTRGDP
GDP	−0.0006*	−0.000	0.001	−0.004	−0.331**	−0.027
	0.0003	0.001	0.001	0.007	0.055	0.020
GDPCAP	0.355*	−0.879*	0.048			
	0.120	0.337	0.226			
SCI	0.002*	0.001	−0.006**	0.004**	−0.020	−0.006
	0.001	0.002	0.001	0.001	0.021	0.007
SPTRADE	−1.824	5.928**	−3.195**	0.516*	2.487*	0.098
	3.009	1.358	0.565	0.199	0.957	0.355
WFDIGDP	0.053	−0.338	0.136**	−0.012	−0.099**	−0.002
	0.118	0.331	0.022	0.007	0.035	0.013
SFDIGDP	−0.005	−0.292**	0.008	0.002	0.003	0.021**
	0.032	0.090	0.060	0.002	0.010	0.004
OECD				1.150**	6.253**	0.557**
				0.254	1.221	0.453
LATIN				0.129	0.805	0.103
				0.200	0.963	0.357
No. Obs.	167	167	167	167	167	167
Adj. R^2	0.06	0.07	0.18	0.17	0.17	0.17

Notes: The standard errors are reported below the coeffient estimates.
  * Significant at the 5% level.
  ** Significant at the 1% level.
  [a] The dependent variable includes investments in all industries with that purpose.

countries with which Spain does not have a high level of international trade and countries with a low level of created assets. Recall that factor-seeking FDI includes investments in raw material production and in cheap factors of production. Therefore, these investments should take place in those countries with a relative advantage in natural rather than created assets. The worldwide stock of FDI in the host country (WFDIGDP) is only significant for factor-seeking investment.

The last three columns of Table 7.3 redefine the dependent variable as the ratio of each type of investment relative to the host country's GDP. This specification avoids the implicit correlation among the dependent variables in the first three columns owing to the restriction that the three dependent variables must sum to 100 per cent. We also believe this normalization to be more consistent with the way in which the exogenous variables have been defined. However, we expect the level of Spanish FDI activity to be higher in certain countries for geographical, regulatory and historical reasons. Therefore, we also include as exogenous variables two dummy variables as controls for OECD countries (OECD) and for Latin America (LATIN).[7] Both dummies are positive as expected.

The results from these regressions confirm the evidence presented above. Asset-seeking investments are more likely to occur in trade-related countries with a high level of scientific activity, while distribution activities occur in countries with a low stock of inward FDI to GDP and with high levels of international trade with Spain. The results for factor-seeking investment are weak. Only the level of Spanish FDI stock in the country (SFDIGDP) is significant with a positive sign.[8]

We also decided to split the sample by the mode in which investment takes place in 27 manufacturing industries.[9] We can distinguish whether the investment involved the establishment of a new company by the foreign investor or the acquisition or the establishment of a long-run relationship with an existing firm in the country.[10] Asset-seeking investments have the goal of acquiring intangible created assets (such as know-how, brand names or name recognition). Market transactions for these assets are often more costly than intra-firm transactions (Caves 1982). This is one of the main reasons for internationalization. Therefore, we would expect this investment to be more likely to occur through the acquisition of an existing firm in the host country. On the other hand, when the intangible asset is the property of the investing

Table 7.4: Outward manufacturing FDI by form of investment and industry[a]

	Total[b]	PANINV	PGREEN	PACQU
PRFRAT	5.911**	0.483**	−0.763	0.397
	0.864	0.051	0.462	0.332
PUBRAT	54.364**	0.041**	−4.761	−3.094
	19.647	0.012	7.557	8.775
C10	−0.286	−0.028	0.444*	−0.523
	0.632	0.037	0.223	0.328
REVADV	30.567	0.021*	0.070	−0.161
	30.104	0.011	0.114	0.137
No. Obs	131	131	124	114
Adj. R^2	0.37	0.57	0.06	0.10

Notes: The standard errors are reported below the coefficient estimates.
* Significant at the 5% level.
** Significant at the 1% level.
[a] Regressions include only observations with positive FDI and industry dummies.
[b] Regression also includes year dummies.

company, i.e. FDI is of the factor-seeking or distribution type, such investment is more likely to be a greenfield investment.

Table 7.4 reports the results of these industry regressions by mode of investment. The dependent variable in the first column is the total value of investment in an industry and year while in the second column the dependent variable is the percentage of investment for that year that took place in that industry. Finally, the last two columns use the percentage of investment in each industry and year that were greenfield investments and the percentage that were acquisitions as the dependent variables.

The first two specifications will help us determine which type of industries are more active in overseas investment. The literature on FDI has consistently found that highly profitable industries (PRFRAT) and those with a high level of intangible assets have more FDI activity. We measure intangible assets using two standard measures (see Caves 1982): the ratio of advertising expenditures to production (PUBRAT), and the ratio of R&D expenditures to production (RDRAT). We only report the results using PUBRAT owing to data problems when using the R&D ratio.[11] A higher PUBRAT implies a higher level of created intangible assets and a larger potential benefit from internationalization. The results in the second column are practically identical: industries with a higher percentage of FDI activity are industries with high levels of profitability and with large intangible assets. In this specification, the measure of revealed comparative advantage (REVADV) is also positive and significant suggesting that export-oriented industries also tend to have large FDI activity.

The distinction between greenfield or acquisitions does not, however, provide much information. In both specifications none of the exogenous variables are ever significant (except for the 10-firm concentration ratio, C10 for greenfield investments). The null hypothesis that all the coefficients of the independent variables (except those of the industry dummies) are equal to zero could not be rejected with an F-test.

INWARD FOREIGN DIRECT INVESTMENT

The rapid increase in inward FDI flows into Spain has been mainly due to non-manufacturing FDI, i.e. finance and service-oriented industries, especially towards the end of the period (see Figure 7.1). Although manufacturing FDI consistently increased after 1986, it did so at a lower rate than overall FDI. Inward manufacturing FDI has increased at a much faster rate than outward manufacturing FDI and by 1993 inward manufacturing flows were nine times larger than outward flows. Given the importance of inward manufacturing FDI activity it will be useful to have a better understanding of the country of origin of FDI, its industry composition and the form in which this FDI takes place. Therefore, we will perform below an analysis similar to that presented in the previous section for outward FDI.[12]

Table 7.5 reports the results of regressing Spanish inward FDI flows from each home country, broken down by the mode of investment as a function of the characteristics of the home country.[13] As in Table 7.4 we report the results using the following dependent variables: total annual investment by home country (TOTAL), percentage of each home country's investment in total annual investment (PANINV), and percentage of the home country's outward FDI flow to Spain that was greenfield (PGREEN) or acquisitions (PACQU).

The results for total investment show that countries with a high income per capita (GDPCAP) and countries relatively well endowed with created assets (SCI) are less likely to perform high levels of

Table 7.5 Inward manufacturing FDI by form of investment and country of origin

	TOTAL	PANINV	PGREEN	PACQU
GDP	0.116**	0.070**	−0.046	−0.003
	0.022	0.011	0.061	0.064
GDPCAP	−38.744**	−0.228*	−0.949*	0.854*
	14.335	0.075	0.403	0.420
SPTRADE	0.029*	0.016*	−0.040	−0.007
	0.257	0.007	0.040	0.040
SCI	−0.562**	−0.338**	0.159	0.250
	0.087	0.046	0.244	0.250
OUTFDI	61.092**	36.883**	−46.035	2.242
	9.794	5.142	27.555	28.662
OECD	90.429**	5.432**		
	32.944	1.730		
LATIN	13.261**	8.154*		
	2.886	1.515		
No. Obs.	132	132	132	132
Adj. R^2	0.42	0.48	0.21	0.01

Notes: The standard errors are reported below the coefficient estimates.
   * Significant at the 5% level.
   ** Significant at the 1% level.

FDI in Spain. These countries will incur FDI when searching for factors in factor-endowed countries or when seeking created assets from equally or more developed countries. To the extent that Spain is an intermediate country in the IDP, its level of created assets is still too low to appeal to most developed countries while, at the same time, Spain has lost comparative advantage with respect to less developed countries in terms of cheap factors of production. Notice that in this regression both dummies OECD and LATIN are positive and significant. If OECD is dropped from the regression then GDPCAP becomes positive and significant indicating the attractiveness of Spain as a destination of FDI from developed countries for locational reasons, although not necessarily from the developed countries with the highest GDP per capita, GDPCAP. We also find the intensity of trade between the home country and Spain (SPTRADE) and the worldwide FDI stock of the home country (OUTFDI) to be positive predictors of the amount of inward FDI originating from those countries.

The last two columns of Table 7.5 report the results of splitting the amount of investment by whether the investment was greenfield or acquisition. Since the variables here are expressed as percentages of each form of investment over total home country investment in Spain, we drop the two dummy variables (OECD and LATIN) from the specification. As was the case for outward FDI the results from these specifications are not very revealing. The only significant variable is the level of the country's per capita income which has a positive effect for acquisitions and a negative effect for greenfield investments. These results suggest that rich countries are more likely to enter FDI through the purchase of existing assets in Spain.[14]

Table 7.6 reports the results of regressing inward FDI by destination industry. As was the case with outward FDI, inward FDI tends to be most intense in manufacturing industries with high levels of profitability (PRFRAT), high levels of intangible assets (PUBRAT), and relatively high export orientation (REVADV). Also, as before, the results are incapable of providing information on the type of industries that are more likely to receive FDI through greenfield investments rather than through the acquisition of existing firms.

Table 7.6: Inward manufacturing FDI by form of investment and industry[a]

	Total[b]	PERC	PGREEN	PACQU
PRFRAT	0.081	0.504*	−0.108	0.258
	0.311	0.025	0.326	0.475
PUBRAT	19.656**	2.988**	−0.181**	5.570
	6.708	0.829	0.063	6.395
C10	−0.202	0.038	−0.077	−0.507
	0.207	0.026	0.198	0.280
REVADV	17.613*	3.121**	−0.077	−3.864
	8.195	1.269	8.889	10.010
No. Obs.	148	148	143	143
Adj. R^2	0.48	0.56	0.17	0.08

Notes: The standard errors are reported below the coefficient estimates.
   * Significant at the 5% level.
   ** Significant at the 1% level.
   [a] Regressions include only observations with positive FDI and industry dummies.
   [b] Regression also includes year dummies.

EXPLANATIONS FOR FDI GROWTH: ECONOMICS AND GOVERNMENT POLICIES

Since the 1980s, Spain has become one of the leading FDI destinations of the world and an emerging source of FDI. What has made Spain such an attractive destination for FDI? This question may be answered from a variety of perspectives. First, time series analyses provide solid macroeconomic evidence in favour of the hypothesis for distribution investments while finding no support for the impact of relative wage and exchange rate levels (Bajo 1991; Bajo and Sosvilla 1992; García de la Cruz 1993). Attracted by the size and growth of the market, foreign investors have flocked to Spain during periods of relative political tranquillity, price stability, and economic and trade liberalization. Second, there is some evidence from the case of the European affiliates of US multinationals that, despite the similar level of sales per employee, they obtain higher returns in Spain than elsewhere in Europe (García de la Cruz 1993).

Third, upgraded assets such as skilled labour, support industries and infrastructures must be playing an increasingly important role given that, simultaneously, Spain has engaged in trade liberalization, reached industrial productivity levels comparable to other EU countries with high FDI inflows (e.g. the UK), and allowed labour costs to rise (United Nations 1992, table 2.7). Inward FDI in non-financial services and in manufacturing, however, has continued to pour into the country.

Fourth, inward FDI is now tilted more towards acquisitions than greenfield investment (Figure 7.3). Why have the most active foreign investors (i.e. EU firms making acquisitions) moved into an increasingly open economy to manufacture or to render non-financial services? In the case of non-financial services, foreign investors have acquired assets in order to overcome industry-level barriers to entry and to gain market share quickly. As regards manufacturing investments, most foreign firms have come to Spain not only to sell in an expanding domestic market (which is by now fairly open to competition from abroad) or to overcome industrial barriers to entry but also to locate value-added activities in the context of a world economy tending towards globalization. Furthermore, foreign firms are finding upgraded assets in Spain such as a skilled workforce, clusters of support industries stimulated in part by prior inward FDI, and an improved infrastructure that allows them to use their Spanish location as an export base (e.g. in automobiles, electronics, electrical appliances and chemicals). Meanwhile, successful Spanish firms have barely shifted production abroad in response to domestic cost increases for the same reason: the continued, yet changing, locational advantages of Spain. Finally, multinational firms in mature industries (e.g. food processing, beverages, auto parts) have been acquiring Spanish firms with an international presence to gain market share not only in Spain but also in other EU countries in which the Spanish firms had a sizeable presence.[15]

Given the tone of our discussion thus far, the political economy of *inward* foreign investment in Spain can only offer a straightforward explanation of the role of the government. In the short run, policies tending towards political and economic stabilization, liberalization of foreign investment legal regimes, and market opening have been the direct contributors to the FDI boom. The stories of the 1960s and 1980s are testimony to this. Arguably, the comparatively smooth transition to democracy in the late 1970s, the containment of inflation during the 1980s, and EU membership in 1986 have been critical to continued foreign inward investment. Beyond the short run, policies have resulted in impressive investments in infrastructure, education and worker training since 1983 and are steadily upgrading the locational advantages of Spain. In the short term these government policies have contributed to economic growth, and thus indirectly to FDI, but they have also tended to feed the public deficit and inflation. As far as *outward* FDI is concerned, there have been some attempts to present the international incursions of state-owned enterprises such as Iberia (the flag air carrier), Telefónica de España, Endesa (electrical utility) and CASA (aircraft construction) as providing a renewed impetus for the internationalization of Spanish firms. While the expansion of Telefónica and CASA abroad have in fact generated much enthusiasm and praise, the small but successful group of Spanish multinationals in industries such as textiles and clothing, food and beverages, luxury goods, electrical appliances, industrial machinery and auto parts have rarely taken advantage of governmental programmes.

R&D AND ASSET CREATION

Spain is unlikely to advance in the IDP without upgrading its creative assets. Countries and firms can upgrade assets and increase the marginal productivity of production factors by investing in infrastructure, support industries, labour skill formation and R&D. During the 1980s private firms have increased investments in labour skills and product differentiation, while the government has invested heavily in infrastructure and professional training. R&D efforts, however, have not been enough to allow Spain to narrow the gap with the more advanced countries. In particular, the role of the government in R&D has not been as forceful as in infrastructure and education. As a result, technology-created assets in Spain play only a minor role in FDI.

Spain is suffering from a yawning gap between payments and receipts for patents, royalties and fees. While since 1960 technological receipts have oscillated between 0.02 and 0.11 per cent of GDP, payments have escalated from 0.17 per cent in 1960 to 0.51 in 1992, roughly one-sixth of FDI inflows during that year (Figure 7.4). Domestic R&D expenditures have been growing faster than net payments for patents, royalties and fees. For every peseta of net payments to other countries in 1980 Spain spent domestically 2 pesetas on R&D. By 1991 the ratio was one to three, still far from the levels of the more advanced countries (INE 1994: 30). The vast majority of the payments go to other OECD countries (60

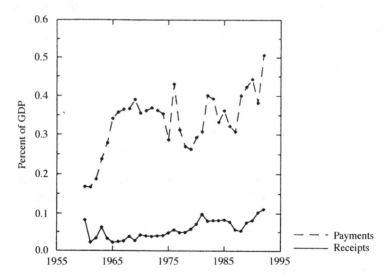

Figure 7.4 Receipts and payments for patents, royalties and fees
Sources: Ministerio de Comercio, *Balanza de pagos de España*; Banco de España, *Balanza de pagos*, several issues.

per cent to the EU and 20 per cent to the United States) while 80 per cent of the receipts come from OECD countries (50 per cent from the EU and 25 per cent from the United States), the remainder mainly from Latin America and, to a lesser extent, South East Asia and the Magreb (Durán Herrera 1992: 242). The fact that 80 per cent of receipts come from countries with a per capita income equal to or higher than Spain's is at odds with the IDP framework. R&D expenditure in Spain has more than quadrupled during the 1980s. But the contribution of the government to total R&D expenditure has fallen from 52 per cent in 1980 to 46 per cent in 1991, while foreign funds have grown from 1 to 6 per cent, and the share of private firms has remained constant. Despite the overall upward trend, in 1991 Spain spent on R&D a mere 0.87 per cent of its GDP, the lowest rate in the OECD except for Greece, Portugal and Turkey (INE 1994: 30, 34). That same year, Spain ranked 19th in terms of cumulative patents granted in the United States (US Patent and Trademark Office 1992:A2), closely followed by countries such as South Africa, Hungary and the former Czechoslovakia, and not much ahead of South Korea, Mexico and New Zealand.

Unlike Portugal, Greece and Ireland, however, Spain has managed to develop three areas of technological strength, as identified in a recent OECD study (Archibugi and Pianta 1992: 76–77): namely, fabricated metals, industrial machinery and motor vehicles, primarily auto parts. Neither funding from the government nor from abroad have contributed significantly to developing distinctive technological capabilities in machinery and motor vehicles: the firms in these industries account for 90 and 98 per cent, respectively, of all R&D expenditure. By contrast, as much as 18 per cent of R&D expenditures in fabricated metals comes from the government (INE 1994: 64). Finally, multinational firms operating in Spain, or Spanish firms with over 50 per cent control by foreign investors, invest in R&D to a greater extent than the rest, and they do so almost exclusively through internally generated resources with little or no governmental funding (INE 1994: 95–96).

INTERNALIZATION ADVANTAGES

The theory of the IDP argues that the higher the economic development of a country and the more advanced it is along the investment path, the more firms are able to exploit whatever ownership advantages they have internally rather than through licensing or

Table 7.7 Internalization advantages of Spanish firms

A Ownership of subsidiaries

Country or area	Authorized outward FDI 1975–1978		Benchmark Survey of FDI stocks 1986	
	Number of subsidiaries	Majority owned	Number of subsidiaries	Majority owned
EU	296	21.6%	946	72.3%
USA	60	18.3%	223	74.4%
Japan	–	–	18	88.9%
OECD	–	–	1332	73.0%
Latin America	382	64.9%	703	51.5%
Asia	–	–	84	71.4%
Africa	–	–	153	38.6%
Total	962	45.3%	2434	65.0%

Note: For 1975–1978 USA includes Canada.
Sources: Nueno Iniesta *et al.* (1981: 106); Secretaría de Estado de Comercio (1989: 107–114).

B Use of proprietary distribution for export by country or area, 1986 and 1992

Country or area	Exports through proprietary distribution channels as % of total Spanish exports in: 1986	1992
EU	7.6	–
USA	14.1	–
Japan	1.3	–
OECD	7.7	–
Latin America	14.5	–
Asia	2.7	–
Africa	2.8	–
Total	7.3	13.4

Note: The numerator includes Spanish-owned firms for 1986 (*n* = 1544), and for 1992 Spanish firms with less than 75% foreign capital participation in the numerator (*n* = 1872) and all firms in the denominator (*n* = 2103).
Sources: For 1986, Secretaría de Estado de Comercio (1989: 225–232). For 1992, authors' calculations from the ICEX 1992 Survey of Exporters (*n* = 2103).

C Use of proprietary distribution for export by type of firm in 1992

Type of firm	No. of firms	% of all exports	% of exports through proprietary distribution	
			Mean	Std dev.
With proprietary distribution	192	62.3	60.9	33.5
Without proprietary distribution	880	37.7	0.0	0.0
All firms	1072	100.0	23.0	36.0

Note: Sample includes Spanish firms with less than 75% foreign capital participation.
Source: Authors' calculations from the ICEX 1992 Survey of Exporters.

joint ownership arrangements. Unfortunately, data limitations to test this aspect of the theory in the case of Spain are tremendous. Official statistics on receipts for patents, royalties and fees from abroad do not specify whether the payer is affiliated with a Spanish parent company or not.[16] There is some limited and outdated information on the ownership of foreign subsidiaries of Spanish companies. Authorizations for new outward FDI between 1975 and 1978 show that 45 per cent of the subsidiaries were majority owned. This compares with overall 65 per cent majority ownership in the 1986 benchmark survey on FDI stocks. It seems, therefore, that Spanish firms have been increasing their ownership share of foreign subsidiaries over time. The rise in majority ownership between the mid-1970s and the mid-1980s has been most remarkable in the case of subsidiaries located in the EU and the United States (from about 20 to over 70 per cent of all subsidiaries), while those located in Latin America have actually become less majority owned (see panel A of Table 7.7). These levels of majority ownership are not much lower than the ones reported by Encarnation (1994: 210) for the subsidiaries of US, EU and Japanese multinationals.

Another way of measuring internalization is to examine whether exports flow into foreign markets through proprietary distribution channels or not. Taking into account Spanish-based parent firms with no more than 75 per cent of foreign capital, the ratio of exports through proprietary channels to total Spanish exports has doubled from 7.3 per cent in 1986 to 13.4 per cent in 1992. The more distant the foreign market (e.g. North and Latin America compared to

Europe), the higher the degree of internalization (panel B of Table 7.7). At the firm level, the degrees of internalization of exports are much lower than for US, EU and Japanese multinationals (Encarnation 1994: 217). Of all Spanish exports originating from firms with less than 75 per cent foreign ownership, 23 per cent are sold through proprietary distribution channels. Firms that do have proprietary distribution channels sell 61 per cent of their exports through them (panel C of Table 7.7).

Finally, no information exists on intra-company shipments of goods other than those for sale through foreign distribution subsidiaries. The fact that outward factor- and raw-material-seeking FDI has remained flat while most of the recent increase has been accounted for by investments in holdings or market access (see, again, lower panel of Figure 7.2) indicates that Spanish firms with investments abroad have not generated the complex patterns of transfers of intermediary and final goods between subsidiaries and parent company or between subsidiaries located in different countries so characteristic of the largest multinational corporations (Encarnation 1994: 221–226).

DISCUSSION AND CONCLUSIONS

The challenge of testing Dunning and Narula's theory in the case of Spain is that since 1960 the country has followed a process of rapid economic development with increasing internationalization of its economy but with few Spanish firms capable of drawing on their ownership and internalization advantages to exploit locational opportunities abroad. Inward FDI grew at a much higher rate than a relatively modest flow of outward FDI. Government policies directed towards encouraging the international integration of the Spanish economy and upgrading the existing infrastructure have stimulated this increasing flow of FDI. The Spanish case can provide some relevant experience to other countries like Mexico which have began a process of international economic integration (see Chapter 8 of this volume).

The case of Spain confirms many of the dynamics typical of countries in the second stage of the IDP. Dunning and Narula (1994) characterize this stage as one in which inward FDI is attracted by natural assets (raw materials, cheap labour), a growing domestic market and the development of technological advantages in certain support industries clustered around primary industries. These phenomena occurred in the Spanish case.

The evolution of outward direct investment also shows a number of patterns that coincide with the predictions of the IDP paradigm. Most Spanish outward investments are in establishing marketing and distribution channels. OECD member countries receive the majority of the value of these investments. However, the percentage of total Spanish FDI that is in distribution is higher for countries with lower per capita incomes and with current high levels of international trade with Spain. Asset-seeking investments take place in countries with higher levels of economic and technological development. However, we find that most of the returns to Spanish-created assets come from investments in countries with development levels equal to or higher than Spain's and not from countries at a lower development stage like the paradigm suggests. Also, direct government incentives to R&D and internalization did not appear to have a direct impact on the level of internationalization of those assets.

The experience of Spain since the mid-1980s shows a rapid increase in inward FDI even as the locational advantages of natural assets have quickly eroded. The importance of a growing domestic market partly explains this growth of inward FDI. Even more important are the acquisitions of companies with established domestic and international positions in their industries or with upgraded assets developed domestically or induced by inward FDI (as in the case of support industries like auto parts). These massive foreign acquisitions will curtail the international expansion of domestically owned firms. Given this acquisition activity, we would expect future outward FDI flows to originate increasingly from a foreign-controlled Spanish firm as part of the overall strategy of the foreign parent company. Outward investment by domestically owned companies will be unlikely to reach the levels of inward FDI activity suggested by further stages of the IDP paradigm. This situation is typical of middle-income countries such as Spain, not because they entirely lack ownership or internalization advantages that they could exploit abroad, but because the existence of both a large, developed and internationally integrated market and a plethora of strategic business assets in the private and state-owned sectors tend to keep the flows of inward FDI at levels and rates of growth higher than those for outward FDI.

NOTES

*   Research funding from the Carnegie-Bosch Institute for Applied Studies in International Management is gratefully acknowledged. We also thank Carlos Pereira and Montserrat Luengo for research assistance.

1   In 1973-1974 and 1976-1977 procedures for inward FDI were clarified and simplified (Muñoz *et al.* 1978: 45–60), while similar changes were introduced for outward FDI beginning with the first comprehensive legislation of 1973 and several liberalizing decrees in 1978 (De Erice 1975; Marín 1982; Aguilar Fernández-Hontoria 1985; Nueno Iniesta *et al.* 1981).

2   Clear problems exist with both measures: (1) certain created assets (such as brand names, organizational advantages, or know-how from traditional industries) are not likely to be highly correlated with these two measures; (2) regulation on industrial property rights differs widely across countries reducing the incentive to register patents; and (3) definitional problems exist across countries for each measure.

3   High protection by a host government can also increase market-seeking FDI activity in production facilities as a way around protection. As explained below, we cannot distinguish this type of investment in our data.

4   Notice that trade to GDP ratios are not necessarily related to degree of protection. An obvious example is the United States which has low rates of protection and a low ratio of international trade to GDP.

5   This classification, although close to the economic phenomena it is intended to capture, does have some problems. For instance, the investment in distribution category does not include the possibility of investments in manufacturing production in a country due to the country's high level of protectionism. This case would likely be an investment in production using Spanish technology which we are classifying as a factor-seeking investment although the economic purpose is likely to be a substitute investment for distribution investment that is not possible because of high import protection.

6   The specific definitions of the variables used and their sources are included in the Data Appendix.

7   A third group of countries, the tax havens, was dropped from the analysis owing to the distortions caused by their tax regimes.

8   We decided to split the factor-seeking group between investments in search for raw materials and investments to produce with Spanish technology. We also included as a regressor the percentage of exports of each country that are minerals and raw materials. As expected, this variable was a significant positive predictor of the level of FDI-seeking raw materials.

9   Ideally one would look at the importance of each form of FDI transaction to each destination country. However, data restrictions do not allow us to identify the transactions in such manner.

10   The raw data classified FDI transactions as: creation of a new company, capital increase in an existing investment, acquisition of an existing domestic company, and a long-term loan with the intention of establish-

ing a management relationship. We aggregate the first two groups and define the aggregate as greenfield investments; we also aggregate the last two and define the new measure as acquisitions of domestic firms. Although a capital increase can be in a domestic company (i.e. an acquisition) as well as in an already foreign-owned company (greenfield) we cannot distinguish between the two. We decided to include all capital increases as greenfields.

11 Missing observations in the R&D data significantly reduce the number of observations in the sample. Also, the R&D data are not directly comparable to the industry classification in the FDI data set. However, when we include this variable in the regression its coefficient is always positive but not always significant.

12 Unfortunately, data limitations do not allow us to distinguish inward FDI by its economic purpose.

13 The home country is the country of residence of the ultimate beneficiary of the investment. We also perform similar regressions by country of immediate origin. In those regressions we decided to exclude certain countries (such as tax havens, The Netherlands, etc.) owing to differences in taxation and government regulations. Owing to the possible noise introduced by this selection criterion we decided not to report those results here.

14 Recall the high level of acquisition activity that has taken place in this period (see Figure 7.3). Most of these acquisitions were done by companies from OECD countries.

15 Recently, Allied-Lyons of the UK has acquired Pedro Domecq, the world's eighth-largest beverages group, Exide Corp. of the United States has taken over Tudor, the third-largest battery manufacturer at the European level, and the Koipe-Elosúa olive oil and foods group has come under the control of Italy's Ferruzzi.

16 Moreno Moré (1975: 101) calculated that intra-firm technological receipts amounted to 5.3 per cent of total receipts in 1969 and 5.5 per cent in 1973.

DATA APPENDIX

The data of outward and inward FDI reflect transactions in which the foreign investor controls at least 20 per cent equity interest in the participated company (10 per cent starting in 1993) or has effective control over the management of the participated foreign company. The data also include FDI long-term loans to or from foreign companies with maturity longer than five years and with the goal of establishing lasting economic links. The data reflect notification of the intent to invest, not of the actual investment. The company has, after its notification of the intention to invest, up to six months to do so. Therefore, an investment might be classified in a calendar year prior to the year in which the investment took place. Also, to the extent that a notification does not end in a transaction, FDI flows may appear in the data that never took place. The overall correlation between notification and actual investments is very high (Aguilar Fernández-Hontoria 1985). Finally, FDI transactions appear in the data (such as reinvested earnings, or contributions in physical assets) that did not result in international capital flows. Therefore, differences exist between our measure of FDI and the values that appear in the capital accounts.

Definitions of variables

$PASSTSK_i$ = percentage of the annual value of Spanish outward FDI in host country i that had the purpose of either producing in country i using non-Spanish technology or starting a joint venture with a foreign company.

$PMRKTSK_i$ = percentage of the annual value of Spanish outward FDI in host country i that was in marketing and distribution.

$PFCTRSK_i$ = percentage of the annual value of Spanish outward FDI in host country i that was in sourcing of raw materials or in manufacturing production using Spanish technology.

$PASSTGDP_i$ = the ratio of the annual value of Spanish outward FDI in host country i that was either a joint venture or an investment in production facilities that will use non-Spanish technology to country i's GDP.

$PMRKTGDP_i$ = the ratio of the annual value of Spanish outward FDI in host country i that was in marketing and distribution to country i's GDP.

$PFCTRGDP_i$ = the ratio of the annual value of Spanish outward FDI in host country i that was either in sourcing of raw material or in production facilities using Spanish technology to country i's GDP.

$PANINV_{i[k]}$ = percentage of the annual value of outward (inward) FDI that took place in (from) country i [or in industry k].

$PGREEN_{i[k]}$ = percentage of the annual value of outward (inward) FDI that took place in (from) country i [or in industry k] that took the form of a new company or an equity increase in an existing foreign company.

$PACQU_{i,[k]}$ = percentage of the annual value of outward (inward) FDI that took place in (from) country i [or in industry k] that took the form of purchase of an existing national company or a long-term loan.

GDP = Gross Domestic Product, in million US$ for 1990.

GDPCAP = GDP/population.

SCI = number of scientists and engineers in the country, latest year.

SCIGDP = SCI/GDP.

SPTRADE = (EXPORTS$_{Spain}$ + IMPORTS$_{Spain}$)/(EXPORTS$_i$ + IMPORTS$_i$), for 1990, where the subscript i indicates the home or host country.

SFDIGDP$_i$ = ratio of Spanish FDI stock in host country i to country i's GDP in 1986.

WFDIGDP$_i$ = ratio of worldwide FDI stock in host country i to country i's GDP in 1990.

OUTFDI$_i$ = ratio of home country i's stock of outward FDI to country i's GDP in 1990.

The source for the variables above is the United Nations *Statistical Yearbook*, except for the values of FDI stocks that come from the United Nations *World Investment Report, 1993* and from Dirección de Transacciones Exteriores *Censo de Inversiones Directas de España en el extranjero*, 1989. The source for Spanish FDI inflow and outflows is the Spanish Economic Ministry, Dirección de Transacciones Exteriores.

PRFRAT$_k$ = the ratio of industry k's real profits to its real production in 1990.

PUBRAT$_k$ = the ratio of industry k's nominal expenditures in advertising to its nominal industry production in 1989.

C10 = 10-firm concentration ratio in 1990, measured in terms of each firm's value of production.

REVADV$_k$ = revealed comparative advantage measured as the difference between industry k's exports and imports as a ratio of the industry production in 1986.

The sources for these variables are Instituto Nacional de Estadística, *Encuesta Industrial*, and Fundación Empresa Pública, Programa de Investigaciones Económicas.

REFERENCES

Agarwal, J. P. (1980) 'Determinants of foreign direct investment: a survey', *Weltwirtschaftliches Archiv* 116 (4), 739–773.

Aguilar Fernández-Hontoria, E. (1985) 'Cinco años de liberalización de las inversiones directas españolas en el exterior, 1980-1984', *Información Comercial Española* August-September, 51–70.

Archibugi, D. and Pianta, M. (1992) *The Technological Specialization of Advanced Countries*, London: Kluwer Academic Publishers.

Bajo, O. (1991) 'Determinantes macroeconómicos y sectoriales de la inversión extranjera directa en España', *Información Comercial Española* 696–697, August-September, 53–74.

—— and Sosvilla, S. (1992) 'Un análisis empírico de los determinantes macroeconómicos de la inversión extranjera directa en España, 1961–1989', *Moneda y Crédito* 194, 107–148.

Campillo, M. (1963) *Las inversiones extranjeras en España, 1850-1950,* Madrid: Manfer.

Castellvi, M. (1973) 'Cataluña abre la puerta del Rosellón', *Actualidad Económica* 30, June, 8–13.

Caves, R. (1982) *Multinational Enterprise and Economic Analysis,* Cambridge: Cambridge University Press.

COCINB (1973) *Las inversiones españolas en el exterior,* Barcelona: Cámara Oficial de Comercio, Industria y Navegación de Barcelona.

De Erice, S. (1975) 'Comentarios al régimen legal de las inversiones españolas en el extranjero', *Información Comercial Española* 499, March, 77–90.

Dunning, J. H. (1979) 'Explaining changing patterns of international production: in defence of the eclectic theory', *Oxford Bulletin of Economics and Statistics* 41, 269–296.

—— (1981) 'Explaining the international direct investment position of countries: towards a dynamic or developmental approach', *Weltwirtschaftliches Archiv* 119, 30–64.

—— (1988) *Explaining International Production,* London: Unwin Hyman.

—— and Narula, R. (1994) *Transpacific Foreign Direct Investment and the Investment Development Path: The Record Assessed,* South Carolina Essays in International Business No. 10, Columbia, South Carolina: Center for International Business Education and Research, University of South Carolina.

Durán Herrera, J. J. (1992) 'Cross-direct investment and technological capability of Spanish domestic firms', in J. Cantwell (ed.) *Multinational Investment in Modern Europe,* Aldershot. Edward Elgar, 214–255.

—— and Muñoz, S. (1984), 'La internacionalización de la economía español via inversión directa 1960–1982', in I. Minian (ed.) *Transnacionalización y Periferia Semiindustrializada,* Mexico: CIDE, Vol. 2, 347–405.

Encarnation, D. (1994) 'Investment and trade by American, European, and Japanese multinationals across the triad', in M. Mason and D. Encarnation (eds) *Does Ownership Matter?,* Oxford: Oxford University Press, 205–227.

García de la Cruz, J. M. (1993) *Empresas multinacionales y economía española,* Ph.D. Thesis, Series No. 141/93, Madrid: Universidad Complutense de Madrid.

González, R. (1989) 'Las inversiones españolas directas e inmobiliarias en el exterior durante 1988', *Boletín Semanal de Información Comercial Española,* 27 February–5 March, 869–879.

Hawkesworth, R. E. (1981) 'The rise of Spain's automobile industry', *National Westminster Bank Quarterly Review* February, 37–48.

INE (1994) *Estadística sobre las actividades en investigación científica y desarrollo tecnológico* (I+D) 1991, Madrid: Instituto Nacional de Estadística.

Marín, J. P. (1982) 'La inversión española en el exterior', *Papeles de Economía Española* 11, 163–184.

Ministerio de Comercio (1993) *Sector exterior en 1992*, Madrid: Ministerio de Comercio.

——— (1994) *Sector exterior en 1993*, Madrid: Ministerio de Comercio.

Moreno Moré, J. L. (1975) 'Quince años de inversiones españolas en el extranjero', *Información Comercial Española* 499, March, 91–107.

Muñoz, J., Roldán, S. and Serrano, A. (1978) *La internacionalización del capital en España, 1959–1977*, Madrid: Edicusa.

Nadal, J. (1975) *El fracaso de la revolución industrial en España, 1814–1913*, Barcelona: Ariel.

Nueno Iniesta, P., Martinez Lapeña, N. and Sarle Guiu J. (1981) *Las inversiones españolas en el extranjero*, Pamplona: Ediciones Universidad de Navarra.

Portillo, L. (1994) 'Las empresas japonesas en Europa ante el mercado único y la recesión', *Boletín Económico de ICE* 2411, 2-8 May, 1139–1145.

Raurich, J. M., Seoane, E. and Sicart, F. (1973) *El marco económico de las inversiones catalanas en el Rosellón*, Barcelona: Condal de Estudios Económicos.

Secretaria de Estado de Comercio (1989) *Censo de inversiones directas de España en el exterior a diciembre de 1986*, Madrid: Secretaria de Estado de Comercio.

Tolentino, P. E. (1993) *Technological Innovation and Third World Multinationals*, New York: Routledge.

Tortella, G. (1994) *El desarrollo de la España contemporánea: Historia económica de los siglos XIX y XX*, Madrid: Alianza.

United Nations (1992) *UN Handbook of Industrial Statistics 1992*, New York: United Nations.

United Nations Conference on Trade and Development (1993) *World Investment Report 1993*, New York: United Nations.

——— (1994) *World Investment Report 1994*, New York: United Nations.

US Patent and Trademark Office (1992) *Industrial Patent Activity in the United States. Part 1: Time Series Profile by Company and Country of Origin, 1969–1991*, Washington, D.C.: US Patent and Trademark Office.

Varela Parache, F. (1972) 'Las inversiones españolas en el extranjero', *Información Comercial Española* 9 (104), August, 59–64.

——— and Rodríguez de Pablo, J. (1974) 'Las inversiones extranjeras en España, 1959–1974: Una vía al desarrollo', *Información Comercial Española* 493, September, 13–20.

Chapter 8

Mexico
Foreign investment as a source of international competitiveness

Alvaro Calderón, Michael Mortimore and Wilson Peres

INTRODUCTION

Foreign direct investment (FDI) has played a crucial role in Mexico's development since the nineteenth century. Investments in mining, oil and public utilities around the turn of the century were followed, after the interruption forced by the 1910 Revolution, by important investments in manufacturing, throughout the import-substituting industrialization (ISI) process. In this context, multinational enterprises (MNEs) have been leaders in some of the most important industries on which the country has based the expansion of its domestic market and its industrial exports. The investment development path (IDP) concept (Dunning and Narula, 1994)[1] is a useful tool to understand and summarize the dynamics of FDI inflows to Mexico, as well as the more recent outflows from the country.

Until the mid-1940s Mexico may be considered as a Stage 1 country in the IDP; its location-specific advantages were insufficient to attract significant direct investment, with the exception of those related to the possession of natural assets. Although some manufacturing MNEs started assembly operations in the country much earlier, it is with the development of the metal-mechanical and chemical industries during the ISI period that the country entered Stage 2 of the IDP. The building up of a basic infrastructure and the upgrading of human resources via education that took place during the previous stage combined with a fast growing domestic market during ISI made it profitable for MNEs to undertake local production with a significant domestic content in parts and components. FDI inflows increased sharply from the 1950s to the 1970s (Table 8.1) basically induced by economic growth, stable macro-economic conditions and government policies that protected the

Table 8.1 Foreign direct investment flows, 1955-1993 (annual averages in million 1985 dollars[a])

	Inflows	Outflows[b]
1955-1961	498	na
1962-1973	731	na
1974-1977	1,271	na
1978-1982	2,347	na
1983-1985	467	176
1986-1988	2,495	140
1989-1993	3,189	235

Notes: [a] Balance of payments flows deflated by the consumer price index in the industrialized countries.
[b] Mexico does not produce data on investment abroad. Outflows recorded in this table refer only to Mexican direct investment in the United States, by far the most important host country for those investments. The large direct investments undertaken by CEMEX in Spain are not included (see below).

Sources: Banco de México, Informe Anual, several years, and OECD, International Direct Investment Statistics Yearbook, 1994.

domestic market, subsidized capital investment and safeguarded the purchasing power of large segments of the urban population.

Although the debt crisis of the 1980s stopped economic growth for a decade, the country experienced a drastic economic restructuring that strengthened some very specific industrial sectors. As is expected for a country well advanced into the second stage of the IDP, some large Mexican firms located in those sectors emerged as significant direct investors abroad. Ownership advantages in the production of some industrial commodities, as well as increasingly important perceived internationalization advantages by such firms, may indicate that there are forces pushing towards Mexico's upgrading from Stage 2 to Stage 3 along the IDP. However, medium-term obstacles (such as the financial crisis surrounding the huge devaluation of the Mexican peso in December 1994) and the increasing dependence of the country on foreign investment inflows to modernize its economic structure will determine that its net outward investment (NOI) position will continue to be negative for a long period in the future.

In this context of change, in which modernization and crisis intertwine permanently, MNEs played, and are playing, a crucial role. The main objective of this chapter is to present the principal features of their dynamics and their impact on Mexico's incorporation into the new international industrial order as well as on its growing competitiveness in some important manufacturing markets. The chapter is divided into five parts that present: (i) a brief description of the most important characteristics of Mexico's process of structural change in the 1980s and the early 1990s, (ii) the role of foreign firms in this process, especially in the areas of outward orientation and international competitiveness, (iii) the dynamics of three industries in which that role is particularly important (automobiles, electric and electronic equipment and in-bond assembly activities, i.e. *maquiladoras*), (iv) the increasingly important process of investing abroad by the largest Mexican industrial corporations, and (v) some conclusions that will consider the new challenges posed by what looks like a new crisis period in the mid-1990s.

MEXICO'S STRUCTURAL CHANGE IN THE 1980s AND EARLY 1990s

When in early 1989 a new Mexican administration announced its target of doubling the stock of foreign investment in the country by the end of its six-year term, scepticism was widespread. The country had been in the midst of a debt crisis since 1982 and the prospects for the future were at most slightly optimistic. At the end of 1993, one year before the end of that administration, the target had been surpassed by over 74 per cent. Foreign investment flows reached $41.7 billion in 1989–1993,[2] increasing the investment stock from $24.1 billion to $65.8 billion in the period (Calderón, Mortimore and Peres, 1994). The context for this spectacular performance was a harsh macroeconomic stabilization programme, radical structural change and an increasingly profound integration in the North American economic area. By mid-1994, Mexico was a member country of the OECD, was implementing the approved North American Free Trade Agreement (NAFTA) with Canada and the United States, and appeared well positioned for a period of renewed economic growth. The plunge in the value of the peso and the collapse of the stock market in December 1994 and January 1995 may result in an important obstacle for renewed growth in the short term, but in a longer-term perspective, the country's prospects for growth continue to be strong.

In spite of a slowdown in the Mexican economy in 1993 when GDP per capita fell, during the 1988–1994 period GDP grew at an annual average of 2.9 per cent and gross fixed investment as a proportion of GDP grew from 17 per cent in 1988 to 20.7 per cent in 1993. Although these figures do not look impressive in comparison to the country's long-term (1950–1980) economic performance, they show an important improvement from the crisis period of 1982–1988. Moreover, other macroeconomic variables also show the results of the stabilization and structural change policies. Inflation decreased from 159 per cent in 1987 to 7 per cent in 1994, public finances showed a surplus in 1992 and 1993, and the ratio of external public debt to GDP declined from 44 per cent in 1988 to 14 per cent at year-end 1993. The net transfer of resources abroad was reversed, and during that period Mexico had net capital inflows of 5 per cent of GDP on average. The capital account balance changed from a deficit of $1.2 billion in 1988 to a surplus of $30.9 billion in 1993, with the accumulated new inflows reaching $86.7 billion in the same period. This process was the result of capital repatriation, foreign investment and the private sector's greatly improved access to international capital markets. Capital inflows combined with a decline in the level of domestic savings and a persistent trend towards the revaluation of the exchange rate implied a current account deficit of $23 billion both in 1992 and 1993 (Banco de México, 1994). By the end of 1994, a deficit of that magnitude proved to be unsustainable and forced a sharp devaluation of the peso and prompted a new macroeconomic stabilization programme.

Mexican exports, especially manufactured exports, have grown continuously since the mid-1980s. In 1985–1993, non-oil exports, measured in current dollars, grew at an annual rate of 17.8 per cent, while manufactured exports did so at an annual rate of 19.4 per cent. As a result the ratio of non-oil exports to GDP increased threefold between 1982 and 1993 (from 4 per cent to 12 per cent). Furthermore, the Mexican economy experienced a significant diversification of its export structure; while in 1982 crude oil accounted for 75 per cent of total merchandise exports, by 1993 this percentage had dropped to 14.3 per cent. Moreover, while in the early 1970s Mexico was mainly an exporter of silver, tomatoes, cotton, seafood and similar goods, by the mid-1990s some of the leading export products were passenger cars, car parts, car engines, electricity distribution equipment, telecommunication and information processing equipment, and television receivers.

These results, both the positive (renewed growth, capital inflows, increased and diversified exports, reduced inflation) and the negative ones (exchange rate revaluation, trade and current account deficit), were basically the outcome of policies oriented towards reducing the role of the state in the economy, dismantling the structure of protection that characterized the import substitution period of industrialization and deregulating important segments of economic activity, which were combined with skilful negotiations with other countries (the United States and Canada) and crucial economic agents in the country (e.g. the automobile-producer MNEs and the largest domestic corporations).

The state's reduced role implied privatization of most state-owned enterprises, with the exception of the oil and electricity state enterprises, and a significant reduction of public investment and expenditures from 42 per cent of GDP in 1982 to 27 per cent in 1993. The protectionist structure was dismantled relatively quickly, and less than 2 per cent of the import schedule is subject to quantitative restrictions in 1993. Even before the NAFTA, the Mexican economy had been transformed into one of the most open economies in the world with an average tariff of about 10 per cent and a maximum tariff of 20 per cent. Deregulation has been especially important in issues related to private and foreign investment, domestic transportation and land ownership. New regulations have been sparse and are concentrated in the field of competition policy.

Regarding the regulatory framework, two government policies, enacted as law, stand out for their potential impact on the country's attraction to foreign investors. In December 1993, the 20-year-old nationalistic foreign investment law was substituted by a new legal framework that incorporated the commitment Mexico undertook in the NAFTA and designed a strategy to reorganize the actions of different government units in charge of the promotion of FDI. The new legislation brought about substantial liberalization in the screening process and opened key sectors of the economy to foreign participation. A closely related law regarding foreign investment in the financial sector was simultaneously approved.[3] As the 1973 law was instrumental for the development of foreign firms in a context of protectionism and ISI, it is to be expected that the new legislation will be instrumental for foreign investors to benefit from Mexico's more recent locational-specific advantages as an export platform to North America.

FOREIGN DIRECT INVESTMENT AND STRUCTURAL CHANGE

Since the beginning of the 1990s, the Latin American countries have received large net amounts of external capital. During the first four years of this decade, the inward flows of capital to the region reached an annual average of $44 billion (ECLAC, 1994). This situation represents a complete turnaround from the 1980s when Latin America had to face a notable restriction of foreign financing as a consequence of the international debt crisis. Although most of the countries in the region benefited from increased foreign capital inflows, these flows were concentrated in only a few countries. The high performer was Mexico whose economy accounts for a quarter of the regional GDP and yet absorbed almost 50 per cent of these net capital inflows from private sources.

Several factors explain the dimension of the capital flows towards Mexico. In terms of external factors, one should take into account the recession in the industrialized countries, especially in the United States, which also resulted in decreased profits in the property market, and the decline in domestic US interest rates on deposits and short-term financial investments (Calvo, Leiderman and Reinhart, 1993). Furthermore, some changes in the regulations of the capital markets in the United States reduced the transaction costs of agents entering foreign markets.[4] The sharp rise in capital inflows also responded to factors in the Mexican economy itself, notably, the high real interest rates, initially closely linked to the stabilization programme and, later on, owing to the policy of partial sterilization of such capital inflows. In addition to offering attractive real yields, progress achieved in the structural reforms had a definite influence in attracting foreign capital owing to the confidence it produced. Particularly, the 1989–1992 external debt restructuring package was a key factor, backing up the perception of reduced country risk (Gurría, 1994).

While shorter-term profitability factors have been central to the explosion of portfolio investment flows to Mexico, FDI flows have responded more to longer-term considerations in terms of MNEs' strategies to improve their competitiveness via production facilities in lower-cost areas, the geographic proximity of Mexico to the huge North American market, the more recent growth potential of the Mexican economy, and the opportunities presented by the NAFTA. FDI has been the preferred instrument of MNEs in these fields.

Since the Second World War, FDI flows to Mexico were closely associated with the import-substituting industrialization process (Fajnzylber and Martínez, 1976; Sepúlveda, Pellicer and Meyer, 1974). For MNEs selling differentiated products in established oligopolistic markets it was important to expand into the larger new markets in developing countries to preserve their advantages (Hymer, 1976). High tariffs kept their exports out, and thus FDI became the only, although inefficient, means of participating in those protected markets. Besides, the Mexican authorities tended to take a defensive approach to FDI, as was manifest in their 1973 Law to Promote Mexican Investment and Regulate Foreign Investment.

By the early 1980s, foreign enterprises accounted for about 27 per cent of the manufacturing industry in the country and their production was concentrated in transport equipment, electrical machinery, foodstuffs and chemicals. Although some foreign firms were efficient, in most sectors their size was well below industrialized countries' standards and optimal economies of scale could not be achieved. Actually most of those industries presented characteristics closely associated with the concept of 'miniature replicas' (Evans, 1977; Peres, 1990a).

The coincidence in time of the breakdown of the ISI process, the domestic impact of the international debt crisis and other severe external shocks (the collapse of the international price of petroleum, etc.) provoked an extensive rethinking of the Mexican development strategy and the official view towards FDI. In the context of the stabilization and structural reform programmes, significant incentives were provided to daring foreign investors by way of the debt-equity conversion programme implemented in the mid-1980s.[5] Debt-equity swaps, for the most part, explained the very peculiar characteristics of FDI to Mexico in the late 1980s: for the first time, FDI flows showed a marked counter-cyclical behaviour. In 1986–1988, although GDP fell the first year and grew very slowly the other two, FDI inflow surpassed even the levels attained during the oil boom of 1978–1981, when GDP grew at about 8 per cent on average (Figure 8.1).

After 1989, FDI flows also showed a counter-cyclical behaviour: as previously mentioned, GDP grew at just 2.9 per cent yearly and the stock of FDI reached a total of $47.9 billion in 1993 (Table 8.2). Foreign investment flows reached a record level in 1993 of $15.6 billion. As well as authorized FDI and registered inflows, the SECOFI (Secretariat of Trade and Industrial Promotion) figures

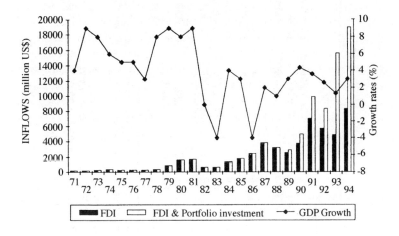

Figure 8.1   Foreign investment and GDP growth
Sources: SECOFI (1993) and Banco de México, *Indicadores Económicos*, several years.

include portfolio investments. These flows consist of $2 billion (12.6 per cent of total inflows in 1993) corresponding to investments authorized by the National Commission on Foreign Investment (CNIE), $2.9 billion (18.8 per cent) corresponding to investments registered by the National Registry of Foreign Investment (RNIE) and portfolio investment in the stock market for a value of $10.7 billion (68.6 per cent).

The largest source of FDI in Mexico has been the United States, with 63.8 per cent, followed by France and the United Kingdom with 4.6 per cent each, Switzerland with 4.5 per cent, Germany with 3.6 per cent, The Netherlands with 2.5 per cent, Japan with 2 per cent, Canada with 1.8 per cent, Spain with 1.1 per cent, and other countries accounting for a total of 11 per cent. Thus, FDI in Mexico continues to show a US-centric character and is a clear signal of the further integration of both countries. In 1993, with the ratification of NAFTA by the US Congress, this tendency increased as North American FDI accounted for 73 per cent of the total inflows for that year. The US share was 71.5 per cent and that of Canada 1.5 per cent.[6]

Table 8.2 Cumulative foreign investment[a] (million dollars)

	New investment					Cumulative direct investment	Cumulative total investment
	Direct Investment						
Year	CNIE[b]	RNIE[c]	Total	Portfolio[d]	Total		
1985	1,337.6	533.4	1,871.0	–	1,871.0	14,628.9	14,628.9
1986	1,563.1	861.1	2,424.2	–	2,424.2	17,053.1	17,053.1
1987	3,260.7	616.5	3,877.2	–	3,877.2	20,930.3	20,930.3
1988	2,448.3	708.8	3,157.1	–	3,157.1	24,087.4	24,087.4
1989	1,231.5	1,268.2	2,499.7	414.0	2,913.7	26,587.1	27,001.1
1990	2,118.6	1,603.8	3,722.4	1,256.0	4,978.4	30,309.5	31,979.5
1991	4,871.7	2,143.5	7,015.2	2,881.0	9,897.0	37,324.7	41,876.5
1992	4,298.5	1,406.6	5,705.1	2,629.7	8,334.8	43,029.8	50,211.3
1993	1,964.8	2,935.9	4,900.7	10,716.3	15,617.0	47,930.5	65,828.3

Notes: [a] Foreign investment flows, as shown in the balance of payments figures, may differ from new foreign investment registered or authorized (due to lags between authorizations and actual investments and because some authorized investments may not be realized).
[b] Investments approved by the National Commission on Foreign Investment (CNIE).
[c] Investments registered by the National Registry of Foreign Investment (RNIE) that do not require prior approval by the CNIE.
[d] The figures for foreign portfolio investment do not reflect the total flows during the year, as part of the flow is recorded as foreign direct investment.

Source: Dirección General de Inversión Extranjera, SECOFI.

During the 1989–1993 period the sectors which attracted most FDI are services (32.1 per cent), followed by manufacturing (31 per cent), communications and transportation (22.3 per cent), commerce (10.8 per cent) and agriculture, mining and construction (3.8 per cent). Over the same period, the accumulated FDI in manufacturing declined from 69 to 50 per cent, while services increased their share from 29 to 48 per cent of the total. The interpretation of this shift away from manufacturing and towards services should be done with caution because several simultaneous processes are taking place: the exit or sale of non-competitive existing foreign firms' operations; the restructuring of existing foreign operations from the ISI period to make them more competitive; and new entrants, both those large MNEs which were not present and small and medium North American firms which are beginning their internationalization process. Mexico is already the second most important developing economy after Hong Kong in terms of the operations of small and medium-sized US MNEs, mainly in the *maquiladora* industry (UNCTAD, 1993; Ortiz, 1993). The key feature is that a strong *specialization* process is taking place and therefore it is more the quality of the FDI than its absolute amount which gives character to it. In a following section reference to the situation in the automotive sector will clarify this assertion.

In the services sector FDI during the 1989–1993 period has been concentrated in property (32 per cent), professional services (30 per cent), financial services (19 per cent) and hotels and restaurants (14 per cent). Part of the rapid growth of FDI in this sector corresponds to the fact that it began from a very small base and new entrants are plentiful in the context of the NAFTA.[7]

Impact on the production structure

The two periods of counter-cyclical foreign investment inflows gave rise to two specific impacts in the Mexican production structure. On one side, the share of FDI in the country's gross fixed investment averaged 9 per cent in 1990–1993, a figure more than three times the average for the oil-boom years (Table 8.3). When direct investment and portfolio investment are both included, the corresponding figure reaches 15 per cent for the early 1990s. Although these data suggest a growing importance of foreign firms in the Mexican economy, the concentration of new investments in the services sector makes it very difficult to determine what is happening with the participation

Table 8.3 Share of foreign investment in Mexico's gross fixed investment (percentages)

	Foreign direct investment	FDI & Stock Exchange investment
1980	3.4	3.4
1981	2.6	2.6
1982	1.6	1.6
1983	2.6	2.6
1984	4.6	4.6
1985	5.3	5.3
1986	9.6	9.6
1987	14.9	14.9
1988	9.4	9.4
1989	6.6	7.7
1990	8.1	10.8
1991	12.5	17.7
1992[a]	8.4	12.3
1993[b]	6.6	20.9

Notes: [a] Preliminary data.
[b] Estimated data.

Sources: SECOFI (1993), Banco de México, *Indicadores Económicos*, several years, *Informe Anual*, several years, and INEGI, *Sistemas de Cuentas Nacionales de México, 1988–1992*, Mexico City, 1993.

of foreign firms in the manufacturing industry. However, information about the most important foreign investment projects,[8] and the net result of the privatization of state-owned firms that accounted for about 7 per cent of manufacturing production, indicate that the long-term ownership pattern prevalent in the Mexican industry might be relatively stable.[9] Foreign firms account for about one-third of production but with a strong presence in consumer durable goods (automobiles, appliances), capital goods (electric and electronic equipment), some modern non-durables (pharmaceuticals and foodstuffs) and some intermediate inputs such as chemicals or paper.[10]

A second characteristic of the industrial sectors that received the most inward FDI was their strong dynamism. As in the 1970s, the sectors with a high presence of foreign firms were the fastest growing in the country. While on average, Mexican manufacturing grew at 5.8 per cent yearly in 1989–1993, the automobile industry grew at 20 per cent, dairy products at 10.8 per cent, beverages at 9.5 per cent, electrical machinery and equipment at 9.3 per cent and miscellaneous chemicals and pharmaceuticals at 8.3 per cent. The only sectors that grew slower than the industrial average were non-electrical machinery (1.2 per cent), pulp and paper (2.2 per cent) and basic chemicals (2.9 per cent). A similar pattern of higher dynamism of sectors with high foreign presence took place in services, particularly regarding communications services (SECOFI, 1993). Although all this information is quite general, it all points towards the long-term stability of two key features of the presence of foreign firms in Mexican industry: their sectoral specialization and their dynamism.

Outward orientation and international competitiveness

While stability characterized the structure of FDI in Mexican industry, extreme dynamism characterizes its behaviour. Mexico is presently in the process of being incorporated into the new international industrial order (Calderón, Mortimore and Peres, 1994; Mortimore, 1992). Structural change combined with the opening up of the economy has produced an intense adjustment on the part of producers, especially manufacturers, operating in Mexico (Mortimore and Huss, 1991). Those that were able to shift to more dynamic activities, to improve significantly their productivity and to modernize their technology have been able to specialize their production and generally have encountered success in exporting their wares or defending their national market share (Casar, 1993, 1994; Shaiken, 1990).

With regard to international trade, export growth has been spectacular and Mexico's international competitiveness has improved enormously over the 1980–1992 period (Table 8.4).[11] Measured by its share of the OECD imports, it rose from 1.26 per cent in 1980 to 1.81 per cent in 1992. Of more importance was the increased market share of OECD imports of manufactures, the dynamic part of international trade, which went from 0.71 to 1.66 per cent over the same period. Moreover, Mexico achieved a massive transformation of the structure of its exports, away from lethargic natural resources and towards dynamic products (especially manufactures not based on natural resources). Manufactures now account for two-thirds of Mexico's exports to the OECD (up from 30.6 per cent in 1980) and natural resource exports declined from two-thirds in 1980 to less than one-third in 1992. In 1980–1992, eight of Mexico's 10 principal exports to the OECD are found on the list of the 50 most dynamic industrial groups in international trade. In other words,

Table 8.4 Indicators of Mexico's international competitiveness (percentages)

	1980	1985	1990	1992
I STRUCTURE OF ITS EXPORTS TO THE OECD	100.0	100.0	100.0	100.0
Natural resources [a + b + c]	67.2	58.2	33.6	29.5
Agricultural products[a]	12.9	9.6	10.2	9.1
Energy[b]	50.3	45.6	21.1	18.5
Other natural resources (textile fibres, crude minerals, etc.)[c]	4.0	3.0	2.3	1.9
Manufactures[d + e]	30.6	39.5	62.5	66.8
Based on natural resources[d]	5.4	3.3	3.4	2.6
Not based on natural resources[e]	25.3	36.2	59.2	64.3
Others[f]	2.2	2.3	4.0	3.7
II MARKET SHARE IN OECD IMPORTS	1.26	1.77	1.59	1.81
Natural resources[a + b + c]	1.94	3.06	2.14	2.20
Agricultural products[a]	1.13	1.30	1.34	1.36
Energy[b]	2.47	4.56	3.22	3.34
Other natural resources (textile fibres, crude minerals, etc.)[c]	1.40	1.87	1.51	1.62
Manufactures[d + e]	0.71	1.09	1.36	1.66
Based on natural resources[d]	1.28	1.28	1.04	1.00
Not based on natural resources[e]	0.65	1.08	1.39	1.70
Others[f]	1.49	1.63	2.55	2.59
III TEN PRINCIPAL EXPORTS TO THE OECD				
(as percentage of total exports)	60.1	62.6	54.9	53.0
333 Crude petroleum	46.1	42.0	19.9	17.5
781 Passenger vehicles[g]	0.3	0.9	6.0	7.7
784 Parts and accessories for vehicles[g]	1.3	2.6	4.3	5.4
773 Equipment for distributing electricity[g]	1.1	2.5	6.6	4.8
931 Unclassified operations and merchandise[g]	2.2	2.2	3.6	3.6
764 Telecommunications equipment and parts[g]	4.6	3.4	3.1	3.1
713 Internal combustion motors and parts[g]	0.6	4.6	3.5	3.0
761 Television receivers[g]	–	0.5	2.6	2.9
772 Electrical apparatus for making/breaking circuits[g]	1.3	1.6	2.6	2.7
054 Vegetables, fresh, chilled, frozen or preserved	2.7	2.3	2.7	2.3

Notes: [a] Sections 0,1 and 4; divisions 21, 22, 23, 24, 25 and 29 of the Standard International Trade Classification (Revision 2).
[b] Section 3.
[c] Divisions 26, 27 and 28.
[d] Divisions 61, 63 and 68; groups 661, 662, 663, 667 and 671.
[e] Sections 5, 6, (except divisions and groups included in 4), 7 and 8.
[f] Section 9.
[g] Industrial groups found on the list of the 50 most dynamic groups in OECD imports, 1980–1992.

Source: Calculated by the authors using the CAN software, version 2.0.

Mexico has dramatically improved its international competitiveness in dynamic products and has linked the dynamism of international trade to its chosen path of economic development.

Mexico had achieved very significant and enviable market positions in certain specific OECD imports by 1992, and these had improved enormously from those held in 1980. The examples of electrical goods, such as equipment for distributing electricity (20.2 per cent), television receivers (12.1 per cent), power machinery (7.7 per cent) and radio receivers (7.2 per cent) as well as engines (5.4 per cent), parts and accessories for vehicles (3.9 per cent) are particularly noteworthy. As a result of these advances in terms of international competitiveness, Mexico now pertains to the small group of 'winners'; that is, countries that have gained at least a 1 per cent OECD import market share for manufactures during the 1971–1992 period. Other members of this select group are Japan, China, South Korea, Taiwan Province of China, Singapore and Spain.

A somewhat similar situation holds in terms of foreign investment, in the sense that Mexico has become significantly more integrated into the international capital markets (ECLAC, 1994). This is true for all aspects of foreign investment: portfolio investment, loans and FDI. If one considers the long-term capital inflows from private sources over the 1989–1993 period, Mexico received US$ 83.7 billion, or 43 per cent of all inflows to Latin American countries. With regard to FDI inflows, Mexico was one of the five principal developing country recipients during 1990–1992 (with China, Singapore, Malaysia and Argentina, which together accounted for 60 per cent of the developing country total). Mexico's share corresponded to one-third of that for Latin American countries, 12 per cent of that for developing countries and 2.5 per cent of the world total.

The importance of foreign firms in improved international competitiveness

At the end of the import substituting period of the 1970s, foreign firms showed much higher labour productivity levels and growth rates than domestically owned firms of similar size and located in similar industries. Foreign firms' share in manufacturing exports was bigger than their share in production, and they accounted for 42 per cent of total exports made by private firms in the economy in 1981 (then, worth only $3.9 billion). In 1986–1987, those firms accounted for 65 per cent of the total of private sector exports (Peres, 1990a). More recent data show that foreign firms continue to have a disproportionate participation in Mexican foreign trade.

Table 8.5 Share of foreign firms in Mexico's foreign trade[a] (million dollars and percentages)

	1990 Amount	%	1991 Amount	%	1992 Amount	%
EXPORTS						
Foreign firms	7,940.4	49.7	9,332.9	51.2	9,903.8	52.7
Total private sector	15,974.4	29.5	18,215.7	34.4	18,792.9	36.0
Total for the country	26,950.3		27,120.2		27,530.8	
IMPORTS						
Foreign firms	11,688.2	43.5	14,613.7	41.4	17,398.7	38.7
Total private sector	26,843.2	37.6	35,331.4	38.3	44,901.7	36.1
Total for the country	31,090.0		38,184.0		48,138.4	
BALANCE						
Foreign firms	-3,747.8	34.5	-5,280.8	30.9	-7,494.9	28.7
Total private sector	-10,868.3	90.5	-17,115.7	47.7	-26,108.8	36.4
Total for the country	-4,139.7		-11,063.8		-20,607.6	

Note: [a] Does not include maquiladora exports.

Source: SECOFI (1993).

The contrast between Tables 8.2 and 8.5 cannot be more apparent. While foreign firms accounted for less than 10 per cent of gross fixed investment in the country, they accounted for more than half of its private exports in 1992 (then, worth $18.8 billion), a proportion equivalent to 36 per cent of all Mexican *non-maquiladora* exports. According to SECOFI (1993), the automobile industry accounted for 61 per cent of total exports by foreign firms, electrical and electronic machinery and equipment for 9.2 per cent, basic chemicals for 8.6 per cent, and non-ferrous basic metals and pharmaceuticals for 2.3 per cent each.

In spite of a higher export propensity, foreign firms' imports also continue to be quite significant and their foreign trade balance shows a deficit of similar proportions to the one reached during the late 1970s. Intra-firm trade, internationalization of production and integration in the North American economy prior to the approval of the NAFTA were the basis for this trade deficit. Naturally, the final explanation of such performance must be found in the dynamics of particular sectors; most specifically it can be found in the performance of the automobile industry.

Regarding labour productivity, data for the late 1980s suggest that foreign firms continued to present a much higher sales/employment ratio than domestic firms, both state-owned and private ones, even in cases where the capital/labour ratio was lower for foreign firms. Particularly, for 1988–1989, the sales/employment ratio for foreign firms was 66 per cent higher than for large private firms, while the capital/labour ratio was 10 per cent smaller for the former than for the latter. This productivity differential is quite compatible with similar indicators available for the late 1970s. Moreover, the presence of foreign firms also continued to be positively correlated with the productivity levels in manufacturing industry, a correlation that seems to have become stronger after trade liberalization in the mid-1980s (Kessel and Samaniego, 1992).

The evidence presented in the last three sections clearly points to a new role for foreign firms in the Mexican economy. Their new export orientation is quite compatible with the counter-cyclical behaviour that FDI has presented in the last decade. Protection and domestic market size and growth are no longer the main determinants of inward FDI. Foreign firms are now the forefront of the integration of the country in the world economy, playing a role quite different from the one they used to play when they were an effective, but usually not efficient, agent of import-substituting industrialization. However, higher productivity and export performance suggest that, as also happened in the previous development stage, foreign firms will continue to be leading agents of change, perhaps the crucial ones, in the Mexican economy.

SECTORAL DYNAMICS

MNEs operating in specific sectoral activities have been a leading force in the structural transformation, the new export orientation and the improved international competitiveness of the Mexican economy (Unger, 1990, 1991). These aspects of the participation of foreign firms in Mexico's development have been particularly noteworthy in the automobile industry, electric machinery and electronic equipment and certain defined in-bond assembly (*maquiladora*) activities. The role of MNEs in these industries will be examined in this section.

The automobile industry

The recovery, expansion and transformation of the Mexican automobile industry has been nothing short of spectacular and has also been an important element in Mexico's structural adjustment, economic reorientation and improved incorporation into the new international industrial order. Foreign direct investment and technology played a central role in that process (Mortimore, 1994; de María y Campos, 1992). The effect was most evident on the trade front where by 1992 automotive industry exports (passenger cars, 7.7 per cent; automobile parts, 5.4 per cent; and internal combustion engines and their parts, 3 per cent) represented 16 per cent of all Mexican exports to the OECD and accounted for three of their five principal exports of manufactures (occupying first, second and fifth spots). In the 1993 list of principal exporters from all of Latin America, the Mexican operations of vehicle producers such as General Motors, Ford, Chrysler, Volkswagen and Nissan occupied the third, fifth, sixth, 10th and 26th spots, respectively, together accounting for exports in the order of $7.8 billion, approximately one-third of the value of the exports of the principal Mexican exporters and over 10 per cent of that of the principal Latin American exporters (*América Economía*, 1994). The automobile industry was evidently one of the principal vehicles by which

Mexico integrated the dynamism of international trade to specific sectoral pursuits.

Figures 8.2 and 8.3 and Tables 8.3 and 8.4 present a profile of the transformation of the industry, viewed primarily from the perspective of overall export performance and the specific situation of passenger cars. Figure 8.2 points out that export performance

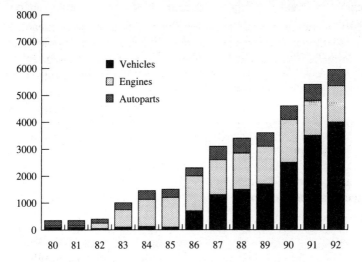

Figure 8.2   Mexico: automotive industry exports, by group, 1980–1992 (millions of dollars)
Source: The authors based on data from the Banco de México.

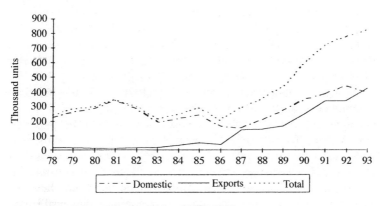

Figure 8.3   Passenger car sales 1978–1993
Source: The authors' estimates based on data from the Mexican Automobile Manufacturers Association (AMIA).

went through three phases. The first was one in which car parts dominated the minor export flows. The second encompassed the export boom associated with the new engine plants which came on stream during the early 1980s. The third phase was based on the explosion of passenger vehicle exports from the new plants built during the late 1980s. Taken together, the growth in engine and vehicle exports was a significant element of the structural change in the Mexican industrialization process.

Figure 8.3, which highlights the domestic and export sales of passenger vehicles, demonstrates that the industry faced two explicit and interrelated challenges. One was to recuperate from the devastating blow associated with the debt crisis in Mexico during the mid-1980s which produced a dramatic decline in domestic demand for passenger vehicles. By 1988, the overall sales of passenger vehicles surpassed the previous high of 1981. The second challenge was to improve the international competitiveness of Mexican automobiles so as to permit the conversion of the industry to an export orientation. As of 1993, exports of passenger cars exceeded domestic sales of such. Thus, the industry met the two challenges put to it.

The automotive industry has lived through three distinct stages, which can be described as the 1978–1982 import substitution boom in which sales for domestic consumption reached an average of 300,000 units a year, the 1983–1987 crisis and reorientation stage in which sales fell to an average of 250,000 units a year but when modern new plants were built, and the 1988–1992 export-based expansion stage when sales jumped to the 570,000 level on average and over 240,000 units were exported annually. In 1993, production surpassed 800,000 units and over half (425,000) were exported. It is necessary to distinguish carefully the nature of these stages in order to appreciate the profound transformation of that industry.

During the import-substituting stage, 1978–1982, the Mexican automobile industry had a radically distinct impact on national development. The fact that automobiles could not be imported into Mexico forced MNEs interested in the national market to make substantial investments to produce locally. This established an oligopolistic market structure for producers and resulted in considerable government intervention via sectoral programmes. The result was a strained negotiating relationship among foreign vehicle producers, national car parts manufacturers and the government (Bennett and Sharpe, 1979a, 1979b; Whiting, 1991) due to the fact that the sector had become so important in the domestic process of industrialization. The difficult relations between vehicle producers and parts producers as well as the complexity of government intervention resulted in an automotive industry characterized by many models and makes, low production runs, high prices and poor quality. Furthermore, the sector negatively impacted the national balance of payments. While unpublished foreign investment data from the Banco de México suggest that over 40 per cent of inward FDI during 1972–1981 went to the transportation equipment sector, it was in no way internationally competitive. As a result, the massive imports of components by vehicle producers and their exceedingly low export propensities in the range of 14–15 per cent during 1977–1982 (US Department of Commerce, 1977, 1982 and 1989) created a yawning trade deficit that even relatively high FDI flows could not eliminate. As a consequence, the government pressured vehicle producers to raise the local content of their vehicles and to export more parts and accessories to compensate for the trade deficit generated by the industry. The foreign producers responded that they could not export by decree, rather they must be given more liberty of action in order to meet this challenge.

Initially, the vehicle producers responded by building modern and internationally competitive engine plants in the early 1980s just as the domestic demand bottomed out. In spite of the fact that the Mexican market collapsed, these companies had great success introducing modern technology into the new Mexican engine plants (Shaiken and Herzenberg, 1987; Moreno, 1988) and this success coincided with the implementation of new corporate strategies on the part of the headquarters of the US vehicle producers operating in Mexico (General Motors, Ford and Chrysler) aimed at defending their national market from import penetration by Japanese and other producers. They concluded that Mexico could become a low-cost export platform for entry-level, front-wheel-drive, four- and six-cylinder small cars. The success of new engine plants, the Mexican government's pressure to relieve the negative balance of payments impact of the automobile industry, and the difficult competitive situation in the US market encouraged the 'Big Three' US automobile producers (General Motors, Ford and Chrysler) to begin major new investments in modern small-vehicle production facilities in Mexico, primarily for export to the US market, in spite of the dismal macroeconomic situation of Mexico and the depressed level of domestic demand for national automobiles. Many of these

producers took advantage of the Mexican programme which subsidized the conversion of external debt paper into direct investments
(Mortimore, 1991). Generally, the new attitude on the part of
government officials was to *facilitate* the new corporate strategies
of the foreign vehicle producers.

The 1988–1992 stage of the development of the Mexican automobile industry witnessed the explosion of vehicle exports from
Mexico creating a trade surplus of $1.3 billion in 1990 (later
reduced by imports). Non-US vehicle producers, Volkswagen and
Nissan, also made significant investments in new plants even though
their export propensities did not approximate those of the US vehicle
manufacturers. As suggested earlier, passenger vehicles, engines and
parts and accessories all enjoyed major improvements in their
international competitiveness, as measured by OECD import market
shares. Car parts corresponded to over one-half of the (low level) of
exports from the automotive industry in 1980, by 1984 engines
accounted for over two-thirds of rising automobile exports, and 10
years later vehicles corresponded to two thirds of such. The transformation of the Mexican automobile industry was clearly a result of
increased *specialization* and technological sophistication by foreign
firms operating in Mexico (Moreno, 1994; Shaiken, 1994).

Table 8.6 Mexico: passenger car sales, by principal market (annual
averages by period, 1978–1992)

	1978–1982	1983–1987	1988–1992
UNITS			
National market[a]	147.1	78.3	70.8
Dual market[b]	138.6	116.9	307.5
Export market[c]	10.5	54.5	199.0
Total	296.1	249.7	577.4
PER CENT			
National market[a]	49.7	31.4	12.3
Dual market[b]	46.8	46.8	53.3
Export market[c]	0.4	21.8	34.4
Total	100.0	100.0	100.0

Source: Mortimore (1994) on the basis of data provided by the Mexican
Automobile Manufacturers Association (AMIA).

Notes: [a] Car models sold only in the domestic market.
[b] Car models with more than 50% of total sales in the domestic
market, less than 50% of sales in export markets.
[c] Car models with more than 50% of total sales in export markets.

Table 8.6 captures the transformation of the automobile industry in terms of the national market, dual market and export market orientations of passenger car sales. During 1978–1982, half of all passenger car models were aimed *exclusively* at the domestic market and export models were virtually non-existent. By the 1988–1992 phase, only 12 per cent of passenger car sales corresponded to models aimed only at the domestic market and export models accounted for more than one-third of all sales. International competitiveness had become a central feature of the transformed industry.

Table 8.7 distinguishes the behaviour of the five passenger car producers in Mexico. This table demonstrates that it was the three US automobile companies which most expanded their Mexican production operations and converted them to an export orientation (US Congress, 1992). Those three companies accounted for over 70 per cent of all exports during the export-based expansion phase and

Table 8.7 Mexico: passenger car sales, in export and domestic markets, 1978–1993[a] (thousands of units)

	1978–1982[c]	1983–1987[c]	1988–1992[c]	1993
EXPORT MARKET SALES				
Ford	–	10.4	87.3	117.2
General Motors	–	17.7	52.6	90.7
Chrysler	–	15.8	53.7	101.7
Volkswagen	14.7	8.3	30.4	77.5
Nissan	–	4.2	18.4	37.4
Total	14.8	56.4	242.4	424.5
DOMESTIC MARKET SALES				
Volkswagen	93.0	64.5	111.3	151.7
Nissan	39.0	45.9	78.0	83.4
Chrysler	49.7	29.1	61.3	59.6
Ford	39.6	25.7	51.4	52.8
General Motors	23.0	15.5	32.9	51.2
Others[b]	37.2	12.6	–	–
Total	281.3	193.3	334.9	398.7

Notes: [a] Does not include imported vehicles. They declined from 6,048 in 1992 to 3,273 units in 1993.
[b] Diesel Nacional SA (Renault) and Vehículos Automotores Mexicanos SA (American Motors).
[c] Annual averages.
Source: Mortimore (1994) on the basis of data provided by the AMIA.

by 1993 all had export propensities above 60 per cent. The non-US automobile producers (Volkswagen and Nissan) concentrated their operations on domestic sales, where together they accounted for over one-half. In other words, the original transformation of the Mexican automobile industry in terms of its international competitiveness was clearly the work of the 'Big Three' US automobile producers.

With regard to the transfer of technology (and new organizational practices), evidence (de María y Campos, 1992) suggests that in terms of productivity and quality the *new* production facilities in Mexico have caught up to and in certain cases surpassed the benchmarks established by the US auto industry, including the Japanese transplants operating there.[12] The experience of Ford in Mexico is particularly revealing in this regard. Ford's engine plant at Chihuahua and its vehicle assembly operations at Hermosillo have been extensively examined and are considered examples of how advanced production processes can be successfully transferred to newly industrializing countries (NICs) (Shaiken, 1991). The Hermosillo plant was designed primarily by Mazda, a major Japanese automobile producer in which Ford has a minority participation, thereby introducing to the Mexican automobile industry many of the best practice production techniques and modern organizational practices of the very competitive Japanese automobile industry. The Hermosillo plant had a defects per vehicle rating (0.276) well below the weighted average for all Mexican automobile producers (0.665) and close to the world optimum (Olea, 1993; Womack, 1990). It is ranked among the five best plants in North America.

The explanation of why this transformation of the Mexican auto industry took place is as important as its dimension. Succinctly, the relevant factors can be combined into three groups: those related to the competitive situation of the international automobile market, those linked to the corporate strategies of the major global producers, and those pertaining to Mexican national policy at the macroeconomic and sectoral levels (Mortimore, 1994). The Japanese challenge to US automobile makers in their own market led the 'Big Three' US producers to alter their corporate strategies with regard to entry-level, front-wheel-drive, small-engine passenger cars. They sought out lower-cost production sites in a few select NICs, one of which was Mexico. The new corporate strategies of these producers led to the transformation of their Mexican production facilities via new plant construction and the restructuring of existing plants so as to integrate them into their North American production system (Ozawa, 1994). The reorientation of Mexican macroeconomic policy during the 1980s, the new Automotive Decrees (1983 and 1989), and the NAFTA negotiations allowed these automobile MNEs to consolidate their advantages (SECOFI, 1994b). In this sense, strategic asset-seeking and efficiency-seeking FDI replaced the former market-seeking FDI in the Mexican automobile industry.

Registered FDI projects in the industry for 1994 alone total $2.5 billion (SECOFI, 1994a). The NAFTA impact was important here, due to the fact that the NAFTA continued the existing limitation of passenger car imports into Mexico that was contained in the 1989 Automotive Decree for a further 10 years to the existing five automobile producers in Mexico. This advantage and the desire to consolidate their Mexican operations into their North American production facilities is reflected in investment projects by Chrysler, General Motors and Ford worth $1.0 billion in 1994. The NAFTA rules of origin (62.5 per cent North American content) inspired investment projects by the non-US producers (Nissan and Volkswagen) in the order of $1.2 billion in order to expand production and consolidate local supplier networks. Furthermore, in spite of the advantages given to original producers, newcomers (BMW and Honda) have registered investments of $246 million in 1994. These facts indicate Mexico's integration into the global or regional production systems of many major automobile producers.

Electrical and electronic equipment and appliances

Another industry which has expanded rapidly in the 1980s is the production of electrical appliances and electronic equipment. As in the automotive industry, the main source of Mexico's comparative advantage for this industry does not lie in the domestic availability of any specific natural resources, but in the abundant supply of high-quality, low-cost labour.[13]

Until the mid-1980s, Mexico's electrical machinery and electronic equipment industry was protected from foreign competition by a number of official programmes, the most important of them being the 1981 'Program for Promoting the Manufacturing of Electronic Computer Systems'. This attempt to develop the industry along import-substituting lines was frustrated by the reluctance of some of the main computer producers (e.g. IBM and Apple) to accept a minority ownership share in the production of personal computers, the speed of technological change, and the fall in domestic disposable incomes caused by the debt crisis which resulted in a sharp contraction in the domestic demand for these goods (Peres, 1990a). Within the electrical machinery industry (excluding electronics), the producers of appliances performed particularly badly during the 1980s. Their combined value added declined by more than 32 per cent between 1980 and 1990, which in turn caused the Mexican value added of the electrical machinery industry as a whole to contract by 3.9 per cent over the decade, despite good performances elsewhere in the industry. The most impressive growth was recorded by producers of accumulators and batteries, whose value added increased by almost 40 per cent between 1980 and 1990 as a result of strong demand from Mexico's thriving car industry, and by producers of electrical bulbs and tubes, whose value added increased by 30 per cent during the same period.

The industry's performance improved following the deregulation of the Mexican economy in the latter half of the 1980s, which prompted a substantial increase in FDI. That situation was fuelled further by the onset of the US recession and the resulting decision of many US firms to relocate to Mexico in an attempt to reduce production costs.

During the early 1990s, new production facilities were created in almost all sectors of the electrical machinery and electronics industry by a number of major international companies, including General Electric, Hitachi, IBM, ITT, Sony and Zenith. They were located mainly in the *maquiladora* sector, with the result that the manufacture of electrical machinery and electronic equipment has become one of the most important *maquiladora* activities (see the next section). This increasing inflow of FDI has also helped to offset the effect of the weakening demand caused by the US recession in the 1990s (UNIDO, 1993).

The biggest gains in the 1990s were made in the production of television sets and other consumer electronics, such as video recorders and camcorders. This sector has attracted large inflows of foreign investment, such as the US-based Zenith, which moved all its colour television assembly and plastic cabinet finishing operations to Mexico. Several Japanese producers, including Sony, Matsushita, Toshiba and Sanyo, have also established production facilities for television sets and related equipment in various parts of Mexico. Important companies from Korea, such as Daewoo

Electronics and Goldstar, opened television manufacturing plants; and the Dutch-owned Philips established a large plant for the production of television sets and compact disc players in Ciudad Juárez, on the US–Mexico border.[14] All these investments implied that the number of colour television sets shipped from Mexico to the United States grew from 1.7 million in 1987 to about 6 million by 1992. The United States remains the main market of the Mexican consumer electronics industry, with about 70 per cent of the output produced by foreign investors in Mexico being exported to the United States.

Another important sector of the electronics industry has been the manufacture of personal computers. As a result of the liberalization process and skilful negotiation with IBM in the mid-1980s, this industry has experienced strong dynamism, mainly through considerable inflows of foreign investment. As in the case of the consumer electronics industry, the computer industry had its origins in the establishment of some assembly and production facilities in the *maquiladora* sector, mainly as a platform for exports into the United States. Many important international firms, such as IBM, Hewlett Packard, Wang, Motorola and Texas Instruments, established plants for the assembly of computers and components in various parts of Mexico, mainly Guadalajara,[15] and by 1993 the country was exporting information processing machines and their parts for a volume worth $826 million.

The third major sector of the electronics industry has been the production of telecommunications equipment. This has been induced mainly by the privatization of the Mexican telephone corporation (TELMEX) in several stages since 1990, which resulted in the introduction of a wide-ranging modernization programme. This naturally generated a considerable increase in demand for telecommunications equipment, which in turn prompted large new investments by suppliers of such equipment from within Mexico and abroad. By the early 1990s, most of the major international telecommunications producers had a significant presence in Mexico, such being the case of the Swedish firm Ericsson (which has played a major role since the 1950s), North-American-based companies like American Telephone & Telegraph (AT&T) and Northern Telecom, Japanese firms like NEC and Panasonic, and the French company Alcatel. Increasingly, Mexico is also being integrated into the production networks of companies based in North America, both indigenous United States and Canadian companies and European and Asian companies with regional headquarters in the United States or Canada.

In summary, during the 1990s the growth of Mexico's electrical machinery and electronic equipment industry has been largely export led, mainly operating under the *maquiladora* scheme, and this process fostered the growing integration of this industry into the world economy, particularly into the economic structure of North America.

The *maquiladora* industry[16]

The in-bond assembly industry in Mexico has experienced explosive growth since the major devaluations of the Mexican peso during the 1980s. The number of plants rose from 620 in 1980 to 2,142 in 1993, the number of jobs increased from 124,000 to 549,000 and the net value added climbed from $772 million to $5,410 million over the same period raising the *maquiladora* share of total exports from 16 to 42 per cent (Table 8.8). This industry is now the second most important source of foreign exchange and the most important creator of new jobs, and is responsible for most of the principal exports of manufactures, especially those with the highest OECD import market shares in 1992. The most important activities were transport equipment, electrical machinery and electronic equipment, textiles, footwear and leather products (Figure 8.4).

Table 8.8 Main economic indicators of the *maquiladora* industry (million dollars and thousand jobs)

	Plants	Value added	Employment
1980	620	771.7	124
1983	600	818.4	151
1985	789	1,267.1	212
1987	1,125	1,598.1	305
1989	1,655	3,047.3	430
1990	1,938	3,606.5	460
1991	1,925	4,118.9	467
1992	2,075	4,808.5	505
1993[a]	2,142	5,410.0	549

Note: [a] Employment data are for October and number-of-plants data are for April.

Sources: Banco de México, *Indicadores Económicos*, May 1994 and March 1990, and INEGI, *Avance de Información Económica, Industria Maquiladora de Exportación*, May 1993 and September 1989.

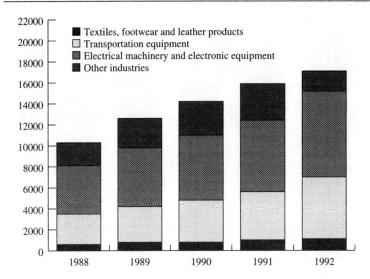

Figure 8.4 Mexico: total exports of in-bond (*maquiladora*) industry, 1988–1992 (millions of dollars)
Source: Banco de México, *Indicadores Económicos*, several years.

As of the early 1990s, about one-half of the *maquiladora* plants pertained in whole or in part to US investors, about 40 per cent were Mexican owned, and the remainder corresponded to Japanese, German and Spanish investors. Ninety per cent of these plants are located in areas close to the US border, which indicates their function: that is, to allow US-based companies to take advantage of the production-sharing provisions 9802.00.60 and 9802.00.80 of the Harmonized Tariff Schedule of the United States. Such companies can obtain reduced tariff treatment for eligible imported goods that are assembled outside of the United States using US-made components and this has been found to be 'an important part of the global competitiveness strategy for many US firms' (USITC, 1991).

It is evident that *maquiladoras* are no longer solely based on the unskilled labour assembly practices of the 1960s and 1970s but have become increasingly intensive in skilled-labour activities keeping up with international competitiveness requirements of US-based MNE operations. The early concentration in the apparel industry has given way definitively to more technology-intensive activities, such as electronic products, electrical equipment and components, and

Table 8.9 Total value of US imports for consumption under HTS provision 9802.00.80 (million dollars and percentages)

	1990				1992			
	All countries	Mexico Amount	As per cent of all countries	Composition	All countries	Mexico Amount	As per cent of all countries	Composition
I Textiles, apparel and footwear	3,526.3	830.1	23.5	6.5	5,363.1	1,304.0	24.3	8.0
II Machinery and equipment	68,986.0	10,548.4	15.3	82.3	47,371.9	13,393.1	28.3	82.4
(a) Electrical machinery and electronic equipment sector	12,619.5	5,388.9	42.7	42.1	12,975.3	6,480.8	49.9	39.9
Television receivers	1,654.3	1,536.5	92.9	12.0	1,944.7	1,918.6	98.7	11.8
Electrical conductors	1,367.9	1,302.3	95.2	10.2	1,834.8	1,660.1	90.5	10.2
Articles for making and breaking electrical circuits	931.6	760.6	81.6	5.9	983.2	830.3	84.5	5.1
Motors and generators; and miscellaneous equipment related to motors, generators and transformers	495.2	440.4	88.9	3.4	656.1	569.4	86.8	3.5
Office machines and parts thereof	2,104.4	337.8	16.1	2.6	2,015.1	392.7	19.5	2.4
Semiconductors	4,961.3	297.4	6.0	2.3	4,353.8	272.0	6.2	1.7
Transformers	170.7	149.6	87.6	1.2	273.3	229.9	83.9	1.4
Radio receivers and transceivers and parts thereof	481.7	260.8	54.1	2.0	344.1	219.9	63.9	1.4
Electric household appliances	286.3	151.2	52.8	1.2	373.6	209.9	56.2	1.3
Electrical capacitors	166.1	152.4	91.7	1.2	196.7	178.8	90.9	1.1

(b) Automobile sector	50,155.8	3,930.9	7.8	30.7	31,097.2	5,585.7	18.0	34.4
Motor vehicles including automobile trucks and truck tractors, motor buses and passenger automobiles	45,184.7	2,602.2	5.8	20.3	27,377.2	3,591.3	13.1	22.1
Motor vehicle parts, industrial vehicles, non-self-propelled vehicles, and motorcycles	2,923.6	1,049.6	35.9	8.2	2,931.5	1,657.9	56.6	10.2
Internal combustion engines, piston-type and parts thereof	2,047.5	279.1	13.6	2.2	788.4	336.5	42.7	2.1
(c) Other machinery and equipment	6,210.7	1,228.5	19.8	9.6	3,299.5	1,326.5	40.2	8.2
III Other articles	2,609.8	1,432.5	54.9	11.2	2,630.0	1,551.1	59.0	9.5
IV Grand total	75,122.1	12,811.0	17.1	100.0	55,365.0	16,248.1	29.3	100.0

Sources: The authors, based on information from *Production sharing: U.S. imports under harmonized tariff schedule provisions 9802.00.60 and 9802.00.80,* various issues, United States International Trade Commission, Washington, DC.

automobile parts, even though the assembly nature of such operations persists. Evidence of the widespread use of modern managerial techniques in the new industrial sectors can be cited (Carrillo, 1989). Just-in-time inventories, statistical process control, zero-defects techniques and work teams are now common practices.

The in-bond assembly operations are a second fundamental aspect of Mexico's integration into the new international industrial order, specifically the North American economy. While the sharp devaluations of the 1980s made Mexican assembly operations much more convenient for foreign companies operating in the US market, the early low-wage advantage seems to have given way to more long-range considerations for corporate strategies in terms of international competitiveness in modern activities, such as electrical distribution equipment, televisions, radios, car parts, electrical apparatus, circuit breakers, telephones and sound equipment, in which the Mexican-assembled products represent a significant share of the US market (Table 8.9).

These sectoral considerations drawn from the automobile, electrical machinery and electronic equipment, and *maquiladora* industries serve to provide a 'taste' for the process of Mexican integration into the North American economy which the statistics alone do not supply. They are especially useful in suggesting the overriding importance of new corporate strategies for improving the international competitiveness of their international or regional production systems in the context of the new international industrial order and the advantages offered by Mexico in that context. Clearly the nature of the advantage sought in terms of FDI has changed over time and in the context of the new development path of Mexico efficiency-seeking and strategic-asset FDI has replaced market-seeking FDI in the automobile, electric and electronic, and, generally, in-bond assembly industries.

MEXICAN OUTWARD FOREIGN DIRECT INVESTMENT

Since the mid-1980s, large Mexican firms have made important market-seeking direct investments in foreign countries. Although Mexican investments abroad are rather diversified, they present two basic features: their concentration in the developed countries (mainly the United States) and their specialization in some key production and service sectors, particularly cement and glass products (Peres, 1993). Most investments have been undertaken through the acquisition of existing firms, and, in some cases, through hostile takeovers.

The most important successful takeover of a US firm by a Mexican conglomerate was by Vitro, a holding company which is the leading producer of glass containers, flat and household glass, glass-making machines, and car windows and windshields, with sales of $3.6 billion in 1994. In 1989, Vitro acquired, through a tender offer, 95 per cent of the Anchor Glass Container Corporation, the second largest glass container manufacturer in the United States. The cost of the acquisition was estimated at more than $900 million, including $460 million of Anchor's debt. According to its CEO, Vitro went abroad because it could no longer be based solely on a strong domestic base coupled with some minor export activity: 'With a more open Mexican economy our strategy had to change' (Peres, 1990b). Although the strategy undertaken by Vitro was quite probably the only way to survive as a world producer in an industry that is under harsh restructuring, the mere fact that such a strategy could be pursued by a Mexican firm before the end of the debt crisis deserves special attention.

In the cement industry, another Mexican conglomerate (Cementos Mexicanos, CEMEX), with sales of $3 billion in 1994, took over its major domestic competitor to prevent its acquisition by one of the largest world producers and CEMEX also went abroad. The focus of CEMEX's first raids was the cement production facilities of the UK-based Blue Circle Industries, both in Mexico and in the United States. When CEMEX's CEO presented an account of the firm's strategy, he argued that the mergers will increase cost efficiency through economies of multi-plant operation, distribution channels will be improved, and transportation costs will be cut (Peres, 1990b). These same reasons, and the access to the European Union market, were also important in CEMEX's acquisition of the two largest Spanish cement producers, which implied that, in 1993, the Mexican conglomerate controlled 29 per cent of Spanish cement production. After these investments (worth $1.8 billion), CEMEX became the fourth largest cement producer in the world.

Although CEMEX and Vitro have been the largest Mexican investors abroad, several other large conglomerates have followed suit, both in the production and service sectors. For example, Synkro (a large producer of panty-hose and women's undergarments) bought Kayser-Roth, DINA (a producer of trucks) acquired Motor Coach Industries, the financial and agro-business Grupo Cabal

Peniche took control of PPI Del Monte Fresh Produce, and the media giant Televisa bought Univision. All these operations took place in the United States.[17]

The size of these firms' investments shows that they are following strategies under which the basic elements that define the structure of their industries and their competitive positions are determined in an integrated Mexican–US economic area. In these cases, we see leading Mexican conglomerates becoming international players in their industries. Some of these conglomerates have a long history in the Mexican economy (e.g. Vitro or Televisa), while others have a relatively recent record (e.g. Cabal Peniche). The strengthening of these conglomerates, both old and new, is in accordance with the pattern that has prevailed in Mexican industry in the long term: foreign firms' control over modern consumer and capital goods, and large Mexican firms' predominance in traditional consumer and intermediate goods. The big change now is that some of the Mexican companies are successfully expanding into regional and global markets and this expansion is gaining speed after the beginning of the implementation of the NAFTA.[18]

CONCLUSIONS

The analysis presented in this chapter suggests that the integration of Mexico in the new industrial order is being fostered by the export orientation of the main foreign firms in the country, which have moved from an inward-looking perspective to using the country as an export platform. This is the case not only of some low-skilled-labour *maquiladoras* but also of such relatively high-value-added activities as the production of passenger cars and electrical and electronic equipment. This relative disengagement of foreign firms from the dynamics of the domestic market has been a result of their own strategy *vis-à-vis* their competitive situations in international markets and of policy decisions that opened and liberalized the country's economy. The structural heterogeneity of the Mexican economy, in particular of its industrial base, allowed foreign firms to develop export-oriented production facilities in quite different sectors, ranging from the extremely high capital-intensive production of chemicals, to the intermediate capital-intensive production of passenger cars and parts, and to the labour-intensive *maquiladora* assembly of electrical appliances.

These 'benefits' of the country's structural heterogeneity suggest that Ozawa's assertion that 'it is imperative for Mexico to keep pushing for labour intensive industrialization until full employment is attained and wages start to rise' (Ozawa, 1991, p. 150) cannot be accepted completely. Although labour-intensive activities should continue to be supported to reduce unemployment, the country already has some quite developed capital-intensive industrial sectors which are competitive exporters to North America or are already in the stage of undertaking foreign investment in the developed countries.

In a long-term perspective, Mexico has been upgrading almost permanently its locational-specific advantages, inducing MNEs to change the main reason for investing in the country. The natural-resources-seeking investments of the early decades of the century have been followed by market-seeking investments during the ISI period, and by efficiency-seeking ones as Mexico becomes an export platform to North America.

Although the evidence tends to point out that some industries in Mexico are moving from Stage 2 to Stage 3 of the IDP, this transition is not clear cut or linear in nature. Owing to the unstable macroeconomic situation of the early to mid-1980s, a result of the international debt crisis, the developmental path of Mexico had more of a convoluted nature. For example, the shift from an inward-looking, import-substituting framework to an outward-looking export orientation was really a sharp break highly compressed in time. For that reason, would-be anomalies such as the growth in labour-seeking FDI in the *maquiladora* sector resulted from the major devaluations demanded by crisis management, yet also coincided with a process of efficiency-seeking and strategic-asset-seeking FDI which produced greater technological sophistication in the electric and electronic equipment industry and the automobile industry. Furthermore, the growth in market-seeking Mexican FDI probably occurred a little bit out of phase according to the IDP. These country-specific factors are a result of the complexity of the Mexican reality. Naturally, the new period of economic uncertainty opened by the December 1994 foreign exchange crisis may reinforce the same complexity.

Finally, Mexico's integration in the North American cluster of the Triad (UNCTC, 1991) has sharply intensified in the last decade. MNEs are central actors in this process and have begun to specialize their Mexican operations, such that they play a progressively more defined role in their global or regional production and marketing systems. Although of a much smaller dimension, large Mexican conglomerates are also globalizing their activities through outward FDI, primarily in the United States. So, Mexico's integration into North America is, at least partially, a two-way process.

Synergy among the changes in the competitive position of countries in international product and capital markets, new globalizing corporate strategies, and reconsidered national policies on the part of most developing countries (including a new attitude towards FDI) has resulted in a new international industrial order. In the case of Mexico, the logic of the globalization process for MNEs, its location in the North American market, and other competitive advantages are replacing the domestic market as the main attraction for foreign investors.

The strategy adopted by the Mexican government in 1995 relies on foreign direct investment inflows to finance almost half of the expected current account deficit, while in the previous years portfolio investment played the predominant role. To induce direct investments of the order of $8 billion per year in an uncertain macroeconomic environment, new locational-specific advantages will be offered, most probably the opening up of new areas for foreign investment (i.e. 100 per cent ownership in banking) and new privatizations (satellite communications, transport infrastructure and possibly, but not probably, some activities related to oil extraction and refining).[19]

NOTES

1 See also the introductory chapter in this volume.
2 Except when otherwise indicated, the currency used for data in this chapter is the US dollar.
3 For a detailed account of these laws and the commitments the country undertook under the NAFTA, see Calderón, Mortimore and Peres (1994).
4 The approval in 1990 of Regulation 'S' and Rule 144A of the US Security and Exchange Comission (SEC) was influential in the decision of portfolio investors to change their investment strategies in response to new offshore opportunities.
5 During a period of foreign investment scarcity in Latin America, the Mexican debt-equity conversion programme succeeded in attracting over $3 billion in FDI (Mortimore, 1991). This FDI went primarily to the tourism (29 per cent), automobile (17 per cent) and *maquiladora* industries (12 per cent). While most of it came from the United States (48 per cent), some diversity by origin was evident: United Kingdom

(14 per cent), Germany (6 per cent), Japan (4 per cent), France (3 per cent) and Spain (3 per cent). This incentive programme carried an initial implicit subsidy (the difference between the cost of Mexican debt paper in secondary markets and the redemption value in pesos offered by the Mexican government) of almost 19 per cent. This incentive programme coupled with macroeconomic considerations, such as the sharp devaluations of the mid-80s, the country's growth potential and its successes in containing inflation, proved very effective in Mexico's eventual return to a more 'normal' FDI inflow situation (Calderón, 1993).

6 In 1993, there were 7,708 firms with foreign investment in Mexico; in 4,783 of them foreign investors owned more than 50 per cent of the capital. Half of the foreign firms operating in the country that year had been established after 1988 (SECOFI, 1993).

7 One notable feature of this service sector FDI, for example, has been the use of joint investments in franchising operations which are spilling over into Mexico from the United States. The number of such operations rose from only 10 in 1990 to 125 (with 950 locals in the country) in 1993.

8 Of total FDI in the manufacturing sector in 1989–1992, 27 per cent went to the metal–mechanical industries, 22 per cent to chemicals and petrochemicals, 21 per cent to foodstuffs, beverages and tobacco, and 17 per cent to non-metallic mineral products (SECOFI, 1993). For a list of new investment projects, see SECOFI (1994a).

9 According to Garrido (1994), most of the privatized manufacturing enterprises were sold to large Mexican conglomerates. Foreign firms did not play a leading role in the privatization process in Mexico, as they actually did in other countries, for example in Argentina.

10 In 1992, foreign firms accounted for 1.1 million jobs in the Mexican economy (total: 7.4 million). More than 773,000 of those jobs were in the manufacturing industries, where such firms accounted for 24 per cent of the total. In the metal–mechanical industries, foreign firms provided 424,000 positions, equivalent to-41 per cent of the total for those industries (SECOFI, 1993). Other data indicate that foreign firms accounted for 456,000 manufacturing jobs in 1980, 19 per cent of total (Peres, 1990a). If, in 1980, foreign firms with 19 per cent of employment explained 27 per cent of industrial production, it is reasonable to expect that in 1992 with 24 per cent of employment they should explain about one-third of production, especially given the relative stability of the sectoral pattern of investment mentioned above.

11 The ECLAC computer software known as Competitive Analysis of Nations (CAN) was used for all calculations regarding international competitiveness. For conceptual and methodological details, see the article by its inventor, Ousmène Mandeng, 'International competitiveness and specialization', *CEPAL Review*, 45, December, 1991.

12 Between 1987 and 1990 the overall production of passenger cars in the United States remained more or less constant at the 6 million unit level; however, the share of the US 'Big Three' fell from 5.5 to 4.8 million while that of the Japanese transplants and joint ventures rose from 0.5

to 1.3 million units (or, from less than 8 to almost 22 per cent of the total). See US Department of Commerce (1991, p. 55).

13 In the early 1990s, labour costs in the electrical and electronics industries in Mexico were not only lower than those of their counterparts in the United States and Japan, but were also below those prevailing in the more advanced Asian countries, such as Taiwan Province of China, the Republic of Korea or Singapore.

14 These inflows of FDI in the sector are for the most part a result of the implementation of anti-dumping duties by the United States against tubes imported from Japan, Republic of Korea, Singapore and Canada in 1988; and more recently in response to the anticipated implementation of the NAFTA.

15 One of the main attractions of Guadalajara as a site for the computer industry has been the decision of IBM to base its Mexican operations in that city, and to establish a major educational and technical centre to train its employees.

16 This section and the folowing one draw heavily on Calderón, Mortimore and Peres (1994).

17 Although Mexican investments in developing countries are much smaller than those in the United States and Europe, important ventures have taken place also in Central and South America. Some examples are the investments of the bread producer Bimbo in Guatemala and Chile, the tortilla producer Maseca in Costa Rica, the airline Aeroméxico in Peru, CEMEX in Venezuela and Televisa in Chile (Peres 1993; *América Economía*, 80, February 1994, p. 27).

18 According to *América Economía* (September 1994), the NAFTA explains the surge in Mexican investment in the United States during the first quarter of 1994. The amount invested in that period $1.4 billion) is bigger than the accumulated Mexican investment in the United States in 1990–1993.

19 'The egg's on Zedillo's face', *The Economist*, 7–13 January 1995, pp. 31–32, and 'México no caerá en la insolvencia', *El Financiero*, 6 January 1995.

REFERENCES

América Economía (1994) 'Los 200 mayores exportadores de América Latina', *América Economía*, Special Issue, September.

Banco de México (1994) *The Mexican Economy 1994*, Mexico City, June.

Bennett, D. and Sharpe, K. (1979a) 'Transnational corporations and the political economy of export promotion: the case of the Mexican automobile industry', *International Organization*, 33, 2, Spring.

——— (1979b) 'Agenda setting and bargaining power: the Mexican state versus transnational automobile corporation', *World Politics*, XXXII, 1, October.

Calderón, A. (1993) 'Inversión extranjera directa e integración regional: la experiencia reciente de América Latina y el Caribe', *Industrialización y desarrollo tecnológico*, 14, CEPAL, División de Desarrollo Productivo y Empresarial, Santiago, Chile, September.

―――― Mortimore, M. and Peres, W. (1994) 'Mexico's integration into the North American economy: the role of foreign investment', in IRELA (ed.) *Foreign Direct Investment in Developing Countries: The Case of Latin America*, IRELA and European Commission, Madrid.

Calvo, G., Leiderman, L. and Reinhart, C. (1993) 'Capital inflows and real exchange rate appreciation in Latin America: the role of external factor', *IMF Staff Papers*, Vol. 40, No. 1, March.

Carrillo, V. (1989) 'Calidad en maquiladoras', *Expansión*, Mexico City, October.

Casar, J. I. (1993) 'La competitividad de la industria manufacturera mexicana: 1980–1980', *El Trimestre Económico*, LX, 237.

―――― (1994) *Un balance de la transformación industrial en México*, ECLAC/IDRC Project on Industrial Organization, Innovation System and International Competitiveness, ECLAC, May.

de María y Campos, M. (1992) *Reestructuración y desarrollo de la industria automotriz mexicana en los años ochenta: Evolución y perspectivas*, Estudios e Informes de la CEPAL, 83, Santiago, Chile.

Dunning, J. and Narula, R. (1994) 'Transpacific foreign direct investment and the investment development path: the record assessed', *Essays in International Business*, 10, College of Business Administration, University of South Carolina, Columbia, SC.

ECLAC (1994) *Latin America and the Caribbean: Policies to Improve Linkages with the Global Economy*, LC/G.1800(SES.25/3), Santiago, Chile.

Evans, P. (1977) 'Direct investment and industrial concentration', *Journal of Development Studies*, 13, 4, July.

Fajnzylber, F. and Martínez, T. (1976) *Las empresas transnacionales: expansión a nivel mundial y proyección en la industria mexicana*, Fondo de Cultura Económica, Mexico City.

Garrido, C. (1994) 'National private groups in Mexico, 1987–1993', *CEPAL Review* 53, Santiago, Chile.

Gurría, J. A. (1994) 'Capital flows: the Mexican case', in R. French-Davis and S. Griffith-Jones (eds) *Coping with Capital Surges: the Return of Finance to Latin America*, Lynne Rienner: Boulder and London.

Hymer, S. (1976) *The International Operations of National Firms: A Study of Direct Foreign Investment*, Cambridge, MA: The MIT Press.

Kessel, G. and Samaniego, R. (1992) *Apertura comercial, productividad y desarrollo tecnológico: el caso de México*, Documentos de Trabajo, 112, Banco Interamericano de Desarrollo, Washington, DC.

Moreno, J.C. (1988) *The Automotive Industry in Mexico in the Eighties*, Working Paper 22, World Employment Programme, International Labor Organization, Geneva.

Mortimore, M. (1994) *La competitividad de la industria automotriz en México*, Mexico City: CEPAL.

―――― (1991) 'Debt/equity conversion', *CEPAL Review*, 44, Santiago, Chile, August.

——— (1992) 'A new international industrial order', *CEPAL Review*, 48, December.

——— (1993) 'Flying geese or sitting ducks? Transnationals and industry in developing countries', *CEPAL Review*, 51, Santiago, Chile, December.

——— (1994) *Transforming Sitting Ducks into Flying Geese: the Example of the Mexican Automobile Industry*, ECLAC/UNCTAD Joint Unit on TNCs, Santiago, Chile.

——— and Huss, T. (1991) 'Encuesta industrial en México', *Comercio Exterior*, 41, 7, Mexico City, July.

Olea, M. A. (1993) 'The Mexican automotive industry in NAFTA negotiations', in C. Molot (ed.) *Driving Continentally: National Policies and the North American Auto Industry*, Ottawa: Carleton University Press.

Ortiz, E. (1993) 'NAFTA and foreign direct investment in Mexico', in A. Rugman (ed.) *Foreign Investment and North American Free Trade*, University of South Carolina, Columbia, SC.

Ozawa, T. (1991) 'The dynamics of Pacific rim industrialization: how Mexico can join the Asian flock of "flying geese"', in R. Roett (ed.) *Mexico's External Relations in the 1990s*, London: Lynne Rienner.

——— (1994) 'The southerly spread of America's automobile industry. Flexible production and foreign direct investment as a corporate restructuring agent', *World Competition*, 17, 4, June.

Peres, W. (1990a) *Foreign Direct Investment and Industrial Development in Mexico*, Paris: OECD Development Centre.

——— (1990b) *From Globalization to Regionalization: the Mexican Case*, OECD Development Centre, Technical Papers, 24, Paris, August.

——— (1993) 'The internationalization of Latin American industrial firms', *CEPAL Review*, 49, Santiago, Chile, April.

SECOFI (1993) *Papel y aportaciones de la inversión extranjera a la economía mexicana*, Subsecretaría de Comercio e Inversión Extranjera, Mexico City, October.

——— (1994a) 'Principales proyectos de inversión extranjera', *Comercio Exterior*, Mexico City, May.

——— (1994b) *Resumen del Tratado de Libre Comercio entre México, Canadá y Estados Unidos,* Mexico City.

Sepúlveda, B., Pellicer, O. and Meyer, L. (1974) *Las empresas transnacionales en México*, Mexico City: El Colegio de México.

Shaiken, H. (1990) *Mexico in the Global Economy: High Technology and Work Organization in Export Industries*, Monograph Series, No. 33, Center for US–Mexican Studies, University of California, San Diego.

——— (1991) 'The universal motors assembly and stamping plant: transferring high-tech production to Mexico', *Columbia Journal of World Business*, XXVI, 11, Summer.

——— (1994) 'Advanced manufacturing and Mexico: a new international division of labor?', *Latin American Research Review*, 29, 2.

——— and Herzenberg, S. (1987) *Automation and Global Production: Automobile Engine Production in Mexico, the US and Canada*, Monograph Series, No. 26, Center for US–Mexican Studies, University of California, San Diego.

UNCTAD (1993) *Small and Medium-Sized Transnational Corporations: Role, Impact and Policy Implications*, ST/CTC/160, New York.

UNCTC (1991) *World Investment Report 1991. The Triad in Foreign Direct Investment*, United Nations Center on Transnational Corporations, E.91.II.A.12, New York.

Unger, K. (1990) *Las exportaciones mexicanas ante la reestructuración industrial internacional. La evidencia de las industrias química y automotriz*, El Colegio de México and Fondo de Cultura Económica, Mexico City.

———— (1991) 'The automotive industry: technological change and sourcing from Mexico', *North American Review of Economics and Finance*, 2, 2.

UNIDO (1993) *Mexico. The Promise of NAFTA*, London: The Economist Intelligence Unit.

US Congress (1992) *US–Mexico Trade: Pulling Together or Pulling Apart?*, Washington, DC: Office of Technology Assessment, October.

US Department of Commerce (1977, 1982 and 1989) *Benchmark Surveys*, Washington, DC.

———— (1991) *Foreign Direct Investment in the United States*, Washington, DC.

US International Trade Commission (1991) *The Likely Impact on the United States of the Free Trade Agreement with Mexico*, USITC publication 2353, Washington, DC.

Whiting, V. (1991) *The Political Economy of Foreign Investment in Mexico. Nationalism, Liberalism and Constraints on Choice*, Baltimore and London: Johns Hopkins University Press.

Womack, J. (1990) *The Machine that Changed the World*, New York: Rawson Associates.

Chapter 9

Taiwan
Foreign direct investment and the transformation of the economy

Roger van Hoesel

INTRODUCTION

It is beyond doubt that Taiwan can be labelled as one of the major post-war development successes in the world. This notion is confirmed by most generally accepted indicators of economic performance. In 1960 its per capita GNP, for instance, only amounted to US$ 141, less than that of Egypt (US$ 160), Malaysia (US$ 275) and the Philippines (US$ 251). An average annual growth rate of real per capita GNP of 9 per cent during the last three decades had resulted in a per capita GNP of US$ 7,959 in 1990, far ahead of most developing nations. In 1993, Taiwan's per capita GNP had increased to US$ 10,556. In the same year, Taiwan ranked as the 14th major trading country in the world representing an export value of US$ 85 billion and an import value of US$ 77 billion. Continuous trade surpluses have resulted in foreign exchange reserves amounting to more than US$ 90 billion, which puts Taiwan in second place in the world behind only Japan. These accomplishments are even more remarkable if Taiwan's international political isolation is taken into account.[1]

As opposed to many other countries that have experienced remarkable economic growth records during the second half of this century, Taiwan's accomplishments have not been confined merely to economic properties but cover a much wider range of features in society.[2] Its distribution of income, for instance, is more equal than in many industrialized countries, whilst – as opposed to any industrialized nation – unemployment is negligible. Life expectancy at present is approximately 74 years, higher than that of many developed countries. Taiwan has built up a sound educational system and illiteracy has virtually disappeared. The abolition in

1987 of martial law has allowed more political freedom, a trend which seems irreversible in present-day Taiwan.

As with the consensus on the scope of Taiwan's success, there also appears to be no disagreement about the important role that the outward orientation of its economy has played in reaching the status of an 'economic miracle' or '(little) dragon'. The *export* orientation of manufacturing has been the prime focus of most analyses in this respect (see for instance Linnemann *et al.*, 1987; Naya, 1988). Much less academic attention has been paid to the pivotal role foreign direct investment (FDI)[3] has played in the rapid transformation of the Taiwan economy during the last three decades. As will be shown in this chapter, this has not been confined to inward FDI but also concerns outward FDI. In terms of the investment development path (IDP), we shall see that Taiwan has gone from Stage 1 to Stage 3 at a remarkably rapid pace and may even have become a net outward investor. This, until recently a seriously underexposed theme, is the topic of this chapter.

First an overview of the impact of inward direct investment on economic development in time will be presented. Special attention will be paid to the continuously changing role of the government in this respect. Subsequently, outward investment from Taiwan will be explored in a similar fashion. Next, the interplay between inward and outward investment in the process of building new comparative and competitive advantages will be investigated in more detail in the case of one of Taiwan's most successful branches of industry, information technology (IT). Finally, some conclusions regarding the interaction between FDI and Taiwan's development are drawn.

DIRECT INVESTMENTS IN TAIWAN

Inward direct investment has had a long history in Taiwan. The first direct investments by foreign companies took place during Japan's colonisation of Taiwan which lasted from 1895 to 1945. The Japanese authorities encouraged Japanese companies to invest in its colony, first primarily in rice and sugar processing for export to Japan, and later in heavy industries meant to support Japan's war efforts.[4] During the one and a half decades after Japan's defeat in 1945, hardly any inward investment was recorded in Taiwan. Most capital inflow was in the form of official concessional aid, especially from the United States. The import-substitution policy pursued by the government in the 1950s implied heavy protection of local entrepreneurs. Potential investors were further deterred by the remote geographical location of the island and the limited size of the home market. Consequently, from 1952 to 1960, annual inward investment flows averaged only US$ 4.1 million (Figure 9.1). By the end of the 1950s the growth potential of first-stage import substitution appeared to have been exhausted. The domestic market became saturated with goods produced in Taiwan, while the heavy import demands (in terms of capital goods and industrial raw materials) of light industry caused serious balance of payments problems. As a result, the government decided to refocus its efforts towards industrial promotion through the export of labour-intensive goods (Clark, 1989).

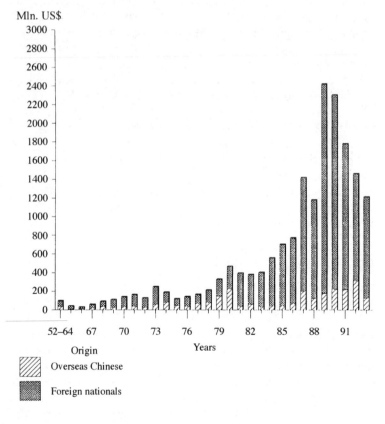

Figure 9.1   Inward direct investment flows (on approval base)
Source: Ministry of Economic Affairs (MOEA).

Export-oriented labour-intensive industrialisation

This policy change towards export-led growth as well as the gradual termination of US aid flows ushered in a more active policy of attracting foreign investors (Gold, 1986). With the help of the US Agency for International Development (USAID) a package of incentives was introduced at a time when Latin American countries showed growing reluctance to hosting MNEs (Wade, 1990). Whereas Latin American countries required the establishment of joint ventures with local companies and threatened expropriation, Taiwan, on the contrary, offered 100 per cent foreign ownership and management as well as guarantees against expropriation. Cheap and well-trained labour, tax concessions, extensive possibilities of profit repatriation, the non-existence of labour strikes and political stability further strengthened Taiwan's position as a potential host economy *vis-à-vis* Latin American countries (Wade, 1990). Persuading foreign companies to invest in Taiwan nevertheless turned out to be a difficult task. A breakthrough was realised when General Instruments, facing increasing competition from Japanese companies using cheap and productive labour, decided to establish an electronics factory near Taipei in 1964. Their success demonstrated the potential of offshore assembly to other US companies (Gold, 1986). Another major step in attracting inward investment was the promulgation in 1965 of the 'Statute for Establishment and Management of Export Processing Zones' (EPZs) and subsequently the establishment of the first EPZ in Kaohsiung in 1966. This EPZ offered modern port facilities, tax incentives and no import duties on equipment and parts as long as they were used to produce output for exports. Moreover, the red tape usually connected with investment approval procedures in Taiwan was considerably limited. In 1969, new EPZs were established in Taichung and Nantze. Kaohsiung and Nantze mainly accommodated the electronics, garment and plastics industries, while the smaller Taichung zone was especially designed for the precision instruments industry.

In 1975 accumulated approved inward FDI amounted to US\$ 1.4 billion. At that time, most inward FDI – in and outside EPZs – took place in labour-intensive operations, especially in electronic and electrical appliances (from 1965 to 1975: 33.5 per cent of total inward FDI flows) and, to a much lesser extent, chemicals (10.2 per cent), textiles and garments and footwear (6.7 per cent). As is shown in Table 9.1,[5] the most important investors in those years

Table 9.1 Approved inward investment flows (in US$ 1,000)

Years	Overseas Chinese	USA	Japan	Europe	Others	Total
1952–64	36,150	47,437	7,771	234	1,514	93,106
	38.8%	50.9%	8.3%	0.3%	1.6%	99.9%
1965–75	374,181	423,298	205,101	178,233	131,328	1,312,141
	28.5%	32.3%	15.6%	13.6%	10.0%	100.0%
1976–80	554,356	310,302	241,784	99,459	107,255	1,312,156
	42.2%	23.6%	18.4%	7.6%	8.2%	100.0%
1981–5	209,795	940,048	672,771	272,765	346,053	2,441,432
	8.6%	38.5%	27.6%	11.2%	14.2%	100.1%
1986–90	779,298	1,570,584	2,552,056	1,042,852	2,146,995	8,091,785
	9.6%	19.4%	31.5%	12.9%	26.5%	99.9%
1991–3	655,109	979,452	1,216,472	536,358	1,065,878	4,453,269
	14.7%	22.0%	27.3%	12.0%	23.9%	99.9%

Source: Ministry of Economic Affairs (MOEA) (see note 5).

were the United States (1965–75: 32.3 per cent) and overseas
Chinese (28.5 per cent). The overseas Chinese, generally from
Hong Kong and South East Asia, were not only driven by economic
considerations, but also had a political motive: investing in Taiwan
showed their support for the anti-communist Kuomintang government (Wade, 1990). Also in terms of sectoral distribution the
investment behaviour of US companies and overseas Chinese
differed considerably. While US firms were primarily active in
electronic and electrical appliances, chemicals and machinery
equipment and instruments, for the overseas Chinese, non-metallic
minerals was the most important sector, followed by services,
construction, textiles and banking and insurance. Initially most
investment projects, especially in the EPZs, implied only little
direct transfer of knowledge (Simon, 1992). The zones to a large
extent acted as foreign enclaves in which assembly-type operations
took place. Therefore, the interaction between MNEs and local
companies was very limited.

Industrial upgrading

In the course of the 1970s it became clear that in the future Taiwan
would be confronted with a gradual erosion of its comparative
advantage in labour-intensive industries (Wu, 1992). New competition emerged from other developing countries with low labour costs,
while in Taiwan full employment and rising living standards started
to push wages up (Gold, 1986). The derecognition of Taiwan by the
United Nations in 1971 followed by Japan in 1972 and the stepwise
approach of the United States towards the People's Republic of
China,[6] were major political shocks to Taiwan with substantial
economic implications such as serious capital flight and the emigra-
tion of human capital to the United States (Wade, 1990). The
worsened relationship between Taiwan and the United States and
the economic and political turmoil on the island resulted in a
decrease of investment flows from the United States during the
second half of the 1970s (its share dropped to 23.6 per cent). This
trend was compensated by increased investments by overseas
Chinese on the island: their share in total inward investment flows
reached an unprecedented 42.2 per cent. Nevertheless, there was an
obvious need to carry out major policy reforms. Investment regulations were further liberalised and in an attempt to upgrade industrial
operations, the authorities started to change their policy towards

attracting FDI in more capital- and technology-intensive sectors. Investment proposals were increasingly evaluated in terms of the extent to which they would open up new markets, bring in new technology and intensify input–output links with local Taiwanese companies (Wade, 1990). The most prestigious project carried out to attract foreign companies and upgrade Taiwan's industry was the construction of the ultra modern Hsinchu Science Based Industrial Park in 1980. Two universities, numerous research institutes and laboratories shape the surroundings for foreign as well as domestic companies that are active in high-priority manufacturing sectors – especially in electronics, the information industry, high-value-added machinery and metal products. Next to an excellent physical infrastructure and vast resources of human capital, companies in the park are also granted a five-year tax holiday, import duty exemptions and certain financial and foreign exchange freedoms (Lim and Fong, 1991). To maximise possible spillover effects, companies also had to meet certain obligations, such as to establish a sizeable research department and train local personnel in advanced technologies. The latter is a clear example of the intensified efforts of the Taiwanese authorities to upgrade the indigenous industry. Another interesting development was the growing awareness that the EPZs were increasingly becoming important sources of local management. The exposure to modern production and management techniques led to the accumulation of know-how in these fields among local employees of MNEs which later on was often utilised by domestic companies.

The 1980s showed a substantial increase in the level of inward FDI as well as a change in the nature of those investments. The size of average annual approved investment flows went from US$ 183 million in the 1970s to US$ 870 million in the 1980s. During the second half of the decade the average annual size of inward FDI amounted to US$ 1,298 million. This growth for a major part can be attributed to the appearance of new investors in Taiwan. Japanese companies, faced with high wage levels at home, increasingly shifted production operations to their former colony – especially in the electronics industry. The size of Japanese FDI flows into Taiwan went from US$ 179 million during the second half of the 1970s to no less than US$ 1.9 billion during the second half of the 1980s. As a result, their share in total inward investment flows grew from 18.4 per cent in 1976–80 to 27.6 per cent in the next five years and even 31.5 per cent in 1986–90 (Table 9.1). Europe also emerged as a substantial investor in Taiwan. The size of their FDI in Taiwan went from a meagre US$ 99 million in 1976–80 to more than US$ 1 billion one decade later. This reflects a share in total inward FDI flows into Taiwan of respectively 7.6 per cent and 12.9 per cent. From the beginning of the 1980s onwards, the relative importance of overseas Chinese investors has dropped. The share of the investment flows of US companies went from 23.6 per cent in 1976–80 to 38.5 per cent during the next five years and – as a result of a rise in Japanese and European investments in Taiwan – 19.4 per cent during the second half of the last decade.

As Table 9.2 shows, during this decade an interesting shift in the industrial distribution of inward FDI took place. Although electronic and electrical appliances remained the most important target sector in the 1980s, its share in total inward FDI flows decreased substantially: from 27.4 per cent in 1981–5 to 20.0 per cent in 1986–90.[7] In the manufacturing sector, chemicals and machinery showed a remarkable growth, especially during the second half of the 1980s. This trend partly reflects a shift from purely export oriented production investments to operations targeted at the local market. British Imperial Chemical Industries (ICI), for instance, invested in a plant producing a chemical (TPA) which is needed to produce polyester fibre (Lim and Fong, 1991, p. 67). Most of the plant's output is sold to Taiwanese manufacturers of polyester fibre, of which Taiwan is the biggest producer in the world. Other examples are the Swiss-based company Ciba Geigy which produces an anti-oxidant additive that is essential in the production of plastics for the Taiwan and East Asian market, and the German company Merck which produces chemical cleaners for ˙the electronics industry, among others for the makers of chips (*Industrial Panorama*, 1993, 1994). Another interesting change concerns the growing importance of trade, finance and service industries during the last few years. While in the past foreign investments in these sectors were severely restricted in Taiwan, they have attracted more than 30 per cent of total FDI flows since 1986. The increasing opening up of its own service and non-service markets has been stimulated by Taiwan's aspirations to become a GATT member. Since Taiwan's economy is heavily dependent on the international economy, it is considered of crucial importance to re-enter GATT in order to enjoy indiscriminate and open business opportunities (Hou and Wang, 1993).[8] An additional incentive to open its markets is rendered by the strong competition of Singapore and Hong Kong which both offer a well-

Table 9.2 Approved inward investment flows per industry (in US$ 1,000)

	1952–64		1965–74		1976–80		1981–5		1986–90		1991–3	
	Amount	Share	Amount	Share	Amount	Share	Amount	Share	Amount	Share	Amount	Share
Agriculture & forestry	742	0.8%	945	0.1%	1,275	0.1%	303	0.0%	2,737	0.0%	386	0.0%
Fishery & animal husbandry	1,264	1.4%	6,801	0.5%	3,390	0.3%	12,230	0.5%	6,886	0.1%	219	0.0%
Mining	73	0.1%	359	0.0%	142	0.0%			12,499	0.2%	88	0.0%
Food & beverage processing	13,449	14.4%	15,685	1.2%	27,093	2.1%	79,849	3.3%	472,814	5.8%	148,778	3.3%
Textile	6,611	7.1%	59,265	4.5%	25,692	2.0%	23,420	1.0%	131,524	1.6%	71,128	1.6%
Garment & footwear	791	0.8%	28,519	2.2%	8,588	0.7%	11,145	0.5%	19,957	0.2%	28,161	0.7%
Lumber & bamboo products	527	0.6%	9,641	0.7%	12,632	1.0%	6,633	0.3%	47,677	0.6%	27,734	0.6%
Pulp paper & products	842	0.9%	12,738	1.0%	2,601	0.2%	12,194	0.5%	67,425	0.8%	14,608	0.3%
Leather & fur products	131	0.1%	9,170	0.7%	1,111	0.1%	4,805	0.2%	7,657	0.1%	5,144	0.1%
Plastic & rubber products	483	0.5%	36,055	2.7%	30,330	2.3%	66,869	2.7%	267,045	3.3%	111,019	2.5%
Chemicals	35,001	37.6%	133,577	10.2%	141,979	10.8%	462,678	19.0%	1,443,425	17.8%	415,162	9.3%
Non-metallic minerals	1,941	2.1%	76,790	5.9%	250,339	19.1%	30,625	1.3%	159,835	2.0%	85,673	1.9%
Basic metals & metal products	1,838	2.0%	107,796	8.2%	66,985	5.1%	173,231	7.1%	598,011	7.4%	246,049	5.5%

Machinery equipment & instruments	2,496	2.7%	112,471	8.6%	48,627	3.7%	339,041	13.9%	554,876	6.9%	383,571	8.6%
Electronic & electrical appliances	4,447	4.8%	439,697	33.5%	407,701	31.0%	668,966	27.4%	1,614,533	20.0%	1,120,058	25.2%
Construction	10,187	10.9%	67,768	5.2%	23,321	1.8%	4,210	0.2%	44,685	0.6%	39,195	0.9%
Trade	366	0.4%	6,323	0.5%	1,179	0.1%	16,199	0.7%	661,345	8.2%	698,491	15.7%
Banking & insurance	2,747	3.0%	61,285	4.7%	37,372	2.8%	131,490	5.4%	611,820	7.6%	419,445	9.4%
Transportation	1,091	1.2%	23,419	1.8%	22,375	1.7%	12,547	0.5%	257,813	3.2%	126,339	2.8%
Services	6,391	6.9%	72,211	5.5%	178,933	13.6%	338,192	13.9%	1,013,123	12.5%	496,902	11.2%
Others	1,685	1.8%	31,638	2.4%	21,500	1.6%	46,795	1.9%	96,100	1.2%	15,119	0.3%
Total	93,103	100.1%	1,312,153	100.1%	1,313,165	100.1%	2,441,422	100.3%	8,091,787	100.1%	4,453,269	99.9%

Source: See Table 9.1.

developed financial and physical infrastructure (Lee, 1993). By 1990, accumulated approved inward FDI had gone up to US$ 13.3 billion.

Towards maturity

The beginning of the 1990s witnessed a major turning point in Taiwan's economy. Its traditional comparative advantage in labour-intensive production had completely disappeared. The democratisation process loosened the control of the government over the labour movement which resulted in a major rise of unit labour costs. Moreover, the high level of education has brought along a serious shortage of low-skilled labour. As a result, for labour-intensive production, attention has moved towards South East Asian countries and during the last few years, also towards the People's Republic of China. Although the export composition suggests that Taiwan's attempts to upgrade its industrial base have been rather successful,[9] further steps are deemed necessary. 'Borrowing technology' from other countries has become a less viable competitive strategy than in the past now that some Taiwan industries gradually approach global technological frontiers (Amsden, 1992). Moreover, developing capital- and technology-intensive industries under one's own steam is a laborious and time-consuming process.

To cope with this new economic reality, the authorities again attempted to shift their policy emphasis. Therefore, Taiwan recently started to promote itself as a 'regional operations centre' for MNEs. The concept reflects Taiwan's intention to persuade MNEs to establish their regional centres on the island, as well as engage in high-value-added activities such as R&D and the manufacturing of high-tech products (*Industrial Panorama*, 1994). Strategic alliances between the MNEs and local companies are expected to lead to a substantial upgrading of Taiwan's industry in terms of technology transfer and a further development of its human capital. Interestingly, because of the vicinity of numerous high-performing economies, Taiwan's geographical location and its knowledge of the region (including mainland China!) have become a major attraction. Moreover, its well-developed industrial base, abundance of high-quality labour and political stability are seen as additional inviting characteristics of the local economy. Recently, Taiwan has initiated ambitious projects (such as the building of a new airport and seaport facilities and a high-speed railway system) to improve its physical infrastructure. By lowering the required minimum investment amount, simplifying the application procedures and offering new tax privileges for MNEs operating in priority sectors, the appeal of Taiwan as a host economy is further reinforced.[10] Although it is too early to render a final judgement on the degree of success, it appears that the results of the authorities' efforts have started to pay off. In 1991, for instance, Hewlett Packard founded an 'Asia Pacific Manufacturing Technology Centre' in Taiwan, while NCR, which already had a service centre there, moved part of its formerly Japan-based R&D operations to the island. By the end of 1993 accumulated approved inward FDI amounted to US$ 17.7 billion.

Non-conventional investments

Until now our analysis has been confined to 'conventional' inward direct investments – although this reflects only part of the business relations of MNEs with Taiwan. As we have seen, the size of these investments was rather modest until the 1980s. This has led some scholars to conclude – somewhat prematurely – that FDI has played a correspondingly minor role in industrialisation (Lim and Fong, 1991, p. 70). As we have shown, the impact of FDI is not only restricted to the direct effect in terms of capital inflows.[11] In addition, it is also important to take into account the so-called 'new' forms of investment (Oman, 1984), since a close relationship exists between both forms of foreign investments. The approach to technology imports in Taiwan has always been conceived as part of a larger state-led strategy of economic development (Simon, 1992). Instead of viewing the acquisition of foreign know-how as a separate goal, the Taiwanese authorities have attempted to take full advantage of the synergies derived from cooperation with foreign firms. As FDI increased in the mid-1960s, so did the number of technical cooperation agreements. Again, a prominent role was reserved for the Taiwanese authorities. In some cases, the government even required the upgrading of local capabilities as part of the approval process for the establishment of foreign-invested factories (Simon, 1992). In addition, the laws concerning capitalization of technology by foreign firms in joint ventures have tightened up in time (Wade, 1990). Also from the viewpoint of the foreign investor, technical cooperation agreements are often advocated or even required as a means of obtaining additional returns on their know-how from their local partners in joint ventures. Based on the number of approved technical cooperation agreements we can determine that Japan and the United States are by far the most important suppliers of technical know-how. Japan concluded about 2.5 times more agreements with Taiwanese companies than US firms did, which underlines Taiwan's dependence on Japanese know-how. Japanese companies have been especially active in electronic and electrical appliances, chemicals, machinery equipment and instruments, and basic metals and metal products, while US firms primarily sold their knowledge in the fields of electronics and chemicals.

In summary, the starting-point of Taiwan, being a relatively small island lacking natural resources, was not very enviable. In the first two decades after its independence in 1945, Taiwan's L advantages were clearly insufficient to attract inward FDI. Only after heavy investments in the physical and human infrastructure, the subsequent termination of US aid and a switch from an import-substitution to an export-oriented industrialisation policy did the situation change. Notwithstanding Taiwan's natural disadvantages, government-induced L advantages (such as EPZs, tax facilities) became relatively successful from the mid-1960s onwards. Inward FDI by that time primarily involved simple assembly-type operations, meant for re-export. Little interaction with local companies took place and spillover effects at that time were almost non-existent. Important benefits of inward FDI at this stage were the creation of low-skilled employment and the access MNEs offered Taiwan to the international market. The 1965–75 period can be considered the heydays of Taiwan's labour-intensive industry. Since then, the first signs of erosion of its traditional L advantages have appeared. This prompted the local government to upgrade its industry. New L advantages, especially in the form of a highly developed knowledge infrastructure (e.g. Hsinchu Science Based Park), were created to attract companies operating in more skill- and capital-intensive industries. At the same time, a policy was observed to maximise more systematically spillover effects for local companies. This clearly led to an increase of O advantages of Taiwanese companies and a deeper integration of MNEs in the Taiwan economy. During the 1980s, when inward FDI really became sizeable, the role of foreign investors continued as a moderator for industrial upgrading. With the growing importance of the Taiwan market, a shift could be observed from resource- to market-seeking investments. The changing role of FDI is illustrated by the share MNEs contributed to total employment, which went from 16.3 in 1977 to 8.8 per cent in 1985 (Riedel, 1992). As Taiwan reached a mature stage of development, more sectors were opened up for foreign companies. In an attempt to catch up with the industrialised world an interesting experiment was designed at the beginning of the 1990s. By becoming a regional centre Taiwan hopes to create new L advantages resulting from the synergy of the O advantages of individual companies.

We can conclude that over the years Taiwan has shown remarkable flexibility with regard to its economic policy and the role of inward direct investment in this. While FDI has played a significant role in keeping the Taiwan economy competitive, the nature of its contribution changed with the transformation of the economy. Crucial in this process was the active participation of the authorities who continuously had to reconsider the potential benefits of the presence of foreign companies and reshape policy regarding inward FDI accordingly.

DIRECT INVESTMENTS FROM TAIWAN

Acquiring an accurate insight into the size and nature of outward FDI from Taiwan is not an easy task. Data on Taiwan investments abroad are notoriously unreliable. A comparison of total outward FDI flow data published by the Central Bank (the *Balance of Payments*) and the Investment Commission of the Ministry of Economic Affairs shows a wide divergence between both sources as is illustrated in Figure 9.2.

While one would expect that approved outflows which are published by the Ministry of Economic Affairs (MOEA) would exceed foreign investments appearing in the balance of payments, the opposite phenomenon is observed (UNCTC, 1992). Owing to the relaxation of foreign exchange controls after the mid-1980s, investment projects representing an amount smaller than US$ 5 million do not need to be registered, however. Many cases of outward investment – often involving smaller-scale companies – therefore did not go through the approval procedures of the Taiwanese authorities. Convincing evidence that actual outward FDI flows are indeed much more substantial than the MOEA figures suggest is rendered by the publications of host countries reflecting inward direct investments from Taiwan (San Gee, 1992). An investigation conducted by the Chung-Hua Institution for Economic Research (CIER) using the latter sources, for instance, put total outward investment in South

Mln. US$

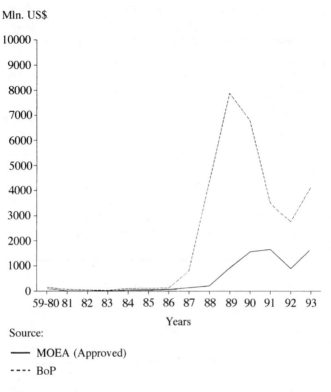

Source:

—— MOEA (Approved)

---- BoP

Figure 9.2   Outward direct investment flows according to balance of payments (BoP) and the Ministry of Economic Affairs (MOEA) respectively.

East Asia at US$ 20 billion, which is 3.5 times the total *official* outward investment figure from Taiwan! An additional complication is that direct investments into mainland China are prohibited and hence not officially known. In early 1991 the Investment Commission stated that all enterprises that have (indirectly) invested in mainland China have to register with the MOEA. In view of the importance of FDI into the People's Republic of China, we shall discuss this phenomenon separately later on in this section. Only the MOEA publishes more detailed information on FDI, including industrial and regional breakdowns, and some of these data are tabulated in Table 9.3 and Table 9.4. Notwithstanding the limitations of the data, we shall therefore, as in the previous section on inward direct investments, base our analysis on this source.

Table 9.3 Destination of approved outward investment flows (in US$ 1,000)

	Asia	USA	Rest America	Europe	Africa	Oceania	Total
1959–64	2,145					895	3,040
	70.6%					29.4%	100.0%
1965–75	17,110	2,101	3,754	35	411		23,411
	73.1%	9.0%	16.0%	0.1%	1.8%		100.0%
1976–80	26,973	41,865	2,048	1,107	24	2,897	74,914
	36.0%	55.9%	2.7%	1.5%	0.0%	3.9%	100.0%
1981–5	33,188	73,223	1,938	3,122	1,800	285	113,556
	29.2%	64.5%	1.7%	2.7%	1.6%	0.3%	100.0%
1986–90	998,295	1,176,782	543,683	110,907	23,675	8,248	2,861,590
	34.9%	41.1%	19.0%	3.9%	0.8%	0.3%	100.0%
1991–3	1,963,088	1,019,884	828,454	362,135	21,813	8,850	4,204,224
	46.7%	24.3%	19.7%	8.6%	0.5%	0.2%	100.0%

Source: See Table 9.1.

Table 9.4 Approved outward investment flows per industry (in US$ 1,000)

	1959–64		1965–75		1976–80		1981–5		1986–90		1991–3	
	Amount	Share	Amount	Share	Amount	Share	Amount	Share	Amount	Share	Amount	Share
Agriculture & forestry			425	1.8%			200	0.2%	5,638	0.2%	8,445	0.2%
Fishery & animal husbandry			13	0.1%	3,781	5.0%	378	0.3%	900	0.0%	675	0.0%
Mining											1,375	0.0%
Food & beverage processing	220	7.2%	7,103	29.6%	273	0.4%	2,250	2.0%	170,615	6.0%	32,206	0.8%
Textile	1,538	50.6%	2,322	9.7%	24	0.0%	7,170	6.3%	92,204	3.2%	216,758	5.2%
Garment & footwear			749	3.1%			826	0.7%	4,745	0.2%	16,072	0.4%
Lumber & bamboo products	147	4.8%	1,268	5.3%	2,550	3.4%	33	0.0%	11,288	0.4%	32,426	0.8%
Pulp paper & products					1,960	2.6%	13,689	12.1%	28,742	1.0%	176,834	4.2%
Leather & fur products							140	0.1%	3,790	0.1%	1,064	0.0%
Plastic & rubber products			1,487	6.2%	6,998	9.3%	1,437	1.3%	68,430	2.4%	77,325	1.8%
Chemicals			508	2.1%	37,568	50.1%	4,253	3.7%	530,872	18.6%	448,793	10.7%
Non-metallic minerals	1,050	34.5%	4,439	18.5%	2,812	3.8%	5,220	4.6%	128,151	4.5%	90,715	2.2%
Basic metals & metal products	86	2.8%	1,532	6.4%	1,383	1.8%	3,669	3.2%	56,320	2.0%	414,913	9.9%

	Value	%	Value	%	Value	%	Value	%	Value	%	Value	%
Machinery equipment & instruments							650	0.6%	13,299	0.5%	193,819	4.6%
Electronic & electrical appliances			122	0.5%	200	0.3%	56,892	50.1%	650,161	22.7%	444,785	10.6%
Construction							758	0.7%	42,067	1.5%	60,372	1.4%
Trade			1,725	7.2%	8,918	11.9%	5,931	5.2%	93,011	3.3%	421,776	10.0%
Banking & insurance			665	2.8%	1,106	1.5%	1,050	0.9%	690,120	24.1%	1,160,894	27.6%
Transportation			1,456	6.1%	7,226	9.6%	8,380	7.4%	27,537	1.0%	33,127	0.8%
Services			50	0.2%			630	0.6%	221,125	7.7%	362,031	8.6%
Others			95	0.4%	114	0.2%			22,576	0.8%	9,819	0.2%
Total	3,041	99.9%	23,959	100.0%	74,913	99.9%	113,556	100.0%	2,861,591	100.2%	4,204,224	100.0%

Source: See Table 9.1.

Although the first Taiwanese investment abroad (in a cement factory in Malaysia) took place as early as 1959, outward direct investment operations have been very modest for many years. Until the beginning of the 1980s they never amounted to more than US$ 10 million per annum. In fact, only since the second half of the 1980s has outward investment from Taiwan really gained momentum. Before that time, modest investments were made in chemicals, electronic and electrical appliances, pulp paper, notably in Asia and the United States. At present, Taiwan, after Japan, is the second biggest outward investor in the Asian region.

The motivations behind the recent surge of outward investments are almost all – directly or indirectly – related to the transformation of the economy and the political system of Taiwan. In fact, this trend was initiated by Taiwan's successful export performance in the past. The export-oriented industrialisation led to the accumulation of enormous foreign exchange reserves in the 1980s, which affected outward direct investments in various ways. As a response to the large trade surplus Taiwan realised with the United States, the US authorities forced the Taiwan government to appreciate substantially the New Taiwan Dollar (NT$) *vis-à-vis* the US Dollar (US$). By the end of 1992 the NT$ had appreciated by 39.7 per cent since 1986. This obviously made exporting from Taiwan less attractive. In addition, the sizeable exchange reserves have put inflationary pressure on the domestic economy and led to high price levels in the non-tradable sector such as real estate and the stock market (San Gee, 1992). This evidently also increased the propensity to invest abroad. Of prime importance to the actual rise of outward investments, however, was the decision of the Taiwanese authorities drastically to liberalise its policy with regard to capital outflows in 1987.

Investments in developing countries

As we can see from Table 9.3, most outward FDI in the *developing world* took place in (South East) Asia. For an important part these investments have resulted from the erosion of Taiwan's traditional comparative advantage in labour-intensive goods. The Labour Standards Law (LSL), promulgated in 1984, has had an important impact on this development (San Gee, 1992). Regulations with regard to minimum wage levels, pension and severance payments, overtime premiums, annual paid vacations, etc., increased the costs of labour substantially. Moreover, as noted earlier, a serious short-age of low-skilled, cheap labour has emerged. As a result of this labour shortage and the promulgation of the LSL, industrial wages have gone up considerably: 13.5 per cent in 1990, 11.0 per cent in 1991 and 10.3 per cent in 1992. As a consequence, a massive shift of labour-intensive production processes to nearby cheaper developing countries took place (Lee, 1993). The countries in South East Asia are not only attractive because of their supply of cheap labour and location near Taiwan, but they are also inhabited by many overseas Chinese which facilitates doing business. Another reason, especially for more capital-intensive companies, to shift production abroad are the increasingly strict regulations with regard to pollution control required by the Taiwanese authorities. In addition, FDI may also offer a possibility to circumvent high tariffs if the host country has preferential trade agreements with important trading partners such as the United States and the European Union (EU).

In Malaysia, the biggest host country in Asia (receiving 33.6 per cent of accumulated Taiwanese FDI in Asia until the end of 1993 – excluding investments in mainland China), most investments went into basic metals and metal products and electronic and electrical appliances. With regard to the latter, it should be noted that espe-cially the more simple operations are shifted abroad while R&D activities and new or more complex production operations remain in Taiwan. Also in Thailand (16.9 per cent of FDI in Asia) electronic and electrical appliances are the most popular target, whereas in Indonesia (10.5 per cent of FDI in Asia) pulp paper products, textiles and non-metallic minerals are the most important sectors. Because of the special intermediary role Hong Kong (15.7 per cent of FDI in Asia) plays in Taiwan–mainland China business activities, Taiwan primarily invests there in trade and services.

The increased investment activities of Taiwanese companies in South East Asia cannot be completely attributed to the transforma-tion of the home economy. During the 1980s, the host countries' authorities started to adopt an open-door policy towards inward direct investment. This has meant a clear abandonment of their policy in the past, when infant-industry protection and the fear of dominance by foreign powers had led to a conservative policy with regard to foreign companies.

An interesting recent phenomenon is the active involvement of Taiwan in the development of a special economic zone in Subic Bay, the Philippines (*Industrial Panorama*, 1994). A joint venture between the Philippine government, the Subic Bay Metropolitan Authority and Taiwan's United Development Co. in 1994 has commenced to build a 300 hectare industrial park in the former US naval base. A satisfactory infrastructure that initially was constructed by the US Army and improved by the joint venture, the availability of cheap labour and various (tax) facilities offered by the Philippine authorities make it fit for export-oriented light industries, such as computer assembly. By the end of 1993, accumulated Taiwanese investment in the Philippines amounted to US$ 248 million. In Vietnam, Taiwan is also involved in establishing industrial zones to house Taiwanese companies. In 1993, Taiwanese investments soared by 685 per cent making Taiwan the largest investor in Vietnam in that year. Accumulated Taiwanese investment in Vietnam amounted to US$ 197 million. These projects illustrate the economic development Taiwan has undergone in the last two and a half decades. While in the second half of the 1960s Taiwan constructed special zones to attract foreign companies, it is now involved in the development of such zones abroad to which production operations in which Taiwan has lost its comparative advantage can be shifted.

The China–Taiwan alliance

The recently changed relation with mainland China has influenced the outward investment pattern from Taiwan, and its international business operations, substantially. Until the end of the 1970s, the People's Republic of China and Taiwan were in a state of serious hostility (Yu, 1993). Since then, the relation has shifted from a military orientation to peaceful coexistence and from economic blockade to trade exchange and (unilateral) investments.[12] In 1979, when Beijing initiated its economic reform programmes, a prudent start of indirect trading activities (via Hong Kong) was made. This trend gained momentum especially after the abolition of martial law in Taiwan after 1987. Table 9.5 shows the recent expansion of trade between both economies.

At present, no less than 54.4 per cent of Taiwan's total trade surplus is realised by its trade with mainland China (Yu, 1993). The (unilateral) FDI figures in Table 9.5 are based on mainland China data.[13] The table indicates an explosive growth of Taiwanese direct investment in the People's Republic during the last few years. The investment flow for 1992 (US$ 5,540 million) almost equals

Table 9.5 Trade (through Hong Kong) and investment between the People's Republic of China (PRC) and Taiwan (in US$ million)

	Commodity trade		Outward investment
	From Taiwan to PRC	From PRC to Taiwan	From Taiwan to PRC
1983–7	3,617	772	190
1988	2,242	478	520
1989	2,896	596	437
1990	3,278	765	892
1991	4,667	1,126	1,391
1992	6,288	1,119	5,540

Source: Taken from Yu (1993).

Taiwan's accumulated approved outward investment in all other countries. Mainland China is not only considered an attractive production location providing cheap labour at a short physical and psychological distance (sharing Chinese culture and history) and abundant raw materials, it also represents one of the fastest growing and potentially biggest markets in the world. In addition, preferential treatments given by the authorities of the People's Republic of China to Taiwanese investors such as tax exemptions and low rental fees and assurances to safeguard Taiwanese property have made the investment climate in mainland China very favourable. Especially for many smaller Taiwanese companies, shifting production to mainland China has meant their survival. The involvement in the mainland is not only beneficial for the investing Taiwanese companies, however. Mainland China, on its side, is able to utilise Taiwan's capital and its management, marketing and production techniques. This combination of interests appears to be highly successful for both economies. The China–Taiwan alliance has not met with full approval in Taiwan, however. Concerned about 'possible adverse effects' from overzealous investments on the Chinese mainland, government officials have already asked larger enterprises either to shelve, temporarily, or at least keep quiet their plans to move capital to the other side of the Taiwan Strait (*The Economic News*, 1993). The fear of a hostage situation refers to the possibility that the government of the People's Republic can impose new conditions or threaten confiscation as a tool for political negotiations (Wang, 1992). The prohibition to invest directly into the People's Republic of China should be considered in this light. Most Taiwanese companies set up a shell company in Hong Kong or elsewhere from which investments in mainland China are made. Since this 'roundaboutness' apparently does not deter potential investors, some authors (e.g. Wang, 1992) have argued in favour of allowing direct investments. While in the beginning most outward FDI took place in nearby Guangdong and Fujian, recently Taiwan companies have also started to invest in Jiangsu, Shandong, Hainan, Shanghai, Wuhan and Sichuan. Important target sectors are: plastic and rubber products, electronic and electrical appliances, and food and beverages.[14] The investment rush into mainland China implies a concurrent drop in 'official' outward investment – as illustrated in Figure 9.2. It should not come as a surprise that investments especially in other (South East) Asian countries have gone down with the rise of investments in mainland China.

'Upward investment'

As we can see from Table 9.3, Taiwan has not restricted itself to investments in developing countries. Perhaps contrary to general expectations, already in the late 1970s the United States was a relatively important host country for Taiwanese investors: during the second half of that decade it even received more than half (55.9 per cent) of the – by that time still modest – total approved outward FDI flows. Investments in *industrialized economies* are motivated by other considerations than those in the developing world. For obvious reasons, investments in labour-intensive industries are of no relevance here. Part of these FDIs reflect mergers and acquisitions (M&As), especially in the United States. M&As can be attractive for several, not mutually exclusive, reasons. The growing reluctance of foreign firms to license advanced technology encourages the takeover of, or merger with, high-technology firms. An example is the acquisition by the Acer group of Counterpart Computers which gave Acer access to the mini-computer business. The lack of brand names and international distribution networks are often serious impediments for the further internationalisation of Taiwanese companies. In order to control its sales network, President Foods Inc., the biggest Taiwanese food processing company, bought Wyndham Foods, the third largest biscuit manufacturer in the United States. Wyse – one of the largest computer terminal manufacturers – was acquired by a Taiwanese venture capital company under the ownership of Mitac, the China Trust and Kuo Chiau (San Gee, 1992). The main motivation was the acquisition of the brand name. Another reason to invest in the industrialised world – by means of greenfield FDI or M&A – is the emergence of regional blocks such as the North American Free Trade Agreement (NAFTA) and the European Union (EU). This development has increased the fear of more protectionist policies *vis-à-vis* countries which are not part of these agreements. This anxiety, as well as the increased attractiveness of a more or less homogeneous market of more than 300 million affluent consumers, recently persuaded some Taiwanese companies to invest in the EU. The first investor was Tatung Co. which established a TV plant in the United Kingdom in 1981. The NAFTA is also expected to attract new FDI to the region, although it is expected that an important part of the new production operations will not be located in Canada or the United States, but in Mexico. Another motive to have affiliates in industrialised countries is the opportunity this offers to scan the local business environment. By hiring qualified local personnel and/ or conducting systematic product and market research, Taiwanese companies can effectively tap technological and commercial know-how, a trend which suggests a shift from 'localised' to 'internationalised learning' (Ozawa, 1992). Many Taiwanese IT companies, for instance, have some type of operation in Silicon Valley for this purpose. Notwithstanding the good reasons which may exist to invest in industrialised economies, the size of greenfield investments there is still limited. One important explanation is the heavy dependence of many Taiwanese companies on Original Equipment Manufacturing (OEM) contracts in the past, which has resulted in little experience in marketing in most lines of business. In addition, the limited size of most companies in Taiwan is a major disadvantage in their further internationalisation as compared to, for instance, the South Korean conglomerates. The latter possess considerable financial backing by the parent company as well as the government which enables them to compensate for possible disappointing financial results during the 'start-up' years.

Although the relative importance of Europe – especially Germany and the United Kingdom – has unmistakably grown during the last few years, the United States is still the most important host country in the industrialised world. An important explanation is the much stronger historical and cultural ties Taiwan has with the United

States than with Europe. As a result, many of the companies which have considered investing in the United States may have done so already, which has resulted in a more 'mature' investment pattern as opposed to Taiwanese direct investments in Europe. By the end of 1993, 31.8 per cent of accumulated approved outward investment was in the United States, whereas Europe had received 18.0 per cent of total outward FDI. This is not the only reason for the higher share of Taiwanese outward FDI in the United States, however. Many important high-tech companies have their origin in the United States. As we saw earlier, a substantial number of them have been an M&A target for Taiwanese companies. The most popular industrial sectors in which Taiwanese companies have invested in the United States are chemicals (28.8 per cent)[15] and electronic and electrical appliances (18.2 per cent). Next to investments in the industrial sector, Taiwan is also very active in banking and insurance operations abroad. In the United States, 24.2 per cent of accumulated approved investment can be found in this sector. The importance of investments in the financial services industry has grown as a response to the worldwide liberalisation of financial markets and the recent deregulation of the financial markets in Taiwan (Lee, 1992).[16] Also in Europe, investments in the tertiary sector are substantial. The shares of banking and insurance services and trade in accumulated Taiwanese investment in Europe respectively are 15.3 per cent, 15.5 per cent and 10.6 per cent. The biggest target, however, has been machinery equipment (36.0 per cent), while direct investments in electronic and electrical appliances are also of a considerable size (13.8 per cent).

The relation between conventional and non-conventional inward investments observed earlier appears to be much less strong in the case of outward investments. For, in spite of the large size of outward FDI, the total number of *outward* technical cooperation agreements until the end of 1992 only amounted to 69 – as compared to 3,769 cases of *inward* technical cooperation agreements. This suggests that the technological capabilities of Taiwanese companies in most industries are not yet advanced enough to be very attractive for foreign companies. This notion is confirmed by the fact that a large majority of the arrangements were concluded with countries at a considerably lower level of development, such as Indonesia, Thailand and the Philippines.

In the foregoing, we have shown that, although Taiwan is a newcomer, it has rapidly gained an important position as an outward investor. This is clearly illustrated by the fact that, whereas accumulated approved outward FDI in 1980 amounted to a meagre US\$ 99 million, by the end of 1993 this amount had increased to US\$ 7.3 billion (Figure 9.4). If we add officially approved indirect FDI in mainland China then accumulated outward FDI amounted to US\$ 10.9 billion! Throughout the colonial era most industrial activities were controlled by Japanese companies. During the 1950s Taiwan started to develop its own business community. In that period, its O advantages on the whole were still very limited and certainly insufficient for outward investment operations. During the first one and a half decades of outward-oriented growth exports in important industries (e.g. electronics) were dominated by MNEs with hardly any spillover effects to local companies. In some industries, however, such as textiles, local firms did build up important O advantages, which were backed by the same favour-able L advantages which attracted MNEs to Taiwan (such as abundant cheap labour). As we saw earlier, from the second half of the 1970s onwards, major structural changes in Taiwan's econ-omy took place. Spillover effects, formal technology transfer arrangements and production linkages commenced to result in the accumulation of O advantages of Taiwanese companies in new industries characterised by a higher knowledge-intensive level and/or a higher capital intensity. In addition, L advantages for traditionally successful labour-intensive industries rapidly wor-sened, which led Taiwanese companies to transplant existing opera-tions to other developing countries that still had abundant cheap labour. Again, the government played a crucial role by drastically liberalising capital outflows in 1987. Because in many industries the O advantages are still rather limited *vis-à-vis* companies in the industrialised world market-seeking greenfield investments in pro-duction units there are not yet very sizeable. In the next section, we shall discuss an exception to this rule.

INWARD AND OUTWARD INVESTMENT AND INDUSTRIAL TRANSFORMATION: THE INFORMATION TECHNOLOGY (IT) INDUSTRY

In this section, the role of inward and outward investment and the government in the industrial upgrading will be analysed in depth in the case of the electronics industry. As Riedel (1992, p. 292) has put it, 'Electronics in Taiwan most vividly illustrates the interaction

Mln. US$

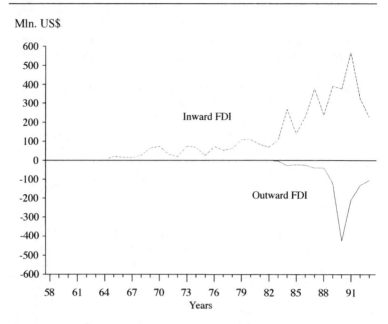

Figure 9.3 Inward and outward investment flows in the electronics and electronic appliances industry
Source: MOEA.

between foreign investment, technology diffusion and changing comparative advantages'. From Figures 9.3 and 9.4 we can see that since 1989 Taiwan's electronics industry has received substantial inward investments but nowadays is also a source for outward direct investments.

This suggests that this industry has reached a rather 'mature' stage of development in Taiwan. Instead of analysing the electronics industry as a whole, we shall focus in this section on the IT industry.[17] Although consumer electronics MNEs gave the initial impetus to Taiwan's electronics industry (Chen and Wang, 1991), indigenous companies have not yet become very successful internationally. The two most important Taiwanese companies do have plants in the industrialized world (Tatung in the United States and the UK and Sampo in the United States), but Japanese and European companies still dominate the market. Therefore, in general we can say that the O advantages of local consumer electronics companies are still too limited to play an important role in the international market.

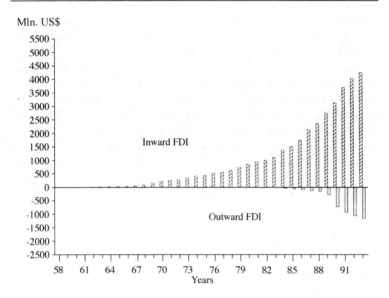

Figure 9.4 Accumulated inward and outward FDI in the electronics and electronic appliances industry
Source: MOEA.

The IT industry, on the other hand, has rapidly become one of Taiwan's key industrial sectors. By the late 1970s, when Taiwan had built up significant experience in the consumer electronics industry, the belief had grown that Taiwan could also become successful in the IT industry. In 1980 the Council for Economic Planning and Development introduced the *Ten Year Development Plan for the Information Industry of Taiwan 1980–89.*[18] In 1982, the IT industry was designated as a 'strategic industry'. As McDermott (1991) rightly points out, Taiwan's L advantages and future policy priorities matched very well with the typical characteristics of this branch of industry. First, Taiwan's shortage of low-cost labour and its abundance of well-trained personnel could serve the knowledge- (and capital-)intensive IT industry very well. Second, IT requires little energy, which fits Taiwan's scarcity of energy resources. Third, as we saw earlier, by the beginning of the 1980s, Taiwan had strong intentions to shift from low-value-added to higher-value-added production operations. The IT industry, especially if vertical integration takes place, could very well suit this goal. Fourth, Taiwan's seriously polluted environment will not further deteriorate by supporting the computer industry which poses minimal threat to the environment.

The knowledge infrastructure in such fields as IT and microelectronics was considerably enhanced by institutes such as the Electronics Research and Service Organisation (ERSO) and the Institute for Information Industry (III). ERSO, located in Hsinchu Park and linked with the Industrial Technology Research Institute (ITRI), is the island's premier research centre in terms of Taiwan's current and future advancements in microelectronics. Through extensive R&D efforts carried out in collaboration with universities and the private sector, the technological gap between Taiwan and the developed nations has narrowed substantially (Chang, 1992). ERSO, for instance, has been the driving force in the establishment of a VLSI company (viz. Taiwan Semiconductor Manufacturing Corporation) in which also Philips and National Chiaotung University are involved (Simon, 1992). III was founded in 1979 with financial support from the government and the private sector. Its principal tasks include software development, assistance in computerisation, collection, analysis, and dissemination of technical and marketing information (Chang, 1992). Knowledge dissemination to local firms takes place on a royalty basis or by some other licensing scheme. The scale advantages realised by institutes like ERSO and III, to some extent at least, compensate for the small size of most Taiwanese companies.

The initiation of the IT industry in Taiwan and its transformation into one of the most successful industries on the island was realised in a remarkably short period. Until the end of the 1970s there were very few local producers in Taiwan and by that time the still limited needs were primarily served by imports from abroad (Chang, 1992). In the first half of the 1980s foreign companies such as Atari, Digital, Philips and Wang were attracted to Taiwan. They established offshore production facilities and dominated the industry (McDermott, 1991). The presence of these MNEs contributed to Taiwan's knowledge regarding information technology in various ways. The training of local personnel, who were later on employed in local companies or who started their own business, is an example of a direct spillover effect. As we saw earlier, Taiwan's requirements regarding potential spillover effects have become more strict in recent years, especially in Hsinchu Park where most companies are located. Moreover, whereas initially the computer business was primarily restricted to assembly operations, later on 'established' companies increasingly started to subcontract (parts of) the production process to smaller local companies to lower production costs. The provision of designs and requirements with regard to quality standards brought along a substantial transfer of knowledge. In addition, the lack of distribution channels and marketing capabilities could thus be bypassed. By 1985, Taiwan's IT industry was characterised by offshore and original equipment manufacturing operations which represented 58 and 37 per cent of total production, respectively. By that time, only 5 per cent of total production could be labelled 'own brand manufacturing' (OBM). More sources can be distinguished which contributed to the initial accumulation of O advantages, however. In September 1982, ERSO, in collaboration with eight local companies, had decided to attempt to build IBM-compatible computers, a mission which was accomplished as soon as March 1983 (Chang, 1992). Also, many Taiwanese who were trained at universities or companies in the United States, returned to the island to apply their know-how in local companies. Matthew Miau, for instance, the chairman of Mitac, was previously a member of the original design team for the 8 bit microprocessor of Intel in the United States. After having started as the representative of Intel in Taiwan, he successfully initiated the production of personal computers and peripherals.

The foregoing should not lead to the conclusion that the road to the establishment of an indigenous IT industry has been shielded from hurdles. One important obstacle has been – and to some extent still is – the high dependence on the imports of key components, especially from Japan and the United States. An emerging shortage of these components may have immediate consequences for Taiwanese IT companies. An example of an attempt to obviate this risk is a joint venture established between Acer, the biggest PC manufacturer in Taiwan, and Texas Instruments (TI). The factory, supplied with TI technology, produces DRAM memory chips which secures Acer's supply of this vital PC component. Similar backward vertical integration initiatives will have to take place on a much wider scale to safeguard the success of Taiwan's IT industry in the future. Another hurdle stems from the fierce price competition in the IT market which recently has resulted in a drastic reduction of the number of companies operating in this business in Taiwan. Companies depending on OEM contracts have to cope with very thin profit margins, which necessitates scale advantages, a requisite that cannot be realised by the many small and medium-sized companies. Moreover, a shift from OEM to OBM not only requires substantial financial means to invest in distribution channels and to build brand awareness among potential consumers, but also a very cautious approach towards OEM buyers. Experience has shown that OEM buyers may consider the emergence of new competitors as a serious threat to their own business performance, which may result in a severance of business relations and, consequently, a considerable drop in sales.

Notwithstanding these hurdles and potential risks, Taiwan's IT industry has been a big success. Exports rose from US$ 105 million in 1981 to US$ 5.5 billion in 1989. For instance, at present, Taiwan is the largest supplier of monitors, hand-held scanners and motherboards in the world. Motherboards made in Taiwan command a world market share of no less than 83 per cent. Taiwan is also among the biggest producers of terminals, control cards, graphic cards, keyboards and PCs (McDermott, 1991). Whereas, in the beginning, Taiwan's success was fully dependent upon offshore and OEM production, nowadays companies such as Acer, Mitac and Tatung sell a considerable share of their products under their own brand names in the international market with growing success. Not only in terms of marketing but also in terms of technology, indigenous companies have significantly improved their capabilities. One of the most convincing pieces of evidence of the latter is the ChipUp technology – a CPU computer upgrade – which Acer in 1993 licensed to Intel. The transformation of the IT industry and the accumulation of O advantages has also resulted in investments abroad. While the more simple production operations are shifted to cheaper countries in the region, investments are also made in the United States and Europe. Because of the rapid changing consumer demands in the PC market, being close to the market has become a prerequisite. This is especially true for those computer companies that do their own marketing. In addition, the leading IT companies have established R&D facilities in the United States to make maximum use of the available knowledge in this field.

Information technology in Taiwan is a fine example of how the interplay between FDI and government policy can lead to the successful development of an industry. This line of business was carefully selected by the government as one of its key industrial sectors to receive an important share of available resources. This choice was based on Taiwan's L advantages, a condition needed to

attract MNEs to initiate operations in this field. Spillover effects –
directed by the government's requirements regarding the activities
of MNEs – formal technology transfer contracts, training elsewhere,
as well as considerable investments in an adequate institutional
environment, led to the accumulation of O advantages of indigenous companies and outward direct investment.

SUMMARY AND CONCLUSIONS

In this chapter we have examined the role of FDI in the industrialisation process of Taiwan. A clear relationship was observed
between the general economic policy objectives and the nature
and role of FDI during the various stages of economic development. While the colonial era involved some inward investment,
mainly in the food processing industry, the import-substitution
policy which was subsequently pursued implied a very limited
role of MNEs in the domestic economy. This period marks Stage
1 of the IDP. The initiation of an export-oriented industrialisation
policy in the 1960s implied a totally different and more positive
attitude towards the role of inward FDI. After a period of investments primarily aimed at relatively simple labour-intensive production operations, from the mid-1970s onwards a gradual upgrading
and expansion of the activities of MNEs in Taiwan took place. We
have seen that the amount of accumulated approved inward FDI
increased more than 10-fold between 1975 and 1993. The change in
the nature of MNE activities was activated by the Taiwanese
authorities who were faced with a decline of the island's traditional
comparative advantages. Because of this transformation of the
domestic economy and its changed position in the international
economy, Taiwan also emerged as an important source of outward
investment itself, since the second half of the 1980s. The pace
with which Taiwan has progressed from Stage 1 to Stage 3 of the
IDP is striking. If we take into account the high outward investment figures as published by the Central Bank, Taiwan may very
well already have entered the fourth stage of the IDP as a net
outward investor.

Although the rise of direct investment from Taiwan is impressive,
it also brought serious risks. The recent drop in the growth rate of
private domestic investment in the manufacturing industries may
lead to an erosion of the domestic industry.[19] Next to urging the
local business community to stop the exodus of indigenous compa-

nies (*Industrial Panorama*, 1994), we observed new attempts in the 1990s to transform Taiwan into a regional centre of economic activities.

The Taiwanese authorities played a considerable role in maximising the potential benefits MNEs can offer. Investments have been guided cautiously by matching the goals of the investing companies with the needs of the Taiwan economy. Also the liberalisation of capital outflows was dictated by a new economic reality. The flexibility with which Taiwan adapted its policy to a continuously changing domestic and international economic environment not only has been highly successful but could also serve as an example for many other developing countries.

NOTES

1   Since the People's Republic of China took over the Republic of China's seat on the Security Council of the United Nations, Taiwan lost most of its memberships of international organisations. Since then all major industrial countries in the world have ceased official diplomatic relationships with Taiwan.

2   Of course there were also serious negative effects of rapid industrialisation, the most important being Taiwan's poor environmental record. It appears, however, that nowadays increasingly attention is being paid to this as well.

3   Taiwan defines FDI to include foreign currency brought in by the investor, imports of machinery and equipment, and reinvested earnings (Lim and Fong, 1991).

4   Japanese companies controlled most of the industrial operations in Taiwan. An excellent analysis of Japan's colonial impact on the Taiwan economy was made by Ho (1978).

5   Tables 9.1–9.4 are based on various issues of *Statistics on Overseas Chinese & Foreign Investment, Technical Cooperation, Outward Investment, Outward Technical Cooperation, Indirect Mainland Investment*, as published by the Investment Commission of the Ministry of Economic Affairs. Some discrepancies may exist between the periodical subtotals based on regional and industry-wise break-ups due to small inconsistencies in the original tables from which the present tables were drawn.

6   On 1 January 1979, the United States and the People's Republic of China established formal diplomatic ties and, as a direct consequence, the embassy in Taiwan was closed.

7   During the last few years, this share has once again increased.

8   Taiwan withdrew from GATT in 1950.

9   The share of labour-intensive products in total exports, for instance, dropped from 47.2 per cent in 1982 to 39.6 per cent in 1992, while the share of high-tech products went up from 25.3 per cent to 37.4 per cent

in the same period. The share of skill-intensive exports went from 18.3 per cent to 28.9 per cent (Lee, 1993).

10 A major hurdle of Taiwan's efforts to attract foreign companies remains the runaway real estate prices resulting from speculation.

11 Also, in some industries, for instance in textiles, MNEs provided Taiwan with access to the industrial markets by purchasing from local companies and taking care of marketing and distribution (Parry, 1988).

12 We do not know of any investments from mainland China in Taiwan.

13 As indicated earlier, a substantial number of Taiwanese companies do not disclose any information on their investment activities to the Taiwanese authorities for fear that the government will utilise this information to probe their capital and income flows (San Gee, 1992). This occurs even more frequently in the case of business relations with the People's Republic of China.

14 Based on MOEA data.

15 Taiwanese investments in the chemical industry mainly represent 'Taiwan public enterprise sourcing of raw materials for the production of energy' (Flowers, 1989, p. 114), including a large-scale investment by state-owned China Petroleum in oil production in Colorado.

16 This has also increased the possibilities for foreign companies in Taiwan. In June 1994, for instance, the ban on foreigners participating in the establishment of new commercial banks was lifted (*Industrial Panorama*, 1994).

17 Unfortunately, no separate FDI data are available for this branch of industry.

18 The plan was designed together with Arthur D. Little, a consultancy company, who have frequently advised the Taiwanese authorities on their industrial policy.

19 This growth rate went down from 25 per cent in 1986 to 10 per cent in 1992 (Lee, 1993). In Japan and in South Korea, for instance, the rates in 1992 amounted to 30 and 20 per cent, respectively.

BIBLIOGRAPHY

Amsden, A. (1992) 'Taiwan in international perspective', in N.T. Wang (ed.) *Taiwan's enterprises in global perspective*, Armonk, NY: M. E. Sharpe.

Chang, C.-C. (1992) 'The development of Taiwan's personal computer industry', in N.T. Wang (ed.) *Taiwan's enterprises in global perspective*, Armonk, NY: M. E. Sharpe.

Chen, T.-J. and Wang, W.-T. (1991) *Globalization of Taiwan's electronics industry*, Paper presented at the Sino-European Conference on Economic Development: Globalization and Regionalization, Taipei.

Clark, C. (1989) *Taiwan's development: implications for contending political economy paradigms*, New York: Greenwood Press.

Flowers, E. B. (1989) 'Taiwan's potential for foreign direct investment in the United States', in C. F. Lee and S.-C. Hu (eds) *Taiwan's foreign investment, export and financial analysis*, Greenwich, CT: JAI Press.

Gold, Th. B. (1986) *State and society in the Taiwan miracle*, Armonk, NY: M. E. Sharpe.

Ho, P. S. (1978) *Economic Development of Taiwan 1860–1970*, New Haven, CT, and London: Yale University Press.

Hou, C. and Wang, C.-N. (1993) *Globalization and regionalization – Taiwan's perspective*, CIER Discussion Papers No. 9301.

Industrial Panorama: Industrial Development and Investment Centre, various issues.

Lee, J. (1992) 'Capital and labor mobility in Taiwan', in G. Ranis (ed.) *Taiwan: from developing to mature economy*, Boulder: Westview Press.

—— (1993) *Taiwan's economy and its international role*, CIER Occasional Paper No. 9303.

Lim, L. Y .C. and Fong, P. E. (1991) *Foreign direct investment and industrialisation in Malaysia, Singapore, Taiwan and Thailand*, Paris: OECD.

Linnemann, H. (ed.), van Dijck, P. and Verbruggen, H. (1987) *Export-oriented industrialization in developing countries*, Manila: Singapore University Press.

McDermott, M. C. (1991) *Taiwan's industry in world markets – target Europe*, London: The Economist Intelligence Unit, Special Report No. 2111.

MOEA, Investment Commission (various issues) *Statistics on Overseas Chinese and foreign investment, technical cooperation, outward investment, outward technical cooperation, indirect mainland investment*.

—— (various issues) *Industrial Panorama*.

Naya, S. (1988) 'The role of trade policies in the industrialization of rapidly growing Asian developing countries', in H. Hughes (ed.) *Achieving industrialization in East Asia*, Cambridge: Cambridge University Press.

Oman, Ch. (1984) *New forms of international investment in developing countries*, Paris: OECD.

Ozawa, T. (1992) 'Foreign direct investment and economic development', *Transnational Corporations*, Vol. 1, No. 1, February: 27–54.

Parry, Th. G. (1988) 'The role of foreign capital in East Asian industrialization, growth and development', in H. Hughes (ed.) *Achieving industrialization in East Asia*, Cambridge: Cambridge University Press.

Riedel, J. (1992) 'International trade in Taiwan's transition from developing to mature economy', in G. Ranis (ed.) *Taiwan: from developing to mature economy*, Boulder: Westview Press.

San Gee (1992) *Taiwanese corporations in globalisation and regionalisation*, Paris: OECD, Technical Papers No. 61.

Simon, F. D. (1992) 'Taiwan's strategy for creating competitive advantage: the role of the state in managing foreign technology', in N.T. Wang (ed.) *Taiwan's enterprises in global perspective*, Armonk, NY: M. E. Sharpe.

The Economic News, various issues (in 1993).

UNCTC (1992) *World Investment Directory – Asia and the Pacific*, New York: United Nations.

Wade, R. (1990) *Economic theory and the role of government in East Asian industrialization*, Princeton, NJ: Princeton U niversity Press.

Wang, N. T. (1992) 'Taiwan's economic relations with Mainland China', in

N. T. Wang (ed.) *Taiwan's enterprises in global perspective*, Armonk, NY: M. E. Sharpe.

Wu, R.-I (1989) 'Economic development strategies and the role of direct foreign investment in Taiwan', in C.F. Lee and S.-C. Hu (eds) *Taiwan's foreign investment, export and financial analysis*, Greenwich, CT: JAI Press.

Wu, Y.-L. (1992) 'Shaping Taiwan's future', in N.T. Wang (ed.) *Taiwan's enterprises in global perspective*, Armonk, NY: M. E. Sharpe.

Yu, T.-S. (1993) *Taiwan's economic development and its economic relationship with Mainland China*, CIER Occasional Paper No. 9307.

Chapter 10

Indonesia
The critical role of government

Donald J. Lecraw

INTRODUCTION

Indonesia provides a fascinating example of the factors that can influence the inflows of foreign direct investment (FDI) and outflows of FDI, by both foreign investors and domestically owned firms. In the analysis, the IDP can well serve as an organizing framework on the one hand, but, on the other hand, the influence of a host of other factors besides GDP per capita immediately becomes apparent. Hence the Indonesian case study can both serve to re-enforce and support the IDP model and to enrich its analytical basis. The Indonesian experience also amply illustrates why simple statistical analysis of net FDI flows as a function of GDP per capita (supplemented by a few other variables) may fail to capture the variety and the dynamics of the factors that influence FDI flows both at one moment and over time.

At the outset, it should also be mentioned that Indonesia, as of 1994, was in the second of the five stages of the IDP model and gradually moving into Stage 3, so that the insights this case study provides on the model cannot be directly used to test and illuminate the factors that determine FDI flows in other stages.

In the description and analysis in this country chapter, the important role that the Indonesian government has played in influencing both inward and outward FDI will be highlighted. This heavy emphasis on the role of government is for two reasons. First, government has, indeed, played a significant role in influencing FDI flows. Second, although the influence of government is firmly embedded in both the eclectic paradigm and the IDP models, its role in influencing macroeconomic variables – growth rates, exchange rates, education levels, infrastructure development and trade barriers

– has received most of the attention. Its role in regulating FDI directly at the industry and firm level through its FDI regulatory system has received relatively less attention. This chapter focuses on this latter role of government by tracing the evolution of the FDI system in Indonesia over time in some detail.

One of the fundamental premises of the IDP model is that the inward and outward flows of FDI are influenced by the state of economic development of the host country and its growth over time. And this state and growth is in turn influenced by government policy and its administration. Hence government has a major role within the IDP framework of analysis. As described below in some detail, the Indonesian case supports the importance of government in influencing FDI flows.

In the introductory chapter to this volume, however, Dunning and Narula have highlighted the government's role in influencing macro, economy-wide variables, such as inflation rates, growth rates, infrastructure development, education and training levels, and the tariff levels and structure. In the case of Indonesia, the government's role in the micro-management of the economy at the firm and industry level has also been an important influence on both the inflows and outflows of FDI. In particular, government regulations on foreign equity ownership (including limitations on the allowed percentage of foreign ownership in an investment project, sectoral restrictions, phase down of foreign ownership over time, and limitations on the duration of foreign investment licences) and government enterprise ownership have had a major impact on FDI flows.

To analyse the impact of various factors on FDI inflows and outflows in Indonesia, this chapter will take a largely historical approach tracing the history of FDI in Indonesia for the past seventy years. Before embarking on this ambitious task, a very brief description of the Indonesian economy and its development over time is necessary.

THE INDONESIAN ECONOMY

Indonesia is the fourth largest country in the world in terms of population (184 million in 1992). It has a rich natural resource base, especially in oil, natural gas, coal, timber and fisheries. After World War II, Indonesia was one of the lowest income countries in the world and during the post-war period through the mid-1960s, economic growth was both sluggish and sporadic. Since 1966, however, with the advent of the New Order government of President Suharto (who was still president as of mid-1995), economic growth has been rapid, averaging over 6 per cent annually from 1966 through 1994. Through the mid-1980s, Indonesia employed a wide array of trade barriers (high tariffs, quotas, import bans, import licensing and sole import agent regulations) to protect its economy from imports as it followed an import substitution development strategy. Starting in the mid-1980s, many of these barriers have been reduced gradually, but, by 1994, the levels of trade protection were still high.

Despite the rapid growth over the 1965–1994 period, by 1994 Indonesia's GNP per capita was still at $620, making Indonesia the poorest among the six ASEAN countries. On a purchasing power parity basis, Indonesia's GDP in 1993 was somewhat larger than that of Canada. In 1994 wage rates in the manufacturing sector were about $2 per day and had not increased markedly in real terms over the past decade.

In short, Indonesia has enjoyed a plentiful supply of natural resources, a relatively large (compared to most other low income countries), fast-growing and protected domestic market, high levels of trade protection, low and steady wage rates, and a stable government. Based on these factors, Indonesia would seem to have been a prime candidate for large inflows of FDI, at least since the mid-1960s. In fact, Indonesia has been the recipient of substantial FDI inflows. But these inflows have been significantly less than any model of FDI inflows would predict. As examples, over the 1970–1980 period, Indonesia ranked seventh among developing countries in FDI inflows and from 1981 to 1991 it fell to twelfth.

A HISTORY OF FDI IN INDONESIA

The colonial period

Foreign direct investment in Indonesia dates well back into the period when Indonesia was a Dutch colony. Prior to World War I, there was substantial foreign investment, largely by the Dutch, in natural resources and plantation agriculture, especially rubber. Before 1920, the modern industrial sector was very small and largely foreign owned and consisted of seasonal cottage industries, such as rice milling and textiles, and semi-processing of raw materials from plantations and mines. In the 1920s, outside of these types of activities, there were only two substantial industrial firms, both foreign owned: a cigarette plant owned by British American Tobacco and an automobile assembly plant owned by General Motors (Soehoed, 1967). This situation illustrates the effect of government intervention even at this early date. Through this period, the Dutch government, at the behest of Dutch interests both in The Netherlands and in Indonesia, maintained strict controls on the establishment of manufacturing facilities and allowed easy access to the Indonesian market for imports, largely from The Netherlands. These policies were not directed towards foreign investors *per se*, but rather were a part of Dutch mercantilist policies towards its colony designed to retard industrial growth in Indonesia in order to promote imports of Dutch-manufactured products to balance exports of Indonesian raw materials to The Netherlands.

The Great Depression forced some changes in the Dutch colonial regulatory policies. From 1929 to 1933, exports from Indonesia declined by almost two-thirds while employment on plantations fell by over one-half (Wertheim, 1956). In response, the government removed some restrictions on investment in the manufacturing sector and imposed some limited tariff protection for domestic manufacturing industries. Although there are no comprehensive statistics on the extent or ownership of the ensuing import substitution industrialization, by 1939, the 'factory sector' had 173,000 employees in food, textiles, metal goods and repair industries and this investment was largely foreign owned.

Under the import substitution regulations of 1933, foreign investment (about half of which was FDI) inflows which had averaged $35 million over the 1925 to 1932 period accelerated to $55 million in 1933, peaked at $99 million in 1934, but then fell abruptly to average less than $9 annually for the rest of the decade as the depression intensified worldwide. By 1939, the total stock of FDI in all industries in Indonesia has been estimated to have been $1.4 billion in current dollars (Callis, 1942), largely in the natural resource sectors.[1]

During the interwar period, although there was little state ownership, the state policy was intimately intertwined with the interests of the private sector in The Netherlands (as exporters of manufactured products) and Dutch-owned investments in the natural resource sectors, especially Shell and Unilever. In a very real sense, the boundaries of state and private enterprise were so blurred that the government acted as the agent of these firms and these firms acted as the arms of government. The net result of this situation was that any investment in the manufacturing sector was small and foreign investment in manufacturing, although large relative to total investment in the sector, was very small in absolute amount. Callis (1942) has estimated that in 1939 63 per cent of FDI was from The Netherlands, 14 per cent from the UK, 7 per cent from the United States and 11 per cent was by 'Island Chinese'. Of Dutch investment, 45 per cent was in agricultural plantations, 20 per cent in mining and petroleum and only 2 per cent in manufacturing.[2]

Increasing restrictions: the post-war period through 1966

During the 1940s, Indonesia was first invaded and colonized by the Japanese and then fought a bloody, but ultimately successful, war of independence from The Netherlands. Foreign assets taken over by the Japanese were returned to their previous owners either in 1945 or at independence in 1949. During this period, there were essentially no inflows of FDI. One estimate of the *stock* of FDI in 1952 put it at $2.24 billion.

Over the next seventeen years (from 1949 to 1966), there was virtually no FDI. After independence, the new government led by President Sukarno sought to follow a path of rapid industrialization. Initially it placed a major reliance on the private sector, especially small industry with *pribumi* (i.e. indigenous, non-Chinese) ownership. This policy was not entirely hostile to FDI, so long as Indonesian ownership in new enterprises was at least 51 per cent. Since there were few *pribumi* entrepreneurs (and even fewer with any training or management expertise) this initiative was not successful either in fostering industrial development or in attracting FDI in partnership with *pribumi* Indonesians.

In response, the government, in formulating its 1955–1960 development plan, shifted emphasis towards industrialization via large scale projects owned by the state. Again FDI was not prohibited, but it was largely restricted to minority joint ventures. Little FDI was forthcoming. Starting in the late 1950s, the government became increasingly nationalistic and socialistic in both its economic and political policies. In 1957 Dutch investments were nationalized; in 1963 British and Malaysian assets were nationalized; and in 1965 some American and other foreign assets (including Bata Shoe of Canada) were nationalized. FDI effectively ended. From 1956 to

1965 there was only $84 million in FDI, entirely by foreign oil companies (Rosendale, 1978). By the end of 1965, state-owned enterprises dominated the economy. Although 'only' 561 of the 27,000 firms listed in the first (1964) Industrial Census were government firms, these firms accounted for 20 per cent of employment and 40 per cent of installed capacity of all firms employing more than five workers 'with power' or ten workers 'without power'. Foreign investment was barred from all mining industries (defined in Indonesia as all extractive industries, including petroleum and natural gas), agriculture, fisheries and land ownership, i.e. in all the industries in which foreign investment had been concentrated prior to 1950.

In summary, to this point in Indonesia's history, during the Dutch regime, private investment, including foreign investment, was welcomed, but the government actively retarded the growth of the manufacturing sector. After independence, the government actively encouraged industrialization, but private investment, especially foreign investment, was discouraged and foreign investment was excluded from all the industries in which it had been concentrated prior to independence. Not surprisingly, given this history, by the end of the period, foreign investment in Indonesia was very low.

The New Order period: 1966 until the present

In the sections that follow, an attempt is made to analyse the rationales for the changes in foreign investment policies, especially in regard to equity ownership, divestment (phase down), and sectoral restrictions through three definite phases of development in the New Order period and to analyse the effects of these restrictions and other factors on the flows of FDI.

Inflows and outflows of FDI in Indonesia over the 1966–1994 period must be placed within the context of Indonesia's situation in the mid-to-late 1960s with the advent of the 'New Order' government of President Suharto. At that time, the Indonesian economy was suffering from the adverse affects of the economic policies of its previous president, President Sukarno. Indonesia faced an economic crisis. Inflation was out of control as were government budgets and the money supply. Indonesia had accumulated substantial international debt; its foreign exchange position was low; it had a substantial trade deficit; and access to foreign loans and credits was difficult. Indonesia desperately needed capital for development and to finance imports. At the same time, with the fall of President Sukarno, capital inflows from the communist bloc ceased while the countries of the West and multilateral economic institutions allied with them, such as the World Bank, acted to assist in the revival of the Indonesian economy via infusions of aid money, loans and grants, and advice about managing the economy. As part of this effort, US-trained Indonesian economists came to positions of influence in government ministries. Their fundamental viewpoint was of economic development via the market system, albeit with government regulation and guidance of basic macroeconomic and industrial structural variables. Within all levels of the New Order government, however, were bureaucrats and politicians with a military background. Their viewpoint was of progress achieved via command: mobilizing and allocating resources directly under their control via state-owned enterprises and regulation of all aspects of the micro economy. As well, these former officers had participated in the war of independence and were sensitive to the issues of foreign control of the economy.

As part of the reorientation of the economy during this period, the Indonesian government turned towards the private sector in general and foreign investment by MNEs in particular. The period 1966–1973 marked a period of 'swings' from restriction to liberalization of both the private sector and foreign investment that has characterized the history of the Indonesian government's policies towards foreign investment until the present. These swings in government policy have had significant effects on the flows of FDI in Indonesia.

Liberalization: 1967–1973

On assuming power in 1966, the New Order government tried to restore macroeconomic stability and changed the orientation of the economy from state-owned enterprises and direct government regulation towards more reliance on market forces. It also made substantial changes in the trade and investment regimes. As part of these initiatives, the government instituted more favourable policies towards private investment in general and foreign investment in particular. The magnitude of the task of trying to accelerate industrialization can be seen from statistics on the size of the manufacturing sector at this time. Although Indonesia was the third largest developing country in terms of population in 1966, the absolute size of its manufacturing sector was smaller than that of many less populous countries such as Hong Kong, Chile, the Philippines and Thailand.

As part of the initiatives to encourage FDI, some nationalized enterprises were returned to their previous owners and a new Law Concerning Foreign Investment (Law #1, 1967) was enacted in 1967. The investment incentives of Law #1 were first provided to foreign investors, but domestic investors were only provided the same incentives a year later (Law Concerning Domestic Investment, 1968).

Professor Dr Sadli, a government minister at that time, has been quoted in Palmer (1979, p. 100) as characterizing Indonesia's stance toward FDI during this period:

> When we started out attracting foreign investment in 1967 everything and everyone was welcome. We did not dare to refuse; we did not even dare to ask for bonafidity of credentials. We needed a list of names and dollar figures of intended investments to give credence to our drive.
>
> (Palmer, 1979)

Law #1 allowed 100 per cent foreign ownership at the time of formation of the PMA project (i.e. a project in which there was *any* foreign equity ownership). At this time, this provision was quite liberal when compared to FDI regulations in most other developing countries. Law #1 also contained 'phase-down' provisions under which the percentage foreign equity ownership share was to be reduced over time. Although Law #1 required phase down of foreign ownership after a 'certain period of time', initially the regulations did not stipulate the length of transfer period or the extent to which the foreign equity percentage would be reduced.

The only limitation on foreign equity ownership was that foreign investment licences were only given for a period of thirty years. After thirty years, the foreign investor was to transfer its shares to an Indonesian investor, otherwise the company would be subject to mandatory liquidation. The regulations also set a minimum investment limit of $1 million for foreign investment projects. The rationale for this regulation was the view by government that the primary benefits of MNEs was their access to large pools of capital that Indonesian investors did not possess. The government believed that Indonesians could undertake smaller investment projects and hence excluded MNEs from investing in these smaller projects.[3]

Although Law #1 was quite liberal for FDI in selected sectors, it also restricted the number of sectors in which foreign companies could invest. The rationales for closing these sectors were the traditional ones of security (e.g. explosives and atomic generation plants), strategic importance (e.g. transportation, the media and telecommunications) and public services (e.g. electricity generation and distribution, water supply). The mining, agricultural and fisheries sectors also were closed to FDI. Closing these sectors flowed from Article 33 (2) of the 1945 Constitution ('branches of production which are important for the state and effect the welfare of the people at large will be undertaken by the state') and Article 33 (3) ('water and natural resources are owned by the state and should be used to benefit all the people'). Interestingly, many of these sectors were also closed to private investors under the same rationales.

As a result of Law #1, twenty-two PMA projects were approved in 1967. By 1970, 177 PMA projects had been approved, of which thirty-seven were 100 per cent foreign-owned projects. It should be mentioned, however, that despite this quite liberal foreign investment system, there were substantial implementation problems within the FDI system, which had a negative impact on the flows of foreign investment.

Increasing restrictions: 1974–1977

Starting in the early 1970s, oil and commodity prices rose substantially. Higher energy prices provided the government with substantial revenues and relaxed the balance of trade and payments problems that had placed constraints on its development efforts. In January 1974, after violent demonstrations during the visit of Japanese Prime Minister Tanaka, the government made the first significant change in Indonesia's FDI system. President Suharto's statement of 22 January 1974 set the standard for the principles governing foreign investment that prevailed for the next twenty years. The President stated the main principles governing foreign investment were: all new foreign investments were to be in the form of joint ventures; Indonesian equity in these investments would be increased to at least a 51 per cent majority share holding within a 'certain period of time' (defined in 1975 as ten years); the number of sectors closed to foreign investment was increased; tax incentives were reduced; and the number of foreign personnel permitted to work at each foreign-owned company was reduced.

At the same time as these changes were being made in the FDI system, growing controls were instituted on all private investment and the financial system, in the form of investment licensing and credit allocation at subsidized interest rates to SOEs. The government, using oil revenues, also expanded the role of state-owned enterprises, and these firms assumed dominance in many sectors, such as petrochemicals and mining. These changes in government policy both towards the private sector as a whole and towards FDI illustrates a recurring theme in government economic policy in Indonesia. When foreign exchange and capital restraints have been reduced, the government has acted to increase the role of the public sector and to decrease the role of the private sector and of FDI.

The impact of this government policy on a model of the determinants of FDI flows is of interest: during relatively expansionary periods the government has increased the restrictiveness of the FDI system thereby retarding FDI inflows; during more difficult periods, the government has liberalized the FDI system in order to attract FDI inflows. Hence any model of FDI flows that does not include government policy will give contradictory results.

During this period an increasing number of sectors were closed to foreign investment (e.g. new weaving mills located on Java). The new investment regulations provided for the possibility to add to the sectors closed to foreign investment. Over the next few years, in accordance with this regulation, a growing number of sectors were deemed closed to foreign investors based on a number of criteria/ rationales: (1) domestic entrepreneurs were deemed capable to undertake the activity; (2) the activity was targeted by state enterprises because of its strategic nature; (3) the activity was targeted for weak or small entrepreneurs.

In 1975–1976, falling oil revenues, combined with the Pertamina Crisis, led to a deterioration of Indonesia's investment climate and exacerbated its external debt situation.[4] To improve the investment climate, the government introduced measures to simplify and facilitate the foreign investment approval process. It also implemented existing restrictions on foreign investment less vigorously. The administrative improvements introduced in 1977 included making the BKPM a 'one-stop service' and the introduction of a Priority Investment List (Daftar Skala Prioritas, DSP).

The government used the annual Priority Investment List as its main instrument to regulate the sectoral composition of investment by the private sector in general and by MNEs in particular. The DSP list covered all economic activities except for oil and gas and the financial sector. The first DSP list was very detailed: 831 sectors in one of the four categories. There were exceptions to the DSP list, however. Foreign companies could invest in activities closed to foreign investment and both foreign and domestic investors could invest in sectors closed to all investment under certain conditions related to the development objectives of the government. The rationales underlying these exceptions were: regional distribution, located outside Java; exports, 100 per cent of production exported; employment creation. These exceptions illustrate how the government relaxed regulations for MNEs if they could provide additional benefits (beyond capital) to the Indonesian economy.

Further restrictions: 1978–1986

The second oil price increase in 1978–1979 again relaxed Indonesia's foreign exchange constraints, accelerated economic growth, and increased government budget revenues. As a direct consequence, the government instituted additional restrictions on foreign investment. In 1981, the government reiterated the requirement that foreign-owned companies were to transfer 51 per cent of their ownership to Indonesian shareholders within ten years. Furthermore, the government appeared to move to implement the phase-down requirements. It stated that, for foreign companies approved prior to February 1974, a minimum of 30 per cent of their equity had to be transferred to Indonesian shareholders by the end of 1984. Also, at this time the government introduced a requirement that, at the time of formation, there would be a minimum 20 per cent Indonesian shareholding for all foreign companies. Starting in 1980, the government closed an increasing number of sectors to foreign investment. The 1981 DSP list reserved additional sectors for cooperatives.

Starting in 1982, Indonesia experienced external shocks from falling oil and commodity prices. Over the 1982–1985 period, the government introduced measures to stabilize the macro economy; introduced some structural reforms to mobilize resources (e.g. tax and financial reforms); and made improvements in customs, ports and shipping.[5] The government's trade and industrial policies, however, became even more inward oriented and interventionist. Against this background, the government also increased the restrictive nature of its foreign investment policies.

Liberalization: 1986–1989

In 1986, the economy again suffered a series of external shocks due to a sharp fall in oil prices and the appreciation of the yen (when a substantial portion of Indonesia's external debt was denominated in yen). These events led to a 34 per cent deterioration in Indonesia's terms of trade and an increase in the debt service ratio from 26 per cent in 1985 to 37 per cent in 1986. In response, the government again undertook macroeconomic stabilization procedures (i.e. fiscal austerity and devaluation) as well as substantial real and financial sector reforms. In the area of foreign investment policy, the government initiated a sustained, but gradual, liberalization on all aspects of the FDI system.

The liberalization of both the economy as a whole and the foreign investment system was linked to the government's policies to promote non-oil exports and to encourage participation by the private sector in the economy. As in the past, under the duress of falling economic growth, strained international credit, and the need for both investment capital and foreign exchange, the government turned once again towards the private sector and foreign investors by relaxing regulations on private and foreign investors.

In May 1986 the government reduced the 20 per cent minimum requirement for Indonesian ownership to 5 per cent for foreign investment in 'high risk' ventures; those located in remote areas (i.e. mainly in Eastern Indonesia); those involved in high technology; those that were export oriented (i.e. exported at least 85 per cent of their production); or investments requiring a large amount of capital (i.e. project costs above $10 million). The phase-down requirements for such projects were: to 20 per cent Indonesian ownership within five years and to 51 per cent Indonesian ownership within ten years (as under the previous regulation). The government relaxed the requirement for foreign investors to phase down their equity ownership to 49 per cent over a ten-year period under certain conditions. The government also confirmed that the licences of joint ventures were valid for thirty years and could be extended another thirty years if the firm increased its capital in order to expand or to diversify its output.

In the 1986 DSP list, the number of activities which were designated open to foreign investment was increased from 475 to 926; open activities increased in the industrial sector from 253 to 596. The government's opening of a number of sectors to invest-

ment to PMA companies reflected a major change in its policy focus
from one in which large sectors of the economy were reserved for
domestic companies to one in which greater emphasis was placed on
attracting foreign investment into these sectors.

In December 1987, the government further relaxed foreign investment restrictions. The minimum Indonesian ownership at the time of
the formation of the company was lowered to 5 per cent for foreign
companies which exported 100 per cent of their production *with no
further obligation to phase down their shares.* The general phase-
down requirement to 51 per cent was also extended to fifteen years.
Furthermore, foreign-owned companies with a minimum capital of
$10 million or located in one of the provinces in Eastern Indonesia
or exporting at least 65 per cent of their production could also be
formed with a 5 per cent minimum Indonesian shareholding. Unlike
the 100 per cent export-oriented PMA companies, however, there
was a phase-down requirement to 20 per cent within ten years and
51 per cent within fifteen years for these companies. The most
significant change in the December 1987 package was the recognition that, in fact, the last three categories of the DSP list functioned
as a 'negative list' for PMA companies.

In May 1989 the DSP list was replaced by a Negative List. In
principle, any sector not on the Negative List was 'open' for
investment by PMA companies. In effect, by this change, the
government effectively further opened additional activities to foreign investment. The original Negative List had sixty-four sectors
closed to foreign investment, although some of these sectors continued to be open under certain conditions, such as for export-
oriented investments. In 1989, the government introduced deregulation packages that lowered the minimum capital investment required
for PMA companies from $1 million to $250,000 if the project were
labour intensive (i.e. employed more than fifty workers), export
oriented, or supported downstream industries which did not compete with existing industries.

In October 1989, the government also liberalized foreign ownership restrictions, albeit in certain areas only: 100 per cent foreign
ownership was allowed in the Batam Economic Zone with 5 per
cent divestment to Indonesian shareholders within five years. For
this type of investment, the October 1989 regulations required no
further divestment, if the PMA company exported 100 per cent of its
products.

The discussion above indicates that, in the late 1980s, the government undertook substantial liberalization with regard to foreign investment policy through several deregulation packages. These deregulation packages were an indication of the seriousness with which government policy-makers pursued structural adjustment measures during this period under the spur of ever-increasing foreign debt and the necessity of increasing exports.

A lull, followed by substantial liberalization: 1990–1994

The government's liberalization efforts experienced a pause during the 1989–1992 period. In part, this pause reflected a boom in foreign and domestic investment that was experienced over this period. As well, during this period, the Indonesian economy expanded rapidly with an average growth rate of 7 per cent annually. With healthy economic growth and increased inflows of FDI (and increased investment by domestic companies), the pressure on the government for further liberalization was reduced.

Two aspects of this period are noteworthy. First, although there was a pause in the liberalization initiatives for foreign investment, the FDI system was not made more restrictive, as it had been in previous periods under similar economic conditions. Second, the government continued to introduce initiatives during this period to deregulate the domestic economy, i.e. the deregulation trajectory of the FDI system diverged from that of the economy as a whole.

In 1991, rapid growth and the resulting accelerating inflation and the increasing current account deficit led the government to institute macro-stabilization measures of tight monetary policies, as well as to impose limits on foreign borrowing by state-related entities. Beginning in 1992, external factors, such as the recession in Japan, the diversion of substantial amounts of foreign investment to China, and the decline in the general investment climate in Indonesia led to a perceived decline in foreign investor interest. As a result, the government introduced two important policy reforms in 1992–1993.

A significant initiative came in the government's 1992 decree, whereby it allowed 100 per cent foreign ownership for certain types of investments: investments of over $50 million, investments located in Eastern Indonesia, and investment located in a bonded zone if all production were exported. For these types of investments, phase down from a maximum 100 per cent foreign ownership to a maximum of 80 per cent foreign ownership was required. The other changes introduced by the government were that for foreign investment in labour-intensive operations (defined as those employing more than fifty persons), export-oriented projects (defined as projects exporting 65 per cent of production) and supplier industries producing raw materials or intermediate goods, the minimum Indonesian shareholding at the time of investment was set at 5 per cent with a phase down to 10 per cent in ten years and 51 per cent in twenty years from the start of commercial production. The lower minimum investment also applied to foreign investment in the services sector, but with 20 per cent minimum Indonesian shareholding at formation and phase down to 51 per cent in twenty years.

The October 1993 package was noteworthy for two reasons. On the one hand, it continued the past trend towards liberalization of the FDI system by allowing initial foreign ownership of 100 per cent for investments of over $2 million in supplier industries. However, the liberalization of the phase-down requirements of the 1992 package were 'taken back' for investments of over $50 million, those located in Eastern Indonesia, and those in bonded zones: phase down had to be to at least 51 per cent Indonesian ownership instead of 20 per cent.

In June 1994, the government announced a dramatic liberalization package for the FDI system: phase-down regulations were essentially removed;[6] FDI with up to 100 per cent foreign ownership was permitted in a wide range of sectors without the previous conditions on investment characteristics that had applied to date; the minimum capital requirements were eliminated; and nine 'public interest' sectors – ports, production, transmission and distribution of electricity, telecommunications, shipping, air transportation, drinking water, railways, atomic generating plants, and mass media – which had previously been closed to FDI were opened to majority, but not 100 per cent, foreign ownership.

Summary

From the colonial period to the present, successive governments in Indonesia have instituted regulations at the industry and firm levels designed to influence the amount and the characteristics of inward FDI. These policies have impacted FDI in (at least) four ways:

1 Sectoral restrictions on FDI have blocked all FDI to those sectors and hence reduced total FDI flows.

2 Foreign equity ownership restrictions have reduced FDI in two ways: by reducing the foreign equity percentages in joint ventures and, probably more importantly, by inducing MNEs for whom investment under those conditions was unattractive to invest elsewhere.

3 The phase-down requirements (even though in general they were not implemented) had two effects: they deterred FDI by making Indonesia a less attractive country in which to invest; and, of the FDI that was attracted, they reduced reinvestment.

4 To the extent that FDI can accelerate economic growth, the effects of reduced FDI due to sectoral and equity restrictions on growth have reduced the attractiveness of Indonesia as a place to invest for MNEs.

DATA AND METHODOLOGY

Before embarking on an analysis of the Indonesian experience and FDI flows, a brief cautionary note about the quality and quantity of the data available concerning FDI inflows and outflows and the FDI stock in Indonesia is necessary. Anyone working with FDI data at the national or industrial level in any country knows that there are problems of varying degrees of severity with FDI stock and flow data.[7] The root cause of these data problems dates back to the establishment of standardized national income accounting and balance of payments accounting. At that time, the focus was on international trade and capital movements and investment in national economies. The sources of this capital and investment were not seen as particularly important or interesting, possibly reflecting the US view (and laws) that made little distinction between foreign and domestic ownership. Hence trade and investment data have been collected down to the five (and sometimes even finer) digit level, but ownership data either of stocks or flows of FDI have not received much attention by government statistics-gathering agencies.

For Indonesia, there is both good and bad news. The bad news is that the statistics concerning flows and stocks of FDI in the aggregate, much less by industry and by source country, are poor. The good news is that they are so poor that anyone who researches the subject of FDI in Indonesia knows how wretched they are and accepts and uses them with extreme caution. This statement is meant to be a warning to readers who are not familiar with these statistics as they appear in the remainder of the chapter.[8]

Beyond the problems with the statistics on *inward* FDI flows and stocks in Indonesia, any systematic statistics on *outward* flows and stocks are essentially non-existent (at least in publicly available form).[9] Hence any comprehensive, systematic analysis of outward flows and stocks is impossible. Anecdotal and limited survey data are available, however, and will be used later on in this chapter.

Based on the history of FDI in Indonesia outlined in the previous section and the IDP theory presented in the introductory chapter of this volume, six hypotheses can be advanced for the 1966–1993 period concerning factors that have affected FDI inflows to Indonesia:

H1: Indonesia's *share* of world FDI should have increased over the 1966–1993 period as its GDP per capita has increased over the period relative to that in (most) other countries.[10]

This hypothesis is directly based on the IDP as put forward by Dunning and Narula. Over this period, Indonesia's GDP per capita became larger and larger relative to that in most other countries. Hence Indonesia should have experienced increasingly large inward FDI flows as it moved through Stage 2 of the IDP, the stage during which FDI flows grow the fastest and the most.

Note that in this hypothesis and the other hypotheses, the dependent variable is Indonesia's *share* of world FDI inflows. The total supply of FDI worldwide has experienced wide swings over the period under study. In part these swings have been influenced by conditions in host countries, such as Indonesia. In part, however, they have also been influenced by conditions in the home countries of major outward investors and hence are not picked up in any model that concentrates on host country conditions.[11]

H2: The more open Indonesia's FDI system, the greater were FDI inflows.

H3: The greater the *change* in Indonesia's FDI system from closed to open (open to closed), the greater (the lower) were the flows of FDI.

H4: The faster the relative growth rate of the Indonesian economy, the greater were FDI inflows.

H5: The higher the real exchange rate, the less competitive the economy and the less attractive it was for FDI.

H6: The higher natural resource prices, the greater were FDI inflows.

In equation form these hypotheses can be modelled by:

$$IS = a + bGRO + cGOV + dDGOV + eNR + fREX + gGDPK \quad (1)$$

where IS = Indonesia's *share* of total world FDI flows; GRO = Indonesia's growth rate relative to other countries, GOV = the restrictiveness of government regulations towards FDI and is scaled from 1 (restrictive) to 7 (open), DGOV = changes in GOV, NR = an index of natural resource prices, REX = real exchange rate (index numbers), and GDPK = gross domestic product in constant dollars.[12] In all cases, IS was related to the independent variables with a one-year lag, i.e. FDI inflows in year X were related to variables in year X - 1.

The data on foreign direct investment, GDP growth and so on used to estimate these equations were gathered from a number of sources: the United Nations, the IMF and Indonesia's Balance of Payments Yearbook.[13] The data for the government policy variables on the restrictiveness of Indonesia's FDI system were based on research done by the author for the Foreign Investment Advisory Service of the World Bank. The data series used was for the twenty-eight years from 1965 to 1992 inclusive.

Data on FDI are notoriously unreliable. This is particularly true for Indonesia's statistics on FDI, especially for the early years in the data series. The FDI flow data collected by the Central Bank used here, however, are better than the stock data, which are based on the BKPM investment approval data.

The results using stepwise linear regression were somewhat encouraging:

$$IS = 2.71GRO^* + 0.72GOV^{**} + 1.85DGOV^{**} + 4.47NR^*$$
$$- 3.55REX^{**} + 0.73GDPK^* \quad (2)$$

where $N = 25$, corrected $R^2 = 0.28$, * = significant at the 0.10 level, and ** = significant at the 0.05 level. The coefficients of GRO, NR, REX and GDPK are standardized beta coefficients (such that a 1 per cent change in these variables impacts on IS by 1 per cent times the coefficient); the coefficients of GOV and DGOV have been standardized such that a change of one unit in these variables impacts on IS by 1 per cent times the coefficient.

This model illustrates the importance of government policy variables in the flows of inward FDI. It also supports the IDP model, since GDPK was significant, albeit only at the 10 per cent level. This marginal support for the IDP model may be due to two factors. The model relates to the absolute amount of FDI flows, not the percentage of FDI flows to Indonesia as a percentage of total world flows. In addition, the restrictive nature of Indonesia's FDI system, especially over the 1979–1985 period, may have acted to negate the effects of the factors behind the IDP model.

Another model can be specified that attempts to isolate the effects of government policies on FDI flows. Instead of Indonesia's investment share in total world FDI, it uses the FDI share in gross domestic capital formation (F/DK) as the dependent variable. There are two potential advantages of using this dependent variable. First, to the extent that foreign investors and domestic firms responded to the same conditions in the Indonesian and world economies in their investment decisions, it can circumvent the problem of not including variables in the equation that proxy for the effects of these variables. In this way the analysis can focus on the effects of government policy variables that differentially impact on foreign investors. Second, to the extent that foreign investors reacted differently to the economic variables in the model, it may be able to identify these impacts. To model the supply side of FDI, the total flows of FDI worldwide can be entered as an independent variable.

This approach leads to somewhat different hypotheses:

H7: The higher the level of government FDI regulation, the lower the share of FDI in gross domestic capital formation (F/DK).

H8: The more open the FDI system (the more it is restricted), the greater (lower) the share of FDI in gross domestic capital formation (F/DK).

MNEs may possess better access to channels of distribution, brand names and technology necessary to produce cost and quality competitive products for export markets than do domestically owned firms and hence they may respond more to changes in real exchange rates.

H9: The higher the real exchange rate, the lower the FDI share in gross domestic capital formation (F/DK).

MNEs are barred from owning natural resources directly (including oil and forest products).

H10: The higher the prices of natural resource products, the lower the share of FDI in gross domestic capital formation (F/DK).

Foreign investors have access to international funds markets, while domestic investors rely more on domestic markets.

H11: The higher real Indonesian interest rates (RI) relative to world interest rates, the higher the share of FDI in gross domestic capital formation (F/DK).

H12: The higher world FDI (WFI), the higher the share of FDI in Indonesia's gross domestic capital formation (F/DK).

H13: The higher Indonesian GDP per capita (GDPK), the greater the FDI share in gross domestic capital formation.

$$F/DK = a + bGOV + cDGOV + dNR + eREX + fGDPK + gWFI + hRI \qquad (3)$$

$$F/DK = 1.08GOV** + 2.21DGOV** - 0.077REX* + 0.98WFI*** + 0.057GDPK* \qquad (4)$$

Note that real interest rates (RI), gross domestic product per capita (GDPK) and natural resource prices (NR) did not enter the equation. Corrected $R^2 = 0.31$, $N = 28$.[14]

Again this model supports the importance of government policy towards FDI in influencing FDI flows. Again the IDP model received some support. Relatively high real interest rates did not seem to impact differentially on domestic capital compared to foreign capital, possibly because Indonesian investors had access to international capital at international rates. There was weak support for the hypothesis that foreign investors responded more strongly to changes in the real exchange rate than did domestic investors. The hypothesis on the effects of restrictions on foreign investors owning natural resources on FDI flows relative to gross domestic capital formation was not supported. Note should be taken that this result does not mean that these restrictions did not impact either FDI flows or FDI flows as a percentage of gross domestic capital formation.[15]

All in all, the results of this statistical analysis give some support to the relationship of FDI flows to GDP per capita in the IDP model and strong support to the influence of government policy on FDI flows within that model. Note, however, that neither model tests the IDP theory directly, i.e. neither model has gross inflows as the dependent variable.

Outward FDI

As mentioned in a previous section, there are no publicly available statistics on outward FDI from Indonesia. Hence perforce the analysis that follows is based on anecdotal evidence and a survey conducted with a sample of Indonesian firms that have invested abroad. The findings of this survey have been reported elsewhere (Lecraw, 1993) and hence only the main results will be reported here. As in the previous section, the emphasis will be on the role of government in influencing the outward projection of Indonesian firms via FDI.

Unlike government policy towards inward FDI, there have been no government policy initiatives directed specifically at outward FDI. In particular, unlike such countries as Korea and Japan, since the late 1970s, Indonesia has had a completely liberal foreign exchange system with no restrictions on capital outflows or rationing of foreign exchange via licences or multiple exchange rates.

The IDP model predicts that for a Stage 2 country, such as Indonesia, there will be little outward FDI by firms based in the country at the beginning of the stage. But, over time, as the country moves through the stage, outward investment should increase as firms in the country develop strategic advantages (O advantages) which they can exploit via FDI.

In the past, the theoretical viewpoint of MNEs was that they possessed some *package* of proprietary firm-specific advantages (ownership advantages) which enabled them to undertake FDI. They were seen as transferring these proprietary advantages via the internal market within the firm rather than via the market based on the internalization advantages of intra-firm transfer compared to transfer via the market for final and intermediate products. Ownership advantages were thought to be in such things as proprietary product and process technologies, brand names, access to or ownership of channels of distribution, management and capital. From this viewpoint, given the stage of development of the Indonesian economy and the firms within this economy, Indonesian firms would not seem to possess any of these ownership advantages, much less some package of them that might enable these firms to compete in markets abroad via FDI.

More recently, however, the theoretical viewpoint of the determinants of FDI has been shifted and broadened somewhat through the resource-based theory of the MNE. According to this theory, a necessary, but not sufficient, condition for FDI is that the subsidiary abroad possesses the resources to compete with other firms in the host country industry. The subsidiary may come to possess these resources via intra-firm transfer from its parent, or from a joint venture partner (or partners) based in the host country or in another source country, or, if the foreign investment is by acquisition, from the subsidiary itself. From the viewpoint of the resource-based theory of the MNE outward FDI by Indonesian firms becomes somewhat more plausible.

Care must be taken here that we are not looking for rationales and explanations for Indonesia's outward FDI to bring it within our accepted theoretical frameworks. The period over which there has been substantial outward FDI from Indonesia has been too short to see if these investments will stand the test of time and competition and hence demonstrate that they were indeed value-creating investments. Perhaps, however, they were based on mistakes and misperceptions and will wither and die over time as they are revealed as value-reducing initiatives.[16]

As mentioned above, the IDP posits that in Stage 2, firms in the host country gradually develop or acquire the necessary firm-specific advantages (ownership advantages) relative to firms abroad that are a necessary, but not sufficient, condition for outward FDI. In Indonesia, government policy has also had a significant influence on the development of ownership advantages by Indonesian-owned firms. As was described in the previous sections, the government's rationale for instituting sectoral, equity ownership and phase-down regulations has been twofold. First, it saw a high cost to foreign control of the Indonesian economy. Second, it envisioned that, over time, Indonesian joint venture partners of foreign firms would acquire the expertise and capital to own and manage these joint ventures as majority (and even sole) owners and that this expertise could be utilized in investments in other industries. This second rationale was a type of 'infant industry' rationale applied to foreign investment: just as trade barriers were envisioned to protect industry as a whole until it could grow up and compete internationally,

investment barriers were envisioned as protecting Indonesian entrepreneurs from foreign competition until they could grow up as well.
In the case of Japan and Korea, this infant industry rationale for
regulation of FDI worked, in that Japanese- and Korean-owned
firms did grow up and eventually could compete directly with
MNEs both at home and abroad. In general, in Indonesia, to date,
this goal has yet to be fulfilled either for the growth of firms in
Indonesia in general or for the growing competitive ability of
Indonesian-owned firms in particular. In part, the abrupt dismantling of the restrictions on FDI in June 1994 was a recognition by the
government of the failure of its past FDI system to achieve this goal
of fostering the development of world-class Indonesian-owned firms
in the manufacturing sector.[17]

The two most important influences of government policy on
outward FDI have been its trade and industrialization policies. As
mentioned in passing in previous sections, through the late 1980s,
Indonesia followed an import-substituting industrialization strategy
whereby industrial development was fostered via high barriers to
trade. High barriers to trade have led to a subscale, inefficient, high
cost industrial structure. Final products have been high cost, not
only due to the inefficient manner in which they have been produced, but also due to high cost inputs either from upstream
domestic manufacturers or imported over high tariff barriers from
abroad. As well, generally trade protection has led to low quality as
well as high cost products.

The effects of trade protection on cost and quality have been re-
enforced by Indonesia's industrial policies. Most notably, the
BKPM has not only regulated entry by foreign investors, but has
also regulated entry and expansion of domestically owned firms.
One of the rationales for this policy was to reduce 'destructive
competition' so as to conserve scarce domestic capital. There
have been three effects of this policy. First, high cost production
has led to even higher-priced products, i.e. higher costs were more
than passed onto consumers. Second, following from the first effect,
the profits from manufacturing operations have been high and have
led to the accumulation of large, but concentrated, pools of capital.
Third, with entry and expansion often blocked in individual sectors,
individual entrepreneurs have sought further growth via conglomerate diversification. One estimate is that the twenty largest conglomerate groups in Indonesia account for well over 30 per cent of
privately owned assets in the Indonesian economy outside land.

The impact of this situation on Indonesia's outward investment is clear. In the manufacturing sector, except for a small enclave of 100 per cent export-oriented firms, firms had no incentive to become cost efficient or to develop proprietary firm-specific advantages which would allow them to export, much less to undertake FDI. As well, given the profits to be made in the Indonesian market, there was little incentive to export or to invest abroad to enhance exports, or to exploit any firm-specific assets, or to acquire firm-specific assets abroad to utilize in the domestic market. Without the means to undertake FDI or the incentive to undertake it, through the mid-to-late 1980s, Indonesian firms in the manufacturing sector did not invest abroad.

Starting in the mid-1980s, the Indonesian government launched a sustained initiative to reorient Indonesian industry from import substitution more towards export promotion. As part of this initiative it sharply devalued the currency twice (and then maintained the real exchange rate at a constant level), began to reduce import restrictions and tariffs, began to deregulate the domestic real and financial markets, and relaxed ownership restrictions for export-oriented foreign investment projects. In these export-oriented segments within industries Indonesian firms began to develop ownership advantages (based on inexpensive labour and access to raw materials) and were able to export. Ironically, these segments were the ones which enjoyed no trade protection (since they were export oriented) and in which 100 per cent foreign ownership had been allowed.

In the late 1980s, several trends and conditions came together that led to a surge of FDI out of Indonesia. As described above, starting in the mid-1980s, Indonesian firms in some industries began to export manufactured products. In general, however, they were caught at the price-competitive end of the market owing to quality problems, lack of product and process technology, and lack of brand names and access to channels of distribution. Despite low cost labour and inputs (for processors of natural and agricultural resources), their costs were high due to scale inefficiencies and lack of expertise and appropriate technology. Import-substituting firms, on the other hand, came under increasing pressure both from imports and from industry deregulation and reduction in FDI restrictions.

In 1988, the government deregulated the banking sector, among other things lowering the capital requirements for starting a bank, removing branching restrictions, and lowering the reserve ratio from 15 per cent to 2 per cent. Money supply growth rates exploded and, although real interest rates were high, domestic credit and loans to the private sector rose dramatically.[18] Since the rupiah was freely convertible and had been devaluing against the dollar by about 4 per cent per year since 1986, this increase in domestic credit could be easily converted into foreign exchange. Since each of the large conglomerates owned at least one bank, this process was made even easier. Hence there existed both a need to invest abroad to acquire resources that they did not possess (to export and to compete domestically) and an opportunity to invest abroad using readily available funding.

Starting in the mid-1980s, the government also began a gradual liberalization of the real sectors of the domestic economy (by, among other things, relaxing its restrictions on domestic investment in many industries in the manufacturing sector). Similarly, starting in the mid-1980s, the government also began to liberalize Indonesia's international trade system by lowering tariffs, reducing the restrictiveness of import licences or removing them entirely, and so on. The first measure facilitated investment in previously 'closed' industries and increased competition from new entrants, both foreign and domestic. The second initiative has gradually exposed Indonesian firms in import-substituting industries to the competitive pressures of imports. As well, in 1986, the government devalued the rupiah sharply and then held its real value more or less constant, thereby fostering sustained export growth.

In the late 1980s, the formation of the free trade area between the United States and Canada, NAFTA between the United States, Canada and Mexico, and the European Union added to the incentive to invest abroad.[19] On the one hand, these trade arrangements were seen by some firms in Indonesia as increasing the competitiveness of their respective markets. Hence there was an incentive to become more competitive in terms of costs, quality and technology in order to continue to export to these markets. On the other hand, there was some anxiety that these trade agreements would lead to a 'fortress' around these important markets. Both these perceptions led some Indonesian firms to invest within these markets.

Taken together these factors have had a substantial influence on outward FDI from Indonesia. Financial deregulation gave Indonesian firms access to plentiful capital with which to make foreign investments. Exports were one way for new entrants to gain the scale economies against larger entrenched rivals. Some firms undertook FDI to acquire the technology, access to channels of distribution, brand names, and management expertise necessary to be competitive on export markets and in their home market. For example, a new entrant into the canned fish market bought a major American firm for this reason.[20] As well, some of the large, entrenched firms in these industries also invested abroad. Some, such as a battery producer, did so both to increase its competitiveness in the domestic market and to enter into export markets. Firms such as those in the examples above invested abroad to acquire strategic assets to increase their competitiveness in the Indonesian market and in export markets.

Other firms invested abroad not to transfer any strategic resources back to Indonesia, but rather to continue expanding even though their sales were under competitive attack at home. As examples, a firm in the beverage industry and one in the pharmaceutical industry invested in a neighbouring country for this reason. Other firms invested abroad not to transfer strategic resources back to Indonesia, but simply to obtain them to be able to compete abroad. A firm in the food products industry invested in one of the former Eastern Bloc countries to acquire processing capacity and process and packaging technology so that its exports would continue to be competitive in Europe.

For some foreign investments there would seem to be no identifiable rationale, besides capital availability. An Indonesian bank became the first foreign investor in banking in a neighbouring country, despite the rapid expansion of the banking industry in Indonesia over this period. A real estate firm invested in a holiday and ski resort in New Zealand. And so on.

Lecraw (1993) found that the impact of these foreign investments on the Indonesian firms which undertook them depended on the type of investment and amount of strategic resources that were transferred from the subsidiary to the parent firm. To summarize these findings, for no investment in his sample were there any identifiable intangible strategic resources transferred from the parent to the subsidiary abroad. For export-promoting FDI, the Indonesian firms *matched* their strategic resources in such things as access to relatively inexpensive inputs and labour with the strategic resources of their acquired subsidiary. Firms in this category also tended to transfer back to Indonesia intangible resources such as management expertise, technology and marketing skills. By this means, the capabilities and competitive position of the parent company were enhanced.

For FDI in import-substituting industries, there was little transfer of any resources in either direction. For these firms, little evidence was found of enhanced capability of the parent firm relative to its competitors in Indonesia.

In early 1991 the government acted incisively to tighten the growth rate of the money supply and to limit credit availability. This action prompted a significant retrenchment among Indonesian firms, bankruptcies in some firms, a decline of the growth rate, and a modest increase in the real exchange rate. As a consequence, some Indonesian foreign investors have drawn back, divested or reduced their ownership percentage. As importantly, the wave of Indonesian FDI that characterized the late 1980s to the early 1990s seems to have abated somewhat, except in the case of China (where Indonesian firms have joined foreign firms based in other countries to throng to invest).

As of 1994, the future path of both inward and outward FDI in Indonesia is uncertain. For inward investment, it can be speculated that the substantial relaxation of the regulatory regimes will, *ceteris paribus*, lead to a significant increase of inward investment as MNEs act to adjust their stocks of FDI to those predicted by the IDP model now that the barriers have been largely removed. For outward investment, the outlook is even less certain. An argument could be made that for outward investments that lead to matching of strategic resources and to flows of those resources, the long run outlook is favourable. For outward FDI that does not have these characteristics, the outlook is less favourable. Only time will tell what the outcome will be. And in time, another research project (perhaps by another researcher) will be able to test these hypotheses concerning the factors that influence the path of inward and outward FDI in Indonesia.

No firm conclusions can be reached concerning any relationship between inward FDI by MNEs and subsequent outward FDI by Indonesian firms. Such a relationship has been observed in a number of countries. (See the papers in Dunning, 1985.) Certainly all the firms in the sample of outward investors had undertaken joint ventures with foreign investors in one or more of the industries in which they operated. They also owned subsidiaries in industries in which foreign investors operated. Hence it is possible that there was some form of direct or indirect transfer of ownership advantages from foreign investors to Indonesian firms that enabled them to develop ownership advantages which formed the basis for their outward investment. The data in this study and the data in the author's study on outward FDI by Indonesian firms, however, cannot be used to address the issue of whether there was a causal link between the two.

Some inferences can be drawn, however. First, a substantial portion of Indonesia's outward FDI has been of the 'strategic asset-seeking' variety, as Indonesian firms have acquired firms abroad in order to enhance their own competitive position. For this type of investment, inward FDI would seem to have had little effect on outward FDI, except possibly as a spur to undertake this outward investment.

There have also been instances in which Indonesian firms which operated in industries in which there was little or no FDI have invested abroad. For example, the Salim Group owns Bimoli, a firm with about 70 per cent of the cooking oil market in Indonesia. The Salim Group has invested in a cooking oil processing and packaging facility in Eastern Europe. Similarly, the Summa Group invested in a bank in Vietnam – and foreign investment in banking in Indonesia is quite small. The Salim Group, through First Pacific Investments based in Hong Kong, has invested in everything from drug stores to rum production. The Dharmala Group has also invested in real estate, engineering consulting and construction abroad. Again there is no foreign investment in these industries in Indonesia. Based on the fragmentary data, there would seem to be no direct causal link between inward foreign investment and much of the outward foreign investment that has been undertaken by Indonesian firms.

As mentioned above, there would seem to be a direct causal link between inward foreign investment and much of Indonesia's outward investment. Indonesia is a natural-resource-rich country, and hence there has been considerable foreign investment in natural-resource-based industries. For example, Filipino logging firms were among the first major investors in the wood products industries. Indonesian firms have also developed in these industries, sometimes initially as joint venture partners with foreign investors. Indonesia's natural-resource-based firms, however, have not generally invested abroad, except for cases such as Manntrust which invested in the United States to acquire brand names and channels of distribution.

In the manufacturing sector, through the mid-1980s, most foreign investment was of the market-seeking type, attracted by Indonesia's growing, but protected, markets. These investment projects were generally scale inefficient and high cost. If anything, they re-enforced Indonesia's shallow industrial structure and lack of competitive advantage on world markets.

Starting in the 1980s, there was considerable foreign investment in export-oriented industries. But this investment tended to use imported inputs intensively and was cut off from the rest of Indonesian industry. Only in the late 1980s did Indonesian manufacturing firms (both foreign and domestically owned) begin to reorient their production from the domestic market towards export markets. In doing so, they began to develop the ownership advantages that subsequently enabled some of them to invest abroad.

In summary, then, it would seem as if foreign investment, to the extent it did have an impact in moving Indonesia along the IDP, had a retarding effect, as it re-enforced the inward-looking nature of Indonesia's industrial structure. This situation may have changed starting in the late 1980s, however, when the Indonesian economy gradually became more outward looking and foreign firms in some industries evolved to become more outward looking as well.

NOTES

1 This estimate may be substantially overstated since it does not account for FDI outflows during these years which, given the depressed state of the Indonesian and world economies, may have been substantial.

2 This share of investment in manufacturing might be compared to 15 per cent of British investment in India at the same period.

3 Professor Sadli has also stated that essentially the government at that time had the wrong idea concerning the benefits that MNEs could bring to Indonesia: large pools of capital. Over time, however, the $1 million requirement was retained, as it was *de facto* reduced by inflation. As described below, in June 1994, the government finally eliminated the minimum capital requirement.

4 Pertamina, the state-owned oil firm with responsibility for all Indonesia's oil and natural gas reserves, was unable to meet its debt obligations. Foreign banks and governments intervened to save Pertamina from default, but, at the same time, required the government to assume responsibility for these debts and to undertake a number of reforms.

5 One aspect of the 1984 tax reforms was the removal of all tax incentives for investment, including FDI in the form of tax holidays and other 'tax expenditures'. Hence, not only was the Indonesian FDI system more restrictive, but it did not provide the 'welcome mat' of tax holidays for foreign investors.

6 'Some' divestment was still mandated, with the amount left undefined, but with strong indications that this amount would be minor, even a token amount. Whatever the exact amount, since 'joint ventures' with a minimum of 5 per cent Indonesian ownership were exempted from any phase down, the conclusion would seem to be that the eventual phase down would at most be to 5 per cent Indonesian ownership.

7 See Rugman (1994) for a particularly scathing, if uninsightful, critique of FDI data.

8 As one illustration, Annex Table 2 of the *World Investment Report 1993* reports that the stock of FDI in Indonesia rose from $10.3 billion in 1980 to $25 billion in 1985. But according to Annex Table 1 of the *World Investment Report 1992*, FDI inflows into Indonesia averaged $227 million per year from 1980 to 1985, or $1.1 billion in total. The lack of consistency arises from the sources of the data: the stock data were from the BKPM (Investment Coordinating Board) while the flow data were from the IMF balance of payments statistics. Both data sets are wrong and are used inappropriately. The IMF data are for net flows (not inflows as they are titled in the annex). The BKPM data are for approvals, exclude the oil, gas, mining and much of the services sectors (most importantly banking and insurance), and do not pick up increases in the stocks of existing FDI due to retained earnings.

9 Some government ministers have stated that the government keeps a 'close watch' on the outflows of FDI. But if so, the results of this watching have not been made public. One of the problems is that the issue is highly political. Much of the private capital in Indonesia is controlled by Indonesian Chinese (who comprise less than 5 per cent of the population) and, although Indonesians are wary of this degree of economic control being exercised by one minority, they are even more wary of outflows of Indonesian capital to fund investment in China, Taiwan, Hong Kong and Singapore.

10 Over the period 1967–1992, Indonesia ranked number five in the world among countries with population over 10 million in terms of growth in GDP.

11 As one example, the substantial increases in FDI to Indonesia, Thailand, Malaysia and Singapore in the late 1980s were not so much a function of changes in their attractiveness as they were attributable to the surge of outward investment from Japan, Korea, Taiwan and Hong Kong over this period due, among other things, to changes in the values of the currencies of these countries.

12 Ideally, *changes* in GRO, NR and REX would also be entered into the model. As it is, however, the degrees of freedom are limited.

13 International Monetary Fund, *International Financial Statistics, Yearbook* (Washington, DC, various years), United Nations Centre on Transnational Corporations, *Transnational Corporations in World Development* (New York: United Nations, various years), Division of Management and Transnational Corporations, *World Development Report* (Geneva: UNCTAD, various years), and Republic of Indonesia, *Balance of Payments Statistics* (Jakarta: Biro Pusat Statistik, various years).

14 The same data sources and time span were used to estimate this equation as for the previous estimation.

15 To see why this conclusion is correct, consider a country in which no foreign ownership of any kind was permitted in natural resources. This restriction would obviously impact on F/DK, but would not be picked up in the regression results.

16 Charles Kindleberger made this point quite strongly in a speech to the annual meeting of the Academy of International Business. Academics have a proclivity to try to bring rationality to what may be a more irrational world than we are prepared to admit. As well, since our jobs are based on the one hand on teaching the 'do's and don'ts' of business management and on the other hand in doing research to uncover the rationales for the regularities behind these do's and don'ts, we may psychologically resist data that suggest that much of business decision making is based on chance or misperceptions and mistakes.

17 Another, more immediate and powerful, reason for this abrupt shift was the fear that if Indonesia did not dismantle its restrictive FDI system, foreign investors would increasingly invest elsewhere, especially in China.

18 Money supply growth rates (as measured by the growth of 'quasi money') grew by 30 per cent in 1988 rising to 65 per cent in 1990. Loans to the private sector and domestic credit roughly followed a similar rate of growth. Real interest rates were 15 per cent in 1988, but fell to 8 per cent in 1989 before rising to 18 per cent in 1990 when the government acted to rein in the growth of the money supply.

19 See Lecraw and Todino (1994) for an analysis of the impact of the European Union on firms in the ASEAN, including Indonesia.

20 In the analysis below, company names have been omitted for reasons of confidentiality of some of the data.

BIBLIOGRAPHY

Callis, H. G. (1942) *Foreign Capital in South East Asia*, New York: Institute of Pacific Relations.

Dunning, J. (ed.) (1985) *Multinational Enterprises, Industrial Structure, and International Competitiveness*, New York: John Wiley and Sons.

Lecraw, D. J. (1993) 'Outward FDI by firms in Indonesia: motivations and effects', *Journal of International Business Studies*, 24, (3), 589–600.

Lecraw, D. J. and Todino, H. (1994) 'The Impact of Europe 1992 on Firms in the ASEAN Region', mimeo, paper given at the Academy of International Business Annual Meeting, Boston.

Palmer, I. (1979) *Textiles in Indonesia: Problems of Import Substitution*, New York: Praeger.

Rosendale, P. (1978) 'The Indonesian Balance of Payments, 1950–1976 – Some New Estimates', unpublished doctoral dissertation, Australian National University, Canberra.

Rugman, A. (1994) 'Book Review: *World Investment Report 1994*', mimeo, University of Toronto, Canada.

Soehoed, A. R. (1967) 'Manufacturing in Indonesia', *Bulletin of Indonesian Economic Studies*, 8, 65–84.

United Nations Centre on Transnational Corporations (1973) *Transnational Corporations in World Development*, New York: United Nations.

United Nations Centre on Transnational Corporations (1983) *Transnational Corporations in World Development: Third Survey*, New York: United Nations.

United Nations Centre on Transnational Corporations (1988) *Transnational Corporations in World Development: Trends and Prospects*, New York: United Nations.

United Nations Centre on Transnational Corporations (1978) *Transnational Corporations in World Development: A Re-Examination*, New York: United Nations.

United Nations Conference on Trade and Development (various years) *World Investment Report*, New York: United Nations.

Wertheim, W. (1956) *Indonesian Society in Transition*, The Hague: van Hoeve.

Chapter 11

India
Industrialization, liberalization and inward and outward foreign direct investment*

Nagesh Kumar

INTRODUCTION

At the time of its independence in 1947, India was a host to a significant stock of foreign direct investment (FDI) largely owed to her erstwhile colonial master: the UK. Soon after independence, India embarked on a strategy of industrialization with active governmental intervention. Domestic enterprises accumulated considerable capability in the process of industrialization, which has influenced not only the pattern of inward FDI in the country in subsequent periods but also led to investments made by Indian enterprises abroad. Recently India liberalized its policy regime with respect to both inward and outward FDI as a part of reforms undertaken to increase the international competitiveness of Indian enterprises.

Dunning's investment development path (IDP) theory explains the evolution of a country's inward and outward FDI position with the level of economic development (see Dunning, 1981, 1993; Dunning and Narula, 1994, among others). This theory focuses on the role of government and economic development in determining the pattern of competitive advantages of foreign investors relative to those of local firms (ownership or 'O' advantages), relative competitiveness of location-bound resources and capability of the country (locational or 'L' advantages), and the propensity of foreign and local firms to utilize the ownership advantages internally rather than through markets (internalization or 'I' advantages). With a country's development and government interventions the configuration of these advantages changes and reflects on the net FDI position of the country.

The IDP provides a useful framework for analysing the evolution of the inward and outward FDI situation of industrialized and developing countries. In India's case, the government has regulated entry of FDI to the country almost all through the post-independence period through a highly selective policy. This has tended to lower the magnitudes of potential inflows of FDI. On the other hand, outward FDI by Indian enterprises which started to emerge in the 1970s, though restricted to investment in kind, was encouraged by the government. Because of this India may have been a net exporter of FDI for a brief period in the late 1970s (Lall, 1985). Therefore, in India's case the relative magnitudes of inward or outward FDI may be somewhat misleading. Instead, the IDP could be used to analyse the changes in the patterns of inward and outward FDI as these are expected to be affected by the changing configuration of OLI advantages. Similarly, in India's case the relatively low per capita income levels tend to mask the level of created assets of enterprises which affect the configuration of their OLI advantages relative to those of foreign enterprises. Therefore, the level of industrialization and other indicators of asset creation may be more relevant indicators of development than those commonly employed.

The Indian government's attitude towards foreign investments has been changing during the post-independence period. Four distinct phases in the evolution of the government's policy are discernible: the period from independence up to the late 1960s, which was marked by a gradual liberalization of attitude; the period from the late 1960s through to the 1970s, which was characterized by a more selective stance; the 1980s, the period marked by limited liberalization of policy; and the 1990s when the policy was liberalized further and made more open and transparent. These phases in government intervention have, indeed, had an important bearing on the pattern of inward as well as outward FDI of India by affecting the configuration of the OLI advantages of local and foreign enterprises (see Figures 11.1 and 11.2). We propose to analyse the evolution of India's FDI position in these four phases of policy in the framework of the IDP.

1948–67: CREATING LOCATIONAL ADVANTAGES WITH IMPORT PROTECTION

In mid-1948, when the first survey of India's international assets and liabilities was undertaken by the Reserve Bank of India (RBI), the stock of foreign investment in the country stood at Rs 2,560 million, largely from the UK. The sectoral pattern of FDI was quite typical

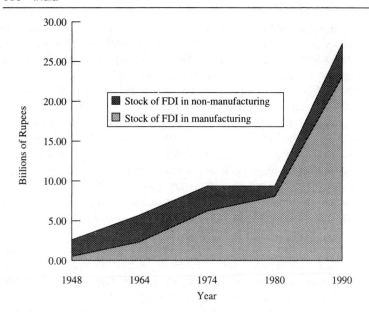

Figure 11.1   Stock of inward FDI in India

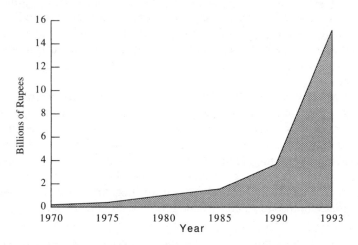

Figure 11.2   Stock of Indian outward FDI

of *Stage 1* of the IDP. The bulk of the FDI stock was of natural-resource-seeking and of a trade-supportive type and was concentrated in raw materials, extractive or service sectors. Tea plantations and jute accounted for a little over a quarter of total FDI (which together accounted for half of India's exports); about 32 per cent was in trading and other services, 9 per cent in petroleum, and only about 20 per cent in manufacturing other than jute (Kidron, 1965: 3).

Soon after independence, India embarked on a strategy of import-substituting industrialization in the framework of development planning. With the Second Five Year Plan which was launched in the mid-1950s, the Indian industrialization strategy focused on the development of local capability in heavy industries including the machinery manufacturing sector. The scope of import substitution extended literally to almost everything that could be manufactured in the country (see Bhagwati and Desai, 1970, for more details). The domestic industry was accorded considerable protection in the form of high tariffs and quantitative restrictions on imports. In order to channel the country's scarce investible resources (the savings rate was just over 10 per cent in 1950) according to Plan priorities, an industrial approval (licensing) system was put into place in the country that regulated all industrial investments beyond a certain minimum. A number of key industries were earmarked for further development in the public sector in view of either their strategic nature or anticipated lack of initiative in the private sector due to large capital requirements. As a part of the development plans, large investments were made in human-resources-creating activities such as the expansion of educational facilities, especially in technical and engineering areas, and the creation of a scientific and technological infrastructure in the form of a network of national and regional laboratories. The government also made investments in the institutional infrastructure for industrial development such as term lending and capital markets development. As the domestic base of 'created' assets, viz. technology, skills, entrepreneurship, was quite limited, the attitude towards FDI was increasingly receptive.

The Foreign Investment Policy Statement made by the Prime Minister in April 1949 considered the foreign investment necessary to supplement Indian capital and for securing 'scientific, technical and industrial knowledge and capital equipment'. FDI was, therefore, encouraged on mutually advantageous terms although majority local ownership was preferred. Foreign investors were assured of no restrictions on the remittance of profits and dividends, fair compensation in the event of acquisition, and were promised 'national treatment'. The foreign exchange crisis of 1957–8 led to further liberalization in the government's attitude towards FDI. In a bid

Table 11.1 Sectorial distribution of the stock of FDI in India (millions of rupees)

Industry group	Mid-1948 %	March 1964 Value	%	March 1974 Value	%	March 1980 Value	%	March 1990 Value	%	Approvals 1991–3 Value	%
I Plantations	25.0	1,059	18.7	1,072	11.7	385	4.1	2,560	9.5	n.a.	n.a.
II Mining	n.a.	47	0.9	64	0.8	78	0.8	80	0.3	n.a.	n.a.
III Petroleum	9.0	1,433	25.3	1,379	14.7	368	3.9	30	0.1	43,290*	32.89
IV Manufacturing	20.0	2,293	40.5	6,256	68.4	8,116	86.9	22,980	84.9	67,400	51.21
1 Food and beverages	n.a.	302	13.2	521	8.3	391	4.8	1,620	7.0	15,720	11.94
2 Textiles	n.a.	166	7.2	356	5.7	320	3.9	920	4.0	2,300	1.75
3 Machinery and machine tools	n.a.	157	6.8	421	6.7	710	8.8	3,540	15.4	4,460	3.39
4 Transport and equipment	n.a.	150	6.5	321	5.1	515	6.3	2,820	12.3	4,710	3.58
5 Metal and metal products	n.a.	331	14.4	867	13.9	1,187	14.6	1,410	6.1	13,210	10.04
6 Electrical goods	n.a.	182	7.9	681	10.9	975	12.0	2,950	12.8	12,830	9.75

7 Chemicals and allied products	n.a.	601	26.2	2,037	32.6	3,018	37.2	7,690	33.4	9,470	7.20
8 Miscellaneous	n.a.	404	17.6	1,050	16.7	1,000	12.3	2,030	8.8	4,700	3.57
V Services	32.0	823	14.6	398	4.4	385	4.1	1,400	5.2	18,380	13.97
Total	2,560	5,655	100.0	9,160	100.0	9,332	100.0	27,050	100.0	131,610	100.0

Notes: Percentages given in the manufacturing subsectors 1 to 8 represent the breakup of FDI in manufacturing.
  * Includes power generation.

Sources: Compiled from RBI, 'India's international investment position', *Reserve Bank of India Bulletin*, July 1975, March 1978, December 1984 and April 1985; and RBI, 'India's foreign liabilities and assets as on March 31, 1990', *Reserve Bank of India Bulletin*, August 1993, pp. 1031–51; and the India Ministry of Industry.

to attract foreign investment to finance the foreign exchange component of projects, a host of incentives and concessions were extended. The Indian Investment Centre, with offices in major investor countries, was set up in 1961 to promote foreign investment in India. Anticipating the foreign exchange bottleneck to continue and affect the Third Five Year Plan projects, the government issued a list of industries in 1961 in which foreign investments were to be welcomed taking into account the gaps in capacity in relation to Plan targets. These included some of the industries earlier reserved for the public sector, such as drugs, aluminium, heavy electrical equipment, fertilizers and synthetic rubber.

Inward FDI

The protection accorded to local manufacturers acted as an important locational advantage encouraging market-seeking FDI. A large number of foreign enterprises serving Indian markets through exports began establishing manufacturing affiliates in the country. The late 1950s and early 1960s was the period when Western multinational enterprises started to show real interest in India. In the early 1950s their response was only lukewarm except in the case of one-shot investment in oil refineries (Kidron, 1965: 102, 157). Most foreign drug companies exporting to India also set up their manufacturing subsidiaries in India during this period. Between 1948 and 1964 the FDI stock in the country more than doubled to Rs 5,655 million from 2,560 million (see Table 11.1). The creation of locational advantages led to a sharp jump in the share of manufacturing in the FDI stock to over 40 per cent from approximately 20 per cent at the time of independence. Within the manufacturing sector, consumer goods industries such as food and beverages (13.2 per cent), medicines and pharmaceuticals (10.9 per cent), textile products (7.2 per cent), and intermediate and capital goods such as metal and metal products (14.4 per cent), electrical goods (7.9 per cent), chemicals and allied products (16 per cent), machinery and machine tools (6. 9 per cent) and transport equipment (6.5 per cent), accounted for the bulk of FDI stock. As Indian enterprises had not accumulated adequate ownership advantages, outward FDI was negligible in the period.

To sum up the above discussion, during this period India was equipping itself with the locational, ownership and internalization advantages necessary to make a transition to *Stage 2* of the IDP.

1968–79: PROTECTING THE DOMESTIC BASE OF 'CREATED' ASSETS

Investments in machinery fabrication facilities, workforce development, scientific and technological infrastructure during the previous period had led to the development of certain 'created' assets in the country. For instance, certain capabilities for process and product adaptations had been built up in the country. A number of local design engineering and project management consultants had accumulated considerable expertise while working for Western contractors on projects within the country. A considerable plant fabrication capability had been built up in the country by the late 1960s. The share of capital goods industry in industrial value added had increased from under 5 per cent in 1950 to nearly 25 per cent by 1970. The share of imported machinery and equipment as a proportion of gross domestic capital formation had gone down from 69 per cent in 1950 to under 25 per cent by 1968–9. However, locally available skills and capabilities needed some sort of infant industry protection as these were not able to withstand competition from more established industrialized country sources. Constraints on the local supply of capital and entrepreneurship had begun to ease somewhat. On the other hand, the outflow, on account of the remittances of dividends, profits, royalties and technical fees, etc., servicing FDI and technology imports from the earlier period, had grown sharply and became a significant proportion of the foreign exchange account of the country.

All these factors prompted the government to streamline the procedures for foreign collaboration approval and adopt a more restrictive attitude towards FDI. A new agency called the Foreign Investment Board (FIB) was created within the government in 1968 to handle all cases involving foreign investment or collaboration with up to 40 per cent foreign equity. Those with more than 40 per cent foreign ownership were to be screened by a Cabinet Committee. Restrictions were put on proposals of FDI unaccompanied by technology transfer. The government listed industries in which FDI was not considered desirable in view of local capabilities. The permissible range of royalty payments and duration of technology transfer agreements with parent companies were also specified for different items. The guidelines evolved for foreign collaborations required exclusive use of Indian consultancy services wherever available. If foreign consultants were required, the Indian consultants had to be retained as prime consultants. Restrictions were imposed on renewals of foreign collaboration agreements. A new Patents Act was enacted in 1970 which abolished 'product' patents in foods, chemicals and drugs and reduced the life of process patents from 16 to 7 years (14 years in some cases). From 1973 onwards further activities of foreign companies (along with those of local large industrial houses) were restricted to a select group of core or high priority industries. In the same year a new Foreign Exchange Regulation Act (FERA) was established which required all foreign companies operating in India to register themselves as Indian companies with up to 40 per cent foreign equity. The Indian companies were also directed to dilute their foreign equity to a maximum of 40 per cent and exceptions were made only for companies operating in high priority or high technology sectors, tea plantations, or those which predominantly produced goods for export. In 1976, a Technical Evaluation Committee with representation from various scientific agencies was set up to assist the FIB in screening foreign collaboration proposals. The Committee was expected to provide a professional input into the decision whether the foreign collaborations or FDI proposals under evaluation were justified in bringing technology unavailable locally into the country.

The government policy encouraged outward FDI by Indian companies as a means of promoting exports of Indian capital goods, technology and consultancy services. A systematic treatment of overseas investments, however, started only in 1974 when an Inter-ministerial Committee on Joint Ventures Abroad was created within the Ministry of Commerce to approve proposals from Indian companies. The guidelines for approval were formulated in 1978 and required Indian participation to be in accordance with the host country regulations. The guidelines encouraged joint ventures with local enterprises and required Indian equity participation by way of capitalization of export of indigenous plant, machinery, capital goods and know-how to the joint venture from India. In view of the scarcity of capital resources in the country, cash remittances of capital to overseas ventures were discouraged but could be allowed in exceptional cases.

The above policies for developing and protecting local expertise strengthened the ownership advantages of local enterprises which in turn was reflected not only in the pattern of inward FDI but also led to significant outward FDI from India as illustrated below. This period marked the completion of India's transition to *Stage 2* of the IDP.

1Inward FDI

The restrictions placed on FDI during the period led to a stagnation of FDI inflows. For instance, FDI stock between 1974 and 1980 increased by only Rs 163 million (Table 11.1). The increase in overall stock of FDI, however, tends to mask the reorganization that took place in the pattern of FDI in the country during this period. One striking trend was the liquidation of FDI stock in the non-manufacturing sector largely due to governmental takeovers of certain activities (such as general insurance companies in 1971 and the petroleum sector between 1974 and 1976). On the other hand, virtually all fresh inflows were directed to the manufacturing sector. As a result, the share of manufacturing in the FDI stock went up from 40.5 per cent in 1964 to 86.9 per cent in 1980. Within the manufacturing sector, new inflows were directed to technology-intensive sectors such as electrical goods, machinery and machine tools, and chemical and allied products (in particular, chemicals and pharmaceuticals). These three broad sectors accounted for nearly 58 per cent of total FDI in manufacturing in 1980 compared to 41 per cent in 1964. The shares of metals and metal products, and transport equipment, showed a decline over the 1964–74 period, but picked up during 1974–80. The increasing importance of technology-intensive products in the FDI stock has been at the expense of traditional consumer goods industries such as food and beverages, textile products and other chemical products.

As domestic enterprises accumulated their created ownership advantages, the inter-industry pattern of market share of foreign enterprises (henceforth foreign shares) changed. The accumulation of local capability in certain industries diminished the competitive edge of foreign enterprises. We have computed elsewhere foreign shares in 54 Indian manufacturing industries in 1980–1 and examined changes over the preceding period (Kumar, 1994a, Chapter 2). In certain branches the foreign shares declined because of increasing public sector participation, e.g. non-ferrous basic metals, fertilizers, heavy organic chemicals, petrochemicals, basic drugs, heavy electrical and non-electrical machinery. In a number of sectors such as jute and cotton textiles, paper, cement, edible and hydrogenated oils, the foreign shares declined because of a loss of ownership advantages by foreign enterprises *vis-à-vis* local enterprises as the latter accumulated capability in these sectors. Foreign shares continued to remain high in a number of industries producing consumer goods sold under brand names, such as processed foods, cigarettes, toiletries and leather goods. This could be explained by the continued dominance of their ownership advantages in the form of well-known international brand names.

To gain further insights into the role of ownership, internalization and locational advantages and policy factors influencing them, determinants of inter-industry variation in foreign shares and intensity of licensing collaborations across 49 branches of Indian manufacturing industry were analysed in 1980–1 (see Kumar, 1987a, 1994a, Chapter 3, for more details). The foreign share and licensing were regressed on the intensity of industry in variables proxying different ownership and locational advantages. In accordance with the hypotheses, FDI was found to be concentrated in advertising and skill intensive industries. Licensing appeared to be a dominant mode in knowledge-intensive industries embodied in capital goods. Access to sources of capital did not appear to be a source of competitive edge for MNEs in the Indian market as it was significant for neither FDI nor licensing. This was partly as a result of the development of local capital markets and term financing institutions in India. The intensity of local R&D was negatively related to foreign shares which was interpreted in terms of the preponderance of Indian R&D activity in the areas of relatively low complexity and maturity. The government's policy factors came up with expected results. Protection appeared to have served as a potent locational advantage favouring local production over market servicing through exports by MNEs. Consumer goods industries appeared to have a lower concentration of foreign shares, other things remaining the same, apparently because of entry regulations which discouraged FDI in industries where local capabilities were available. The high priority industries in industrial policy attracted both FDI and licensing.

Outward FDI

The import-substituting industrialization followed by India had created a reasonably diversified industrial base in the country with a substantial machinery manufacturing capability by the early 1970s. The accumulation of considerable learning and technological capability had taken place in Indian enterprises as protection policies restricted technology imports. Indian enterprises learned to trouble-shoot, to adapt the processes and products imported originally from their Western counterparts to Indian conditions, to substitute imported raw materials by locally available ones, and made them more rugged to withstand frequent power failures (see for example Desai, 1984; and Lall, 1987, for analyses of the acquisition of technological capability by Indian enterprises). Indian chemical and pharmaceutical enterprises developed indigenous processes for manufacturing known chemical compounds and bulk drugs as product patents had been abolished. The increasing technological capability of Indian enterprises was reflected in terms of rising Indian exports of manufactures, in particular of chemical and engineering goods. The share of chemical and engineering goods in India's total exports nearly doubled from 7.9 per cent to 15.5 per cent over 1969–70 to 1980–1 (Kumar, 1987b). By the beginning of the 1980s, India had emerged as a significant exporter among developing countries of capital goods including turnkey plants, consultancy services, licensing of know-how (see Lall, 1982, 1983; Kumar, 1987c). The 1970s also marked the emergence of outward FDI by Indian enterprises in a significant manner. After taking off in the early 1970s, outward FDI grew at a faster pace in the second half of the 1970s. According to Lall (1983) India had emerged as the third largest exporter of 'industrial' FDI among developing countries after Hong Kong and Singapore by about 1980. Therefore, by the mid-1970s Indian enterprises had acquired 'created' ownership advantages in the form of technology adaptations, capital goods fabrication capability, human resources, etc., that are prerequisites for outward investment. The bulk of Indian FDI during this period went to developing countries in Africa, South East Asia and South Asia. In these countries, the ethnic and cultural links with Indian enterprises also served as ownership advantages.

Table 11.2 provides the number and magnitude of investments made by Indian enterprises in their wholly owned subsidiaries and joint ventures by the year of government approval on the basis of firm-wise unpublished data collected from the Indian Ministry of Commerce. This data set includes only those investments which are either in operation or under implementation and excludes the abandoned ones. The latter is an important limitation in that it tends to underplay the scale of operation especially during the earlier period. The figures for more recent years can be expected to

Table 11.2 Investments made by Indian enterprises in overseas subsidiaries and joint ventures by year of approval (value in millions of Rs)

Region	<1970		1970–5		1976–80		1981–5		1986–90		1991–3		Total	
	No.	Indian equity	No.	Indian equity	No.	Indian equity	No.	Indian equity	No.	Indian equity	No.	Indian equity	No.	Indian equity
South East and East Asia	**3**	**62.319**	**13**	**57.972**	**27**	**323.17**	**8**	**32.616**	**27**	**466.504**	**67**	**1,635.949**	**145**	**2,578.53**
Singapore	2	59.884	5	14.173	9	25.147	4	20.406	6	274.884	32	689.711	51	1,010.148
Malaysia	1	2.435	2	12.072	5	60.702	3	6.21	8	90.113	17	566.358	40	797.44
Thailand					4	120.841			8	92.252	6	25.822	21	253.422
Hong Kong			1	0.26	3	0.307			4	9.046	9	90.289	17	99.902
Others			5	31.462	6	116.173	1	6.0	1	0.209	3	263.769	16	417.618
South Asia	**1**	**0.23**	**1**	**0.699**	**7**	**95.143**	**14**	**31.141**	**8**	**96.884**	**29**	**845.813**	**60**	**1,069.91**
Sri Lanka	1	0.23	1	0.699	3	52.303	8	12.243	4	35.658	12	675.921	29	776.054
Nepal					4	42.84	6	19.898	3	31.146	9	137.555	22	231.439
Bangladesh									1	30.08	7	16.837	8	46.917
Maldives											1	15.5	1	15.5
Pacific Islands					**1**	**1.403**	**2**	**0.728**			**1**	**1.398**	**4**	**3.529**
Fiji					1	1.403							1	1.403
Solomon Isl.							1	0.529					1	0.529
Tonga							1	0.199					1	0.199
Vanuatu											1	1.398	1	1.398
Africa	**3**	**77.997**	**2**	**186.61**	**10**	**94.317**	**13**	**210.61**	**7**	**16.506**	**27**	**916.874**	**62**	**1,502.914**
Mauritius	1	55.545					2	4.123	2	7.089	12	782.711	14	789.8
Kenya			1	186.196	4	31.549			1	1.404	3	6.954	12	285.771
Senegal							1	142.18					1	142.18
Egypt							3	13.523			3	68.292	6	81.815
Others	2	22.452	1	0.414	6	62.768	7	50.784	4	8.013	9	58.917	29	203.348

	No.	Value	No.	Value	No.	Value	No.	Value	No.	Value	No.	Value	No.	Value
Middle East	7	140.546	3	2.9	5	9.65	7	21.574	6	345.85	31	4,556.043	52	4,936.017
UAE	7	52.609	2	0.9	4	6.657	2	12.639	2	1.75	22	3,263.028	32	3,284.974
Israel							2	5.538			1	677.164	1	677.164
Saudi Arabia	1	0.033	1	2.0	1	2.993					3	590.65	7	601.181
Jordan							3	3.397	2	265.07			2	265.070
Others									2	79.03	5	25.201	10	107.628
E and C Europe					1	19.4			14	662.521	53	794.036	68	1,475.947
Russia									8	94.942	25	466.257	33	561.199
Kazakhstan									2	523.500	1	5.013	3	528.513
Uzbekistan									1	12.000	9	152.452	10	164.452
Turkmenis									1	28.600	3	7.844	4	36.444
Others					1	19.4			2	3.479	15	162.47	18	185.339
Latin America									2	2.701	4	230.75	6	233.451
Mexico											2	162.278	2	162.278
Panama									2	2.701	2	68.472	4	71.173
Developing Countries			19	248.181	51	543.083	44	296.669	64	1590.966	212	8,980.863	397	11,800.398
Western Europe			1	0.359	11	33.439	13	10.698	14	248.135	73	1,547.686	119	1,892.926
UK			1	0.359	11	33.439	10	7.664	8	240.682	36	698.882	67	981.059
Ireland											2	172.35	2	172.35
Netherlands									2	2.654	6	147.588	8	150.242
Germany	3	10.403					1	0.35	1	2.3	8	109.06	13	122.113
Switzerland	3	42.173					1	0.162			2	78.32	6	120.655
Others							1	2.522	3	2.499	19	341.486	23	346.507
North America			1	0.037	3	4.426	7	31.086	13	190.647	55	915.688	79	1,141.884
USA			1	0.037	3	4.426	7	31.086	13	190.647	53	876.079	77	1,102.275
Canada											2	39.609	2	39.609

Table 11.2 (continued)

Region	< 1970		1970–5		1976–80		1981–5		1986–90		1991–3		Total	
	No.	Indian equity	No.	Indian equity	No.	Indian equity	No.	Indian equity	No.	Indian equity	No.	Indian equity	No.	Indian equity
Japan and Australia			**1**	**0.72**							**4**	**206.327**	**5**	**207.047**
Japan											2	201.010	2	201.01
Australia			1	0.72							2	5.317	3	6.037
Industrialized countries	7	52.609	3	1.116	14	37.865	20	41.784	27	438.782	133	2,669.701	203	3,241.857
Grand Total	14	193.155	22	249.297	65	580.948	64	338.453	91	2,029.748	344	11,650.564	600	15,042.165

be closer to actual approvals as potential failures may not yet be apparent. Keeping in mind the above limitation of the data set available it would appear that in the second half of the 1970s the outward FDI from India showed considerable growth. During this period, 64 new investments were made with a total Indian investment of Rs 581 million in contrast to just 36 ventures existing in 1975 with a cumulative investment of Rs 442 million. These figures tend to underestimate the scale of outward investment activity since quite a few ventures set up during the period failed.

It is clear from Table 11.2 that the bulk of Indian FDI (80 per cent in number and 95 per cent in terms of value) in the 1970s went to other developing countries. In fact much of Indian FDI was concentrated in Malaysia, Indonesia and Singapore within South East Asia, Kenya and Nigeria in Africa, and Sri Lanka and Nepal in South Asia. Most of these countries were at a lower stage of development in terms of 'created' ownership assets than India as predicted by the IDP. Table 11.3 provides the industrial composition of Indian outward FDI. The bulk (73 per cent in terms of value) of Indian FDI made during the 1970s was in the manufacturing sector. The most prominent branches of industry were light engineering, textiles, and chemicals and pharmaceuticals. Among the service sector, hotels, restaurants and consultancy services were the most prominent.

It would appear from this pattern that Indian outward FDI during this period was designed to exploit the created assets of Indian enterprises in the form of adapted, and sometimes scaled down, processes and products, human resources, equipment fabrication capabilities, etc. Hence, these were concentrated in countries at a lower stage of the IDP and in relatively lower technology-intensive and mature industries. In the case of India's inward FDI, the knowledge embodied in capital goods or machinery was found to have low internalization advantages as performance guarantees given by equipment manufacturers are usually adequate to take care of the buyer's uncertainties. In the case of Indian enterprises operating abroad, buyer's uncertainty may have persisted despite guarantees because of the lack of an established reputation. Rajiv Lall (1986) in a survey of 17 Indian enterprises investing abroad conducted in the course of 1982 found the 'managerial and technical expertise as embodied in Indian personnel' abroad was the main source of competitive advantage of Indian enterprises. His quantitative analysis of the decision to invest abroad for a sample of 162

Table 11.3 Investments made by Indian enterprises in overseas subsidiaries and joint ventures by industry and year of approval (value in millions of Rs)

Industry	< 1970 No.	< 1970 Indian equity	1970–5 No.	1970–5 Indian equity	1976–80 No.	1976–80 Indian equity	1981–5 No.	1981–5 Indian equity	1986–90 No.	1986–90 Indian equity	1991–3 No.	1991–3 Indian equity	Total No.	Total Indian equity
Extractive			**1**	**0.8**	**2**	**33.835**	**1**	**0.313**			**1**	**3,117.6**	**5**	**3,152.548**
Light engineering	4	31.765	4	7.816	13	162.155	7	32.882	7	59.915	30	1,189.852	65	1,484.385
Textiles	3	64.995	5	39.137	5	61.545			3	30.038	11	214.261	27	409.976
Chemicals and pharmaceuticals					5	31.254	11	162.093	13	463.851	34	1,848.427	63	2,505.625
Food Products					1	0.573	5	13.448	3	21.269	6	68.575	15	103.865
Leather and Rubber			1	2.0	1	0.7	2	11.591	7	488.166	6	514.161	17	1,016.618
Others	1	46.786	6	197.754	4	104.217	5	32.216	4	44.948	32	1,284.037	52	1,709.958
Manufacturing Total	**8**	**143.546**	**16**	**246.707**	**29**	**360.444**	**30**	**252.23**	**37**	**1,108.187**	**119**	**5,119.31**	**239**	**7,230.427**
Hotels and restaurants			2	7.57	7	84.096	4	29.71	10	144.578	11	104.804	34	363.945
Engineering services	1	0.26			1	2.6	1	0.59	2	69.302	18	212.695	23	285.447
Trading	1	5.1	1	0.359	10	11.239	4	23.752	12	103.717	78	992.262	106	1,136.429
Consultancy	1	0.403	1	0.414	4	29.153	6	2.505	7	138.326	9	121.208	28	292.009
Others	4	44.106			12	59.581	18	29.353	23	465.638	108	1,982.683	165	2,581.36
Services total	**6**	**49.609**	**5**	**1.79**	**34**	**186.669**	**33**	**85.910**	**54**	**921.561**	**224**	**3,413.652**	**356**	**4,659.105**
Grand total	14	193.155	22	249.297	65	580.948	64	338.453	91	2,029.748	344	11,650.564	600	15,042.165

Source: Own computations on the basis of unpublished data from Ministry of Commerce, Government of India.

Indian enterprises of which 24 were foreign investors for the years 1977–9 revealed that firm size was an important determinant of outward investment. Impediments to exports appeared to provide an incentive for outward FDI suggesting the market defensive nature of Indian investments. Dasgupta and Siddharthan (1985) and Agarwal (1985) found an interdependence between Indian exports and outward FDI in the late 1970s and early 1980s and found it to be concentrated in sectors comprising largely standardized goods and with relatively low skill and technological content.

1980s: 'HALTING REFORMS' TO IMPROVE INTERNATIONAL COMPETITIVENESS

Towards the end of the 1970s India's failure to increase significantly the volume and proportion of her manufactured exports against the background of the second Oil Price Shock began to worry the policy-makers. It led to the realization that international competitiveness of Indian goods had suffered from growing technological obsolescence and inferior product quality, limited range and high cost which in turn were due to the highly protected local market. Another limiting factor for Indian manufactured exports was the fact that marketing channels in industrialized countries were substantially dominated by MNEs. The government intended to address the situation by (i) emphasizing the modernization of plants and equipment through liberalized imports of capital goods and technology, (ii) exposing Indian industry to competition by gradually reducing import restrictions and tariffs, and (iii) assigning a greater role to MNEs in the promotion of manufactured exports by encouraging them to set up export-oriented units. This strategy was reflected in the policy pronouncements that were made in the 1980s. The Industrial Policy Statements of 1980 and 1982, for instance, announced a liberalization of industrial licensing (approval) rules, a host of incentives and exemption from foreign equity restrictions under FERA to 100 per cent export-oriented units. It was decided that four more export processing zones (EPZs) would be established, in addition to the two existing ones (Kandla and Santacruz set up in 1965 and 1972 respectively), to attract MNEs to set up export-oriented units. The trade policies in this period gradually liberalized the imports of raw materials and capital goods by gradually expanding the list of items on the Open General Licence (OGL). Between 1984 and 1985, 150 items and 200 types of capital goods were added to the OGL list. Tariffs on imported capital goods were also slashed. Imports of designs, drawings and capital goods were permitted under a liberalized Technical Development Fund Scheme. The liberalization of industrial and trade policies was accompanied by an increasingly receptive attitude towards FDI and foreign licensing collaborations. Policy guidelines were issued to streamline the foreign collaboration approval. The rules concerning the payments of royalties and lump-sum technical fees were also relaxed. Tax rates on royalties were reduced from 40 per cent to 30 per cent in 1986. A degree of flexibility was introduced in the policy concerning foreign equity participation, and exceptions from the general ceiling of 40 per cent on foreign equity were allowed on the merits of individual investment proposals. The approvals for opening liaison offices by foreign companies in India were liberalized and procedures for the outward remittance of royalties, technical fees and dividends, etc., were streamlined. New procedures were introduced enabling direct application by a foreign investor even before choosing an Indian partner. A 'fast channel' was set up in 1988 for expediting the clearance of FDI proposals from major investing countries such as Japan, Germany, the United States and the UK.

The focus of policies in this period, therefore, was on sharpening the international competitiveness of Indian enterprises by exposing them to increased domestic and international competition. Bhagwati (1993) has termed these policy changes as 'halting reforms' because they were not comprehensive in their scope and did not go far enough to make a significant impact.

Inward FDI

The liberalization of industrial, trade and foreign collaboration policies in the period improved the investment climate and helped the country attract increasing inflows of FDI. The restrictions put on FDI during the 1970s had virtually neutralized the internalization incentives for potential foreign investors in the country. As a result of easing these restrictions, the stock of FDI nearly tripled during the 1980s (see Table 11.1 and Figure 11.1) to Rs 27 billion. The liberalization also eased the near total restriction on FDI flows to technology-intensive manufacturing and manufacturing's share in total FDI stock in 1990 actually declined slightly. The share of services and plantations increased over the period. Within manufacturing, the food and beverages, machinery and machine tools, and transport equipment industries improved their share. The share of metal products and chemicals declined during this period. The period also witnessed the further diversification of sources of FDI to the country with the emergence of Japan as the fourth largest source of FDI in India after the UK, the United States, and Germany.

Outward FDI

The initial enthusiasm of Indian enterprises in international operations in the late 1970s waned slightly in the early 1980s when the magnitude of FDI declined to Rs 338 million from Rs 581 million in the previous period, although an equal number of investments were made (Table 11.2). In the second half of the 1980s, overseas investment activity picked up again to 91 ventures abroad with a total Indian investment of Rs 2,030 million. Around the mid-1980s the geographical pattern of Indian FDI abroad had also registered a shift coinciding with an increase in magnitude that took place. Until the mid-1980s, India's FDI had tended to concentrate on developing countries. Since then, however, the share of industrialized countries has gone up steadily. In the second half of the 1980s, industrialized countries hosted 27 of the 91 new Indian ventures with 21.6 per cent of investments. Continuing the trend observed in the 1970s, African countries were most prominent as hosts to Indian outward FDI in the early 1980s accounting for 62.22 per cent of all investments made during that period. South and South East Asian and Middle Eastern countries accounted for much of the rest of India's FDI outflow. In the late 1980s, the Eastern and Central European countries, which had been important markets for Indian exports, emerged as important hosts of Indian FDI with 14 ventures accounting for 32.6 per cent of Indian FDI in the period. The South East Asian countries hosted another 23 per cent of FDI for the period in 27 ventures. The Middle East was another region which attracted considerable (17 per cent) investment in the period. African countries received a negligible share of FDI in the late 1980s. Among the industrialized countries, the United States and Western Europe accounted for all the FDI made by Indian enterprises in the 1980s. Therefore, the geographical spread of Indian outward FDI expanded during the late 1980s with the inclusion of countries at a higher stage of the IDP than India, viz. industrialized countries, Eastern and Central

Table 11.4: Indian outward FDI by region and sector (values in millions of Rs)

Region of destination	Extractive Total	Manufacturing Light engineering	Textiles	Chemicals and pharmaceuticals	Food products	Leather and rubber	Others	Manufacturing subtotal	Services Hotels and restaurants	Engineering services	Trading	Consultancy	Financial and others	Services subtotal	Total
South East and East Asia		712.757 (27.6)	169.036 (6.56)	228.666 (8.87)		17.632 (0.68)	260.893 (10.1)	1388.984 (53.87)	10.974 (0.43)	0.26 (0.01)	404.225 (15.7)	52.924 (2.05)	721.163 (28.0)	1189.546 (46.13)	2578.53 (100)
South Asia	33.835 (3.16)	7.595 (0.71)	29.51 (2.76)	101.928 (9.53)	30.364 (2.8)	8.491 (0.79)	709.721 (66.3)	887.609 (82.96)	61.267 (5.72)	0.59 (0.06)	4.575 (0.43)		82.034 (7.67)	148.466 (13.88)	1069.91 (100)
Pacific Islands				3.529 (100)				3.529 (100)							3.529 (100)
Africa		65.062 (4.3)	123.398 (8.21)	150.348 (10.0)	3.203 (C.21)	488.569 (32.5)	229.547 (15.3)	1060.127 (70.54)	34.055 (2.27)	2.726 (0.18)	39.747 (2.64)	29.926 (1.99)	336.333 (22.4)	442.787 (29.46)	1502.91 (100)
Middle East	3118.4 (63.18)	33.186 (0.67)	45.396 (0.92)	1511.844 (30.6)	13.918 (0.28)	2.0 (0.04)	31.563 (0.11)	1637.907 (33.18)	2.993 (1.65)	5.194 (0.11)	5.483 (0.11)	81.317 (1.65)	84.723 (1.72)	179.71 (3.64)	4936.02 (100)
Eastern and Central Europe		219.192 (14.9)		46.99 (3.18)	23.418 (1.59)	497.6 (33.7)	241.753 (16.38)	1028.953 (69.71)	206.01 (13.6)		125.8 (8.52)	10.588 (0.72)	104.61 (7.1)	447.008 (30.29)	1475.95 (100)
Latin America		1.773 (0.76)					160.0 (68.54)	161.773 (69.3)			2.278 (0.98)		69.4 (29.73)	71.678 (30.70)	233.451 (100)

Developing countries total	3152.24 (26.71)	1039.565 (8.81)	367.34 (3.11)	2043.305 (17.32)	70.903 (0.60)	1014.29 (8.60)	1631.68 (13.83)	6168.882 (52.28)	315.299 (2.67)	8.77 (0.07)	582.108 (4.93)	174.55 (1.48)	1398.263 (11.85)	2479.195 (21.01)	11800.3 (100)
Western Europe	0.313 (0.02)	332.489 (17.6)	23.371 (1.23)	229.467 (12.1)	32.662 (1.72)	2.3 (0.12)	69.399 (3.67)	689.688 (36.43)	7.735 (0.4)	64.652 (3.42)	406.8 (21.5)	25.946 (1.37)	697.792 (36.86)	1202.925 (63.55)	1892.93 (100)
North America		112.331 (9.84)	19.265 (1.69)	227.566 (19.93)	0.3 (0.03)		7.082 (0.62)	366.544 (32.10)	37.091 (3.25)	212.025 (18.57)	147.521 (12.92)	91.308 (8.00)	287.395 (25.17)	775.34 (67.9)	1375.34 (100)
Japan and Australia				5.317 (2.57)				5.317 (2.57)	3.82 (1.84)				197.91 (95.59)	201.73 (97.43)	207.047 (100)
Industrialized countries total	0.313 (0.01)	444.82 (13.72)	42.636 (1.32)	462.35 (14.26)	32.962 (1.02)	2.3 (0.07)	76.481 (2.35)	1061.549 (32.75)	48.646 (1.50)	276.677 (8.53)	554.321 (17.10)	117.254 (3.62)	1183.097 (36.49)	2179.995 (67.25)	3241.86 (100)
Grand total	3152.55 (20.96)	1484.385 (9.86)	409.976 (2.72)	2505.63 (16.7)	103.865 (0.69)	1016.6 (6.76)	1709.96 (11.37)	7230.416 (48.1)	363.945 (2.42)	285.447 (1.90)	1136.43 (7.56)	292.009 (1.94)	2381.36 (15.8)	4659.19 (29.6)	15042.2 (100)

Source: Own computation on the basis of unpublished data from Ministry of Commerce, Government of India.

European countries and some more South East and East Asian countries.

The increasing geographical diversification of Indian FDI in the late 1980s coincided with sectoral diversification to cover more services and trading activities as compared to near total domination of the manufacturing sector until the mid-1980s. This is because India's FDI in the more industrialized countries has been of a different sectoral composition than that in developing countries at a lower stage of the IDP. The shift in terms of sectoral composition also came about in the mid-1980s when the share of manufacturing in total FDI outflow declined from nearly 75 per cent in the early 1980s to about 55 per cent in the late 1980s (Table 11.3). The fact that the bulk (nearly 70 per cent) of FDI outflows to industrialized countries is in services and not in manufacturing is clear from Table 11.4 which shows the sectoral breakup of Indian outward FDI hosted by different regions. Apart from the industrialized countries, the share of services is also considerable in South East and East Asian countries (46.13 per cent), a region constituting countries at a higher stage of their IDP than India.

A significant proportion of FDI in the service sector was in trading, usually in the form of a subsidiary set up in major export markets of the firm to support the export activity. These subsidiaries are meant to create a marketing network and also serve as the exporter's 'listening posts' to gather market information. As international competitiveness is increasingly determined by non-price factors such as access to information and market presence, these investments can be seen as strategic investments made by Indian enterprises in improving their international competitiveness. Obviously such subsidiaries will be set up in major markets and those that are growing. Besides, Indian enterprises have also developed ownership advantages in certain services that are human resource intensive because of a vast pool of trained labour available in India. These services include engineering and construction, consultancy, software, finance, and hotels and restaurants.

Within the manufacturing sector, there also appears to be a shift in the focus of Indian enterprises in the 1980s. The chemical and pharmaceutical industry emerged in the first half of the 1980s as the most important industry accounting for 47.8 per cent of all FDI. In the second half of the 1980s, the chemical and pharmaceutical industry occupied second place with 22 per cent of FDI after leather and rubber products which had a slightly higher share.

This reflects the increasing technological capability of Indian enterprises in the chemical and pharmaceutical sector. A number of dynamic Indian chemical and pharmaceutical companies, e.g. Ranbaxy, Lupin, Dr Reddy's Labs, have built up ownership advantages in the form of cheaper indigenous processes of the production of off-the-patent bulk drugs, increasingly known brand names and cheaper formulations. In the ethical pharmaceutical sector market, presence is an important factor for market penetration. This has prompted Indian pharmaceutical enterprises to make outward investments in developing countries. The emergence of the leather products sector in the late 1980s was due to a large leather project in Central Europe presumably established to protect Indian companies' market in the former Soviet Union.

Therefore, the decade of the 1980s was marked by important changes in the policy regime existing in the country geared to improve the international competitiveness of Indian enterprises. The policy changes eased the restrictions on FDI inflows that were neutralizing the internalization advantages for most deals for the transfer of technology between Indian and foreign enterprises. Increasing emphasis on international competitiveness made Indian enterprises make strategic asset-seeking types of investments in trading and other services in industrialized countries.

THE 1990s: STRUCTURAL ADJUSTMENT AND GLOBALIZATION

In the financial year 1990–1, India entered a period of severe balance of payments crises and political uncertainty. A rapid increase in India's external debt coupled with political uncertainty led international credit rating agencies to lower India's rating for both short and long term borrowing. This made borrowing in international commercial markets difficult and also led to an outflow of foreign currency deposits kept in India by non-resident Indians. The situation was worsened by the Gulf War in so far as it led to increased petroleum prices and caused the virtual stoppage of remittances from Indian workers in the Gulf. These developments brought the country almost to the verge of default in respect of external payments liability which could only be averted by borrowing from the IMF under standby arrangements and other emergency measures taken by the government to restrict imports. In June 1991 a new government headed by Mr P.V. Narasimha Rao came into power following the mid-term elections. This government initiated a programme of macro-economic stabilization and structural adjustment supported by the IMF and the World Bank. As a part of this programme the Indian rupee was devalued and a New Industrial Policy (NIP) was announced on 24 July 1991 in the parliament.

The NIP and subsequent policy amendments have significantly liberalized the industrial policy regime in the country especially as it applies to FDI. The industrial approval system in all industries has been abolished except for 18 strategic or environmentally sensitive industries. In 34 high priority industries FDI up to 51 per cent is approved automatically if certain norms are satisfied. FDI proposals do not necessarily have to be accompanied by technology transfer agreements. Trading companies engaged primarily in export activities are also allowed up to 51 per cent foreign equity. To attract MNEs in the energy sector, 100 per cent foreign equity was permitted in power generation. International companies were allowed to explore non-associated natural gas and develop gasfields including laying down pipelines and setting up liquefied petroleum gas projects. A new package for 100 per cent export-oriented projects and companies in export processing zones was announced. A Foreign Investment Promotion Board (FIPB) authorised to provide a single window clearance has been set up in the Prime Minister's office to invite and facilitate investment in India by international companies. Existing companies are also allowed to raise foreign equity levels to 51 per cent for proposed expansion in priority industries. The use of foreign brand names for goods manufactured by domestic industry which had earlier been restricted was also liberalized. India became a signatory to the Convention of the Multilateral Investment Guarantee Agency (MIGA) for the protection of foreign investments. The Foreign Exchange Regulation Act of 1973 has been amended and restrictions placed on foreign companies by the FERA have been lifted. Companies with more than 40 per cent of foreign equity are now treated on a par with fully Indian-owned companies. New sectors such as mining, banking, telecommunications, highway construction and management have been opened to private, including foreign-owned, companies. These relaxations and reforms of policies have been accompanied by the active courting of foreign investors at the highest levels. The international trade policy regime has been considerably liberalized too, with lower tariffs on most types of imports and sharp pruning of the negative list for imports. The rupee was made convertible first on the trade and finally on the current account.

As a part of this reform the government also removed some of the restrictions on Indian outward FDI. The modified Guidelines for Indian Direct Investment in Joint Ventures and Wholly Owned Subsidiaries Abroad issued in October 1992 provide for automatic approval for proposals where the total value of Indian investment does not exceed US$ 2 million of which up to US$ 500,000 could be in cash and the rest by capitalization of Indian exports of plant, machinery, equipment, know-how, or other services and goods. Approval for other outward-FDI-related proposals including external borrowing, use of export receipts blocked abroad, etc., will be made within 90 days after due consideration of the track record of the Indian party in terms of external orientation and financial viability of proposed investments, etc. Another modification to the guidelines has been with respect to the export of second-hand or reconditioned machinery which is now allowed but was earlier prohibited.

Inward FDI

Comparable figures for FDI inflows for the early 1990s are not yet available. However, some trends can be discerned from the figures of approvals of FDI in the 1991–3 period. The liberalization of the policy regime seems to have led to considerable improvement in the investment climate in the country. For instance, FDI approvals over the three-year period totalled Rs 131 billion in contrast to the total stock of FDI existing in March 1990 valued at Rs 27 billion (Table 11.1). The approvals, however, have been slow in materializing into actual inflows and are still much lower than FDI inflows received by other developing countries such as China. The share of manufacturing in these approvals has gone down to 51.2 per cent largely because of the opening up of new areas such as power generation, petroleum refining, a number of services which have claimed a large chunk of approved FDI. Within the manufacturing sector, the processed food and beverages sector has claimed the largest chunk of FDI accounting for 23.3 per cent of approved FDI in manufacturing. It appears that the created assets of foreign enterprises in a consumer goods industry such as food processing in the form of internationally well-known brand names have considerable appeal in the local markets. Metal and metal products, electrical goods, and chemicals and pharmaceuticals are other important sectors.

Another noticeable trend in this period is with respect to the organizational structure. The liberalization of policy removed the policy barriers that were neutralizing the internalization advantages of foreign investors to the country. Table 11.5 shows that the proportion of foreign collaborations that are internalized through FDI in total approved has gone up from just over 16 per cent in the 1970s to over 44 per cent during the early 1990s. Therefore, the balance between FDI and licensing has begun to shift in favour of FDI. Furthermore, majority foreign ownership, which had become restricted to certain exceptional cases during the 1970s, is becoming more popular again. Table 11.6 shows that the majority of approvals over the past three years have been in the 50–74 per cent range. A number of MNEs have taken advantage of the new rules to increase their stake in their existing affiliates in the country.

One of the objectives of the current reforms of policies is to remove impediments for export-oriented manufacture in general and to attract MNEs to locate efficiency-seeking FDI in the country. These investments could help India to expand manufactured exports by using it as an export platform. The majority of the recent approvals of FDI, however, aim to explore India's sizeable and expanding domestic market. Efficiency-seeking FDI has yet to start flowing into the country in a considerable manner. It may be too

Table 11.5 Summary of foreign collaboration approvals, 1948–93

| Period | Average number of collaborations approved per year | Those with foreign equity | | Average foreign investment involved per year (Rs million) |
		Average number per year	Proportion in total	
1948–58	50	n.a.	n.a.	n.a.
1959–66	297	108[*]	36.36	n.a.
1967–79	242	39	16.11	53.62
1980–8	744	170	22.80	930.84
1989–90	635	194	30.55	2,224.95
1991–3	1,315	589	44.76	44,280.40

Note: [*]On the basis of 1961–6.
Source: Kumar (1994a), Table 1.4.

Table 11.6 FDI approvals by foreign equity ownership

Foreign ownership (%) Year	Number of approvals	Amount (millions of Rs)	%
1991			
0–26	57	1,058.9	22.47
26–50	119	1,713.1	36.35
50–74	24	1,893.5	40.18
75–100	3	47.4	1.01
1992			
0–26	185	7,298.1	19.10
26–50	290	9,869.5	25.83
50–74	173	12,374.1	32.29
75–100	45	8,664.6	22.68
1993			
0–26	276	22,735.8	25.66
26–50	259	14,055.3	15.86
50–74	151	34,476.8	38.92
75–100	99	17,350.1	19.58

Source: India, Ministry of Industry (Secretariat for Industrial Approvals).

early to expect such FDI to start flooding the country. Yet in an era of stiff competition among developing countries to attract export-oriented FDI, liberalization of policies alone may not be enough to win the race. More active negotiations and bargaining with MNEs may be required. India should use her bargaining advantages such as a large domestic market, an abundant supply of trained and low wage labour, a vast pool of technical professionals, well-developed capital markets, etc., more effectively to attract a greater proportion of efficiency-seeking FDI (see Kumar, 1994a, Postscript; Kumar, 1994b).

Outward FDI

The 1991–3 period has also witnessed the liberalization of restrictions to remit cash abroad for making outward FDI. The removal of these restrictions as well as the improved transparency of the policy regime perhaps explain a record 345 outward investment projects being approved with a projected Indian equity of Rs 11.65 billion.

Thus 57.3 per cent of the 600 ventures abroad at the end of 1993 (accounting for 77.5 per cent of total Indian outward FDI) have been committed between 1991 and 1993 (Table 11.2). The liberalization of the FDI codes seems to have made a more dramatic difference to outward than inward FDI.

The Middle East accounts for a large portion (39 per cent) of India's FDI in the period. However, the bulk (26 per cent) of it is on account of a single, large natural-resource-seeking (petroleum exploration) project in the UAE as well as the emergence of Israel as a host to a fertilizer project. South East Asia hosts 67 ventures with a 14 per cent share of all FDI abroad. African countries hosted 27 projects with 7.86 per cent of FDI. India's contiguous neighbours in South Asia which had been trailing behind South East Asia and Africa in terms of their importance as hosts of Indian FDI, attracted 29 ventures with 7.2 per cent of total investments. Indian investment in this region had been restricted to Nepal and Sri Lanka. Since the mid-1980s, however, Bangladesh and, more recently, the Maldives have played hosts to Indian enterprises. East and Central European countries have retained their place as significant hosts of Indian FDI with 53 ventures and 6.81 per cent of FDI. Among the manufacturing sectors, chemicals and pharmaceuticals continue to dominate as in the 1980s (Table 11.3). These are followed by light engineering which has been a traditionally important sector for Indian FDI.

The trend of the emergence of industrialized countries as significant hosts of Indian FDI which was visible in the late 1980s gathered momentum during the 1991–3 period: 133 of the 345 ventures representing nearly 23 per cent of India's FDI during that period were set up in the industrialized countries. Western European (mainly EC member states) countries have hosted the bulk (nearly 58 per cent) of Indian FDI in the industrialized world in the early 1990s. The formation of a Single European Market in the EC protected from the outside world by common external tariffs has prompted MNEs worldwide to make market-defensive FDI in one of the member states (see Kumar, 1994c, for an analysis of the response of MNEs from different regions to European integration). Indian outward FDI appeared to follow the current trend of FDI by non-EU corporations to set up trading subsidiaries to protect and strengthen its presence in the EC market. A considerable proportion of Indian FDI in North America has been in engineering and consultancy services (Table 11.4). These FDIs have something to do with the growing internationalization of the Indian software industry. In this industry the country is fast emerging as a global player. This has attracted considerable investments by the world's largest information technology enterprises to locate software development centres in India. A number of Indian software enterprises have also set up affiliates in the United States to market their own products but also to benefit from the agglomeration economies and spillovers from more established firms in Silicon Valley. The latter are, to some extent, examples of strategic asset-seeking investments.

CONCLUDING REMARKS

The above analysis has examined the trends and patterns of FDI inflows into India over the post-independence period as well as the emergence of Indian enterprises as direct investors abroad against the background of a changing policy regime. The sectoral pattern of FDI in India reveals a shift in favour of more technology- and skill-intensive industries as the country industrialized itself. The Indian government's policies appear to have played an important role in shaping this pattern by affecting the relative configuration of ownership, internalization and locational advantages of foreign investors in the country. Indian investments have been made over the years in a large number of countries all over the world. However, a clear divergence is seen between India's FDI in countries below India in the levels of economic development and in those above it. In the former, the ownership advantages of Indian enterprises in the form of technology and product adaptations, human resources, experience of operating in a developing country environment and ethnic links have led to investments in manufacturing. In industrialized countries and increasingly in South East and East Asian newly industrializing countries these ownership advantages cannot provide a competitive edge to Indian enterprises *vis-à-vis* host country enterprises. In these countries Indian FDI largely represents strategic investments made in trading subsidiaries to provide a marketing backup to Indian exports or those in human-resource-intensive services where Indian enterprises have accumulated some advantages and capability. Over the years Indian outward FDI appears to have grown in terms of skill content as in terms of geographical and sectoral coverage.

Thus the IDP is found to be a useful framework for analysing the evolution of India's inward and outward FDI position over the post-independence period. India graduated to the second stage of the IDP some time in the 1970s by which time local enterprises had accumulated certain created assets to be able to operate abroad. The current reforms are geared to sharpen the competitiveness of the country's enterprises and to improve its place in the international division of labour and move to the third stage of the IDP. Export platform production (or efficiency-seeking FDI) in India by MNEs could be an important means of their expanding manufactured exports from India. The recent liberalization of the policy regime has not yet succeeded in attracting efficiency-seeking FDI in a considerable manner. In the current environment of intense competition among developing countries to attract such FDI, just the liberalization of policies may not be adequate. More effective use of India's bargaining advantages with respect to MNEs, such as the large domestic market, abundant supply of skilled labour and technical professionals as well as low wages, may be desirable to attract a greater proportion of such FDI.

NOTES

* The research assistance of Anne Hogenbirk is gratefully acknowledged.

REFERENCES

Agarwal, J. P. (1985) *Pros and Cons of Third World Multinationals: A Case Study of India*, Kieler Studien 195, Tubingen: JCB Mohr.

Bhagwati, J. (1993) *India in Transition*, New Delhi: Oxford University Press.

———— and Desai, P. (1970) *India: Planning for Industrialization*, Oxford: Oxford University Press.

Dasgupta, A. and Siddharthan, N.S. (1985) 'Industrial distribution of Indian exports and joint ventures abroad', *Development and Change*, 16, 159–74.

Desai, A. V. (1984) 'India's technological capability: an analysis of its achievements and limits', *Research Policy*, 13, 303–10.

Dunning, J. (1981) 'Explaining the international direct investment position of countries: towards a dynamic or developmental approach', *Weltwirtschaftliches Archiv*, 117, 30–64.

———— (1993) *Multinational Enterprises and the Global Economy*, Reading: Addison-Wesley.

———— and Narula, R. (1994) 'Transpacific FDI and the investment development path: the record assessed', *University of South Carolina Essays in International Business*, No. 10.

Kidron, M. (1965) *Foreign Investments in India*, London: Oxford University Press.

Kumar, N. (1987a) 'Intangible assets, internalization and foreign production: direct investments and licensing in Indian manufacturing', *Weltwirtschaftliches Archiv*, 123, 325–45.

—— (1987b) 'Foreign investment and export-orientation: the case of India', in S. Naya et al. (eds) *Direct Foreign Investment and Export Promotion: Policies and Experiences in Asia*, Honolulu, Hawaii: East West Center, 357–82.

—— (1987c) 'India's economic and technical cooperation with the co-developing countries', in G. R. Agrawal et al. (eds) *South–South Economic Cooperation: Problems and Prospects*, New Delhi: Radiant Publishers, 181–220.

—— (1994a) *Multinational Enterprises and Industrial Organization: The Case of India*, New Delhi: Sage (a revised and updated edition of *Multinational Enterprises in India*, London and New York: Routledge, 1990).

—— (1994b) 'Determinants of export orientation of foreign production by US multinationals: an inter-country analysis', *Journal of International Business Studies*, 25(1), 141–56.

—— (1994c) 'Regional trading blocks, industrial reorganization and foreign direct investments: the case of a single European market', *World Competition*, 18(2).

Lall, R. B. (1986) *Multinationals from the Third World: Indian Firms Investing Abroad*, Delhi: Oxford University Press.

Lall, S. (1982) *Developing Countries as Exporters of Technology: A First Look at the Indian Experience*, London: Macmillan Press.

—— (1983) 'Multinationals from India', in S. Lall et al. (eds) *The New Multinationals: The Spread of Third World Enterprises*, Chichester: John Wiley, 21–87.'

—— (1985) 'India', in J. Dunning (ed.) *Multinational Enterprises, Economic Structure and International Competitiveness*, Chichester: John Wiley.

—— (1987) *Learning to Industrialize: Acquisition of Technological Capability by India*, London: Macmillan.

Wells, L. T. (1983) *Third World Multinationals*, Cambridge, Mass.: MIT Press.

Chapter 12

China
Rapid changes in the investment development path

Hai-Yan Zhang and Danny Van Den Bulcke

INTRODUCTION

In this chapter the evolution and patterns of the inward and outward foreign direct investment (FDI) of China will be examined in the framework of Dunning's investment development path (IDP) (1981, 1986, 1993). The main objective is to capture the dynamic changes in the OLI (Ownership, Location and Internalization) variables of China and their interaction with the Chinese economic development during the last 15 years. The chapter consists of three parts. The first part states the position and growth of Chinese inward and outward FDI, while the second part emphasizes the changing pattern of the OLI configuration of China and the role of the Chinese government in creating new capabilities and stimulating the competitiveness of their international investment link-ups and initiatives. The dynamic inter-action between inward and outward FDI is examined, in particular with regard to the sequential development of different Chinese regions as a gradual process in upgrading China's IDP. Attention is also given to some specific features of the Chinese outward FDI operations, e.g. the rapid 'take-off' in the internationalization process and the high concentration in 'upstream' countries. In the third part, the impact of FDI on China's global economic development process is analysed, particularly with regard to the contribution to capital formation, technology accumulation and integration within the world economy.

CHANGING PATTERNS OF CHINA'S INVESTMENT DEVELOPMENT PATH

After 30 years of isolation China decided in 1979 to open up again for FDI.[1] Since then it has gradually taken a number of measures to improve its investment climate and its attractiveness to existing and potential foreign investors. The competitiveness of the domestic enterprises has been systematically upgraded because of the decentralization of corporate decision making and the introduction and extension of the market mechanism in the Chinese economic system. As a result of the ensuing improvement of the L advantages, the accumulated inflow of FDI amounted to more than US$63 billion at the end of 1993 (in current value), while China ranked second in the list of recipients of FDI in the world (following the United States of America) and became the single largest host country among the developing nations (UNCTAD, 1994: 68). The relative importance of inward FDI in China's GDP increased from 0.31 per cent in 1983 and 1.01 per cent in 1990 to 5.42 per cent in 1993. On the other hand, the development of the O advantages of Chinese firms resulted in the emergence and growth of Chinese outward FDI. The Chinese outward FDI in more than 120 countries almost reached US$1.85 billion – of which US$1.59 billion was in non-trade sectors[2] – at the end of 1992 (Table 12.1). The ratio of inward to outward FDI was 37 during the whole period of China's 'open door policy', but declined somewhat between 1987 and 1991 because of the higher growth rate of outward FDI. That the net outward FDI position of China expanded from US$2.6 billion in 1983 to US$61.9 billion in 1993 seems to indicate that the general trend of Chinese direct investment corresponds to the first two stages of the investment development path (Figure 12.1).

Between 1980 and 1992, China's GNP per capita increased by 7.6 per cent per year from US$270 to US$470 (World Bank, 1994: 162). With the increasing importance of inward and outward FDI, the proportion of the national economy that is subject to external influences expanded rapidly. The share of inward FDI in the total gross domestic investment of China increased from 1.3 per cent in 1983 to 13.6 per cent in 1993, while its proportion of the total investment of state-owned enterprises progressed from 1.9 per cent in 1983 to 11.9 per cent in 1992. Moreover, by 1992 and continuing in 1993, FDI became the single most important source of external capital for China (more than 57 per cent). It surpassed the combination of the loans from foreign commercial banks, foreign governments and international organizations, the export credits and the issues of bonds in international financial markets (Nicholas, 1994: 63). The exports of foreign affiliates reached US$25.2 billion in 1993 and represented 27.5 per cent of the total

Table 12.1 Inward and outward foreign direct investment of China (US$ million) (1979–1993)

Year	Inward FDI						Outward FDI				Net FDI position**	
	No. of projects	Contracted amount	Growth rate (%)	Current amount	Growth rate (%)	% of GDP	No. of projects	Approved amount	Growth rate (%)	% of GDP	I/O*	NOI*
1979–1982	922	4,958.00	–	1,769.00	–	0.645	43	37.00	–	0.013	47.81	–1,732.00
1983	470	1,916.90	–	915.96	–	0.312	33	13.00	–	0.004	53.70	–2,634.96
1984	1,856	2,874.94	49.98	1,418.85	54.90	0.474	37	100.00	669.23	0.033	27.36	–3,953.81
1985	3,073	6,333.21	120.29	1,956.15	37.87	0.672	76	47.00	–53.00	0.016	30.76	–5,862.96
1986	1,498	3,330.37	–47.41	2,243.73	14.70	0.799	88	33.00	–29.79	0.012	36.10	–8,073.69
1987	2,233	4,319.12	29.69	2,646.61	17.96	0.869	108	410.00	1,142.42	0.135	17.11	–10,310.30
1988	5,945	6,190.72	43.33	3,739.66	41.30	0.991	141	75.00	–81.71	0.020	20.55	–13,975.00
1989	5,779	6,294.09	1.67	3,773.45	0.90	0.889	119	236.00	214.67	0.056	19.41	–17,512.40
1990	7,273	6,986.32	10.99	3,754.87	–0.49	1.012	156	77.00	–67.37	0.021	21.61	–21,190.30
1991	12,978	12,421.73	77.80	4,666.61	24.28	1.257	207	362.00	370.13	0.098	19.34	–25,494.90
1992	48,764	58,123.51	367.92	11,007.51	135.88	2.624	355	195.00	–46.13	0.046	23.91	–36,307.40
1993	83,265	110,852.00	90.92	25,759.00	134.01	5.415	380	120.00	–38.46	0.025	37.33	–61,946.40
Total	174,056	224,600.91	74.50	63,651.40	46.13	–	1743	1705.00	207.99	–	37.33	–61,946.40

Notes: * Calculated on the basis of current inward FDI and approved outward FDI.
   ** Cumulative.
Sources: MOFTEC (1984–1994), World Bank (1994).

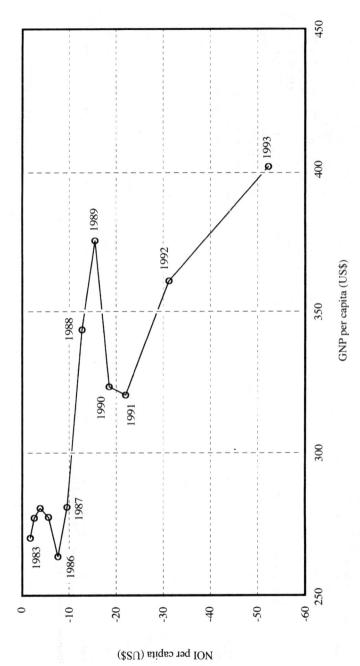

Figure 12.1 Evolution of the Chinese investment development path 1983–1993

Table 12.2 Some indications of the impact of inward foreign direct investment on the Chinese economy (1979–1993)

	Exports		Capital formation		Employment	
	Exports of foreign affiliates (US$ million)	As % of total exports	FDI as % of total gross domestic investment*	FDI as % of investment in state-owned enterprises	FDI as % of total inward foreign capital*	Foreign affiliates as % of total employment in urban area
1983	–	–	1.27	1.90	46.25	–
1984	–	–	1.80	2.78	52.46	–
1985	320	1.2	2.26	3.42	43.84	–
1986	480	1.6	2.57	3.91	30.91	–
1987	1,000	2.5	2.71	4.29	31.32	0.65
1988	1,750	3.7	3.10	5.04	36.57	1.24
1989	3,590	6.8	2.43	5.60	37.51	1.71
1990	7,810	12.6	4.04	7.44	36.49	2.32
1991	12,100	16.8	4.71	6.98	40.39	3.33
1992	17,360	20.4	7.71	11.90	57.32	4.05
1993	25,200	27.5	13.59	–	–	–

Note: *Calculated on the basis of the average exchange rate of the year.

Sources: Moftec (1993–1994), World Bank (1992: 185), Harrold and Lall (1993), Zhan (1993: 137).

Chinese exports (see further). At the end of 1993, the employment of foreign enterprises in China totalled about 6 million, or 4.05 per cent of the total urban employment of China (Table 12.2).

OLI CONFIGURATION AND CHINESE INWARD AND OUTWARD FDI

Initial conditions

Even after China opened up for FDI, its L advantages were strongly influenced and – from the point of view of potential investors heavily distorted – by its development ideology of self-reliance and the centrally controlled economic management system. At the beginning, the importance of the external sector in the national economy was quite small, as exports and imports only accounted for 5.6 per cent and 6.3 per cent of GDP in 1978. China exported mainly primary products (53.5 per cent in 1978), while its principal imports consisted of machines and equipment (17.5 per cent) or industrial components and raw materials (57.6 per cent).[3] The resource allocation was decided and the distribution system totally controlled by institutions belonging to the central government, while the production process itself was based on physical planning and the preoccupation to achieve correspondence between output and input in the so-called 'material balances' of the state plan. The absence of a market mechanism and the lack of an entrepreneurial climate – which are two basic conditions for economic development – were not conducive to the creation of O advantages or firm-specific advantages by Chinese companies.

However, the initial conditions under which China entered into the so-called 'first stage' of its IDP, i.e. when only the natural resources are sufficient to attract inward FDI (Dunning, 1986), were quite different from the situation in other developing countries. Several factors might have positively affected the rapid growth and satisfactory results of its inward and outward FDI activities after 1979.

Industrial infrastructure

About 30 years of massive industrialization since the 1950s resulted in China having established a relatively well-developed and integrated industrial sector, of which the share in the GNP increased from 20 per cent in 1952 to 49 per cent in 1978. The annual growth rate of industrial production was more than 10 per cent during the period 1965-1980, while GDP expanded at a rate of 6.4 per cent during the same period (World Bank, 1988). As China especially focused on the development of heavy industry, the share of this sector in the total industrial output amounted to more than 57 per cent in 1978. The existence of this basic industrial structure in China was quite significant, as it provided an essential industrial platform and enormous opportunities for the development of light industry, once investment decision making became decentralized (Harrold, 1992).

Technological capabilities

China developed its own industrial infrastructure to a large extent on the basis of a non-equity foreign (advanced) technology transfer. In the early 1950s, China imported 304 'turnkey' plants and 64 sets of equipment from the Soviet Union for a total contract value of US$2.7 billion, which represented 90 per cent of the total imports of China during that period. From 1962 to 1968, China purchased 84 plants (US$260 million) from Japan and West European countries, in the sectors of petroleum and chemicals, metallurgy, mining, electronics and precision machinery, etc. During 1973–1978, 232 technology contracts were concluded with Western countries for a total value of US$7 billion (Macdougall, 1982: 152, Liu, 1986: 23). Between 1978 and 1993, China signed about 5,000 technology transfer projects for a value of US$40 billion (Gu, 1994). This amount represented more than 65 per cent of the total inward FDI during this same period. Even more relevant for China's technological transformation is its capacity to imitate and modify the imported technology. These innovatory and assimilatory capabilities later facilitated the technology transfer by foreign investors in establishing production facilities in China and had a positive impact on the outward FDI of Chinese enterprises, especially with regard to the transfer of appropriate technology to neighbouring developing countries.

The existence of a dramatic technological disparity within China's industrial structure may also have influenced FDI. While the large and medium-sized enterprises constituted only 2 per cent of all Chinese industrial enterprises, they represented one-third of the country's industrial labour force and two-thirds of its fixed capital stock and contributed half of the national gross value of industrial output (GVIO) in 1987 (Kueh, 1989: 431). The average capital intensity, as measured by the capital–labour ratio, is therefore much higher in this special group of larger firms. The lack of sophisticated or international standardized technology in the small-sized enterprises resulted in a certain rigidity of Chinese light industry and a deficiency in intra-industrial cooperation, in particular between state-owned enterprises (SOEs) and town and village enterprises (TVEs). Yet, this skewed industrial structure offered specific opportunities for the foreign investors from the newly industrializing countries (NICs) and other developing nations to transfer small scale and labour-intensive technology to these smaller production units.

Cultural and ethnic ties with Overseas Chinese

The successful performance of Overseas Chinese in the South-east Asian economies and the economic complementarities among mainland China, Hong Kong, Taiwan and other South-east Asian countries increases the interest for Chinese- and Overseas-Chinese-owned enterprise to integrate their capital, technology, marketing expertise and human resources in a single economic region, which is sometimes called the 'Greater China Economic Region'. The realization of these economic complementarities is to a large extent based on the cultural and ethnic ties with Overseas Chinese. This provides China with a set of specific L advantages that are not present in most other countries, at least not to the same extent.

To the initial specific L advantages of China also belong the relatively high rate of gross domestic saving and investment rates, i.e. respectively 32.5 per cent and 34.2 per cent of national income between 1971 and 1980 (ADB, 1991: 284–285), its balanced fiscal and external accounts and its equal income distribution. Also the high investment in, and cheap access to, health and education contributed to the L advantages created by the Chinese government.

The O advantages and disadvantages of the Chinese domestic enterprises during this period were mainly linked with the strengths and weaknesses of government ownership. This resulted on the one hand in a high political profile and rapid resource mobilization and on the other hand in deficient management, unprofessional managers and low motivation of the employees. Also these firms lacked marketing expertise and competitive experience, because they were accustomed to operate in the protected national market. Apart from these well-known general features of SOEs (Blanc and Anastassopoulos, 1983: 177, Kumar, 1981: 196), Chinese enterprises also suffered from other specific weaknesses linked to the centrally controlled economy, such as the rigid state planning system, the parallel decision making process and the intervention by the administration in corporate operations (Schermerhorn and Nyaw, 1992: 11–17). These 'system- and policy-induced' characteristics were major obstacles for the SOEs to develop their O advantages and successfully compete in domestic and foreign markets.

However, a few large Chinese SOEs were privileged, at least *vis-à-vis* other domestic firms, in terms of the allocation of domestic and foreign resources, their monopoly status in related sectors and specific tax and tariff conditions. Although these country-specific assets tend to disappear or are reduced during transactions across national borders, they form the basis of the so-called 'created assets' that are firm specific, such as technological and innovatory capabilities, production skills, marketing expertise, human resource development, organizational and managerial knowledge, etc. These latter assets can to a certain extent be more easily transferred abroad, e.g. into outsourcing operations. The development of non-home-country-bound (or non-policy-induced) O advantages on the basis of home-country-bound (or policy-induced) advantages might even be regarded as an important specific feature of Chinese multinationals (CHMNEs) (Zhang and Van Den Bulcke, 1994a, 1994b).

Because of the policy- and system-induced 'distortion' of the locational factor endowments in China and the specific ownership characteristics of Chinese enterprises, the government's actions in enhancing and upgrading the country's L advantages as well as in influencing the O advantages of its own multinational enterprises are likely to be quite significant. The Chinese government influenced the locational attractiveness of China for international investment and the competitiveness of its enterprises in a gradual way. The process of liberalization and upgrading of locational resources, the so-called 'marketization'[4] of resource allocation, the building up of a legal infrastructure for market transactions, the decentralization of macro-economic management and the improvement of the efficiency of SOEs were major aspects of this development.

Changes of L advantages and inward FDI patterns

1979–1982: deregulation of FDI policy

The Chinese government ended its prohibition of inward FDI by the promulgation of the Joint Venture Law in 1979 and the creation of four special economic zones (SEZs) in two coastal provinces in 1980.[5] The L advantages for foreign investors in this period were mainly related to the specific geographic position of these SEZs, i.e. (1) the proximity to Hong Kong, which facilitated the importation of raw materials and semi-finished products for export processing and assembly operations and reduced the transportation cost by using Hong Kong's infrastructural resources, particularly as a transit port and marketing base; (2) the lower labour costs as compared to neighbouring Asian countries, which permitted Asian NICs to relocate their labour-intensive production in a more profitable location; (3) the 'diaspora' of about 55 million Overseas Chinese who had both economic and political interests to invest in China, their original homeland.

The specific L advantages of the SEZs seemed to be most suitable for foreign investors from Hong Kong, for whom the O advantages were mainly related to their access to export and outsourcing networks, labour-intensive processing technology, geographic proximity, trade facilities, etc. The so-called 'social knowledge', i.e. similar cultural and language background, personal contacts, family links and past experience of doing business with the Chinese bureaucracy, could also be regarded as important assets of these investors as compared with companies which had no previous experience in operating in such an institutional environment.

The I advantages of foreign investors are mainly linked to their rationalized low cost labour-seeking strategies. The outsourcing of export-oriented production in the SEZs allowed these enterprises to reduce significantly the production costs with minimal additional costs of transportation, communication and administration. However, as the political situation was still uncertain, they preferred to minimize their resource and management commitment by using flexible arrangements, such as contractual joint ventures (CJVs), subcontracting, compensatory trade, etc. During 1979–1982, the number of CJVs in the total number of FDI projects accounted for 86 per cent, while their contracted value amounted to about 55 per cent of the total investment (Table 12.3). Even the equity joint

Table 12.3 Forms of inward FDI in China (% of contracted value) (1979–1992)

	1979–1982	1983–1985	1986–1988	1989–1991	1992	Total
Equity joint venture	2.82	29.52	46.71	44.52	49.59	44.12
Contractual joint venture	54.98	49.28	30.81	17.41	22.57	26.41
Wholly owned enterprises	7.40	1.66	7.01	30.21	26.73	21.85
Joint (oil) exploration	20.15	12.23	1.01	1.91	0.07	2.66
Other	14.62	7.30	14.46	5.95	1.04	4.97
Total (US$ million)	4,958.00	11,125.05	13,840.21	25,702.14	58,129.00	114,359.95

Source: MOFTEC (1984–1993).

ventures (EJVs) approved during this period were mostly character-ized by their small size, high ownership control (as a result of their low integration with the local market) and rather short term nature. At the end of 1982, only 1,399 projects had been approved with an accumulated contracted capital of US$4,958 million.

1983–1985: introduction of market mechanisms

Although the Chinese government gradually introduced a new set of regulations since 1979 (e.g. labour use, foreign exchange control, dispute settlements, taxation, etc.), the operating environment in China was regarded by foreign investors as quite restrictive, because these regulations were still dominated by bureaucratic control mechanisms, rather than by considerations of market effi-ciency. The domestic resources, such as raw materials, capital goods, labour and distribution networks, were allocated by the state planning system, as the Chinese government did not carry out any significant reforms in the industrial sector before 1983. Therefore, the complex bureaucracy and the administrative control which was associated with the SEZs' incentives, discouraged many foreign investors.

Based on the experience of the SEZs, a set of new regulatory measures (e.g. Joint Venture Implementing Regulations) was intro-duced in 1983, not only to improve the investment environment by liberalizing FDI policy and introducing tax and tariff incentives, but also to provide a set of concrete operational measures with regard to, for instance, repatriation of profits, transfer of technology, foreign exchange transactions, accounting methods, contract regulations, etc. On the other hand, the opening up of the 14 coastal cities in 1984 provided foreign investors with more extensive locational opportunities, because of the access to a relatively well-developed industrial infrastructure, a larger geographic and densely populated area, a better educational and living environment, higher trained technicians and labour force, cities with a tradition in foreign trade, better transportation and communication systems, etc. In 1984 the industrial production of the 14 coastal cities amounted to 23 per cent of the total production of China, while their share in total exports reached almost 40 per cent. In 1985, the so-called three River Deltas, i.e. Pearl River Delta, Yangtze River Delta and Fujian Delta, were also opened to foreign investors in order to encourage the integration of the foreign companies' export processing manufacturing activities with the small labour-intensive domestic enterprises, especially with the TVEs.

It was of great importance that all these FDI deregulatory measures were carried out at the same time as the economic reforms in the urban areas in 1983–1984, in particular with regard to the 'marketization' of resource allocation and the decentralization of the Chinese economic management system. The influence of the state plan on the production quotas and the use of the material supply system for the allocation of inputs was gradually reduced. For example, the proportion of the investments in fixed assets which were financed by the state budget in SOEs declined from more than 60 per cent in 1979 to 35 per cent in 1984 and even 21 per cent in 1987, while the number of key raw materials allocated through the central material supply system diminished from around 211 in 1978 to only 23 in 1988. Decentralization was not limited to macro-economic decisions, however. It was extended to practically all spheres of economic activity and included tax and price reform in SOEs and the foreign trade and banking system. The abolition of centralized decision making allowed for more market creation by a gradual process, i.e. the government released administrative control only as markets developed (Singh, 1992: 13–18). The reduction of the state planning system in general and the decentralization of the decision making to local governments greatly benefited the growth of inward FDI in the industrial sectors and contributed to its geographic diversification towards the 14 coastal cities.

As the result of the improvement of the location endowments and the general business climate, the contracted inward FDI increased by 50 per cent in 1984 and 120 per cent in 1985 (Table 12.1). The location pattern of foreign investors significantly changed, as the proportion of the Eastern region with its 14 coastal cities increased its total contracted FDI from 40 per cent in 1983 to nearly 78 per cent in 1984–1985, while the relative share of the Guangdong and Fujian provinces in particular expanded from 32 per cent to 46 per cent (Table 12.4). It is interesting to notice that the proportion of FDI, which was contracted directly by the various ministries of the central government (e.g. MOFTEC, Ministry of Finance), declined from 59 per cent to 12 per cent during this particular period, as a result of the decentralization of the Chinese economic system. With regard to the sectoral distribution, FDI in the service sectors diminished significantly during 1983–1985, especially in tourism-related activities, such as hotels, restaurants, taxi services, etc.

Table 12.4 Location pattern of inward FDI in China (% of contracted value) (1983–1992)

	1983	1984–1985	1986–1988	1989–1991	1992	Total
Eastern region	40.03	77.75	80.07	87.41	88.70	85.59
Guangdong and Fujian	32.38	45.84	42.34	56.04	43.37	46.18
Western region	0.77	6.72	6.39	1.95	3.49	3.70
Central region	0.20	3.30	5.26	4.08	7.38	5.89
Ministries	59.00	12.23	8.29	6.55	0.43	4.82
Total (US$ million)	1,916.90	9,208.15	11,840.24	24,172.69	58,123.51	105,261.49

Source: MOFTEC (1984–1993).

Table 12.5 Sectoral distribution of inward FDI in China (% of contracted value) (1983–1992)

	1983	1984–1985	1986–1988	1989–1991	1992	Total
Agriculture	0.93	2.23	3.35	1.92	1.17	1.67
Industry	13.58	32.73	55.59	82.14	56.20	59.26
Commerce	2.05	6.91	1.64	1.44	2.48	2.53
Finance	0.00	0.69	0.10	0.00	0.01	0.08
Real estate	0.00	24.66	30.56	10.26	31.11	25.13
Service	64.54	19.18	4.30	3.42	6.78	7.86
Other	18.91	13.60	4.47	0.82	2.25	3.47
Total (in US$ million)	1,916.9	9,208.15	11,840.24	24,172.69	58,123.51	105,261.49

Source: MOFTEC (1984–1993).

Meanwhile the proportion of the investment in the manufacturing sector expanded from 14 per cent to 33 per cent during the same period (Table 12.5).

The government regulations of the period 1983–1985 not only determined the location and industrial patterns of FDI in general, but also influenced the investment behaviour and resource commitment of foreign investors in particular. The opening of the coastal cities allowed Western foreign investors to engage in more local-market-oriented production and to transfer their higher human-resource- and capital-intensive technology into their export processing operations (e.g. electronics). The three River Deltas provided them with lower cost local sourcing options and increased the integration of these regions into the outsourcing production system of Hong Kong and later of Taiwan, notably in the textile industry. The relocation of whole production processes and complete plants into these regions further improved the technological range and capabilities of the local enterprises. On the other hand, the technological and organizational capabilities of the Hong Kong and Taiwanese parent companies were also upgraded because they were able to concentrate more on marketing strategy, product design, quality control, inventory systems, management and technical supervision, and financial arrangements and control (Sit, 1989, Ash and Kueh, 1993: 738).

The I advantages of the FDI operations in the 14 coastal cities were quite different from those in the SEZs. Foreign investors not only expected to benefit from their internalization by reducing production costs, but hoped to acquire a sizeable local market share and to build up a strategic position in the world's largest potential market. As FDI became more local market oriented, the proportion of EJVs in the total value of the contracted capital went up from about 3 per cent in 1979–1982 to 30 per cent in 1983–1985. EJVs seemed to be more suitable for foreign investors who wanted to acquire specific local knowledge, such as access to domestic market resources and information, political links, improved bureaucratic accessibility and more favourable government decisions.

1986–1988: introduction of performance requirements

The tremendous growth of inward FDI during 1984–1985 was stopped in its tracks in 1986 when it declined by about 47 per cent (in terms of contracted value), because of the changes involved in both the market situation and the general business environment.

First, the difficulties for foreign investors to balance their foreign exchange became extremely severe, especially when their sales were concentrated in the domestic market. Also they often needed to import components or raw materials as inputs which were not yet available or not sufficiently competitive in the local market. Domestic buyers and customers could not pay the foreign enterprises in foreign currency, as a result of exchange control which was set up by the government to limit the deficit in the Chinese balance of payments during the period 1985–1986 (Pearson, 1991: 75).

Second, the increased decentralization of the Chinese economic system and the extension of the decision making authority allowed the provincial and other local governments to shield their own markets from outside competitors by the establishment of all kinds of trade and non-trade barriers. These local protectionist measures fragmented the market for both consumer and industrial goods in China very seriously. Market-seeking foreign investors were confronted with increased difficulties to operate efficiently in the Chinese market. On the other hand, within the context of the liberalization of FDI policy, certain (especially Japanese) overseas suppliers relied on dumping to achieve market penetration in China. Consequently many local-market-oriented manufacturing companies came under heavy competitive pressure.

In order to improve the overall investment climate and to provide special incentives for foreign investors operating in preferential sectors – especially for those engaged in import substitution and export-oriented advanced technology projects – the State Council issued in late 1986 the 'Provisions for the Encouragement of Foreign Investment', or the so-called '22 regulations'. These new measures attempted to improve the operating environment of FDI by: facilitating exports, providing foreign companies with additional options to solve their foreign exchange imbalances, guaranteeing the autonomy of EJVs from external bureaucratic interference and eliminating unfair local costs. In particular, the establishment of swap centres was an important institutional change which allowed foreign investors, especially those oriented towards the domestic market, more flexibility and possibilities to balance their foreign exchange operations. At the same time, the Chinese FDI regulations became more selective with regard to the 'quality' of FDI, as the '22 regulations' introduced a set of specific performance criteria, e.g. in terms of export share, technology transfer, sector specificity, production requirements, etc. With the extension of the market system, the government also set up a certain basic legal framework (e.g. commercial law in 1986 and copyright law in 1990), which is generally regarded as an essential characteristic of a market-efficient system.

To a certain extent the relationship between the foreign investors and the Chinese government became more bargaining oriented during this period. For instance, the commitment of O advantages by foreign enterprises to their local joint ventures not merely focused on the appropriation of rents, but most importantly, intended to acquire strategic influence and control (Casson and Zheng, 1990: 2). The transfer of technology and the concession by Western MNEs to develop export markets for their EJVs in China were more and more considered as a bargaining item in the negotiation process of EJVs. It can generally be expected that the larger the stream of quasi-rents which is generated by the O advantages of foreign MNEs, the stronger will be the MNEs' bargaining position to obtain, for instance, a significant and higher equity stake, a longer duration of the agreement, and a stricter control of the management operations of the joint venture. Of course, the MNEs' strengths are counterbalanced by the position of the Chinese partners in the local market and the political support they can obtain. The more important the local market for the MNE and the larger the necessity to get local political support, the more the firm will favour participation by Chinese partners (Van Den Bulcke and Zhang, 1992, 1994).

The increasing confidence of the foreign investors resulted in an expansion of the contracted FDI by more than 36 per cent during 1987–1988, while the foreign capital committed to these EJVs went up by more than 50 per cent. The sources of origin of FDI in China also became more diversified. The proportion of Hong Kong in the total FDI gradually declined from 66 per cent in 1979–1982 to 59 per cent in 1986–1988, while the FDI originating from other countries (especially from the EC) increased significantly (Table 12.6). Although enterprises from Taiwan and South Korea were formally prohibited by the authorities of their home countries to invest in mainland China, their FDI was routed via Hong Kong and Singapore and expanded rapidly after 1987. By the end of 1988, the total investment from Taiwan reached US$660 million (Tai, 1990: 76). The industrial composition of FDI in China also changed significantly, as the proportion of manufacturing in the total FDI increased from 33 per cent in 1984–1985 to about 56 per cent in

Table 12.6 Foreign direct investment in China by countries of origin (% of contracted value) (1979–1992)

	1979–1982	1983–1985	1986–1988	1989–1991	1992	Total
Hong Kong and Macau	66.42	62.41	59.17	60.79	71.45	66.65
Japan	15.54	6.90	6.65	7.07	3.74	5.68
Singapore	0.69	1.39	2.90	1.53	1.71	1.72
EC-12	6.25	6.02	7.44	5.27	1.56	3.68
USA and Canada	6.92	16.77	11.77	6.76	5.91	7.87
Taiwan*	0.00	0.00	5.49	10.59	9.54	5.00
ASEAN-4	0.08	0.77	0.85	1.04	1.92	1.41
Other	4.10	5.75	5.73	6.95	4.16	7.99
Total in (US$ million)	5,535.75	11,139.60	11,840.22	24,172.58	58,123.51	110,811.66

Note: *The proportion of Taiwan in China's total inward FDI during 1986–1991 was estimated on the basis of data of Taiwan's Chung Hua Institution for Economic Research (*Far Eastern Economic Review*, 17 September 1992).

Source: MOFTEC (1984–1993).

1986–1988. The foreign investment in the service activities continually decreased to less than 5 per cent, as a result of the more selective Chinese FDI policy.

1989–1991: political crisis

The increasing FDI influx of 1987–1988 was dramatically broken off after June 1989 due to the government's military intervention against student activists in Tiananmen Square. Although the contracted and utilized FDI inflow during the first half of 1989 rose respectively by 44 per cent and 22 per cent over the same period in 1988, the growth rate for the whole year was only 5.6 per cent and 3.6 per cent respectively. The political instability suddenly became a deterrent that seriously undermined the willingness to invest for foreign (especially Western) companies. The proportion of the European Union and North America in the total FDI in China decreased respectively from 7.4 per cent and 11.8 per cent in 1986–1988 to 5.3 per cent and 6.8 per cent in 1989–1991. At the same time, the relative shares of the Asian investors significantly expanded. For instance, the investment from Taiwan practically doubled from US$460 million in 1989 to US$900 million in 1990 and continued to grow to US$1,200 million in 1991 (*Far Eastern Economic Review*, 1992: 23). The proportion of Taiwanese investment in the total Chinese inward FDI rose from 5.5 per cent in 1986–1988 to 10.6 per cent in 1989–1991. The growth of Taiwanese and other Overseas Chinese investment during this period was probably related to the nature of the O advantages of these firms. First, Asian enterprises are more likely to be risk takers than Western MNEs, because of the similarities between the political, social and cultural heritage of the home and host countries. Second, since most of the Asian enterprises are at the early stages of internationalization, they have fewer organizational capabilities and less resources to switch to alternative locations.

The expansion of Taiwan's FDI in export processing manufacturing in mainland China affected the location patterns and forms of FDI. The proportion of the Eastern provinces of Fujian and Guangdong in the total FDI of China increased from 42 per cent in 1986–1988 to 56 per cent in 1989–1991, while the share of FDI in the form of wholly owned foreign enterprises went up from 7 per cent to 30 per cent. The concentration of Taiwanese investment in these two provinces and their preference for wholly owned subsidiaries because of their high export ratio (i.e. less linkages with the domestic market and less need for local involvement) clearly influenced these changes. While about 77 per cent of the number of Taiwanese enterprises in Xiamen were wholly owned affiliates, full ownership represented even 90 per cent in terms of value. Also, 86 per cent of their total output value was exported in 1990. The relative export ratio of other foreign subsidiaries was more than half as high (35 per cent) (Qi and Howe, 1993: 753).

During 1989–1991, when an overall economic restructuring programme was carried out, neither significant FDI incentives nor restrictive measures were taken. The Joint Venture Law of 1979 was reviewed in 1990, however. The most important modifications were the elimination of the contract duration applied to some joint ventures, and permission for a foreigner to become chairman of the board of directors of a joint venture. The recentralization of macroeconomic decision making and the political and economic 'isolation' measures by Western countries benefited local-market-oriented MNEs as it allowed them to build up and strengthen their 'insider position' during this controversial period.

1992 on: towards global liberalization

Western FDI started to flow back to China with the improvement of the country's overall economic performance (real growth rate of GDP of 13 per cent in 1992) and with the renewed relaxation of investment policies. The contracted inward FDI in 1992 amounted to US$58 billion, i.e. more than the total of all FDI commitments between 1979 and 1991. In June 1992, the FDI incentives were extended to 18 inland provincial-capital cities, five cities along the Yangtze river and 13 border cities in the North East, South West and North West regions. New sectors, such as real estate, transportation, communication, port development, retailing, insurance, accounting, etc., were also gradually opened to foreign investors in the context of the liberalization of the service sectors, put forward as a condition to rejoin GATT (Lardy, 1994: 66–70). The FDI inflows continued to grow in 1993. The number of FDI projects, the contracted and the current capital expenditures rose respectively by 70 per cent, 91 per cent and 134 per cent as compared to 1992[6] (Table 12.1).

The policy changes of 1992 were very relevant to the locational factor endowments of China and its business climate. First, the opening of inland cities provided foreign firms with better access to the domestic interior market. An increasing number of foreign subsidiaries actually moved their production units from the coastal to the inland region to benefit from lower labour costs, cheaper raw materials, less competition (of both imports and local products), larger market size, more tax incentives, etc.[7] The proportion of the Western and Central region in the total value of FDI increased from 6 per cent in 1989–1991 to 11 per cent in 1992.

Second, the local factor endowments (such as technological and managerial capabilities, availability of the inputs, trade and production infrastructure, business standards, service quality, etc.) were significantly upgraded through the building up of forward and backward linkages between local firms and foreign subsidiaries (especially in export processing production) and the liberalization of the service sector and infrastructure development to foreign investors.

Third, the opening of previously 'prohibited' sectors such as highway construction, power generation, harbour and airport infrastructure and telecom service extended the opportunities for foreign enterprises. The introduction of new FDI forms, such as 'umbrella enterprises', BOT (Build, Operate and Transfer) and 'B' shares provided foreign investors with more latitude for establishing and operating companies in China.[8] The reform of the tax system and the elimination of the dual exchange rate system are further considered by the Chinese government as important regulatory measures towards the 'national treatment' of foreign affiliates in order to reduce market distortions, to ensure fair competition, to provide foreign investors with easier access to financial resources and to expose domestic enterprises to more competitive pressure (Zhan, 1993). Regulatory measures were also taken with regard to the evaluation of the non-cash contribution to the equity capital by foreign investors[9] and the manipulation of transfer prices.

The opening of the inland regions and the booming demand convinced a number of leading Western multinationals – such as Motorola, Bell Alcatel, Philips, IBM, AT&T, Siemens, etc. – to establish large scale production units and to introduce capital-intensive technology in their ventures in China. Some well-established foreign enterprises in China expanded their investment or diversified into other related and unrelated business lines. The O advantages of these enterprises *vis-à-vis* local firms were no longer only related to their high financial and technological profile, but also and in particular to their product and process technology in large scale production and in the manufacturing of a wide range of products. The organizational capabilities (such as experience with inventory control, flexibility of production, quality control, etc.) allowed these 'global' MNEs to benefit from the I advantages based both on economies of scale and economies of scope realized within the Chinese market. On the other hand, the domestic market became more fragmented because of the multiplication of local trade and non-trade barriers (geographic segmentation) and the extension of product differentiation (consumer segmentation). These changes resulted in the foreign investors' increased adaptation to local market conditions. Many MNEs developed consumer-oriented options by establishing local marketing facilities and by introducing new product ranges in different Chinese regions. Therefore, the O advantages related to the capabilities of the foreign subsidiaries in local marketing development and the coordination of different business lines within China became quite important (Van Den Bulcke and Zhang, 1994).

Changes in the O advantages of Chinese enterprises and outward FDI patterns

Outward FDI from China in the early 1980s was carried out by a small number of centrally administered enterprises and organizations. However, while the local governments at various levels obtained autonomy in their economic operations through the process of the decentralization of macro-economic management since 1983–1984, they also engaged in outward FDI to speed up local economic development by pursuing internationalization. Many non-centrally controlled, and even non-state-owned firms such as TVEs, invested relatively large amounts of capital into overseas operations.

The major destinations of Chinese outward FDI are the industrial countries. They received more than 69 per cent of the value of the Chinese approved outward FDI in non-trade sectors or 34 per cent in terms of the number of projects at the end of 1992 (Table 12.7). Apart from some large projects, such as the Portland Aluminium Smelter Company in Australia (CITIC), the Hierroperu SA in Peru (Shougang) and UA Agri-Chemicals in the USA (SINOCHEM), the Chinese overseas subsidiaries are generally quite small, as the average Chinese foreign investment project amounted to less than US$1.2 million. Yet, Chinese subsidiaries located in industrial

Table 12.7 Geographic pattern of Chinese outward non-trade FDI (1979–1992) (US$ million and numbers)

	Chinese investment	%	Total investment	%	Number of projects	%	Average Chinese investment	Chinese equity share
USA and Canada	672.75	42.28	1,089.83	31.09	228	16.73	2.95	61.73
EC-12	32.89	2.07	82.34	2.35	72	5.28	0.46	39.94
Japan	12.02	0.76	37.95	1.08	71	5.21	0.17	31.67
Hong Kong and Macau	143.98	9.05	227.09	6.48	141	10.34	1.02	63.40
ASEAN-5	68.30	4.29	178.91	5.10	158	11.59	0.43	38.17
Other industrial countries	371.06	23.32	1,340.38	38.24	96	7.04	3.87	27.68
Other developing countries	290.02	18.23	548.41	15.65	597	43.80	0.49	52.88
Total	1,591.01	100.00	3,504.91	100.00	1,363	100.00	1.17	45.39

Source: MOFTEC (1984–1993).

countries are much larger than their counterparts in the developing countries.

In terms of the sectoral pattern, nearly 86 per cent of the total amount of Chinese outward FDI was concentrated in non-trade sectors as compared with 41 per cent of the number of projects at the end of 1992. Most of the Chinese non-trade subsidiaries are engaged in manufacturing and resource extraction. Of the 64 Chinese overseas subsidiaries established during 1985–1990 in Australia and New Zealand, about 28 per cent were in manufacturing, 17 per cent in resource extraction, 16 per cent in agriculture and forestry, and 17 per cent in the restaurant business. An empirical survey of 31 Chinese overseas manufacturing subsidiaries showed that they are mainly in chemicals (26 per cent), metalworking (23 per cent), machinery (13 per cent), textiles and clothing (13 per cent). A large number of smaller Chinese subsidiaries are engaged in both simple manufacturing activities (e.g. assembly) and trading activities (Zhang and Van Den Bulcke, 1994a).

1979–1983: centrally driven foreign direct investment

During 1979–1983 outward FDI by Chinese enterprises was still insignificant. Only 77 non-trade projects with a total investment of US$50 million were approved (Table 12.1). These pioneering outward FDI operations were mostly undertaken by a number of long-established state-owned foreign trade corporations (FTCs) and newly created foreign business oriented corporations (FBOCs) (e.g. CITIC). The O advantages of the FTCs at that time were mainly related to their monopoly position in foreign trade, their administrative connections and business contacts and their experience in foreign markets,[10] while the FBOCs were granted more decision making authority and were allowed to use flexible management systems. In addition they were able to benefit from their high political profile and extensive personal contacts abroad.

The early overseas operations of these enterprises were closely linked with the government's political interests, and their overseas subsidiaries were mainly intended to acquire the necessary financial and technological leverage to launch and improve domestic investment projects. Most of these companies were also directly or indirectly involved in the development of industrial infrastructure and the creation of joint production plants together with foreign investors in the SEZs (e.g. CITIC, China Everbright Holdings Co.

Ltd, Conic Investment Co. Ltd). On the other hand, these companies later also became involved in overseas resource-seeking ventures. The politically induced investment behaviour of FTCs and FBOCs can also be illustrated by their strong investment presence in Hong Kong's public utility and infrastructure sectors, which is based on China's desire to stimulate political and economic confidence in Hong Kong.

1984–1988: beginning internationalization of local and industrial enterprises

With the decentralization of the economic system after 1984, the provincial and municipal governments 'pushed' a large number of local FTCs and FBOCs into FDI operations (especially in Hong Kong) in order to provide capital, technology and trade support for their local development strategy. A growing number of trade companies which were set up during the early 1980s by different ministries, inland provinces and cities in the SEZ of Shenzhen also started to expand abroad on the basis of their own strategic considerations. As a result, the number of Chinese affiliates in Hong Kong was estimated to surpass 2,000 in 1987 with a substantial Chinese investment of about US$10 billion, which was higher than the US investment of about US$6 billion. China had then emerged as the major 'foreign' investor in Hong Kong (Salem, 1988: 64).

The most important change during this period was the entry of Chinese industrial enterprises into the internationalization process. The O advantages of these industrial enterprises were quite different from those of the FTCs and FBOCs. The former firms rely more on their strengths in production technology and skills, while the latter companies are more competent in providing access to foreign business connections and in getting bureaucratic approval for their outward investment plans. It is not surprising that in establishing foreign manufacturing subsidiaries, Chinese FTCs and FBOCs often convinced other domestic industrial enterprises to join them in their investment projects abroad in order to tap into their production technology and experience. On the other hand, the industrial enterprises also involved FTCs and FBOCs in order to facilitate bureaucratic approval procedures with regard to their foreign investment activities and to link up with their overseas business antennas. These alliances to enter into new foreign markets were clearly intended to enhance the O advantages of the investing companies which belonged to the same industrial or administrative ministries. To some extent these joint initiatives may be specific for the Chinese enterprises in the early stages of the internationalization process (Zhang and Van Den Bulcke, 1994a). The entry strategy of Chinese multinationals into foreign markets varies also with the O advantages of the parent companies. The FBOCs and FTCs preferred to use mergers and acquisitions (M&As) to invest in advanced technological firms in industrial countries and large projects in resource extraction, because of their expertise in international financial operations and better business information system, while the small and middle-sized industrial firms tended to expand abroad by establishing new plants, especially in developing countries. Twenty-two per cent of all Chinese overseas subsidiaries were set up via M&As, while all the other initiatives to establish a foreign plant were the result of traditional 'greenfield' investments (Luo, Chen and Yang, 1993).

The motives of the Chinese enterprises to invest abroad evolved over the years and gradually became more concerned with additional factors, such as the need to expand into new markets, to advance the parent company's exports, to locate close to export markets, to get access to information abroad and to build up international business experience (Ye, 1992, Zhang and Van Den Bulcke, 1994a, 1994b). Although the Chinese investors seem to be seeking markets and export facilities rather more often than resources through their overseas expansion, foreign investment in resource-intensive projects by Chinese FBOCs and FTCs is nonetheless important, particularly in terms of its size. However, there are two specific features to be mentioned. First, the industrial enterprises – which are mostly market seekers in order to earn foreign exchange – are less influenced by the home government's policy than the FBOCs and FTCs which sometimes have to engage in unrelated resource-seeking investment. Second, apart from some large Chinese enterprises, the motives for Chinese investment abroad are still largely determined by changes in the external and internal environment, rather than by efficiency and strategy considerations.

The rapid and frequent changes within the context of 'marketization' of the Chinese economic system might have greatly affected the investment behaviour and the development of the O advantages of CHMNEs. On the one hand, while the production and transaction activities of the state-owned enterprises have gradually been reorganized from state planning into a market system, enterprises were obliged to adapt their supply, production and distribution methods to the market approach. In view of this, the overseas operations of Chinese enterprises can be considered as engaging in new business dimensions in order to safeguard the survival or growth of the firm in the turbulent business conditions in the domestic and international markets. On the other hand, the government–business relationship has been transformed from administrative governance into contract-based dependence. This has encouraged the emergence of a professional managerial class with the necessary experience and decision making authority.

However, the Chinese market mechanism is still in a preliminary stage. The legal system is underdeveloped and the state ownership is merely reconstitutionalized into a contract system without a real change in the nature of state ownership (Lu and Child, 1994: 5). The 'mixture of the quasi market mechanism system' and the 'decentralized or personalized' state ownership of firms tends to transform the Chinese market into a fragmented and uncoordinated structure and to increase the complexity, uncertainty and cost of transacting activities of the domestic operations. This situation of uncertainty might generate opportunistic behaviour where personal interests might even affect the outward FDI decisions of CHMNEs.

1989–1991: strategic development options

In order to override provincial and local constraints and to improve the performance of inefficient enterprises, the government carried out several reforms with regard to the organizational structure and ownership of state-owned enterprises through mergers, creation of enterprise groups and shareholding companies.[11] While the mergers and formation of enterprise groups were generally carried out by administrative decisions, it allowed these firms to diversify more rapidly into related and unrelated business lines and to acquire additional technology and financial capabilities without significant resource commitment at the company level. Enterprise groups controlled by the central government were even granted 'separate planning status', which meant that they could significantly reduce bureaucratic interference and operate in a more independent way. The introduction of these reforms provided Chinese state-owned enterprises with more management autonomy than under the so-called contract responsibility system (CRS). Yet the influence of the related administration was still evident, because all important corporate agreements (e.g. mergers or enterprise groups) resulted from negotiations between enterprises and the government.

The expansion of their technological, financial and organizational capabilities allowed large Chinese SOEs to reorganize their business activities and adopt a more global strategic approach in order to exploit the economies of integration. On the one hand, the FTCs attempted to 'take over' or set up production and service enterprises and to extend their business activities forward and backward (e.g. manufacturing, warehouses, harbour infrastructure, transport, distribution, retail, insurance, financial services, etc.). On the other hand, the industrial enterprises tended to integrate into related and unrelated production and service (especially in trade and finance) companies via different cooperative arrangements. The internationalization of these Chinese enterprises therefore went more in the direction of strategic asset seeking, at least as compared with their early overseas expansion, when the internationalization process was only regarded as a way for rapid expansion and diversification.

1992 on: increasing liberalization

After 1992, enterprise reforms were continued with the promulgation of the 'Regulations for Transforming the Operating Mechanism of the State-Owned Enterprises' in order to protect the autonomy of SOEs by law. Company managers were granted decision making autonomy in 14 key managerial areas, such as production, pricing, distribution, purchasing, import and export, investment and finance, joint venture initiatives or mergers, etc. It is very likely that the extension of the decision making authority of the managers stimulated the overseas expansion of Chinese enterprises. Anyway, while the number of outward investment projects increased by 71.5 per cent in 1992 and 7 per cent in 1993, the total value of Chinese investment in these projects decreased by 46 per cent in 1992 and 38.5 per cent in 1993 (Table 12.1). This could possibly be explained by the establishment of a large number of rather small scale overseas subsidiaries by industrial enterprises, in particular by TVEs.

By developing EJVs and concluding subcontracting agreements with state-owned enterprises and foreign firms, TVEs have upgraded their technological and organizational capabilities and started on the road towards internationalization. The proportion of the exports of TVEs in the total of China's exports increased from 29.7 per cent in 1991 to 42.4 per cent in 1992. By the end of 1992, more than 15,000

Chinese TVEs had entered into joint ventures with foreign partners. This amounted to 18 per cent of all Chinese inward FDI projects. The number of overseas subsidiaries established by TVEs increased from 15 in 1991 to 130 in 1992 (*China Statistic Bureau*, 1993). Most of the outward FDI of the TVEs is trade oriented and is mainly located in neighbouring countries, such as Thailand, Russia and other republics of the former Soviet Union.

A specific feature of Chinese outward FDI is that the reverse investment by Chinese subsidiaries in Hong Kong has become more and more important for the capital inflows of China (Zhan, 1993). In the first nine months of 1993, for instance, four Chinese subsidiaries in Hong Kong invested about US$1.5 billion in China, which came to 14 per cent of China's total utilized FDI inflow during this period (Lin, 1994). On the one hand, this particular group of companies has the advantage – as compared with foreign investors – of having greater local market knowledge, better access to the state bureaucracy, lower cost production facilities and more Chinese business experience. On the other hand – as compared to the purely domestic firms – they have access to favourable tax and tariff treatment, better access to business information and export markets, better managerial skills and superior production technology. The direct participation of the CHMNEs in China's inward FDI occurred under different sequential stages. At the early stage, the outward FDI by Chinese FTCs and FBOCs in Hong Kong was regarded by Western and other foreign investors as a confirmation of the Chinese 'open door' policy. The presence of SOEs in a foreign market provided not only political confidence, but also an 'intermediate' function for foreign enterprises to invest in China. With the reinforcement of their competitive position abroad, a number of these firms got increasingly involved with foreign enterprises as partners in the creation of international joint ventures and strategic alliances for investing in China as well as in third countries.

Regional aspects of IDP and dynamic interaction between inward and outward FDI

The recent nature of FDI in and from China makes it difficult to assess the dynamic interaction between inward and outward FDI at this stage. However, in view of the fact that China gradually implemented its FDI policy from coastal provinces to inland regions, a preliminary evaluation seems to be possible by comparing the investment scenario of different regions and provinces.

The early opened 12 coastal provinces in Eastern China received more than 92 per cent of the total inward FDI (in terms of current value) and committed more than 70 per cent of the Chinese outward FDI at the end of 1992, while the later opened Central and Western regions only acquired a relative share of 5.2 per cent and 2.7 per cent in inward and 11.9 per cent and 17.8 per cent in outward FDI. On the other hand, the regional trends show that the importance of FDI (measured by the NOI) of a particular region or province was positively related to its gross regional product (GRP), i.e. the higher its GRP level, the more important was its inward FDI. These trends correspond perfectly to the main characteristics of the first two stages of the IDP. For instance, the three independent municipalities Shanghai, Beijing, Tianjin and the province of Guangdong already distinguished themselves from other Chinese provinces in 1986, while other provinces, such as Hainan, Fujian, Liaoning and Shaanxi only emerged in the cycle in 1992 (Figure 12.2). The rapid expansion of Hainan, Fujian and Guangdong provinces both in the level of GRP and the FDI positions can be mainly explained by their 'privileged' geographic position and special incentives to attract export processing investors, while the competitive position of the 'traditional' industrial cities and provinces such as Shanghai, Tianjin and Liaoning have relatively more to do with 'created' locational resources and market potential. Also it has been observed that the impact of the FDI on GRP level was quite evident – especially in the case of Guangdong and Fujian – and that the more a province was involved in FDI activities, the higher was its speed of development.

Another specific feature of China's IDP is the high level of Chinese outward FDI as compared to other countries at similar stages of development and its high concentration in 'upstream' countries. Table 12.8 shows China's foreign investment position vis-à-vis 14 countries that are its principal foreign direct investment and trade partners. The FDI from these countries accounted for 80 per cent of the total Chinese inward FDI and their relative participation in Chinese outward FDI and exports reached about the same proportion, i.e. respectively 77.3 per cent and 83.5 per cent in 1993.

The ratio of Chinese inward to outward FDI illustrates that Chinese firms tended to invest in countries with high technological and innovatory capacities and abundant natural resources, such as the USA, Australia and Canada. These policy-induced resource-seeking

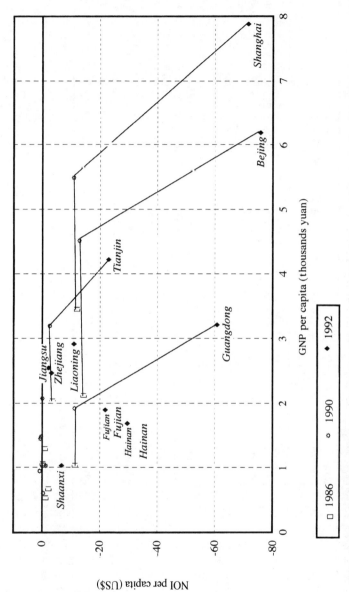

Figure 12.2 Regional pattern of the investment development path in China by major municipalities and provinces (1986–1992).

Table 12.8 China's foreign investment position by country 1979–1992 (in US$ million)

	% of Chinese exports	Inward FDI (current value)	% of total	Outward FDI	% of total	I/O*	NOI*
Hong Kong	44.16	20,320.34	53.63	128.10	8.05	158.63	−20,192.24
Japan	13.75	3,577.26	9.44	12.02	0.76	297.62	− 3,565.24
USA	10.12	3,001.61	7.92	307.02	19.3	9.78	− 2,694.59
Taiwan	0.82	1,050.50	2.77	0.00	0.00	–	− 1,050.50
Germany	2.88	464.00	1.22	7.63	0.48	60.83	−456.37
Macau	0.62	395.00	1.04	15.88	1.00	24.87	−379.12
Singapore	2.39	388.87	1.03	10.72	0.67	36.29	−378.15
UK	1.09	350.39	0.92	5.07	0.32	69.13	−345.32
France	0.90	213.69	0.56	8.86	0.56	24.13	−204.83
Australia	0.78	203.27	0.54	315.21	19.81	0.64	111.94
Italy	1.29	190.63	0.50	2.99	0.19	63.84	−187.64
Thailand	1.05	161.78	0.43	45.39	2.85	3.56	−116.39
Canada	0.77	119.63	0.32	365.73	22.99	0.33	246.10
South Korea	2.83	119.48	0.32	4.86	0.31	24.56	−114.62
World	84,940.06	37,892.40	100.00	1,591.01	100.00	23.82	−36,301.39

*Calculated on the basis of current inward FDI and approved outward FDI.

Source: MOFTEC (1984–1993).

(raw materials, technology, capital) investors and market-seeking operations changed the general profile of the Chinese IDP which featured a short 'gap' in time between inward and outward investment and a rapid catching up with industrial countries in particular. Such characteristics completed the theoretical prediction of the IDP, especially with regard to its application to the 'government-controlled investment scenario'.

FDI-INDUCED CHANGES AND THEIR IMPACT ON THE CHINESE ECONOMY

The FDI-induced changes and their impact on the Chinese OLI configuration within the context of the transition of a centrally controlled to a market economic system can be evaluated from three angles. First, FDI has helped to develop market mechanisms in the overall economic system by 'pushing' the government to create market infrastructure and a legal framework for business transactions and by introducing international business standards into forward and backward sectors. These effects greatly contributed to the upgrading of the Chinese L advantages, especially with regard to market creation and efficiency. Second, FDI allowed a restructuring of production (e.g. industrial sectors) from a pattern dictated by political–ideological priorities towards a structure more firmly based on economic realities (McMillan, 1993). In a number of sectors this has resulted in the development of competitive labour-intensive export manufacturing activities and the upgrading of capital- and technology-intensive industries, such as telecommunications, automobiles, informatics, etc. Third, FDI upgraded the competitive assets of Chinese enterprises in terms of capital, technology, management skills, business experience, etc., and improved their efficiency and stimulated their competitive behaviour.

Export performance

The most significant impact of FDI on the Chinese economy resulted in the enormous expansion of Chinese exports. The proportion of China in world exports rose from 0.9 per cent in 1980 to 2.3 per cent in 1992, while its annual growth rate was about 13 per cent. The contribution of foreign affiliates in the export performance of China became more and more evident, as their relative share in total Chinese exports augmented from 1.2 per cent in 1985 to 27.5 per cent in 1993 with an annual growth rate of more than 78 per cent during this period (Table 12.2). Also the shift of Chinese exports from primary products to (unskilled and later skilled) labour-intensive manufacturing products can be largely attributed to the export processing operations of the foreign affiliates, which gradually integrated the Chinese economy into the so-called South-east Asian 'flying geese' pattern of the development of international trade and investment. As a result, manufactured products in total Chinese exports increased from less than 50 per cent to nearly 80 per cent during the period 1980–1992. More particular exports of machines and transport equipment progressed from 4.6 per cent to 15.6 per cent of the total. The growth of inward FDI from Hong Kong, Taiwan and other Asian neighbouring countries has encouraged the creation of cross-border networks of intra-industry and intra-firm specialization, which in themselves stimulated the regionalization of FDI-induced trade flows of intermediate and capital goods as well as consumer goods (Kirkpatrick, 1994: 193). The exports of mainland China to and its imports from Hong Kong increased by 24 per cent and 32 per cent per year during the period of 1980–1991 and China's indirect imports from and exports to Taiwan (through Hong Kong) actually rose by 27 per cent and 24 per cent (Ash and Kueh, 1993: 717–719). The direct and indirect trade flows between mainland China and Hong Kong and Taiwan reached US$64.6 billion, or almost 40 per cent of China's foreign trade value in 1992 (MOFTEC, 1994: 482–483). On the other hand, although the official data are incomplete, an estimation based on the difference between FDI-related imports and exports in 1991 and 1992 showed that nearly half of the exports (in terms of value) of the foreign affiliates in China was made up of local added value. However, this proportion was much lower in the Fujian and Guangdong provinces, as it was only 18 per cent and 41 per cent during 1989–1991. This might be explained by the concentration of export processing FDI in these regions and their relatively lower local sourcing activities.

Capital contribution

The capital contribution of inward FDI in the total investment of state-owned enterprises reached more than 11 per cent in 1992 (see Table 12.2). This resulted in a positive impact on enterprise reform and investment, as it helped to diversify the financial system of domestic enterprises. During 1981–1988 the investment funds pro-

vided by the government as a percentage of the total investment of
SOEs declined from 44 per cent to 15 per cent, while the foreign
investment participation gradually increased from less than 2 per
cent in 1983 to 9 per cent in 1988 (UNIDO, 1994: 111). The relative
share of foreign investors in the equity capital is much higher in the
regions which were opened first. It reached 18 per cent in the 14
coastal cities and 38 per cent in the SEZs in 1992 (Zhan, 1993). The
direct capital contribution by foreign investors in the creation of
joint ventures allowed domestic enterprises to bypass financial
constraints and/or to launch new investment initiatives. The recent
introduction of 'B' shares for foreign investors has aimed at attracting foreign capital and increasing the financial capabilities of SOEs.

While the overseas operations of some large Chinese FBOCs
were initially aimed at attracting capital from foreign markets, their
contribution to the financial position of domestic firms is important,
especially in infrastructure development, e.g. power stations, mining
and telecommunications. The recent entry of several industrial
enterprises and FTCs into foreign financial operations under specific arrangements with the government has allowed them to
strengthen their overall financial position. However, the direct
capital contribution of overseas subsidiaries set up by small and
medium-sized enterprises (SMEs) is quite limited and may be
negative because of unfair practices and shortcomings in management operations. This may result in 'capital flight' and reinvestment
for purposes of tax evasion.

Technology accumulation

In 1992, the imports of equipment, machinery and materials as
equity capital by foreign affiliates reached US$8.2 billion, i.e. an
increase by 71 per cent as compared to 1991. This represented 73
per cent of the total FDI inflows (in current value) and nearly 10 per
cent of the total Chinese imports of that year (China Statistics
Bureau, 1993: 190). Yet, the contribution of inward FDI to China's
technological transformation is regarded as quite limited before
1992, especially with respect to advanced technology (Conroy,
1992: 212). The most evident impact of FDI on technology upgrading in China probably occurred in the SMEs which operate in the
export processing and assembling industries. While the transfer of
technology to these SMEs was mainly concerned with the
development of an international standardized product and process

technology, it mainly benefited the technological development of Chinese light industry and the TVEs from the south of China. The recent entry of leading multinationals in China was expected to contribute to the development of high technology in industrial sectors, such as telecommunications, transport equipment, chemicals, etc. With the increasing insistence of the central government on a higher proportion of 'localization' of inputs, a number of MNEs tended to develop their local sourcing capability by investing in related downstream industries or by establishing their own local supply networks. For instance, the proportion of local components of the 10 foreign automobile producers in China reached nearly 54 per cent in 1992 (China Statistics Bureau, 1993).

The technological contribution of Chinese overseas subsidiaries to their parent companies was quite limited, apart from certain FBOCs which are especially engaged in technology transfer operations. Yet, most of the Chinese foreign investors are concentrated in 'upstream' countries. The reason is that on the one hand, almost all Chinese subsidiaries are operating in export supporting activities (market seeking), and on the other hand, that they are still in a 'stand-alone' position, i.e. they have few linkages with their parent companies, as their operations are not really integrated in the group as a whole. However, Chinese outward FDI facilitated the exportation of complete Chinese plants and production technology to developing countries. In fact, most of the equity contribution in foreign ventures was made up of equipment and machines (Chai and Tang, 1993: 10–11).

CONCLUSION

This chapter has tried to use the IDP to emphasize the changing patterns of inward and outward FDI in China and their interaction with the development of the Chinese economy in its transition to a market economy during the last 15 years. Two specific aspects of the IDP have been illustrated. The first is that the national government is an important explanatory variable in determining the OLI configuration and its impact on the level, structure and geographic location of FDI. The second aspect consists of the changes of the O advantages of Chinese state-owned enterprises and their internationalization process under a government-controlled investment scenario.

The policy- and system-induced factor distortions have made the

Chinese government a very important factor in liberalizing and upgrading the national factor endowments and in creating competitive assets for its own multinationals. The political actions of the Chinese government *vis-à-vis* FDI consisted not only of specific regulatory measures – such as tax and tariff incentives, approval procedures, ownership control, sector specifications, location limits, export measures, etc. – but also of global development strategies for market creation and efficient business transactions in the context of the reform of the overall economic system.

The Chinese locational resources have been gradually opened to foreign investors under a government-controlled investment scenario, i.e. from limited geographic location to countrywide access, from production-oriented to market-oriented operations and from natural resources to more human- and capital-intensive assets. The shift in the resource allocation (foreign exchange, raw materials, labour, etc.) – from a direct command by administrative authorities to market transactions and from a controlled and unified pricing system to pricing as a function of production costs and market demand – has resulted in the creation of a more efficient market system and a more competitive business climate.

Along with the home-specific (or non-policy-induced) advantages, Chinese firms have tended to build up their own competitive assets (such as technological and innovatory capabilities, organizational knowledge and entrepreneurship) with the implementations of 'corporate mechanisms' by state-owned enterprises and the diversification of ownership structure. These assets are increasingly transferred into their international operations.

The outward FDI of Chinese enterprises was originally 'pushed' by the central and local governments as a component of the 'open door' policy to get the confidence of foreign investors and to support the domestic development strategy by acquiring capital, technology and raw materials from abroad. However, with increasing management autonomy and ownership control, more and more firms engaged in an internationalization process based on their own objectives, i.e. market seeking in general and efficiency and strategy seeking in particular. In fact, these changing patterns reflect the evolution in the O and I advantages of Chinese enterprises from policy-induced considerations to more corporate and strategic approaches.

The resource commitment of foreign affiliates in China became increasingly based on organizational and process knowledge, as they extended their activities from labour-intensive and outsourcing export processing operations to more local-market-oriented technology-driven and human-resource-intensive industries. The linkages of the foreign subsidiaries with the local market are reinforced by upstream and downstream integration. The shift and/or expansion from natural resource seeking (e.g. low labour costs) to market efficiency- and strategic-seeking operations means that certain foreign investors are starting to reorganize their stand-alone Chinese operations into more globalized and diversified activities.

The rapid upgrading of the Chinese OLI advantages in the global economy and the enormous expansion of FDI in China confirm the prediction about the role of the national government in the early stages of the IDP. While the importance of the Chinese government in the future will likely continue to be significant, the way in which it controls the investment path will undoubtedly change over time as the Chinese economic system becomes even more market oriented.

NOTES

1 In 1894 China had to open its coastal cities to foreign direct investors under the 'Treaty of Shimonoseki' following its defeat in the Chia-Wu War against Japan. As a result the inward FDI which was carried out before World War II was subject to much political opposition from the Chinese government (Cao, 1991: 382–400). After 1949, China's policy-makers even prohibited inward FDI completely as they regarded private foreign capital as opposed to socialist development goals and feared for a loss of control over the country's economic development and political independence. Even in 1977, one year before the 'open door' policy was announced, the Chinese government reaffirmed: 'We have never joined capitalist countries in exploring our natural resources; nor will we explore other countries' resources. We never did, nor will we ever, embark on joint ventures with foreign capitalists' (Red Flag, Beijing, March, 1977, cited by Kleinberg, 1990: 1).

2 The Ministry of Foreign Trade and Economic Cooperation (MOFTEC) classifies Chinese outward investment projects into two main types, i.e. trade and non-trade projects. The first category includes investment in service sectors such as banking, commercial offices, travel agencies, etc., while the second category covers projects in industrial manufacturing and resource extraction. The administration of these two kinds of overseas investment projects is organized in different ways, in particular with regard to the investment regulations and the approval procedure. This latter procedure is generally easier for overseas trade enterprises.

3 This trade structure showed that the priority of the Chinese economic external policy was industrialization and that imports of the necessary

industrial inputs were completely dependent on the exports of primary products.

4 Term used by McMillan (1993) to designate the creation of institutional infrastructure that allows the renaissance of the market mechanism in the economic system.

5 The Hainan province was granted the status of SEZ in 1988.

6 In the first nine months of 1994 the volume of contracted new FDI reached US$22.72 billion, up 49 per cent as compared with the corresponding period of the year before. Meanwhile the number of new projects declined by 46 per cent (*Financial Times*, 1994) which can be explained by the growth of the investment of Western MNEs in large projects.

7 The local governments of inland towns and cities also created their own development zones in order to attract foreign and domestic investors, as the total number of such zones increased from 117 at the end of 1991 to about 10,000 at the end of 1992. Since 1993, the government restricted the initiatives of local governments to establish development zones, because of the resulting uncoordinated local investment regulations (Harrold and Lall, 1993: 5–6).

8 For more details about these new forms of FDI in China, see International Economic Review (1994: 14–17).

9 The overvaluation of machinery and equipment by foreign investors in creating EJVs was estimated to be US$500 million between January 1991 and June 1994. For 4,940 inspected shipments, about 25 per cent of the equipment was found to be overvalued (*Financial Times*, 1994).

10 For instance, SINOCHEM had a monopoly position in the import and export of chemicals and realized nearly 20 per cent of China's total import and export value in 1984.

11 By the end of 1992, there were 55 centrally controlled and 1,600 locally controlled enterprise groups and 3,700 shareholding companies at various levels. Also about 4,000 mergers occurred in 1992, involving more thatn 8,000 enterprises (Harrold and Lall, 1993).

BIBLIOGRAPHY

ADB–Asian Development Bank (1991) *Asia Development Outlook*, Manila: Asian Development Bank.

Ash, R. F. and Kueh, Y. Y. (1993) 'Economic integration within greater China: trade and investment flows between China, Hong Kong and Taiwan', *The China Quarterly*, No. 136: 711–745.

Blanc, G. and Anastassopoulos, J.-P. (1983) 'Les multinationales publiques', in A. Cotta and M. Ghertman (eds) *Les Multinationales en Mutation*, Paris: IRM, 161–193.

Cao, J.W. (1991) *Modern China and the Making Use of Foreign Capital*, Shanghai: Shanghai Academy of Social Sciences Press (in Chinese).

Casson, M. and Zheng, J. (1990) 'Western joint ventures in China', *Discussion Paper*, University of Reading.

Chai, L. and Tang, N. (1993) 'Faced with the World: China develops actively its foreign direct investment', *International Economic Cooperation*, No. 3: 9–12 (in Chinese).

China Development Report (1993) *China Statistics Bureau*, Beijing: ZhongGuo TongJi ChuBanShe (in Chinese).

Conroy, R. (1992) *Technological Change in China*, Paris: OECD.

Dunning, J. H. (1981) 'Explaining the international direct investment position of countries: towards a dynamic or development approach', *Weltwirtschaftliches Archiv*, No. 119: 30–64.

—— (1986) 'The investment development cycle and third world multinationals', in K. M. Khan (ed.) *Multinational of the South: New Actors in the International Economy*, London: Frances Printer, 15–47.

—— (1993) *Multinational Enterprises and the Global Economy*, Wokingham, UK, and Reading, MA: Addison-Wesley.

Far Eastern Economic Review (1992) 'Flags follow trade', *Far Eastern Economic Review*, 17 September.

Financial Times (1994) 'China', *Financial Times Survey*, November 7.

Gu, S. L. (1994) 'A review of reform policy for science and technology system in China: from paid transactions for technology to organizational restructuring', *UNU/INTECH Working Papers*, No.17, Maastricht: UNU/INTECH.

Harrold, P. (1992) 'China's reform experience to date', *World Bank Discussion Papers*, No. 180, China and Mongolia Department, Washington, DC: World Bank.

Harrold, P. and Lall, R. (1993) 'China: reform and development in 1992–93', *World Bank Discussion Papers*, No. 215, China and Mongolia Department, Washington, DC: World Bank.

International Economic Review (1994) 'Foreign Investment in China', July: 12–17.

Khan, Z. S. (1991) 'Patterns of direct foreign investment in China', *World Bank Discussion Papers*, No. 130, China and Mongolia Department, Washington, DC: World Bank.

Kirkpatrick, C. (1994) 'Regionalisation, regionalism and East Asian economic cooperation', *The World Economy*, Vol. 17, No. 2, 191–202.

Kleinberg, R. (1990) *China's opening to the outside world: the experiment with foreign capitalism*, Oxford: Westview Press.

Kueh, Y. Y. (1989) 'China's new industrialization strategy', *The China Quarterly*, No. 119: 421–447.

Kumar, K. (1981) 'Multinationalization of third world public sector enterprises', in K. Kumar and M. G. Mcleod (eds) *Multinationals from Developing Countries*, Lexington, MA, and Toronto: Lexington Books, 187–201.

Lardy, N. R. (1994) *China in the World Economy*, Washington, DC: Institute for International Economics.

Lin, D. (1994) 'Hong Kong's China-invested companies and their reverse investment in China', *Paper presented at the Conference 'Management Issues for China in the 1990s'*, University of Cambridge, 23–25 March.

Liu, H. (1986) 'Importation de technologies', *Beijing Information*, No. 10: 23–26.

Lu, Y. and Child, J. (1994) 'Decentralization of decision making in China's state enterprises', *Paper presented at the conference 'Management Issues for China in the 1990s'*, University of Cambridge, 23–25 March.

Luo, L., Chen, Y. and Yang, R. (1993) 'Some consideration on the management of Chinese multinationals', *World Economy*, No. 5: 46–50 (in Chinese).

Macdougall, C. (1982) 'Policy changes in China's foreign trade since the death of Mao, 1976–1980', in J. Gray and G. White (eds) *China's New Strategy*, London: Academic Press, 148–171.

McMillan, C. H. (1993) 'The role of foreign direct investment in the transition from planned to market economies', *Transnational Corporations*, No. 3: 97–119.

MOFTEC (1984–1994) *Almanac of China's foreign economic relations and trade*, Hong Kong.

Nicholas, R. I. (1994) *China in the World Economy*, Washington, DC: Institute for International Economics.

Pearson, M. M. (1991) *Joint Ventures in the People's Republic of China: The Control of Foreign Direct Investment Under Socialism*, Princeton, NJ.: Princeton University Press.

Qi, L. and Howe, Ch. (1993) 'Direct investment and economic integration in the Asia Pacific: the case of Taiwanese investment in Xiamen', *The China Quarterly*, No. 136: 746–769.

Salem, E. (1988) 'The China syndrome: Peking pours money into Hong Kong – for its own benefit', *Far Eastern Economic Review*, No. 23: 66.

Schermerhorn, Jr, J. R. and Nyaw, M. (1992) 'Managerial leadership in Chinese industrial enterprises', in O. Shenkar (ed.) *Organization and Management in China 1979–1990*, Armonk, NY: Sharpe, 9–22.

Singh, I. (1992) 'China: industrial policies for an economy in transition', *World Bank Discussion Papers*, No. 143, Washington, DC: World Bank.

Sit, Victor F. S. (1989) 'Industrial out-processing – Hong Kong's new relationship with the Pearl River Delta', *Asian Profile*, Vol. 19, No. 1.

Tai, M. C. (1990) 'China–Taiwan trade growth suffers a setback: the water margin', *Far Eastern Economic Review*, No. 15: 76–77.

UNCTAD (1994) *World Investment Report 1994*, New York: United Nations.

UNIDO (1994) *Industry and Development: Global Report 1992/93*, Vienna: UNIDO.

Van Den Bulcke, D. and Zhang, H. (1992) 'Belgian equity joint ventures in China, some considerations and evidence', *CIMDA Discussion Paper*, No. 1992/E7, to be published in S. Stewart (ed.) *Joint Ventures in the PRC, Advances in Chinese Industrial Studies*, Vol. 4, Greenwich, CT: JAI Press.

—— (1994) 'The development of local marketing knowledge within joint ventures: an analysis of the performance of Belgian multinationals in China', in K. Obloj (ed.) *High Speed Competition in a New Europe, Proceedings of the 20th Annual Conference of EIBA*, Vol. 2, Warsaw: International Postgraduate Management Center, University of Warsaw, 129–162.

World Bank (1988–1994) *World Development Report 1994*, Washington, DC: The World Bank.

—— (1994) *China: Reform and the Role of the Plan in the 1990s, A World Bank Country Study*, Washington, DC: The World Bank.

Ye, G. (1992) 'Chinese transnational corporations', *Transnational Corporations*, No. 2: 125–133

Zhan, X. J. (1993) 'The role of foreign direct investment in market-oriented reforms and economic development, the case of China', *Transnational Corporations*, No. 3: 121–148.

Zhang, H. and Van Den Bulcke, D. (1994a) 'International management strategies of Chinese multinational firms', *CIMDA Discussion Paper*, No. E17, University of Antwerp, to be published in J. Child and Yuan Lu (eds) *Management Issues for China in the 1990s*, Cambridge University Press.

—— (1994b) 'Strategic management of international diversification: the case of three Chinese multinational enterprises', *Paper presented at the 20th Annual Conference of EIBA*, 11–13 December 1994, Warsaw, Poland.

Chapter 13

The investment development path
Some conclusions

Sanjaya Lall

INTRODUCTION

This chapter seeks to highlight some of the main findings of this volume. It notes some features of the analytical approach, presents some comparable data on FDI flows by the countries concerned, and tries to identify common patterns in their engagement in international production. It reflects the interest and specialisation of the present author in development economics and, in particular, in industrialisation and the role of government in promoting industrial development.

Let us start with the investment development path. The IDP approach is based on two premises: first, that there are consistent patterns of structural change with development; and, second, that these changes have systematic relations with patterns of FDI. Both are supported by different branches of the economics literature, but neither is part of mainstream neoclassical economics. The process of structural change as a central feature of economic development is assumed away by the market efficiency and equilibrium assumptions of neoclassical theory. Yet the structuralist approach of Chenery and others establishes that development is systematically associated with important structural shifts that are independent determinants of the growth processes.[1] Chenery points to the growing share in GDP of manufacturing and modern services, greater capital- and skill-intensity of production, a shift in consumption patterns from simple to sophisticated, differentiated products, and the appearance of new sources of comparative advantage in trade. He also finds that patterns of structural change are not uniform. They differ by size of the country, initial resource endowments and trade orientation: small, resource-poor and outward-oriented countries experienced the fastest rate of structural transformation.

This supports the IDP approach that patterns of ownership and locational advantages, which are closely related to the structural factors traced by Chenery, tend to develop in a predictable pattern with income growth. In the comparative advantage literature, a similar approach is used by 'neo-technology' theories of trade, which, in contrast to neoclassical trade analyses, are based on market imperfections in the creation of technology and where competitive advantages accrue to firms rather than to nations. Again, the approach is similar to that used in the theory of international production, though neo-technology trade theories are not concerned with systematic patterns of change in competitive advantages in relation to income levels.

The IDP approach is more comprehensive and ambitious than these other analyses, since it goes on to consider how structural changes in locational and ownership factors affect patterns of international capital flows, corporate behaviour and government policies. This is a theoretical advance and provides important insights into the process of internationalisation. However, systematic and predictable relations are more difficult to establish here. There seem to be many *subpatterns* of structural change within the broadly similar evolution of skills and technologies from the simple to the complex. Different countries at similar levels of income may have very different patterns of ownership advantages in activities that go multinational, depending on their initial conditions and government strategies as well as accidents of history. Though each country may evolve over time along the lines postulated by the IDP (from being net importers to being net exporters and finally achieving balance) the differences between countries may remain quite large.

The Dunning and Narula analysis takes this into account when it talks of the '*character* of growth of GNP' of particular countries and the possibility that investment flows are driven by the quest for new ownership advantages rather than by the possession of such advantages. The content of the 'character' of income growth needs to be further explored, since it is likely to yield further refinements of the theory. It is possible, for instance, that these patterns lead to permanent asymmetries in FDI flows for some countries. Or that the role of FDI in the economy differs greatly between different countries because of earlier strategies and the nature of economic structures and institutions developed over time – these differences are not the concern of the IDP model, which is only concerned with overall flows, but they are important if the model were taken into more normative and prescriptive areas. Certainly, as far as developing countries are concerned, the policy implications of the model are of significance.

As Dunning and Narula note in the first part of Chapter 1, the eclectic paradigm does offer insights on how FDI flows affect national development. These effects can be positive or negative, though they are difficult to attribute to FDI *per se*. They are strongly affected by many other factors that determine how well any particular country is able to use the resources offered by MNEs. Given the market failures within which MNEs come into existence, the effects of FDI must depend largely on how each country, or its government, is able to improve the functioning of markets, develop its skills and technological resources and extract greater spillovers from the presence of MNEs. However, something that the IDP recognises implicitly but does not develop is the fact that MNEs can transfer their advantages (technology, skills and so on) to other countries in many different ways apart from direct investment. The choice of modes of technology and skill transfer may itself affect how much and how well the host country creates its own base of assets, and so its potential for long-term development. This gives rise to two interesting possibilities. First, it may be possible that the IDP could be better measured by the international transfer of intangible assets rather than only by direct investment. Second, since the effects of FDI on the creation of ownership and locational advantages can vary by the policy context, the model may try to endogenise these policies by differentiating broadly different approaches.

The country studies in this volume show that the investment path is highly variegated, and that progress along it is strongly conditioned by a host of exogenous factors not related to levels of per capita incomes. Given differences in initial endowments such as size, location and natural resources, the most important conditioning influence seems to be that of *government policies*. In the introductory chapter Dunning and Narula note that policy differences seem to play a larger role than was initially expected. To someone like the present author, who is primarily a development economist, the role of policy interventions has always been taken as crucially important in the growth process. In the present context, policies (apart from those related to FDI noted above) can influence the underlying determinants of OLI factors that in turn determine how and how much each country participates in international production.

The empirical analysis by Dunning and Narula (Part 2 of Chapter 1), carefully conducted and suitably qualified, shows how difficult it is to establish systematic investment development paths on a cross-section basis when these differences cannot be controlled for. The authors also note that at higher stages of development, the activities of MNEs reflect conditions in all countries that they operate in and not just the home country: ownership advantages tend to become more firm specific and less country specific as MNEs become more internationalised. This is an interesting and persuasive idea, one that analysts like Vernon have been propagating for some time. The growth of 'alliance capitalism' is also a useful encapsulation of a trend that has been widely noted.

Another interesting finding of the statistical analysis, the focus of much concern in the development literature, is the growing gap between the least developed countries and the newly industrialising and developed ones. This is showing up in the formers' increasing marginalisation from FDI flows as in their lack of competitive advantages and inability to diversify their economies. There are many explanations for this, but the most apt ones seem to relate to the small base of human capital and the inability of their governments to mount the sort of industrial support policies and institutions that the NIEs were able to. Note that these policies were often highly selective and targeted, building up infant industries and promoting indigenous enterprises, and not just 'market supportive' in the sense of being non-selective strengthening of market institutions.[2]

The statistical analysis stresses that countries are highly idiosyncratic in the engagement in FDI. As with Chenery, systematic differences are traced to size, resources, trade strategy and the role of government. With respect to government policies, the chapter notes that increasing economic specialisation leads to increasing market failures and so increases the potential benefits of interventions to remedy these failures (i.e. developed countries need to intervene more than developing ones). While it may well be true that specialisation leads to a greater incidence of certain forms of market failure, however, it should be noted that different, and possibly more pervasive, market failure occurs at lower levels of development. In fact, the process of development may be characterised as the effective use of policies and institutions to overcome market failures, including the ability to use FDI flows for furthering the growth of national ownership and locational advantages.

PATTERNS OF FDI

It may be useful to look at some data, patchy and imperfect as they may be, on the inflows, outflows and net investment positions of the countries covered in this book. Table 13.1 shows patterns of FDI flows, based on data from the *World Investment Report 1994*. The figures for inflows are available for all the countries for the period 1982–92 (those for 1982–7 are annual averages), but for outflows there are some gaps for the developing countries. The country papers do, however, give some of these data from national sources; these have not been drawn upon here for the sake of consistency.

There are large annual variations for several countries, and significant differences in patterns and values of FDI between them. Take the two main investing countries, the UK and the United States. The UK goes from being the largest investor overseas in the group in 1982–7 to being the largest importer, with its net FDI position being consistently positive in the 1980s to being consistently negative in the 1990s. The United States moves in exactly the reverse direction, with its massive net inflows converting into large net outflows over the decade. Sweden and Japan are consistently biased towards capital exports and receive relatively little FDI in relation to the size and competitive positions of their economies. Both show large declines in overseas investment in the last year, because of recession and associated problems. New Zealand is a fairly minor player as both capital exporter and importer, and its outward investment has declined steadily after a burst of activity around the turn of the decade.

Spain and Mexico are large capital importers with some outward investment activity, conforming nicely to Stage 3 of the IDP. Taiwan is similar, except that it is far more outwards oriented in FDI than the data indicate – the official data understate actual outward investments by a factor of 10 or more. This makes it possibly the largest overseas investor in the developing world (though Hong Kong, with its own investments and its growing *entrepôt* role in China, is running neck and neck). Its net investment position has been positive (i.e., it is a net capital exporter) for a considerable time, an unusual position for a developing country. At

Table 13.1 Foreign direct investment: inflows and outflows (1982–92) (US$ million)

	Inflows						Outflows					
	1982–7	1988	1989	1990	1991	1992	1982–7	1988	1989	1990	1991	1992
UK	6,665	21,414	30,553	32,436	16,158	18,182	13,713	37,287	35,484	19,419	15,944	16,089
USA	26,927	58,571	69,010	48,422	25,446	3,388	12,428	14,324	33,826	23,932	33,100	33,089
Sweden	464	1,514	1,522	1,972	5,751	329	2,364	7,233	9,694	14,034	6,988	1,405
Japan	480	−520	−1,060	1,760	1,370	2,720	9,093	34,210	44,160	48,050	30,740	17,240
New Zealand	296	441	1,365	1,754	682	70	175	152	1,791	998	−44	−22
Spain	2,528	7,021	8,428	13,841	10,503	8,058	396	1,235	1,473	2,937	3,584	1,300
Mexico	1,294	2,594	3,037	2,632	4,762	5,366						
Taiwan	306	1,105	1,775	2,444	2,014	2,116	162	4,120	6,951	5,243	1,854	1,701
Indonesia	282	576	682	1,093	1,482	1,774						
India	89	91	252	236	145	140						
China	1,362	3,194	3,393	3,487	4,366	11,156	333	850	780	830	913	4,000

Net outflows

	1982–7	1988	1989	1990	1991	1992
UK	7,048	15,873	4,931	−13,017	−214	−2,093
USA	−13,499	−44,247	−35,184	−24,490	7,654	29,701
Sweden	1,900	5,719	8,172	12,062	1,237	1,076
Japan	8,613	34,730	45,220	46,290	29,370	14,520
New Zealand	−121	−289	426	−756	−726	−92
Spain	−2,132	−5,786	−6,955	−10,904	−6,919	−6,758
Taiwan	−144	3,015	5,176	2,799	−160	−415
China	−1,029	−2,344	−2,613	−2,657	−3,453	−7,156

the macroeconomic level, this is backed by enormous foreign exchange reserves and high savings rates. At the enterprise level, it reveals a large and diverse base of 'created assets' in the form of technological capabilities and a growing research base, more substantial than all the others in the sample with the exception of the mature industrial powers.

Indonesia is the least industrially developed of the group and is primarily a capital importer. Some of its enterprises, led by some large and well-endowed private conglomerate groups, do invest abroad in areas like textiles and food processing, as well as in services and real estate. But they lack the created assets of the more advanced NIEs and their performance conforms well to the IDP model. India and China are somewhat unusual for low income countries because they have built up large, diverse and in parts quite productive industrial sectors. Their enterprises therefore possess much greater ownership advantages than would be expected on a straightforward application of theory. However, both are net capital importers. India is a small one, since it has persisted till very recently with nationalistic policies that have deterred inward investments; this is now changing, but the data in the table do not capture this. China, on the other hand, is the developing world's largest capital importer, and may well become the world's largest. Much of this capital flows from (or through) overseas Chinese (and some of it is 'roundtripping' by local enterprises which send capital to Hong Kong and bring it back as FDI to avoid taxes), which makes it difficult to judge the *relative* competitive advantages of China as a host country. At the same time, large state-owned Chinese enterprises are becoming large overseas investors in a number of heavy and resource-seeking industries, testifying to their own created assets.

In spite of the individual variations and fluctuations, these patterns are basically reassuring for the IDP approach. After all, the approach is intended to analyse broad tendencies rather than providing well-specified predictions of where exactly a country will be with respect to FDI at any given level of income. Clearly ownership and locational factors evolve systematically with development, even if income levels do not capture the multifaceted nature of the development process. The evolution of the middle level developing countries is the best illustration of this. Given this underlying tendency, the significance of policy differences is very large, as is shown in the individual country studies.

DEVELOPED COUNTRIES

The developed country group falls naturally into three discrete groups. The two traditional overseas investors, the UK and United States, are in a class by themselves. They are among the largest investors over this century, though Japan overtook them in the late 1980s, and their MNEs are perhaps the best established and best known. Japan and Sweden may be placed together, though the former is now the second largest overseas investor in the world (and was the largest in 1989–90) while the latter is a relatively small player (though in relation to the size of its economy its enterprises are among the most international). Their affinity rests more on their specialisation in certain areas of advanced industrial technologies and some common features in the development of their MNEs. Finally, New Zealand and Spain may be put together even though the latter is a much bigger economy, more centrally located and industrially more developed, than the former, which remains essentially a primary producer and a small recipient and exporter of FDI. However, both are economies without a strong set of ownership advantages based on technology generation, and both have relatively passive attitudes to the attraction and promotion of inward and outward investments.

The *UK* has experienced a decline in both inward and outward flows in recent years, a reflection of the general decline in OECD FDI. In the course of this, from being a large net exporter of capital it has become a net importer. Clegg's chapter on the UK traces this evolution in great detail, and concludes that while in the short term there are evident disequilibria, and that there is a subcycle in investment behaviour with respect to the United States, over the longer term the IDP provides a useful explanation of the UK's investment patterns. While the direct role of the government in promoting or restricting FDI flows has been relatively small, the indirect effects are much more significant. The membership of the EU may have increased the incentive to export from the UK rather than to invest in Europe, reducing outward investment; at the same time, this may have stimulated inward investment to take advantage of the country's improving locational advantages. The recent privatisation of large utilities has also created new sources of investment overseas. The government has also played a role in this locational improvement. However, it may be argued that the improvement has in effect downgraded the innovatory capabilities of many parts of

UK industry (with obvious exceptions like pharmaceuticals, aerospace, food processing and some other industries in which UK firms retain a global position). Instead of attracting investments in the highest value-added end of the spectrum it has often led to FDI that involves lower grade assembly-type activities. The causes of this 'hollowing out' of Britain's industrial capabilities, along with its marked long term deindustrialisation, are not well understood and so are difficult to attribute to particular policies or political regimes. However, the possibility that a balance is being reached in international investment flows at a 'lower' level with industrial maturity is an interesting one and needs exploration.

The *United States* has been the dominant source of FDI in the world for a long time, and its experience is particularly interesting for the IDP in a mature industrial country. Graham's chapter shows the fluctuations that US net investment flows have experienced since the 1950s, and finds that there is a distinct cycle in which the former dominance of outward investment is followed by a move towards greater balance, followed again by a resurgence of outward flows since the late 1980s. He concludes that there is no clear evidence of an 'equilibrium' emerging in net FDI flows.

A range of factors can be adduced to explain this cycle in US net FDI, but simple explanations do not do justice to such a complex phenomenon. Graham notes the impact of government policies on FDI inflows and, to a lesser extent, on outflows, and finds that direct FDI policies may have had some effect in making foreign investors feel a little less welcome than before. However, the swings of the cycle are based less on direct policies to restrict inward and encourage outward FDI and more on swings in competitiveness of the United States *vis à vis* leading developed countries, and these are based on such fundamentals like human capital formation, technology investments and corporate strategies, as well as macroeconomic variables like exchange and interest rates. The government has an important role to play in determining these underlying factors in US competitiveness, of course, and Graham touches on some of these. He does not, however, go into the early (and in some cases recent) development of industrial competitiveness in the United States, when the government had a larger role to play through such interventions as infant industry protection, infrastructure development, procurement, education, R&D (directly and by its space and defence programmes).

The main conclusion of the US chapter is that there is no clear trend towards net balance in FDI flows, and that the competitiveness of US investors does not show any distinct signs of regressing. The evidence is thus rather mixed and difficult to interpret in terms of a simple IDP analysis. One of the more interesting aspects of the US case is that its MNEs are looking for new ownership advantages from competitors abroad, especially in Europe, by takeovers and alliances. There are thus many twists and turns possible in the evolution of competitiveness, and the impression at present is that idiosyncratic national and historical factors are more important than deterministic rules on the rise and fall of advantages.

Japan is naturally a very interesting and unusual case for the study of the IDP, as for many other issues, and Ozawa's chapter brings out some of its most fascinating aspects by looking at the evolution of industry-level advantages over time. For a start, Japan developed its ownership advantages by a deliberate strategy of keeping out foreign MNEs and importing technology from them by licensing, copying, reverse engineering and research. The development of its own capabilities was based on protecting national enterprises and stimulating them to increase skills and R&D investments by a variety of pressures and incentives: the restrictions placed on the import of internalised technology were a critical element of building up indigenous technology. This attitude to FDI inflows persists now and is institutionalised, even though the government does not directly intervene to discourage foreign investors. Thus, there is little noticeable tendency towards the kind of balance predicted by the IDP. However, there is more of a 'balance' if total technology trade is taken into account, suggesting again that this may be an alternative way to formulate the hypothesis.

Japan's progress in developing its ownership advantages is broken down into four phases by Ozawa: these he terms factor driven, scale driven, components intensive and innovation driven. These rise greatly in sophistication and complexity, the move in each stage necessitating an enormous investment in human capital and technological effort. While this is a normal part of industrial development, the speed, spread and autonomy of the transformation were made possible in Japan only by interventionist government policies. It went international relatively late, when its enterprises started to invest abroad, initially to seek low cost locations (rather than to exploit advanced technological advantages). Over time, the pattern shifted to technologically driven FDI while activities in which Japan is losing competitiveness are relocated overseas or phased out. The role of the government in resource allocation is much less now, but it retains some in co-ordinating research effort. There is still little sign that FDI flows inwards will approach the size of flows outwards.

Sweden also has relatively low inward FDI and shows little sign of achieving 'balance' of in- and outflows. But in Sweden's case, unlike Japan, there has not been an overt policy of restricting investment by foreign enterprises (except for a ban on foreign ownership of natural resources), and many Swedish enterprises were founded by foreigners settled there. Many Swedish technological innovations, that later founded the basis of the expansion of its industrial competitiveness and the ownership advantages of its MNEs, drew upon ideas created elsewhere. The government did help by creating a large base of skilled technical labour, but this was indirect. The role of MNEs has been small and has stayed constant over time; for instance, they account for 7 per cent of employment now, as they did in 1900.

This raises two interesting questions. First, why has inward FDI been so low, despite the obvious skill and technological advantages possessed by the country? And, second, has the development of Swedish technological capabilities been conditional on keeping a secure domestic market? The chapter by Ivo and Udo Zander casts some light on this. There was a cluster of innovations in the early part of this century in Sweden, drawing, as noted, on foreign ideas and basing their utilisation on the base of skilled technical labour. This historic accident gave its enterprises a head start in establishing world class competitive advantages. The base of national ownership of national resources may have helped by providing a base of capital and a testing ground for many innovations, thus starting an 'innovation culture'. The growth of a diverse and competent supplier base must have helped in all activities based on engineering technologies. The rise of a few large enterprises led to a political economy in which the state had very close connections with national business and defended its interests. Thus there may have been subtle pressures limiting FDI inflows into Sweden.

The second question is more difficult to answer. Many innovations in Sweden have been aimed from the start at world markets, since the small domestic economy could not sustain scale- and technology-intensive activities on its own. However, it is also possible that the secure domestic base was important as a testing and 'learning' ground for Swedish firms, and that interactions with local networks of suppliers, universities and research institutions helped in developing production capabilities. As the authors of the chapter note, the domestic innovation base remains of primary importance for Swedish MNEs, and there are few instances of their investing overseas to seek new technologies.

Spain has developed rapidly in recent years, building upon a diverse industrial base left by a period of import substitution in which there was relatively low inward FDI. However, the earlier period did not leave Spain with a technological base that had autonomous dynamism; the economy was always highly dependent on technology inflows from the advanced countries of Europe. With the opening up of the economy (and later admission into the EU), inwards FDI increased significantly. Much of it was directed at using the relatively cheap skilled base of labour, serving the growing domestic market (especially for services) or acquiring local firms with established market position. The government helped inward FDI by investing in infrastructure and training. Campa and Guillén provide many important insights into the nature of FDI into and out of Spain by their careful use of statistical tests. Their access to what seems to be a unique base of data for the country studies in this volume is a major asset of their chapter.

Little FDI into Spain has gone into technology-intensive activities despite government efforts to raise the technological level of Spanish industry. R&D levels remain well below those of neighbouring industrialized countries. Areas of technological strength for Spain are activities at medium levels of technology such as fabricated metals, industrial machinery and automobiles, of which the last is overwhelmingly foreign owned. There *is* local R&D in these industries, and MNEs spend more on this than local firms, but in general terms the country remains at technologically a much lower level than, say, the larger East Asian NIEs. Probably as a consequence, Spain remains primarily a capital importer, and its outward investments, while not insignificant, are low for a country of its size and income levels.

Finally, *New Zealand* is unique in the present group of developed countries in that it is highly resource based and rather peripheral to international trade and investment flows. Its development in the last century was driven by unrestricted FDI into agro-based activities, with the farmer-dominated government providing research and marketing support. The state welcomed foreign investments and helped by investing in education and infrastructure. Later the country tried a long period of import-substituting industrialisation but the local market was too small, the location too unfavourable and (despite the efforts of the government) the base of technology too weak to enable New Zealand to become a successful exporter of manufactures. With the decline in agricultural exports and the consequent recession, the government moved to sweeping liberalisation of the economy. FDI into infrastructure was freely allowed, the banking sector became entirely foreign owned and outward FDI by large, local resource-based enterprises was encouraged. The prospects for the New Zealand economy remain unclear.

Akoorie notes in concluding her chapter that government policies towards industrialisation and FDI were unsuccessful in creating a base for sustained growth, unlike East Asia. She does not specify just what the government did wrong, but clearly industrial policy did not work well in New Zealand. While ownership and location advantages did change over time, and there seems to be evolving a 'balance' in inward and outward FDI flows, it is taking place at a low level. Could this be a case similar to the UK, even though in New Zealand there is no industrial dominance from which to retreat?

DEVELOPING COUNTRIES

The developing countries fall into three groups, again with large differences within each group. The two richest are Mexico and Taiwan, upper middle income countries in World Bank terms, with large industrial sectors and a large presence in international trade and investment. One has been traditionally import substituting, with large domestic conglomerates and public enterprises and highly dependent on inward FDI, the other highly export oriented with a strong indigenous industrial sector consisting largely of small enterprises. Taiwan has emerged as possibly the largest overseas investor in the developing world, and has used FDI consciously to promote its objectives of developing its own capabilities and advantages. The second group are the two giant economies, China and India, formerly closed or hostile to FDI and now opening up. China has been spectacularly successful and is the largest host for investment flows among developing countries and may become the largest in the world. India is still lagging, but the signs are optimistic. Both are low income countries with large industrial bases and considerable technological capabilities; thus, their enterprises are investing abroad to a greater extent than their income levels would predict. Finally, there is Indonesia – with a large economy and ample natural resources, low wages and a strategic location to attract the relocation of industries from East Asia. It has switched from inward- to outward-oriented trade strategies but retains a lot of intervention, much of it not economic or well implemented. However, its location, low wages and resources make it a large recipient of FDI; some of its large conglomerates, flush with funds and with a base in certain technologies, are starting to invest overseas.

Mexico has always been a large recipient of FDI, and until the debt crisis of the 1980s was the second largest destination for foreign investors in the developing world, drawing them primarily to serve a large and protected domestic market. It changed economic direction drastically after 1985, switching from import substitution to completely liberalised trade, open door policies to MNEs, sweeping privatisation of public enterprises (except in petroleum) and a commitment to join the North American Free Trade Area. This switch resulted in a rapid growth of exports, led by the multinational-dominated automobile industry and chemicals, as well as much simpler, labour-intensive *maquiladora* industries near the US border.[3] It also led to an increase in FDI inflows and an even faster rise in imports, with much of the inward investment going into upgrading existing industries and into services. There has been relatively little FDI into new high skill or high technology activities for export, a pattern different from recent FDI in East Asia.

This is in effect increasing the duality of the Mexican industrial sector, with parts upgrading into higher value-added level activities (e.g. import-substituting activities like automotives that have matured into competitiveness) while others remain at relatively low level assembly stages (the *maquila* industries). Mexico also has some large, domestic industrial conglomerates, especially in heavy intermediates like paper, glass, steel and cement, which have also developed considerable capabilities over the years. These are now investing overseas (mostly in the United States), both to exploit their mastery of complex but stable technologies in larger markets and to gain access to new technologies by joining up with or taking over foreign companies. This pattern conforms nicely to the IDP.

There is an interesting point to note about Mexico. Its unique location and its traditional dependence on FDI and technology inflows mean that its industrial sector has grown without developing significant indigenous technological capabilities. R&D is very low and has fallen since liberalisation took place. While liberalisation and NAFTA are forcing industries to restructure and upgrade their technologies, the lack of a 'research culture' may not as a consequence lead to as much upgrading into new high technology activities as seen, for instance, in Taiwan. The role of the government in this evolution of advantages has been crucial, though not always to the country's benefit. Mexico has not been able to mount the kinds of effective industrial policies that characterise East Asia, and so has not been able to extract all the benefits from FDI for local 'asset creation' that the latter did.

Taiwan is one of the great success stories of industrialisation in East Asia. By the use of careful selective interventions since 1960 in the context of strong export orientation, it has built up a highly flexible, efficient and skill-based industrial sector.[4] Its capabilities show up in the largest volume of manufactured exports in the developing world. It has some world class indigenous firms with the capability to set up foreign ventures in activities like computers, video recorders, TV sets and other electronics, but its strength lies in the large number of small and medium-sized enterprises that use its base of skilled technical labour and the technical support services offered by the government to sell a diversity of products to world markets. It has exercised selectivity in the entry of MNEs, and has imposed various conditions to maximise their spillovers and linkages, and to raise the technological content of their manufacturing activity. The chapter by van Hoesel describes well the evolution of the strategies pursued by Taiwan to upgrade its industrial structure, with a prominent recent element being encouragement to its low to medium technology industries to relocate to cheaper countries in order to retain their comparative edge while allowing domestic operations to move to more sophisticated activities.

Taiwan has been a net capital exporter for some years, even though the official statistics do not show this. Its rising technological competence has provided the ownership advantages to go abroad, while rising costs, an appreciating currency and enormous reserves (and the search for political friends) have encouraged diversification overseas. The 'Chinese connection' has helped its firms to lower the transactions costs of setting up in mainland China and in many South East Asian countries. The fact that it has been a net investor at relatively low levels of income may be explained by the promotion by the government of its competitive capabilities and its selectivity on FDI inflows. Otherwise it conforms rather nicely to the IDP model.

The experience of *India* is so strongly affected by inefficient government interventions that it is difficult to assess with general models. As traced in Kumar's chapter, it has pursued nationalistic and inward-oriented policies assiduously for a long period, and its insipid performance is a reflection of this. It has kept out inward FDI for a long period by restrictive policies, part of its larger effort to control large private firms. It has permitted overseas investment in the form of capital goods and know-how, and outward FDI boomed in the early 1980s as companies took advantage of this facility to promote their exports and escape the constrictions in the domestic economy. However, this enthusiasm cooled after a while; Kumar's data suggest that there is now renewed activity. The total stock of Indian equity overseas (around $500 million at current exchange rates) is relatively small.

The fact that Indian enterprises invest abroad at all, and in a broad variety of industries, attests to the capabilities that have been fostered within the protectionist walls, and exceed those of most other low income countries. The low rate of growth of industry, exports and FDI attests, on the other hand, to the fact that interventions in general retarded the fuller development and exploitation of the potential. It certainly led to a much worse performance than the NIEs of East Asia, which started with roughly the same income levels in the 1960s.

China is rather similar to India, except that its initial isolation was greater than India's and its subsequent opening up more rapid (at least in the special zones). In addition, the existence of large Chinese business communities abroad, with large amounts of capital and established industrial and other capabilities, gives China a unique advantage in terms of attracting FDI. The pattern of FDI is shifting from simple labour-intensive operations to heavy industry aimed at the domestic market and to more complex export-oriented activities. State-owned and mixed-ownership enterprises are participating enthusiastically in its rapid industrial and export growth, and are also proving to be aggressive foreign investors.

FDI is clearly playing a catalytic role in China's industrial and export growth, but local enterprises are more concerned to learn from MNEs and gain access to their proprietary technologies and their markets than to be passive recipients of capital and know-how. In this the pattern resembles that of the larger NIEs in the region.

Indonesia is another import-substituting country that is switching to more open policies, but its industrial development is at a lower level than its neighbours in the region. Its large market and enormous natural resources have proved a magnet for large amounts of FDI, while its low wages have attracted simple export-oriented FDI (mostly in garments, shoes and plywood) in the past decade from the NIEs. Some of its large business houses have developed sufficient expertise and are endowed with sufficient capital to start investing overseas. In this, the pattern conforms to the IDP.

To sum up, the country experiences reviewed here support the investment development path analysis, but there are large deviations depending mainly on the pattern and efficacy of government interventions. Countries have long term departures from the predicted path, with little real sign of returning to it. This suggests that the theory itself may need to be extended and modified, to take these subpatterns into account.

SOME POLICY IMPLICATIONS

The IDP as such is not intended to be normative: it simply describes systematic relationships between development and patterns of ownership and locational advantages. Nevertheless, there is some expectation in related writings that FDI influences the development of these advantages over time, generally in a positive direction. This is clearly true. Locational and ownership advantages interact with MNE presence in a variety of ways, and FDI has the potential for enormous benefit to host countries – the 'created assets' that it can transfer can dynamise the development of those and related assets.

However, the kind of assets (i.e. the level of technology and skills) that MNEs decide to transfer to a particular location, the impact that this has on the development of local capabilities and local firms (both suppliers and competitors), and the ability of the host economy to tap other externalities that may result, all vary. They depend on the efficiency of local markets and the level of local skills and institutions. In the presence of market failures, especially of the deep structural kinds that characterise underdevelopment, the role of the government in alleviating or exacerbating these market failures is crucial to the effects that FDI has.

Apart from the traditional leaders in FDI, which did not need to adopt particular strategies, there seem to be three broad approaches:

1 Passive open door policies to FDI and to local technological development.

2 Pro-active policies to attract and guide FDI to activities that most benefit local development.

3 Selective policies to FDI, using it as one of a range of possible ways to access foreign 'created assets' while intervening to promote the development of local competitive capabilities.

These strategies have broadly different effects on the development of local advantages. Passive policies can attract FDI to exploit existing locational advantages like domestic markets, natural resources or low cost labour. They will yield certain externalities and growth benefits but, in the absence of specific measures to overcome market failures in the host country, will not lead to a maximisation of the benefits that MNEs have to offer. Pro-active FDI strategies, if accompanied by appropriate measures to provide the skills, technological backup and infrastructure that more complex activities need, can have much greater benefits on development and locational advantages. By choosing to depend on FDI, however, they may not lead to the development of *national* capabilities. Finally, a more selective strategy of choosing different modes of asset transfer and combining it with efforts to develop the skills and technological capabilities of local enterprises can lead to larger benefits to long term development of ownership as well as locational advantages. However, this sort of industrial policy can only be conducted successfully in an export-oriented setting where interventions are counter-balanced by competitive pressures from world markets.[5]

Examples of these strategies can be found in the sample, though most countries have mixtures of different strategic elements. Spain and Mexico veer towards the passive strategy. Taiwan has elements of pro-active strategy, with some selective nationalist strategy thrown in. The best example of pro-active FDI strategy, however, is Singapore, which has the highest level of dependence on MNEs in the world by almost any measure and has used a battery of interventions to ensure that they meet its development objectives. Unfortunately, it is not in the current group, and so cannot be analysed at any length. Japan is the best example of the selective nationalist strategy. Again, another good case is not in the present group – Korea, which promoted its hand-picked local firms to giant conglomerate size and forced them into high technology industries with a minimal reliance on FDI.[6] In the process, it developed the deepest and broadest base of technological capabilities anywhere in the developing world and has the largest investments in R&D.

The inclusion of such considerations (drawn from the current literature on industrial policy in development economics) can enrich the IDP analysis, taking it beyond the purely deterministic framework that links changes only to levels of income. In turn, the IDP approach has many insights that can help the development analyst (like the present author) and lead to a better understanding of the process of participation of developing countries in international production.

NOTES

1 For the most comprehensive exposition of this see Chenery *et al.* (1986). Chenery poses his structuralism in strong contrast to the neoclassical approach under which all markets function perfectly at all levels of income, with no adjustment lags and no differences in factor returns in different activities. Under neoclassical assumptions, therefore, structural change does not appear as an independent factor. The IDP approach is also very structuralist in this sense, since ownership advantages and internalisation are manifestations of market failure that are ruled out by neoclassical economics.
2 See Lall (1994).
3 The growth of exports has, however, been more the result of massive devaluations and domestic recession than of the restructuring of the manufacturing sector as a result of import competition. See Ros (1994). The restructuring process is under way now, led by MNEs, large local conglomerates and privatised public enterprises.
4 See Wade (1990) and Lall (1994).
5 Lall (1994).
6 Amsden (1989).

REFERENCES

Amsden, A. (1989) *Asia's Next Giant*, New York: Oxford University Press.
Chenery, H. B., Robinson, S. and Syrquin, M. (1986) *Industrialization and Growth: A Comparative Study*, New York: Oxford University Press.
Lall, S. (1994) 'Industrial policy: the role of government in promoting industrial and technological development', *UNCTAD Review 1994*: 65–89.
Ros, J. (1994) 'Mexico's trade and industrialisation experience since 1960', in G. K. Helleiner (ed.) *Trade Policy and Industrialization in Turbulent Times*, London: Routledge.
Wade, R. (1990) *Governing the Market: Economic Theory and the Role of Government in East Asian Industrialization*, Princeton, NJ: Princeton University Press.

Index

ABB 117, 121
Abramowitz, M. 8
Acergroup 302, 309, 310
acquisitions *see* mergers and
   acquisitions
Advanced Research Projects
   Agency 94
Advanced Technology Program 94
Africa 57
AGA 107, 114, 133
Agarwal, J. P. 207, 365
Agricultural Producer Boards
   177–8, 184, 190, 202
agriculture (New Zealand) 176–9,
   183–5, 190, 194–5, 197, 202,
   434–5
Aguilar Fernández-Hontoria, E. 236
Ahlström, G. 108, 113
Akamatsu, Kaname 144, 146, 148
Akoorie, M. 184, 192, 199–200,
   201
Alam, M. S. 8
Alcatel 265, 401
Alfa Laval 107, 109, 114, 117, 133
alliance-seeking investment 163–4
alliance capitalism 16–18, 21, 426;
   see also cooperative ventures,
   strategic alliances
American Telephone and Telegraph
   93–4, 265, 401
Ammebergs Zinkgruvor 110
Amsden, A. 290
Anastassopoulos, J. - P. 388

Anchor Glass Container
   Corporation 271
Andersson, T. 116, 117, 119
Archibugi, D. 229
Arendal 112
Arisawa, H. 152
ASEA 107, 109, 114, 116–17, 121,
   133
ASEAN-4 148–9, 167
ASEAN region 298, 318
Ash, R. F. 395, 414
Asia 57, 192, 198, 199; NIEs 24,
   148–9, 167, 189, 377, 389;
   Taiwan and 298–9
Asia Development Bank 387
Asia Pacific Manufacturing
   Technology Centre 291
assembly-based manufacturing
   161–3
asset creation439–40; China 388;
   IDP theory 2, 5, 8–10, 13, 16, 22,
   26, 28–30, 33–7; India 351,
   355–65; Spain 218, 221, 227–9,
   233; Taiwan 429; UK 80–1
Atari 308
Atlas Copco 114, 117
Australia 184–8, 191, 194, 197–9,
   201
Austria 60
automobile industry: Japan 161,
   162; Mexico 256–63, 436

'B'shares 401, 415
Bahco 107, 133

Baird, M. 190
Bajo, M. 190
balance of payments (UK) 69–70
Banco de Mexico 243, 259
Bank of New Zealand196
banks/banking: India 349;
    Indonesia 339–41; Japan 163;
    Mexico 243, 259; New Zealand
    196–7, 201, 202; Sweden 109,
    126
Bata Shoe 320
Batam Economic Zone 328
Baumol, W. 8
Bell System 152, 196, 401
Bennett, D. 258
Bergstrom, V. 122
Bhagwati, J. 351, 366
bilateral country IDP (UK) 65–7
bilateral FDI cycles 63–5
Bimoli 343
BKPM 325, 333, 338
Blanc, G. 388
BMW 263
Boatwright, B. D. 51
Bofors 133
Bolinders 134
Bollard, A. 180–1, 190, 197
Bonacich, E. 158
Bosworth, B. P. 122
BOT (Build, Operate and Transfer)
    401
brand names 336, 339, 341, 343,
    358, 371, 373; own brands
    (OBM) 309, 310
Bretton Woods system 52
British American Tobacco 319
Brown Boveri 117, 121
Buckley, P. J. 43, 45, 63
Bureau of Economic Analysis
    (USA) 81
Bureau of Industry Economics
    (New Zealand) 185, 186–7, 189
Bush administration 94

Cabal Peniche 271–2
Calderón, A. 242, 251
Callen, L. 183
Callis, H. G. 319–20
Calvo, G. 245

Campillo, M. 211
Cantwell, J. 8–9, 10, 21, 96
capital: contribution (China)
    414–15; flight 415; -labour ratio
    387
capital goods 146, 272, 355, 365–6
Carlsson, S. 108
Carrillo, V. 270
Carter Holt Harvey 195
CASA 227
Casar, J. I. 251
Casson, M. C. 43, 45, 397
Castellvi, M. 212
'catching-up' effect 8, 21, 24, 30;
    Japan 143, 149. 56
Caves, R. 221–2
CBS 158
CEMEX 241, 271
Chai, L. 416
Chalmers Institute of Technology
    111
Chang, C.-C. 308, 309
chemical industry (Japan) 159–61
Chen, T.-J. 306
Chen, Y. 406
Chenery, H. B. 423–4, 426
Child, J. 407
'chilling effect' 87–8
China 429, 435, 438; changing IDP
    patterns 380–5; FDI-induced-
    changes 413–16; OLI
    configuration 385–413; role of
    national government 416–18;
    Taiwan alliance 285, 290, 294,
    300–2, 399–400, 437
China Development Report (1993)
    409
China Everbright Holdings 404–5
China Trust 303
ChipUp 310
Chrysler 256, 259, 263
Chung-Hua Institution for
    Economic Research (CIER) 293
Ciba Geigy 287
CITIC 404
Civil War (Spain) 211
Clark, C. 282
Clinton administration 94

Closer Economic Relations
    agreement 186–7, 191, 197
COCINB 212
colonial period (Indonesia) 318–20
Combustion Engineering 117
Commerce Department?, US 80,
    85, 88, 259
commodity prices 177, 324, 326
common external tariffs 376
comparative advantage 4, 6, 10, 25,
    29, 47, 148, 424
competitive advantage 5–6, 10–11,
    13, 14, 21, 424; China 429;
    Sweden 101, 107–9, 113–15,
    117–18
competitiveness: Mexico 240–74;
    UK industry 48–51
components-intensive
    manufacturing (Japan) 161–3
computer-integrated manufacturing
    163
computer industry 308–10, 376–7
Condliffe, J. 183
Conic Investment Company 405
Conroy, R. 415
consumer electronics 161, 162
consumer goods 146, 186, 200, 272,
    358
contract responsibility system 407
contractual joint ventures 389–90
cooperative ventures 7; alliance
    capitalism 16–18, 21, 426; see
    also joint ventures
copper industry (Sweden) 105–6,
    108, 110–11
'corporate mechanisms' (by SOEs)
    417
Cort process 105
Council for Economic Planning and
    Development (Taiwan) 307
Counterpart Computers 302
countries: development of UK's
    IDP by 51–67; idiosyncratic
    nature of 24–8; specific
    differences (non-market) 18–20;
    specific factors (IDP) 12–22
Crafts, N. F. R. 50
created assets see asset creation
'creative destruction' 148

Crocombe, G. 183, 186
cross-border: knowledge absorption
    149; learning curve 143, 144
culturalties (Chinese with overseas
    Chinese) 387–8

Daewoo Electronics 264–5
Daftar Skala Prioritas 325–6, 327–9
Dahmén, E. 113
dairy industry (New Zealand)
    177–8, 184, 200
Dasgupta, A. 365
Deane, R. 179, 181, 182, 184
debt: crisis (Mexico) 241–2, 245–6,
    258, 271, 436; -equity swaps 246;
    India 371; Indonesia 325, 327
decentralization (China) 392, 396,
    405
De Erice, S. 214
Defense Advanced Research
    Projects Agency (DARPA) 94
de Greer, Louis 108
demand management policies 52
de Maria Y Campos, M. 256, 262
de Pablo, J. R. 212
deregulation: China 389–92;
    Indonesia 329, 339–40; Mexico
    264; New Zealand 196, 201;
    Spain 244; Taiwan 304; USA
    93–4
Desai, A. V. 351, 359
devaluation: Indonesia 340; Mexico
    270; Sweden 122
developed countries: IDP and 430–
    5; see also individual countries
developed market economies
    (DMEs) 53
developed regions, UK and 53–7
developing countries: IDP and
    435–9; see also individual
    countries
Dharmala Group 343
Dickson family 108
Digital 308
Dobson, W. 200
Douglas, R. 183
'downsizing' policies (USA) 93
Dowrick, S. 8, 24
Dunlop Rubber 151

Dunning, John H. 142, 240; IDP
  theory 1, 6–7, 9–10, 12–14, 18,
  21, 424–6; statistical evaluation
  21–2, 28–9, 35
Dunstall, G. 179
Durán Herrera, J. J. 216, 229
Durkheim, Emile 28
'Dutch disease' 161
Dutch mercantilism 319

Ebashi, M. 196
ECLAC 245, 253
economic growth (Indonesia)
  317–18
economic integration (Spain)
  207–33
economic liberalization (Spain)
  212–14
economic specialization 426
economic system 27; impact of FDI
  (China) 413–16
economies of scale 5, 9, 15, 18, 26,
  116, 197, 402
economies of scope 9, 15, 196–7,
  402
education systems 95, 179
EFTA 8, 56, 58–9, 60, 66
Electrolux 113, 114, 116
electronics industry: Japan 161,
  162; Mexico 263–6; Taiwan
  305–11
Electronics Research and Service
  Organisation 308, 309
Employment Contracts Act (New
  Zealand) 190
Encarnation, D. 231–2
Enderwick, P. 184, 192, 199
English Electric 151
Enskilada Bank 109, 126
enterprise groups 407, 408
entrepreneurship 43, 125, 355
equity joint ventures 389–91, 395,
  396, 397, 408
Ericsson 107, 114, 133
Eriksberg 112, 134
ESAB 107, 112, 114, 116
ethnic ties (Chinese with overseas
  Chinese) 387–8
Europe: countries outside EU 60–1;

EFTA 8, 56, 58–9, 60, 66; market
  integration 44, 51, 53–7
European Union 8, 44; New
  Zealand and 198–9, 201; Single
  European Market 54, 199, 376;
  Spain in 212–17; Sweden and
  119, 121, 123, 124; Taiwan and
  299, 303–4; UK in 51–60, 65–7
Evans, P. 246
exchange rate: China 401; controls
  51–2, 178–9, 212, 293; crisis
  (India) 351; Indonesia 336, 339;
  mechanism (ERM) 52; Sweden
  122; UK 48, 67, 69
export-orientation: New Zealand
  176–202; Taiwan 283–5
Export Processing Zones: India
  365; Taiwan 283, 285–6
exports 29; manufactured (Mexico)
  243; maquiladora (Mexico)
  266–7; performance (China)
  413–14; promotion (in Indonesia)
  339–41; proprietary distribution
  (Spain) 230–2
Exxon-Florio amendment 88

factor-price-magnification effect
  148
factor-seeking investment 219,
  221–2
Fagersta Secoroc 117
Fajnzylber, F. 246
'falling-behind' effect 24, 30
Falu Copper Mine 109–10
Falu Mining School 111
Far Eastern Economic Review 399
FDI see foreign direct investment;
  foreign direct investment
  (country studies)
Filipstad Mining School 111
financial institutions (UK) 68–9
financial services sector (New
  Zealand) 196–7, 201, 202
Findus 120
Finlay family 108
firm-specific knowledge (Sweden)
  113, 117–18, 126
First Pacific Investments 343
Fisher, A. 176

Fletcher Challenge Limited 186, 195
flexible production (Japan) 163–4
'fluctuating equilibrium' 9, 96–7, 99
'flying geese' paradigm 144–50, 414
Fong, P. E. 286, 287, 291
Ford 256, 259, 262, 263
foreign business oriented corporations 404–6, 409, 415, 416
foreign collaboration (India) 374
foreign direct investment: developed countries 430–5; developing countries 435–9; IDP approach 1–22, 423–7; inward see inward FDI; outward see outward FDI; patterns 427–9; shifts (rationale) 14–16; statistical evaluation 22–36
foreign direct investment (country studies): China 380–418; India 348–78; Indonesia 316–44; Japan 142–67; Mexico 240–74; New Zealand 174–204; Spain 207–33; Sweden 101–22; Taiwan 280–312; UK 53–67; USA 78–99
foreign firms, importance of (Mexican competitiveness) 253–6
Foreign Investment Board (India) 355–6
Foreign Investment Promotion Board (India) 372
forestry industry: New Zealand 194–5, 200; Sweden 106, 111
Forestry Institute (Sweden) 111
Forsgren, M. 117
France 58, 66
Freeman, C. 24
FTCs 404–6, 408–9, 415

Gallivareverken 110
Gambro 116
Garcia de la Cruz, J. M. 226
GATT 52, 287, 400
GDP 37, 423; China 385–6; evaluating IDP 28–36; Mexico 242–7; net outward investment 29–33; New Zealand 174–5, 177, 185, 187–9, 192; Spain 212, 214–15, 219–21, 223–4, 228; Taiwan 280; UK 23, 45; USA 23
Gemmell, N. 8, 24
General Electric 151, 264
General Instruments 283
General Motors 93, 151, 256, 259, 263, 319
Gerlach, M. L. 17
Germany 58, 66
Ghauri, P. N. 119
GKN 115
Glete, J. 109
global liberalization (China) 400–2
globalization 83, 371–7
GNP 11, 12, 16, 424; China 411; Indonesia 318
Gold, T. B. 283, 285
Goldstar 265
Goodman Fielder Wattie 197, 200
Goodrich, B. F. (Rubber) 151
goods: capital 146, 272, 355, 365–6; consumer 146, 186, 200, 272, 358; intermediate 272
Götaverken 112
government intervention/policies 3, 27, 425–6; Japan 432–3; Spain 226–7; Sweden 110–11, 113–15, 121–3; USA 431–2
Government Printing 196
Graham, E. M. 64, 85
Grängesberg 106
Granstrand, O. 117
Gray, H. P. 36
Great Depression 177, 211, 319
Greater China Economic Region 387
greenfield investment 16, 222–6 passim, 303, 305, 406
gross value of industrial output (in China) 387
GRP (China) 410
Gulf War 371
Gurría, J. A. 245
Gustavson, C. G. 107

Hagedoorn, J. 24
Hakanson, L. 118

Hall family 108
Hamalainen, T. 28
Handelsbank 109
Harmonized Tariff Schedule (USA) 267
Harper, D. 196
Harrold, P. 386
Hawke, G. 177, 179, 181, 185
Hawkesworth, R. E. 212
heavy industries (Japan) 159–61
Heckscher, E. F. 105, 107
Heckscher-Ohlin trade 7, 157
Heinz, H. J. 197
Herzenberg, S. 259
Hewlett Packard 265, 291
hierarchical capitalism 17
hierarchical development (Japan) 142–50
Hierroperu SA 402
Hine, S. 163
Hitachi 264
Honda 263
horizontal integration 182, 200
Hörnell, E. 117
Howe, C. 400
Hsinchu Science Based Industrial Park 286, 292, 308
Huss, T. 251
Hymer, S. 246

I advantages see internalization advantages
Iberia 227
IBM 115, 120, 164, 264, 265, 401
ICI 287
IG Farben 151
IKEA 116
IMF 333, 371–2
import protection: India 349–55; licensing 178–9, 181, 191; see also tariffs
import substitution: India 351, 358–9; Indonesia 318, 319, 339; Mexico 240, 244, 246, 249, 255–6; New Zealand 176–88, 202, 435; Taiwan 281–2; UK 53, 54
in-bond assembly industry
(Mexico) 242, 249, 256, 264–70, 272, 273, 436
India 429, 435, 438; created assets 355–65; IDP framework 348–9, 377–8; international competitiveness 365–71; locational advantages 349–55; structural adjustment 371–7
Indian Investment Centre 354
Indonesia 429, 436, 439; data/ methodology 331–44; economic growth 317–18; government role 316–17; history of FDI 318–31
industrial activity (Sweden) 104–23
Industrial Development Fund (Sweden) 123
industrial enterprises (internationalization of Chinese) 405–7
industrial infrastructure (China) 385–6, 391, 404–5
Industrial Panorama 290, 299, 312
Industrial Policy Statement 365
Industrial Revolution 42, 105
industrial sector, outward FDI by (New Zealand) 199
Industrial Technology Research Institute (Taiwan) 308
industrial transformation (Taiwan) 305–11
industrial upgrading (Taiwan) 285–90
industrialization: India 348–78; Japan 159–61; Sweden 107–15; Taiwan 437
industry: evolution of (UK) 67–9; mature (Sweden) 111–15; structure (New Zealand) 180–1
INE (Spain) 228, 229
infant industry protection 3, 7, 147, 299, 337–8, 355, 426
information technology 281, 305–11
infrastructure development: China 385–6, 391, 404–5; Mexico 240; New Zealand 176, 186, 202, 434–5; USA 95
innovation 14, 15, 93, 122, 433–4;

see also inventions (Sweden); research and development
Institute for Information Industry 308
Intel 310
Inter-Ministerial Committee on Joint Ventures Abroad (India) 356
Inter Innovation 116
interest rate (New Zealand) 196
intermediate goods 272
internalization advantages 1, 4, 63, 80, 348; China 389, 395, 402, 417; Spain 229–32; *see also* OLI configuration
international competitiveness: India 365–71; Mexico 240–74; UK 48–51
International Paper195
internationalization 424; of industrial activity (Sweden) 115–23, 126–7; of local and industrial enterprises (in China) 405–7
intra-industry trade 7
inventions (Sweden) 107, 116, 133
investment: factor-seeking 219, 221–2; foreign direct *see main entries*; greenfield 16, 222–6 *passim*, 303, 305, 406; net outward *see* net outward investment (NOI); non-conventional (Taiwan) 291–3; non-resource based 196–7; resource-based 194–6; strategically networking phase 163–4
investment development path: country-specific factors 12–22; evaluating 28–36; idiosyncratic nature of countries 24–8; nature of (stages) 1–12; structural changes and 22–4
investment development path (country studies): China 380–418; India 348–78; Indonesia 316–44; Japan 142–67; Mexico 240–74; New Zealand

174–204; Spain 207–33; Sweden 101–27; UK 53–67; USA 78–99
inward FDI: China 380–2, 384–416; IDP theory 2–6, 9, 11–12, 14, 16, 18–21, 23; India 348–9, 354–5, 357–8, 366–75, 377; Indonesia 316–21, 329, 330–6; Japan 143, 145, 148–53, 169; Mexico 240–1, 245–56, 259; New Zealand 174–6, 179, 181, 186–9, 191–7; Spain 207–10, 212–14, 216, 223–7, 232–3; Sweden 101–4, 109–10, 118–21, 124–5, 127, 136–7; Taiwan 281–93, 305–11; UK 46–7, 54, 56, 58, 63–7, 69–70, 74; USA 82–3, 85–7, 96, 99
iron industry (Sweden) 105–6, 108, 110–11
Italy 58
ITT 115, 264
ITT Rayonier 195
IWK 29, 35

Japan 427, 432–3; catch-up experience 150–6; economic development 164–7; Indonesia and 398; industrial hierarchy 142–50; stages (FDI) 156–64; Taiwan and 281, 286–7, 292; UK and 64–5, 72
Japan Development Bank 161
Jennings family 108
Johanson, J. 114
Johansson, C. E. 133
Johansson, H. 119
Johansson-Grahn, G. 116, 119
joint ventures 24, 151–2, 201; China 389–91, 395–7, 400, 408; contractual 389–90; cooperative ventures 7, 16–18, 21, 426; equity (EJVs) 389–91, 395, 396, 397, 408; India 356, 359–62, 364, 373; Indonesia 324, 337, 342; Taiwan 291, 299–300
Jones, D. T. 162
Jonsereds 134
Jörberg, L. 105

Kayser-Roth 271
Keiller (Götaverken) 134
Kessel, G. 255
Kidron, M. 351, 354
Kinnwall, M. 116, 119
Kirkpatrick, Colin 414
Klotenverken 110
knowledge: firm-specific 113,
  117–18, 126; intensification
  156–64; seeking acquisitions 93,
  96
Kock-Cronström 108
Kockrums 112, 134
Kokusaka Pulp 195
Korea 210, 338, 440–1
Krugman, P. 85
Kueh, Y. Y. 387, 395, 414
Kumar, K. 357–9, 375, 376, 388
Kuo Chiau 303
Kuomintang government 285

L advantages see locational
  advantages
labour: driven development (Japan)
  158–9; intensive industrialization
  (Taiwan) 283–5; productivity
  (Mexico) 255
Labour Standards Law (Taiwan)
  298–9
Lall, Rajiv 363
Lall, S. 349, 359
Lardy, N. R. 400
Larsson, A. 105, 117
Law Concerning Domestic
  Investment (Indonesia) 323
Law Concerning Foreign
  Investment (Indonesia) 323–4
Law to Promote Mexican
  Investment and Regulate Foreign
  Investment 246
lean production techniques 93, 162
Lecraw, D. J. 336, 341
Lee, J. 290, 299, 304
Le Heron, R. 184
Leiderman, L. 245
liberalization: China 400–2, 408–9;
  India 348–78; Indonesia 322–4,
  327–30; Spain 212–14

licensing 358; of imports 178–9,
  181, 191; of technology 48–50
Lim, L. Y. C. 286, 287, 291
Lin, D. 409
Lindholmen 112, 134
Linnemann, H. 281
Litton 119
Liu, H. 386
local enterprise, internationalization
  of (China) 405–7
location pattern (China) 392–3
locational advantages 1–6, 9, 12,
  15, 21, 25, 424, 425, 429; China
  381, 385, 387–402, 413; India
  349–55; New Zealand 182,
  187–8, 194–7, 200, 202; Taiwan
  292–3, 305, 307, 310; UK 52, 63,
  65; see also OLI configuration
Lu, Y. 407
Lund, H. 119
Lundström, R. 114
Luo, L. 406

McDermott, M. C. 307, 308, 310
Macdougall, C. 386
Machine Industry Law (Japan) 161
McMillan, C. H. 116
McQueen, D. 116
macro-economic strategy 28
macro-organizational strategy 28
macro-IDP 149, 150, 165
macro-motivated FDI 158–9
macro-organizational policy 28
Malaysia 299
Manntrust 343
manufacturing sector: China 394–5;
  India 365, 370–1; Indonesia
  322–3, 339, 343–4; Japan 161–3;
  New Zealand 180–1, 197; Spain
  212–13, 223–6; USA 83–5, 94
Manufacturing Extension Program
  94
maquiladora industry 242, 249,
  256, 264–70, 272, 273, 436
market: failure 28, 425–7, 439;
  imperfections 6, 7, 28, 424;
  integration 44, 51, 53–7;
  mechanisms 381, 385, 388,
  391–5, 406–7, 413; size 26–7

Marlene 158
Martinez, T. 246
Mason, Mark 151–2
mass production 161–3
Matsushita 264
Maui Gas and Synfuel 196
mechanical engineering workshops
(in Sweden) 108, 111–12, 120,
134
Meiji Restoration (1868) 146
Merck 287
mergers and acquisitions 10, 15, 16;
in China 406, 407; New Zealand
190, 196–7; Spain 223, 225–6;
Sweden 116–17, 120–1; Taiwan
302, 303–4; UK 52, 61; USA 93
meso-IDP 144–50, 164
Mexico 427, 435, 436–7; FDI (role)
240–2; FDI and structural change
245–56; integration process
272–4; outward FDI 270–2;
sectoral dynamics 256–70;
structural change 242–4
Meyer, L. 246
Miau, Matthew 309
militarism 153, 399
Mines Authority (Sweden) 110
'miniature replicas' 246
Ministry of Commerce (India) 359
Ministry of Commerce (Spain) 214
Ministry of Communications
(Japan) 152
Ministry of Economic Affairs
(Taiwan) 293, 294
Ministry of Finance (China) 392,
414
Ministry of Industry (Japan) 152,
153
Ministry of Industry (Sweden) 122
Mitac 303, 309, 310
MODO 117
Monetary and Economic Council
(New Zealand) 183
Moreno, J. C. 259, 260
Moreno More, J. L. 212
Mortimore, M. 242, 251, 256, 260,
262
Motala 134
Motor Coach Industries 271

Motorola 265, 401
Multilateral Investment Guarantee
Agency (India) 372
multinational enterprises: China
388, 397, 400–2, 406–7, 409,
416, 438; IDP theory 7–16, 22–5,
36, 425–6; India 358, 365, 372,
374–5, 378; Indonesia 322–3,
325–6, 331, 334–8, 342; Japan
146–52, 163–4, 167, 430, 432;
Mexico 240–1, 244–6, 249,
256–70, 273–4; New Zealand
175, 181, 201, 202; Sweden 101,
114–19, 124–7, 433–4; Taiwan
283–6, 290–2, 305–6, 311–12;
UK 43–4, 47, 50–2, 64, 69, 71–2;
USA 78, 90, 432
Munktells 134
Muñoz, J. 212

Nadal, J. 211
Napoleonic Wars 106
Narasimha Rao, P. V. 371–2
Narula, Rajneesh: IDP theory 1, 13,
21, 424–6; statistical evaluation
21–4
National Board for Technical
Development (Sweden) 123
National Chiaotung University 308
National Commissionon Foreign
Investment (Mexico) 247–8
National Registry of Foreign
Investment (Mexico) 247–8
natural resources/assets: IDP theory
2, 8–9, 11, 13, 23, 25–30, 33–7;
Indonesia 317–18, 343; New
Zealand 180; Sweden 104–11
Naya, S. 281
NCR 291
Negative List 328
neo-imperialism 78
neo-technology theories of trade
424
neoclassical theory 423, 424
Nestle 119, 120
net outward investment (NOI):
China 410, 412; IDP theory 2, 4,
7–8, 11–12, 16, 36–7; Japan 154,
164, 169–70; Mexico 241;

statistical evaluation 23, 25–6,
29–33; UK 45–6, 48, 50, 53, 56,
58, 63, 65–6, 69–72, 74
Netherlands 58, 319, 320
New Industrial Policy (India) 372
New Order period (Indonesia)
321–2
New Zealand 427, 434–5; devel-
opment 174–6; 1870–1938
period 176; 1938–67 period
176–82; 1967–84 period 183–8;
1984–94 period 188–201;
summary and conclusions 202–4
New Zealand Australia Free Trade
Agreement (NAFTA) 184
New Zealand Dairy Board 178, 182,
199
New Zealand Forestry Corporation
196
New Zealand Planning Council
185, 190
New Zealand Railways Corporation
196
New Zealand Reserve Bank 190
New Zealand Tourism Board 195
Nicholas, R. L. 381
NICs 32–4, 44, 262, 387, 426, 429,
438–9; Asia 24, 148–9, 167, 189,
377, 389
Nippon Electric Company 151–2,
265
Nissan 256, 260, 262, 263
Nitro Nobel 107
Nobel 109
Nobel, R. 118
non-conventional investments
(Taiwan) 291–3
non-market country-specific
differences (in IDP) 18–20
non-resource-based investment
196–7
non-tariff barriers 3, 52, 53, 212
Nordlund, S. 110
North American Free Trade
Agreement 15, 242, 244–5, 247,
249, 255, 263, 272, ¤303, 340,
436, 437
Northern Telecom 265
Nueno Iniesta, P. 216

Nyaw, M. 388
NZ Steel 196

O advantages see ownership
advantages
OECD 44, 123, 188–9, 221, 224–5,
228–9, 233, 242, 251–3, 256,
260, 266, 430
Ohmae, K. 13
oil prices 160, 185, 324, 326–7, 365
Oki Paper 152, 195
Olea, M. A. 262
OLI configuration 44–5, 51, 54,
56–7, 63–6, 72, 174–5, 178, 182,
202 3, 349, 358, 380, 385–418,
426
Olsson, U. 105, 109
Oman, C. 291
Omnibus Trade and Competitiveness Act (1988) 88
open door policy: China 381, 409,
417; Mexico 436, 440
Open General Licence (India)
365–6
Original Equipment Manufacturing
(OEM) contracts 303, 309–10
Ortiz, E. 249
Otis Elevator 151
outward FDI: China 380–2,
385–413, 416; IDP theory 4–6, 9,
11–12, 14, 16, 18–21, 23; India
348–50, 356–65, 367–71, 373,
375–7; Indonesia 316–17, 321,
332, 336–44; Japan 148–51, 153,
158–64, 167, 169–70; Mexico
241, 270–2, 274; New Zealand
174–6, 191–2, 197–201; Spain
207–10, 212–23, 227, 230–3;
Sweden 101–4, 109–10, 114,
118–21, 123–4, 136–7; Taiwan
281, 293–311; UK 44–7, 54,
57–8, 65–6, 69–70; USA 82–3,
90–2, 95, 99
Overseas Investment Commission
(New Zealand) 191, 194–5, 197
Overseas Takeover Regulations
(New Zealand) 179
Owen, S. 108
OWK 29, 35

own brand manufacturing (OBM)
309, 310
ownership advantages 22–3, 27,
424–5; China 381, 385, 387–8,
397, 401–9, 416–17, 429; IDP
theory1, 3–6, 8, 10–12, 14–16,
21; India 429; Indonesia 336–7;
New Zealand 178, 181–2, 186–8,
197, 199–201; Spain 207;
Sweden 433; Taiwan 292–3,
305–6, 309–11; UK 52, 63, 65;
USA 80, 83, 93, 432; see also
OLI configuration
Ozawa, T. 13, 21, 27, 148, 151, 155,
157, 159–60, 162–4, 263, 273,
303

Palmer, I. 323
Panasonic 265
patents 228–9, 231, 356
Pearce, R. D. 45
Pearson, M. M. 396
Pellicer, O. 246
percentage of total exports 29
Peres, W. 242, 246, 251, 253, 264,
270–1
performance requirements (China)
395–9
Perstorp 109
Pertamina Crisis 325
Philippines 299–300
Philips 115, 265, 308, 401
Pianta, M. 229
PMA project (Indonesia) 323–4,
328
political crisis (China) 399–400
Porter, M. E. 13, 111
Portillo, L. 214
Portland Aluminium Smelter
Company 402
Post Bank 196
President Foods Inc. 302
pribumi entrepreneurs 320
prices: commodity 177, 324, 326;
oil 160, 185, 324, 326–7, 365
primary exports 29
Priority Investment List (Indonesia)
325
privatization 244, 250, 430

privileges system (Sweden) 110
pro-active policies 440–1
processing technologies 180
Producer Boards 177–8, 184, 190,
202
product cycle 164
production structure (Mexico)
249–51
proprietary distribution channels
(Spain) 230–2
protectionism: India 355, 358–9;
Indonesia 337–8; infant industries 3, 7, 147, 299, 337–8, 355,
426; Japan 147, 153, 162;
Mexico 244; New Zealand 182;
Spain 211; Taiwan 299
pulp industry (Sweden) 106–7, 111

Qi, L. 400

Randaccio, F. 8
Raurich, J. M. 212
Reagan administration 94
Regal Accessories 158
regional aspects of IDP: China
409–13; UK 51–67
'regional operations centre'
(Taiwan) 290
Reinhart, C. 245
Renault 117
'renewal funds' (Sweden) 123
Renton, G. A. 51
rents 162
Republic Cellini 158
research and development 94, 441;
India 358; Japan 162, 432;
Mexico 437; New Zealand 178;
Spain 218, 222, 227–9, 233, 434;
Sweden 113, 116–18, 120–3,
125–7, 135; Taiwan 299, 310;
USA 431
Reserve Bank of India 349
resource: based investments 194–6,
199–200; endowments (character
of) 25–7; -rich economy (New
Zealand) 174–204; structure
25–6; see also natural resources/
assets
Riedel, J. 293, 305

Rivlin, A. M. 122
Robson, P. 52
Roche, M. 180, 184, 195
Roos, D. 162
Rosenberg, W. 177
Rosendale, P. 321
Rostow, W. W. 144
Royal Institute of Technology
    (Sweden) 111
Royal Swedish Academy of
    Engineering Sciences 113
royalties 48–9, 228–9, 231, 355,
    366

SAAB-Scania 93, 112–13, 116–17
Salem, E. 405
Salim Group 343
Samaniego, R. 255
Sampo 306
Samuelsson, K. 107, 119
Sandvik 109, 114, 117
San Gee 293, 298, 303
Sanna-Randaccio, F. 96
Sanyo 195, 264
SCA 117
Scania-Vabis 133
Schermerhorn, J. R. 388
SECOFI 246–7, 251, 255, 263
selective policies 440
SEMATECH consortium 94
Sepulveda, B. 246
services sector 249
Shaiken, H. 251, 259, 260, 262
Sharpe, K. 258
Shell 319
Shipping Corporation 196
shipping/shipyard industries
    111–12
Siddharthan, N. S. 365
Siemens 151, 164, 401
Silentz 108
Simkin, C. 177
Simon, F. D. 285, 291, 308
Singapore 440
Single European Market 54, 199,
    376
Sit, V. F. S. 395
SKF 107, 109, 114

small and medium-sized enterprises
    415
Smith, Adam 142
'social knowledge' 389
Söderberg, T. 105
Soehoed, A. R. 319
software industry (India) 376–7
Sölvell, O. 107, 111
Sony 264
Sosvilla, S. 226
SOU 109, 114, 118, 119
Spain 58, 427, 434; data 235–7;
    economic growth 207–10, 232–3;
    FDI growth 226–7; historical
    overview 211–17;
    internationalization advantages
    229–32; inward FDI 223–5;
    outward FDI 217–23; research
    and development 227–9
Spartan Mayro 158
special economic zones 389, 391,
    395, 404, 405, 415
specialization process 249, 260
stage 5 hypothesis 95–9
Stal-Laval 133
State Council (China) 396
state monopolies 54, 56
state owned enterprises: China
    387–8, 392, 407–8, 409, 415–17;
    Indonesia 325; Mexico 244; New
    Zealand 190
statistical evaluation 22–36
Stora 117
strategic alliances 10, 16–17, 23–4,
    37–8, 93; see also cooperative
    ventures
strategic asset-seeking acquisition
    15–16, 21, 93, 96
strategic development options
    407–8
structural adjustment 6, 23, 27;
    India 371–7; New Zealand
    188–91
structural change: IDP and 14–20,
    22, 423–4; Japan 164, 166;
    Mexico 242–56; New Zealand
    188–91; in world economy 22–4
subcontracting 17, 162, 408

Subic Bay Metropolitan Authority 299–300
subsidiaries: China 499–402, 404, 409, 416, 418; India 356, 359–62, 364, 376; Indonesia 337, 342
Suharto, President 318, 321, 324
Sukarno, President 320, 321–2
Summa Group 343
Sutch, W. B. 178
Sweden 60, 66, 427, 433–4; economic development 123–7; IDP framework 101–4, 123–4; industrial activity 104–11, 115–23; maturing of industry 111–15; natural resources 104–11
Swedenborg, B. 116, 117, 119
Swedish Institute for Metals Research 113
Swedish Iron Masters' Association 111
Swedish Match 107, 113, 114, 133
Switzerland 60, 66

Tai, M. C. 397
Taiwan 427, 435, 438; China alliance 285, 290, 294, 300–2, 399–400, 437; direct investments in 281–93; direct investments from 293–305; economic growth 280–1, 311–12; inward/outward FDI 305–11
Taiwan Semiconductor Manufacturing Corporation 308
takeover activity (USA) 85, 87–8, 96
Tanaka, Prime Minister 324
Tang, N. 416
tariffs 3, 53, 54, 212, 244, 267, 338; common external 376; GATT 52, 287, 400
Tatung Company 303, 306, 310
taxation (China) 401, 415
Technical Development Fund Scheme (India) 366
Technical Evaluations Committee 356
technical fees 228–9, 231, 366
technology: accumulation (China)

415; competitiveness 48–51, 94–6; development path 153–6; dual-use 94; gap (Japan) 143, 153; licensing 48–50; trade (Japan) 154–6, 171; see also patents; research and development
technology transfer 425; China 386, 415–16; India 355, 372; Mexico 262; Sweden 116; Taiwan 290, 305, 311
Telecom NZ 191, 196
Telefónica de España 227
Televisa 272
TELMEX 265
Tetra Pak 116, 117
Texas Instruments 265, 309
textile industry (Japan) 146–7, 157–8
Thomas, M. 50
Thomas-Gilchrist process 106
Tiananmen Square 399
Tolentino, P. 21, 207
Tortella, G. 211
Toshiba 164, 264
tourism (New Zealand) 195–6
town and village enterprises (TVEs) 387, 392, 402, 408–9, 416
Toyota Motor Company 162
Trafikaktiebolaget Grangesberg-Oxelösund (TGO) 110
transaction costs 7
transnational corporations 78
Triad countries 8–9, 11, 15, 19, 24, 44, 273
Trollhättan (NOHAB) 134
22 regulations (China) 396

UA-Agri-Chemicals 402
Uddevallavarvet 112
ultimate beneficial owners 71
'umbrella enterprises' 401
UNCTAD 11, 29, 44, 195, 249, 381
UNCTC 52, 273, 293
Unger, K. 256
UNIDO 264, 415
Unilever 119, 319
United Development Company 300
United Kingdom 427, 430–1;

competitive industries 48–51;
economic development 42–5;
FDI flows 69–72; future
developments 72–4; IDP position
45–8, 51–69; New Zealand and
198–9, 201
United Nations 226, 285, 333
United States 427, 431–2; IDP
81–95; Japan and 153, 155;
Mexico and 267–70, 273–4; postwar dominance 78–81; stage 5
hypothesis 95–9; and Sweden
119; Taiwan and 284–5, 292,
298, 302–4; UK and 61–4, 66–8,
72
UNTCMD 52
'upward investment' 302–5
USAID 283
USITC 267

Vahlne, J.-E. 117, 120
Van Den Bulcke, D. 388, 397, 402,
404, 406
van Swinderen 108
Varela Parache, F. 212
Vautier, K. 187–8
vent-for surplus theory 148
Vernon, R. 164
Verspagen, B. 24
vertical integration 180, 187, 200,
307, 309
vicious cycles 10, 21, 27
Victor Talking Machine 151
Vieille Montagne 110
Vietnam 300
virtuous cycles 10, 21
Vitro 271, 272
Volkswagen 256, 260, 262, 263
Volvo 112–13, 114, 116–17

Wade, R. 283, 285–6, 291
wages: Japan 148, 158–9; Sweden
122, 124
Wallenberg family 109, 126
Waller, D. 158
Wallmark, T. 116
Walloons 108
Wang 265, 308
Wang, N.-T. 301–2
Wang, W.-T. 306
Wertheim, W. 319
Western Electric 151, 152
Westinghouse 117
Whiting, V. 258
Wicanders Korkfabriker 109
Wiedersheim-Paul, F. 114
Womack, J. P. 162, 262
Wood Pulp Research Association
(Sweden) 113
World Bank 29, 322, 333, 372, 381,
386, 435
world economy, structural changes
in 22–4
World Investment Report (1994)
427
Wu, Y.-L. 285
Wyndham Foods 302
Wyse 302–3

Yang, R. 406
Ye, G. 406
Yu, T.-S. 300

Zander, I. 111, 113
Zander, U. 116
Zenith 264
Zhan, X. J. 401, 409, 415
Zhang, H. 388, 397, 402, 404, 406
Zheng, J. 397

ح